CT 788 .S53 D3 1967
Davies, David William,
Elizabethans errant

DATE

Spring Valley Library
Colorado Mountain College
3000 County Road 114
Glenwood Springs, CO 81601

ELIZABETHANS ERRANT

The Strange Fortunes of

Sir Thomas Sherley and His Three Sons

ELIZABETHANS

ERRANT

The Strange Fortunes of Sir Thomas Sherley and His Three Sons  *As Well in the Dutch Wars as in Muscovy, Morocco, Persia, Spain, and the Indies*

BY D. W. DAVIES

Cornell University Press

Ithaca, New York

Copyright © 1967 by Cornell University

All rights reserved. Except for brief quotations in a review, this book, or parts thereof, must not be reproduced in any form without permission in writing from the publisher. For information address Cornell University Press, 124 Roberts Place, Ithaca, New York 14850.

First published 1967

Library of Congress Catalog Card Number: 67-16462

PRINTED IN THE UNITED STATES OF AMERICA
BY VAIL-BALLOU PRESS, INC.

This book is for Thelma

Acknowledgments

THE three Sherley brothers ranged widely over the earth, and the records and documents of their escapades are to be found in a great number of places. As a consequence, this book may possibly contain the longest list of acknowledgments for services rendered of any work extant.

The manuscripts and printed materials that were unearthed help to explain some Sherley adventures that have seemed improbable or inexplicable. The connection of Sir Thomas Sherley the elder with the lands of Norwich Cathedral, for example, has been clothed in mystery. Actually there is no mystery. The documents in the case have been printed, a fact I discovered only after I had transcribed the original manuscripts, which are in the British Museum.

The journey of Anthony and Robert Sherley to Persia appears to be without reason or motive until one connects it with the Earl of Essex' interest in the Dutch voyage of Cornelis de Houtman. The sojourn of Sir Anthony at Venice has been spoken of as his period of unemployment, but the manuscripts in Venetian archives gathered at the time of his trial, and Spanish manuscripts, chiefly those containing information furnished by Sir Anthony's servant, Pagliarini, show that, far from enjoying a period of unemployment, Sir Anthony was at this time the secret agent of King James, the Emperor, and the King of Spain, and possibly drew stipends from all three at the same time. Sir Anthony's sojourn in Spain, a span of more than twenty years, has usually been disposed of in a few pages or paragraphs. By utilizing the hundreds of documents concerning Sherley in the Archivo General de Simancas, I have been able to give a fairly full account of Sir Anthony's last days.

It is customarily assumed that Wiston, the ancestral estate, passed from the Sherleys to the Faggs and Gorings. The uncalendared and unpublished Sherley manuscripts in the Cranfield collection make it clear, however, that the Sherley estates were owned by the crown, by Robert Carr, Earl of Somerset, by relatives of the Wiston Sherleys, and by Lionel Cranfield, Earl of Middlesex, between the time they were lost by the Sherleys and the time they passed into the hands of the Fagg family.

Many of the materials documenting the strange fortunes of Sir Thomas Sherley and his sons are to be found in the British Museum. The staff of the Museum was consistently courteous and kind during the many months I used their library, and particular thanks are due to Mr. Richard Bancroft and Mr. Howard Nixon, who were unfailingly helpful. The Sherley manuscripts in the Cranfield collection on deposit at the Historical Manuscripts Commission and the Bodleian Library have been particularly valuable. I am grateful to Mr. R. H. Ellis and Mr. H. M. Baillie, who not only obtained permission from Mr. Lionel Sackville-West for me to use the manuscripts, but provided a comfortable room in the Historical Manuscripts Commission's quarters in which to consult them. I would like also to thank Mr. Lionel Sackville-West for granting permission to use the Cranfield Papers. The staff of the Public Record Office has been kind, helpful, and able, and I appreciate the generous treatment accorded me during the two months I worked there.

Miss Clare Talbot, Librarian of Hatfield House, has contributed most generous assistance, and to her I owe a great deal. I must also thank the Librarian of the Inner Temple Library for permission to use the valuable Sherley document in that library. My friends Marjorie Bindoff and Professor S. T. Bindoff of Queen Mary College, University of London, have read the manuscript with great care and attention to detail, saving me from many a grievous error. I am much indebted to Professor Ann K. S. Lambton, Professor of Persian in the School of Oriental and African Studies, University of London, who explored the possibility of finding references to the Sherleys in Persian sources. Mr. Norman Sainsbury, Keeper of Oriental Books, Bodleian Library, also endeavored to find for me references to the Sherleys in Persian literature. I am also much indebted to my three friends, all enthusiasts for Persian literature, Mas' uud Farzaad, Cultural Attaché, Persian Embassy, London; Robert Cecil, Head of the Cultural Relations Department, the Foreign Office; and Major John Bowen of the Indian Army. These three have guided the writer in all things Persian, a subject on which he was, and still is, utterly ignorant. Mr. E. F. D. Roberts, Assistant Keeper, Department of Manuscripts, National Library of Scotland, not only furnished upon request photostats of Sherley letters, but also sent along photostats of other Sherley letters which the author had overlooked. The county archivists of Berkshire and Lincolnshire were also most obliging in making photostats of Sherley letters, and Mr. E. C. Earl, Archivist for the Isle of Wight, was kind enough to search through the papers of Sir John Oglander for additional references to Sir Thomas Sherley the younger.

One of the pleasantest interludes in the work was a visit to Wiston, the Sherley ancestral home, now used by the Foreign Office, and known to the Foreign Office as Wilton Park. The visit was arranged by Mr. Basil Bleck, Information Officer, British Consulate General, Los Angeles, and Mr. Robert Cecil. The Warden of Wilton Park, Dr. H. Koeppler, was kind and hospitable in entertaining my wife and myself during our visit to Wiston, and I must thank all three, Basil Bleck, Robert Cecil, and Dr. Koeppler, for one of the pleasantest times of our lives. During the writer's several stays in England, he has on each occasion enjoyed the help, encouragement, and hospitality of that illustrious contemporary member of the Shirley family, Earl Ferrers, and to him I express my thanks and appreciation.

In the Netherlands, the writer is indebted to his friends at the University of Utrecht who helped him on the present task, as they have assisted him on previous ones. My thanks and gratitude go to Professor W. Ph. Coolhaas of the Historical Institute, to Miss D. J. Kohlbrugge, Professor of Persian, and to Dr. D. Grosheide, University Librarian. Special thanks are due to Professor Willem Heckscher, who provided in the Institute for Art History a warm, comfortable room in which to work.

In Spain, the assistance of Señora Adela Gonsales Vega of the Archivo General de Simancas was invaluable, and this book owes a great deal to her. The writer is also indebted to the staff of the Biblioteca Nacional, Madrid, for many courtesies. In Torremolinos, Sr. Felipe Perez Currea provided many needed translations, and in Churiana, Mrs. Gerald Brenan saved the writer from a grievous error in identifying the town in which Anthony Sherley lived. Mr. Gerald Brenan put me in touch with Professor Emilio Orozco Diaz of the University of Granada, who ascertained the date of death of Anthony Sherley.

Mr. Jean Prinet of the staff of the Bibliothèque Nationale examined a number of manuscripts concerning Sir Anthony Sherley in that library. Fr. Emmanuel of the Discalced Carmelites, London, and Fr. Bede of the same order in Rome checked the archives of the Order for possible additional Sherley material. Professor Marcel de Grève of the École Militaire, Brussels, and Dr. Dorothy Thickett, London, went to a great deal of trouble to explore possible sources of Sherley material in Belgium; Professor R. F. Leslie of Queen Mary College, University of London, did his best to do the same in Poland.

The Folger Shakespeare Library contains important Sherley letters, and I wish to thank the Director, Dr. Louis B. Wright, and also Miss Eleanor Pitcher, Miss Virginia LaMar, and Miss Lilly Stone for much assistance and many kindnesses during the time I worked there. I am indebted also to Miss Mary Isabel Fry and to other members of the staff of the Henry E. Huntington Library.

My colleagues in the Claremont Colleges have been most helpful and patient with me. Mr. Philip Merlan and Mr. H. J. Carroll translated a number of Latin documents concerned with Sir Anthony's tax schemes for Sicily and with his venture into alchemy. Miss Bertha Ward, Mr. H. T. Young, and Mr. G. V. Ricapito have given invaluable help in translating both Italian and Spanish. Mrs. Renata Gould provided numerous translations of Italian letters. Mr. Edwin Fussell photographed in Rome the Sherley plaques in the Church of Santa Maria della Scala. Mr. F. L. Mulhauser kindly put me in touch with research workers in both Florentine and Venetian archives. The manuscript was read entirely by Mrs. Margaret G. Davies and by Mr. W. T. Jones, Mr. J. H. Gleason, and Mr. Leland Carlson. The first six chapters were read by President M. H. Curtis of Scripps College, and Mr. H. C. Herring struggled manfully through the first six sentences.

The book has actually been written three times. Fortunately, no one read the first version but the author. The typescript of the second edition was proofread by Virginia Dunbar, who also checked numerous citations. The typescript of the third recension was proofread and criticized by Thelma Cikovsky. Umbra James assisted me in numberless ways, as she has for many years. My wife spent a long, hard month checking citations in the British Museum, and checked all the copy before it went to the typists. To my wife, my colleagues, Mrs. James, Mrs. Dunbar, Mrs. Gould, and Mrs. Cikovsky I am deeply indebted.

Finally, I must express gratitude and thanks to the President, Mr. Gordon Ray, and to the Trustees of the John Simon Guggenheim Foundation for the fellowship which made the research possible.

D. W. DAVIES

Honnold Library
November 1966

Contents

Illustrations

ELIZABETHANS ERRANT

The Strange Fortunes of
Sir Thomas Sherley and His Three Sons

CHAPTER I

The Family of Shirley and the Sherleys of Wiston

SIR THOMAS SHERLEY and his three sons lived in the England of Elizabeth I and James I. Though of a well-established family, they refused to remain established. Like so many of their contemporaries they were gentlemen on the make. Chicanery, larceny, adultery, heroism, and treachery figured in their story. Such peccadilloes were to be found in the lives of many of their peers, but the Sherleys possessed a talent for carrying such matters to extremes. Courtiers spiced their letters with Sherley stories, and the vulgar multitude read pamphlets about them. A play dramatized their lives, and their travels were embalmed in Hakluyt and Purchas. As the ultimate tribute to their fame a book has been written to prove that Shakespeare's plays were written by Anthony Sherley, surely the least plausible of all the men who have been put forward as the authors of those works.[1] France, Holland, Austria, Spain, and Italy preserve records of their frequently distressing visits. The histories of Virginia, Jamaica, and Morocco cannot be written without reference to the Sherleys, and Persian children read about them in school.

Though by no means the first or the last members of this remarkable line to create a stir—a later Shirley, for example, was the last peer hanged in England—Sir Thomas and his family are perhaps the best known. They lived in Sussex, but the Sherleys were originally a Warwickshire family. They were established in England by the time Domesday Book was compiled, and some believe that they were Anglo-Saxon landowners who had survived the Conquest. The first member of the family of whom there is a record was called Seswalo, but his grandson, Sewallis,

Spring Valley Library
Colorado Mountain College
3000 County Road 114
Glenwood Springs, CO 81601

took the name of his manor, and was known as Sewallis de Scyrle, or Shirley, or Sherley, and so the family has been known ever since.[2] From this beginning the Sherleys spread over England. Through the centuries they have held lands, houses, and manors in the counties of Warwick, Leicester, Middlesex, Bucks, Nottingham, Bedford, Hereford, Oxford, Gloucester, Huntingdon, Derby, Sussex, and Somerset, and lesser properties in other places.

The family came into Sussex through the marriage of Sir Hugh Shirley to Beatrix de Braose, who inherited the manor of Wiston, which became the Shirley home. Sir Hugh valiantly fought and died for his king at Shrewsbury in 1403, and it is he who is referred to in Prince Henry's speech to Douglas in the first part of *Henry IV:*

> Hold up thy head, vile Scot, or thou art like
> Never to hold it up again! the spirits
> of Valiant Shirley, Stafford, Blount, are in my arms.
> It is the Prince of Wales that threatens thee
> Who never promiseth but he means to pay.

Wiston, the home of the Sussex Sherleys, is presently used for conferences by the Foreign Office, and is familiar to diplomats, journalists, professors, and politicians all over the world. It is a charming country house; some parts are Elizabethan, others Restoration, and other parts were added in the nineteenth century. The South Downs rise up behind it, and the Weald of Sussex stretches before it. There are more striking settings and grander views, but few houses give such a sense of tranquility. The manor is very old. In the early nineteenth century it comprised 2,750 acres of arable land, pasture, and woodland, and formerly had been larger.[3] Before the Conquest it was in the possession of a prominent landowner, Azor, who held it of Earl Godwin, and later held it of Godwin's son, King Harold. After Harold's defeat at Hastings, William the Conqueror gave it to Ralph de Braose,[4] and its history can be traced continuously since that time.

Steyning, more charming than most villages, is a mile away. Though now an inland town, at the time of the Conquest it was

a thriving port. Its prosperity continued until the fourteenth century. It had a market, a mint, and two churches. It returned two members to Parliament, and indeed continued to do so until 1832. In Elizabethan times the Sherleys of Wiston held extensive properties in Steyning. It was their pocket borough and they frequently represented it in Parliament. Since then it has had a number of distinguished inhabitants, including William Butler Yeats, but its quaint thatched cottages now are usually out of the reach of all except the wealthy few who can afford such charming but expensive antiques.

The history of the Sussex Sherleys was unspectacular until the time of Sir Thomas. They lived quietly at Wiston for more than a century, as many another family lived quietly in the country for decades or centuries, but Sir Thomas was restless. While he rusticated at Wiston, others made fortunes raiding Spanish commerce, and still others did even better raiding the national treasury or the lands of holy church. Sir Thomas' contemporaries voyaged to the far corners of the earth. They were famous seamen, dauntless soldiers, and gifted poets. He longed to be like them and eventually could endure the life of a Sussex gentleman no longer. He projected himself on the national scene, and thereafter the activities of the Sherleys interested the whole of England.

Sir Thomas was probably born in 1542, and matriculated as a fellow commoner from Queen's College, Cambridge, in 1561; that is to say, he lived as a student but dined with the dons. Returning to Sussex, he assumed the honors and duties accorded and expected of the head of a prominent family. He was knighted at Rye in 1573 and served as a member of Parliament, sheriff, and justice of the peace, and as a deputy lieutenant of the county. Aside from such facts, what one can know about Sir Thomas before 1585 is tenuous. He appears to have had two characteristics worth remarking: he was inclined to be extravagant rather than parsimonious, and he made friends easily, traits which are not unrelated. As a young man he did two things which cost a good deal of money, both of which perhaps could have been avoided: he remodeled Wiston, and he became sheriff of Sussex and Surrey. There are pictures extant of his home after he had remodeled it, notably a painting at Wiston. After that transformation it was not the charming house of a country gentleman but a rambling, grand, important house, much bigger than it is now. Sherley's steward declared that the remodeling had cost his master a thousand pounds. In Sir Thomas' defense it should be said that at the time extravagance was endemic in England. Camden noted in 1574 that "our apish nation" not only "jetted up and down in silks glittering with gold and silver" but began to indulge in a "riot of banquetting" and "bravery in building" to the "great ornament of the kingdom, but to the decay of the glory of hospitality." [5] Probably Sir Thomas could not really afford his extravagances, but then neither could the great majority of his contemporaries.

As to the office of sheriff which Sir Thomas filled, it was such an expensive burden that gentlemen frequently did all they could to avoid it, pleading they were too old, too frail, or too burdened with other royal duties to accept the honor. Sir Francis Coke wrote Sir John Coke imploring him to keep a "loving neighbor and friend" from being appointed sheriff. The friends of Sir W. Malorye petitioned that he be excused from serving because he was "in every way unmeet for it," and in the next reign a courtier wrote to a country friend who was in danger of being chosen for the post that "when laboring to get you off, I perceived that my Lord Keeper distasted you, having resolved that you should be sheriff." [6] There is no indication that Sir Thomas labored to be let off; he accepted the honor, the duty, and the expenses, which were numerous. A sheriff paid fees when he entered office and fees when he left it. There were fees to barons of the Exchequer, masters in chancery, attorneys, marshals, clerks, criers, tipstaves, and many others "which to record would be long, and so he is quit." [7] He had to maintain a representative at Westminster, and on his twice-yearly visits to that place the sheriff was expected to provide dinners for hordes of gentlemen, food for their numberless servants, and tips for the swarming hangers-on. He had to go about the county followed by an imposing retinue. One sheriff of Sussex was followed by one hundred and sixteen men in silken doublets, but thirty or forty retainers was a respectable number. If the Queen, great nobles, or foreign ambassadors visited the county, the sheriff was expected to entertain them, but Wiston was a large house and the gregarious Sir Thomas may have enjoyed the splendid guests. The day-to-day duties may even have had a certain zest. Since the sheriff was the chief executive of the Queen's courts in his county, the bulk of his work comprised the execution of writs issuing from both the local courts and those at Westminster. The sheriff himself presided at the county court, and though no criminal matters were punishable there, nor could civil suits be brought which were for sums greater than forty shillings, still the details of the chicanery, malfeasance, and petty larcenies inflicted by his neighbors on one another might have been entertaining.

In addition to his work for the courts, the sheriff was charged with many police duties. He was to examine idlers, vagrants, and suchlike suspect persons and place them in the stocks. He was charged to take swords and daggers from laborers and the servants of craftsmen. He was to seek out all mortal enemies of the Queen and her councilors; all counterfeiters, murderers, thieves, sorcerers, witches, and traitors; all people who burned other people's corn and houses; and all who had abjured the realm and returned by stealth. He also had financial duties. He collected fines imposed by the county court, and certain small taxes and debts due the crown. He kept an account of who owed the Queen, the amount involved, and how the debt was incurred; and by this means Sir Thomas may have accumulated information useful to him later when he obtained a patent to collect small debts.

Religious questions doubtless impinged upon Sir Thomas' life, as they did on the lives of Elizabethans generally. The Shirleys have the reputation of being a recusant family, and certainly in Elizabethan times and afterwards many of them were Roman Catholics. The life of Sir Thomas overlapped by some years that of his young relative and namesake, Sir Thomas Shirley of Bottlebridge. This latter gentleman, himself a Catholic, declared that his kinsman, Sir Thomas of Wiston, had begun life in the Roman church and attributed the misfortunes which later befell him to the fact that he had deserted the ancient religion. Since our Sir Thomas spent his youth under the reign of Queen Mary, when the country was officially Catholic, it could very well be, as his relative declared, that he had begun life in that faith; but there is no evidence for his alleged Romanism other than the statement of his kinsman and the fact that many Shirleys were Catholics. Actually, many Shirleys also were zealous protestants, such as that Elizabethan Calvinist Shirley who, when making his will, declared, "I rest assured of the free remission of all my sins, with full assurance of resting both soul and body in the highest comfortable heaven of heavens, which my sweet Saviour hath prepared for me and all the select saints of God on the earth, of which number I assuredly account myself to be one." [8] Since there were both devout Catholics and zealous Calvinists among Elizabethan Shirleys, what one can safely say about the religion of Sir Thomas is very little. One can, in fact, only make the remarkably nonstartling statement that the Sherleys, like numerous other Elizabethan families, were, generally speaking, deeply moved and influenced by religion.

Sir Thomas was several times a member of Parliament for Steyning; he also represented Sussex in Parliament in 1572 and was a candidate for re-election in 1584. It was comparatively easy to enter the Commons as the member for a borough such as Steyning, but representing the county was an honor reserved for the leading families. Although ostensibly county members were elected, actually they were usually named by the great men of the shire. At the Sussex election of 1584 two gentlemen whom the magnates had not agreed to support put themselves forward for election, whereupon Lord Buckhurst stirred into action. This noble lord was not only a power in Sussex, but a famous Englishman. A Privy Councilor, a barrister, and a writer, he achieved such renown that he still has an important place in literary history. "Cousin Calvert," he wrote to the then Sussex sheriff, "I hear that Mr. Herbert Pelham and Mr. G. Goring do stand to be the knights of the shire; and as you friendly offered me your furtherance if need were, so now, though I doubt not of any great need, yet would I be glad to use the help of my friends in this cause for Sir Thomas Shirley and my son." A few days later the sheriff also received a letter from Viscount Montagu of Cowdray. "I have thought good to signify unto you," the Viscount wrote, "that both sundry noblemen and gentlemen, with myself, have thought Mr. Robert Sackville [Buckhurst's son] and Sir Thomas Shirley most fit . . . if the country shall like so to make choice . . . I pray you to make my wish and desire to be known to the freeholders there." The Pelhams and the Gorings were also old and prominent Sussex families—the Pelhams, at least, older in Sussex than the Sherleys—but the noble lords were for Sherley and Sackville, and it was they who represented Sussex in the Commons.[9]

As Sir Thomas sat in Parliament he must have been continually reminded of the necessity of opposing Romanists and Spaniards. In the first Parliament to which he was elected, that of 1572 (which lasted incidentally until 1581), he could have heard, had he been diligent in attendance (a dangerous assumption to make of any legislator then), a speech by the Lord Keeper in which Parliament was exhorted to provide funds for defense against the Catholic menace abroad. In 1576 Sir Walter Mildmay, Chancellor of the Exchequer, made an eloquent oration against Catholics. He was an ardent Puritan, and his heart was in his work. He reminded Parliament that the Queen "hath delivered us from the tyrannous yoke of Rome, and restored again the most holy religion of the Gospel." But even though they have been saved, "wise mariners in calm weather do then most diligently prepare their tackle and provide to withstand a tempest that may happen." He therefore prayed that Parliament would leave the Queen, "not unfurnished of that which shall be sufficient to maintain both her and us against the privy or open malice of enemies." It was a nicely balanced effort, and on this occasion Sir Thomas Sherley was himself named a member of the committee appointed to draw up a bill voting the Queen a subsidy.[10]

It is evident that mention of the menace of Spain and Catholicism in the Elizabethan age was as effective a means of extracting money from a legislature as the mention of the Communist menace has been in our time. In 1581 Mildmay was more specific in asking for funds than he had been in the previous session. He plainly identified the Pope as the foreign enemy and referred to certain princes who were his confederates. The Pontiff and his accomplices, Mildmay declared, not only manifested open hostility, but secretly sought to engender disloyalty within the country by sending into England Popish priests and monkish Jesuits. Parliament ought, he concluded, to consider seriously how best to restrain evilly disposed subjects and how to provide adequate forces, "so that England's enemies, seeing their minds so willing and their hands so ready to defend their country, would be discouraged from attempting anything against it." [11] Sherley was again a member of the committee charged to frame the bill voting subsidies.

Four years later, in 1585, the House again pondered the twin dangers threatening the kingdom, the Jesuits secretly lurking within the realm and the Pope and his confederates without, the accomplices being now plainly labeled as Spain and the Catholic League in France. For the third time Sir Thomas was named to the committee which considered in what measure and manner Her Majesty should be supplied by subsidy.[12]

Sir Thomas was also made increasingly aware of the menace of Spain and Catholicism as he performed his duties as a deputy lieutenant of the county, an office which he frequently held. The deputy's principal duty was to assist the lieutenant in bringing the county into a state of military readiness. He maintained a muster of the able men in the shire and took charge of "all the store and powder, metals and bullet." [13] Sir Thomas was first appointed in 1569 and was not finally removed from the list of deputies until 1601. As the antagonism to Catholics increased, and the war with Spain changed from cold to hot, the duties of deputy lieutenants became increasingly arduous and important. Sir Thomas also held other offices which directly concerned Elizabethan Catholics. In 1580 he was a commissioner for recusancy, and in 1585 a commissioner for disarming the Sussex recusants. After the Throgmorton conspiracy, the Countess of Arundel was committed to his custody and he kept her at Wiston as his official prisoner for a year. During that time he questioned her on her speeches against the government, her remarks against the Queen, her having Catholic priests in her house, and the fact that she attended mass.[14]

The turning point in Sir Thomas' career came in 1585 when he accompanied the forces sent to the Low Countries to aid the Netherlanders in their rebellion against Spain. The dispatch of the force was an English blow against Spain and Roman Catholicism, and to take part in it was a highly respectable adventure for an aspiring knight. By that time Sir Thomas had tasted about all that the life of a Sussex gentleman had to offer. He had served as member of Parliament, sheriff, justice of the peace, deputy lieutenant, and had shown himself an industrious servant of the Queen in other ways. He had been knighted and had married the daughter of a knight. In addition to his three sons, he had at that time six daughters, all of whom, as one would say, later married well. Mary was to marry Sir John Crofts, Isabel became the wife of Sir Edward Onslow, Elizabeth the wife of Sir Pexel Brocas, and Jane of Sir John Shurley. Two married into the nobility: Anne later became the wife of Viscount Tracy, and Cecilia of Baron de la Warr, the first governor of Virginia. Sir Thomas' affairs were in order. He was rich, well thought of, and probably bored. With his two elder sons he embarked with Leicester for the Low Countries and a life of adventure, excitement, and possibly large, quick profits.

CHAPTER II

The Sherleys Take Up Arms

WAR has usually been profitable to someone, and Elizabethan war had the virtue that some of the soldiers who fought it had an opportunity to turn a profit. Sir Thomas Sherley was perhaps determined to do so, for he showed amazing skill in making money. His sons, aged twenty and twenty-one, like their father were commanders of companies. With the edifying example of their parent before them, they were quickly initiated into the forms of petty theft and grand larceny customarily practised by captains. Actually, although he commanded a company, Sir Thomas was the staff-officer type. Presumably he was not averse to doing his part in the business of killing and being killed, but his great talents would have been wasted in such simple matters; he owed it to his country to do more important things. He quickly became the confidant of the commander-in-chief and gravitated to administration. His eldest son, Thomas, was that Elizabethan counterpart of the Piccadilly or Washington commando, a "court captain," by which was meant a gentleman who left his company fighting in the Low Countries while he enjoyed the pleasures of the court. The judgment may wrong young Thomas, but he was absent during the only action in which his company took part of which there is any record, and he undeniably enjoyed courtly pleasures. The second son, Anthony, was one of those who did the actual fighting, an indispensable, if somewhat awkward, type in any army. Like many of his kind, his conduct off the battlefield was not exemplary.

The war which Sir Thomas and two of his sons entered was the Eighty Years War (1568–1648) between Spain and her rebellious subjects in the Netherlands. For approximately seventeen years Elizabeth and her advisors debated whether the country should adopt a policy of intervention or nonintervention, or should induce the belligerents to make peace. The Queen hated rebels, but she feared Spain. Personally tolerant, she was alarmed by Catholic power. Loving peace and hating expense, she was yet unwilling that the Dutch should have French rather than English allies. She knew the evils of an ever-changing policy, but she loved to change her mind. Yet, though she might swing from side to side, she never got far off the course dictated by considering what was best and most advantageous for her country. This consideration was also the lodestone guiding some of her councilors, but there were others. Some, notably those of the Puritan persuasion, believed in the inevitable conflict, and desired it. Of the puritans, Sir Francis Walsingham, the Secretary of State, was the most influential, and the Earl of Leicester was married to the daughter of another powerful puritan, Sir Francis Knollys. While the Queen and her councilors debated, from 1572 onward, whole companies of English were fighting in the Dutch forces, and individual adventurers slipped away daily to join one side or the other.

In 1584 and 1585 when Walsingham and Leicester, the leaders of the war party, dominated the Council, two events forced the hands of the Queen and the shrewd, temporizing councilors. In the first of those years the Prince of Orange was murdered. The following year Antwerp, so convenient a port for the invasion of England, fell to the Spanish. Now Catholics and Spanish clearly appeared to be the enemy and the war party appeared just as obviously to be right. Elizabeth was shocked into making a treaty with the Dutch. She agreed in August 1585 to send an army of 6,000 foot and 1,000 horse to the Netherlands. The States of the Netherlands agreed to hand over to the English as "cautionary towns" Flushing, Brielle, and the fortress of Rammekens near Flushing. When the English had been repaid for the cost of their soldiery, the towns were to be handed back. The man the Queen appointed to lead the army was the man she loved, the Earl of Leicester.

She had loved him as a young man when he was handsome and fearless; she loved him now when he was red faced and potbellied, but still fearless. But having agreed to send an army to the Low Countries, at the last moment she doubted, wavered, and could not part with Leicester.

He hurried to her. "You can consider," he wrote Walsingham, "what manner of persuasion this must be from me to her . . . [I] did comfort her as much as I could, only I did let her know how far I had gone in preparation. . . . I do think for all this she will let me go, for she would not have me speak of it to the contrary to anybody." [1] Finally Leicester was allowed to depart, and many fine gentlemen with him, including the three Sherleys; some troops also went—but not very many. Disembarking in the Netherlands, the expedition was enthusiastically welcomed at Flushing, Middelburg, Rotterdam, and Delft. It was a delightful experience and the business in hand was postponed while English and Dutch expressed mutual love and admiration. "Concerning the wars," Sherley wrote to Burghley about a month after landing, "there is yet little done since our coming nor is not like to be until there be a supply of men from England." [2] As a matter of fact, Leicester's first spectacular action was not military but political. He had barely arrived in the Netherlands before the Dutch offered to make him their governor. One morning a solemn delegation, heralded by trumpets, appeared at his house at The Hague. Leicester, not quite dressed, received the Dutch leaders in his great room, but when the intentions of the delegation were whispered to him he invited the gentlemen into the privacy of his bedroom. There, said Leicester, the deputation proceeded "to offer to me with many good words, for Her Majesty's sake, the absolute government of the whole of the provinces and to proclaim the same immediately." Leicester had no intention of refusing. He waited a few days before accepting, not because he wished to consult the Queen or secure her permission, but apparently hoping the Dutch would improve their terms. He then accepted and became governor of the Netherlands. "They have given him the absolute authority to govern," Sir Thomas Sherley reported to Walsingham, "which surely was their wisest [course]." [3]

Sherley may have thought so, but Queen Elizabeth did not. She was furious that a creature, "raised up by ourself and extraordinarily favored," should treat her wishes with contempt. Burghley and Walsingham endeavored to calm her but her blood was up. In February she sent Sir Thomas Heneage to Leicester with a demand that he resign his governorship forthwith, and in the same month Leicester sent Sherley to the Queen to intercede for him. Sir Thomas' success was not brilliant. The Queen refused either to receive Sherley or the letter from Leicester which he brought. "I find," Sir Thomas reported to his commander, "that the Queen continueth near in the same humour of mislike of your Lordship's acceptance of the government there," but he doubted not "in the end but all will be well, and Her Majesty will be reduced by reason to allow well of that which your Lordship hath done." [4] He was too sanguine. About a week later Sherley succeeded in seeing the Queen, and reported the interview to Leicester. "May it please your good Lordship," he wrote, "after eight days I spoke with Her Majesty, being brought unto her by Mr. Vice Chamberlain into the privy chamber when she used most bitter words against your Lordship for your receiving that government, affirming that she did expressly forbid it unto your Lordship in the presence and hearing of divers of her Council." [5] Sir Thomas used every possible argument to justify Leicester's action. "I told her," he said, "how those countries did expect you as a governor at your first landing and that the States durst do no other but to satisfy the people . . . and that the States . . . conferred the authority upon your Lordship with incessant suit unto you to receive it . . . and . . . when you had seen into their estates your Lordship found great profit and commodity like to come unto Her Majesty by your acceptance of it . . . how Her Highness might have garrisons of English in as many of their towns as pleased her . . . how no peace can at any time hereafter be made with Spain but through her and by her. I put Her Majesty also into remembrance that, if any of another nation had been chosen it might have wrought great danger." [6] The Queen reminded Sherley that she had published an eloquent pamphlet in which she declared to the world she would never take the sovereignty of the Netherlands. Now the general of her forces had accepted it. "Your Lordship's proceedings," Sherley reported her as saying, "was sufficient to make her infamous . . . and that your Lordship, being her servant, ought not, in your duty towards her, to have entered into that course without her knowledge and good allowance." The Queen was fearful that Leicester's action would embroil her in difficulties with Spain. Sherley most respectfully and humbly pointed out that by sending Leicester to fight the Spanish in the Netherlands, and Drake to strike at Spain in the Indies, the Queen was inevitably embroiled with Spain anyway, and of the two actions the depredations of Drake were the more direct affront to Spain. To this argument the Queen replied that she "could very well answer for Sir Francis, but if need be the gentleman careth not if I should disavow him." "Even so," replied Sherley, "standeth my lord, if your disavowing of him may also stand with Your Highness' favor toward him." Sherley besought the Queen to receive Leicester's letter which he had been charged to deliver. She refused to receive it. She questioned Sir Thomas about events in the Netherlands and the activities of her forces, whereupon he became wily. "In divers things that she asked of me," he wrote Leicester, "I seemed more ignorant than I was, and told her that I thought your Lordship had written thereof, because I would have her to receive your letter, but it would not be." Sherley continued his efforts to justify Leicester's acceptance of the governorship. Having used the good arguments, he turned to a poor one. He averred that upon the acceptance of the governorship by Leicester the authority of the States General of the Low Countries was "dissolved," and if the Queen insisted on Leicester's resignation then the country would be left without a government. The argument was nonsense and the Queen knew it. "She knew well enough," she gave him to understand, "that the States did remain the States still and said she meant not to do harm unto the cause but only to reform that which your Lordship had done beyond your warrant from her, and so she left me." [7]

Sherley made one more attempt on Leicester's behalf, relying on prevarication and pity rather than on his meager knowledge of statecraft. "Upon Friday last," he wrote Leicester, "as Her Majesty walked in the garden, I thought to test her affection unto your Lordship by another means." He told the Queen that Leicester was ill. In fact, he alleged, the fictitious affliction was a recurrence of one which had previously been cured by the Queen's physician, Goodrowse. Would it be possible, he begged, to send Goodrowse to the Low Countries to cure Leicester? "I assure your Lordship," he wrote, "it moved her much, and she answered me that with all her heart you should have him and that she was sorry that your Lordship had that need of him." [8] The dialogue proved the fact that the Queen had a warm heart, which was already known, but it did not alter her attitude toward Leicester's governorship, which could have been predicted.

In the meantime there was the problem of the business in hand, the fighting of the war. It is remarkable how many English expeditionary forces have gone off gaily to foreign parts and have been quickly forced into an agonizing reappraisal. Leicester's force was one of them. Among his fine gentlemen there was no one capable of handling an army, and in fact he did not really have an army. His was a collection of infantry and cavalry companies, with only the rudiments, if that, of the staff and logistical organization necessary for a unified fighting force. His opponent, the Spanish General Alessandro Farnese, Duke of Parma, outclassed any leader the Dutch or English could produce, and the hard-bitten Spanish regiments were the best troops in Europe. The moment of truth came when the fighting began. "How barbarous that common opinion is," observed Thomas Digges, who became muster master of Leicester's forces, "that an Englishman will be trained in a few weeks to be a perfect soldier." [9] "I am ashamed to think," Leicester wrote, "much more to speak, of the young men that have come over. Believe me you will all repent the cockney kind of bringing up at this day of our young men. . . . Our simplest men in show have been our best men, and your gallant blood and ruffian men the worst of all others." [10] A famous English soldier, Sir Roger Williams, observed that although arquebuses and muskets had been in general use by European infantry for fifty years and twenty-five years previously, the first English soldiers who really knew how to handle them were those who learned in the

Low Countries. The English soldier's habit of carrying his powder loose in his pocket was dismissed contemptuously by one of his countrymen as "more apt for the show of a triumph and wanton skirmish before Ladies and Gentlewomen than fit for the field." [11]

The English learned to fight the war the hard way and it was a painful process. Leicester and his officers were also hampered in their desire to create an effective fighting force by their ambition to make war profitable, since profits implied a minimum force at a maximum expenditure. The simplest way to make money was to be a company commander. The post of captain of a company was so lucrative that no man, considering his wife and children and what he owed himself, had the heart to forego it. Leicester, for example, was the commander-in-chief, but he was also the captain of a company. Sir Thomas Sherley became Treasurer at War, but he retained a company. The muster master had a company, the commanders of garrisons had companies; in fact, all staff or general officers, as far as there were any, had companies. The versatility of the company commanders in devising ways of making money was astounding. There were many of them working at the task, and they traded information. The most common and time-honored way was to draw pay for more men than were actually present. A certain number of "dead pays" was considered legitimate, say 10 per cent,[12] but by exercising ingenuity one could increase that percentage without actually seeming to do so. As early as the winter of 1586–1587 the army was short two thousand men, and that accomplishment was improved upon as the captains gained experience.[13] In 1589 it was found that, although a cavalry troop at strength was a hundred troopers, Barrows' troop was twenty-two strong, twelve at the most fit for service; Sir Christopher Blount had forty in his, half of whom were fit for service; Anthony Sherley had forty-two; Sir John Burgh had thirty-nine.[14] In fact, when six hundred cavalry were withdrawn to go with Drake and Norris on the expedition to Portugal, it was found that unfortunately there were only four hundred and fifty. When they arrived in England they were counted again, and unaccountably the number had shrunk to two hundred and sixty-seven, of whom more than fifty had no horses and so were called cavalrymen by courtesy only.[15]

There were ways of inflating the muster rolls other than by counting the dead, wounded, prisoners, or missing, or adding the legitimate 10 per cent. In return for a pass to England and a certificate that he was sick, for example, a soldier would agree that the captain was to draw his pay as though he were still in Holland.[16] This counting of men who were not there was the most elementary device for profit taking. The theory of the old mercenary companies was that the captain would pay the soldiers, who would undertake to feed, clothe, and arm themselves, but there were many variations on this basic understanding. The captain might and did furnish cloth to his men, and on this he could make a profit. He contracted with victualers to feed his men, and as a reward for this kindly concern received presents from the victualers and profits on the food. In the Netherlands, happily, it was sometimes possible to obtain food and supplies from the Dutch authorities, municipal, provincial, or central, by signing notes for them. At the same time the captain would deduct ("defalk" it was then called) the cost of the food from the soldiers' pay. Of course, the notes which the captains signed were ultimately presented to someone for payment, but the captains relied on the muddled bookkeeping in vogue in the English forces to keep them safe from exposure, or at least from too much exposure, and this confidence was seldom misplaced. As one moved up in the hierarchy of the army one's opportunities, of course, improved. For example, Leicester began his career as a general in the Netherlands by ordering a raise in pay for all officers, including himself, a change which his brother officers accepted with soldierlike obedience.[17] At first both the commander-in-chief and the captains were harassed by a paymaster, Richard Huddlestone, who evinced a certain lack of flexibility. By June 1586 Leicester avowed that he would deal with Huddlestone no longer.[18] The Treasurer at War was called home and examined on the charge that he had defrauded the Queen and the troops.[19] The charge could not be proved, but about seven months later Huddlestone, for his alleged but unproved sins, was dismissed. It is worth noting in passing that when a treasurer was needed for the expedition to Portugal two years later Huddlestone was chosen, and he died a poor man.

Huddlestone was replaced by Leicester's old friend and confidant, Sir Thomas Sherley, and thereafter things went much more smoothly, and the money much more quickly.[20] In June 1587 Burghley noted that £30,000 had been given to Sherley to pay the debts of the expedition, restore the cavalry to good condition, and pay all lendings (half pay for the soldiery) until 12 September; but the debts were not paid, the cavalry not rehabilitated, and when Leicester returned to the Netherlands in the last days of June, Sherley had only £3,000 instead of the £18,000 he should have had.[21] Leicester had been given an additional £30,000 to take with him to the Low Countries, but £8,000 disappeared before he left England, "for leaving money and other necessities," he explained. Two thousand pounds even disappeared between the lines of his letter, for having explained away eight of the £30,000, he goes on to say, "how little a while twenty thousand pounds will last among so many [here] your good Lordships may consider." [22] At the end of July Leicester reported that the money on hand would only last until 12 August, so the Queen saved the situation by sending another £30,000.[23] This additional largesse arrived in September, but the following month the situation was worse than ever. "The wants and discontentment of the old companies is wonderful, having received no full pay in twelve months," Sir Thomas wrote, "their exclamations . . . maketh me weary of my life here." [24]

Sir Thomas had one grave fault from the captains' viewpoint. He was far more versatile than they were, and they were soon murmuring against such versatility. "Although I had engaged myself for some sums of money to the relieving of the companies in Her Majesty's pay in the time of their necessity," wrote Sir John Norris, "whereof by my last I advertized the Lords of Her Highness' Council, yet am I not appointed to reimburse one penny and as for the repartition of the treasure of all such as was now brought out by Sir Thomas Sherley I have received both for my horse and footmen *not ten days pay.*" [25]

Arthur Champernowne, a captain at Utrecht, complained directly to Walsingham. "The Treasurer," he fumed, "presumes so far on the patience of such horse and foot companies as lies in these quarters as every two months or six weeks, he makes us fast fifteen days. . . . He makes us follow the Popish fastings and yet the most part of my men are Christian Welshmen who take no delight in such lean ceremonies." [26] Champernowne added that the cash intended to pay the troops had been loaned out by Sir Thomas at interest. Willoughby, who succeeded Leicester as commander-in-chief, almost instantly "conceived some misliking against the Treasurer," and his steward wrote Burghley that "it falleth out most strangely, by what device none knoweth, that the companies at Utrecht . . . are clean without money, and the Treasurer's man there answereth he hath none. I fear the fault springeth from some avarice in some of the Treasurer's men, who peradventure have put out the same for profit, and now suffer the soldiers to starve." [27] Willoughby drew up for Burghley an estimate of what he thought Sherley might be making. First there were his legitimate emoluments, his entertainment or pay, and the 1 per cent he received from the Queen on all funds he disbursed, plus the 1 per cent he exacted from all soldiers for having disbursed the funds to them. These sources, thought Willoughby, amounted to £4,120 per year, or double the amount paid the commanding general. In addition he had the money he could embezzle, to use a crude word, in the time-honored and respectable way as a captain of an infantry company which, in Sherley's case, could be augmented by what he could get out of the companies commanded by his sons. Then there were the gratuities from grateful officers who were paid before their pay was due, and tokens of gratitude from victualers who were paid before their fellow victualers. Sherley could also pick up a few pounds by buying up from merchants the debts owed them by captains and soldiers. Whereas merchants might despair of collecting, for Sherley it was an easy matter. He stopped the debts out of the soldiers' pay. He also bought up soldiers' claims to back pay, for whereas soldiers might give up hope of being paid it was a simple matter for the paymaster to pay to himself the full amount due the soldier. By no means to be discounted was the money to be made by loaning the Queen's fund at interest. Putting these various devices together, Willoughby believed that Sherley was making £20,000 per annum, or nearly a fifth of the amount necessary to maintain the English forces in the Netherlands for a year.[28] Later Willoughby, Thomas Lord Burgh, Sir John Burgh, and Sir William Russell begged the Queen to examine Sherley's accounts. "If," they wrote, "it be not found upon due examination that there is, and hath long been, in his hands of your Majesty's treasure, many thousands more than would pay all due to ourselves, we will still forbear to solicit Your Majesty for our own due." [29]

Because of such dastardly charges Burghley began to get uneasy. In May 1589 he asked Sherley what his income was. Sir Thomas claimed to be drawing a modest £1,700, but the details were vague, so vague, in fact, that Burghley felt impelled to continue to ask questions.[30] Sherley was hurt that anyone could believe that he reaped large sums from his office. Such suspicions, he felt, had originated in the guilty minds of some officers who were themselves appropriating the Queen's money. He asked for an audit of his accounts. If it were found that they were in good order he would continue to serve, for the Queen's favor was more desirable to him than any joy save the joys of heaven.[31] Burghley remained almost rudely persistent, and two and a half years later Sir Thomas was again explaining his income. His latest statement was that he really received only £700 per year, and even then his office entailed certain expenses (amount unspecified) which were fortunately offset by additional sources of income, also not indicated.[32] The situation was opaque and to be on the safe side the Queen reduced his stipend. About a year later he was again explaining his income. It had recently been said that the merchants with whom he worked made £11,000 per annum on the monetary exchange, and that he himself made £3,000 annually from his office. He replied that, far from making £3,000, he spent on his office £135 more than his income every year. What his friends the merchants made he was not sure, but he felt it could not be £11,000.[33]

When so many were receiving more than they were entitled to, it might be expected that others received less than they ought to. These latter were Queen Elizabeth, the private soldiers, and the United Provinces. It did not take long for the careful Queen to sense that something was wrong. Only four months from the time Sir Thomas first began to oversee the disbursement of funds she complained that, "God knows by whose default," but she could never get an accounting of her money.[34] The army, she exclaimed, "is a sieve that spends as it receives to little purpose." [35] In June 1586, scarcely half a year after Leicester arrived in the Netherlands, she wrote him, somewhat ungrammatically, "It frets me not a little that the poor soldier that hourly ventures life should want their due, that well deserve rather reward." She admonished Leicester to "look in whom the fault may duly be proved; let them smart therefore." [36] Still no one smarted very much except the Queen and the soldiers. About a year later she had had enough. She declared "peremptorily," wrote Burghley, "that she will send no more money until she shall have . . . a good declaration made in particular how Sir Thomas Sherley hath paid such great sums as (she saith) he hath had." [37] Though she employed a treasurer, an auditor, and a muster master, she was never able to learn what the monthly expenses were, "so as though it be continually alleged that great sums are due, yet why such sums are due, . . . and who are paid and who not paid . . . is never certified." [38]

The Dutch had contracted to pay for a certain number of troops (6,000), and they were so impolite and distrustful as to count the English soldiers present. In 1589 a Dutch official checking on the strength of the English companies came to the conclusion that he was dealing with people without either sense or discretion, and the States General later in that year sent commissioners to England to complain that many companies were only at two-thirds of their alleged strength.[39]

The private soldiers even more than the Queen or the Dutch were aware that something was rotten in Leicester's army. The reason that such large sums could find their way into private pockets was that although the cost of the army had originally been reckoned on the basis of full pay for the soldiers, actually the men seldom got more than lendings, or half pay, enough to keep them from starving, at least in most cases. Sometimes even the lendings failed. In March 1587 Lord Buckhurst was besieged with the complaints of captains and soldiers in Bergen op Zoom that there was little money and no credit, and he implored the home government for Jesus' sake to take cognizance of the situation.[40] Sherley wrote Burghley a month later that if a supply of money were not sent the situation would become dangerous, and a few days later in one town the soldiers, in desperation, took to robbing the townspeople.[41] In October 1588 the States of Zeeland with some concern called to Burghley's attention the fact that for the past two years the garrisons of Flushing and Brielle had not received a full monthly pay.[42] About the same time the garrison at Ostend mutinied. The mutineers declared that many companies in their garrison had not received a month's pay for two and a half years. They were ready to prove that on one occasion seven and a half months' pay had been brought into the garrison and the men had not received a penny of it. The captains were paid for full-strength companies which were actually at half strength. Each man, then, did the work of two. They were continually on guard and they were breaking under the strain.[43]

When mutiny threatened, the brass became frightened. Sherley pleaded with the Privy Council that he might have fourteen or fifteen thousand pounds for "lendings," for without them were was no way for the soldiers to live and the men would "fall into arms with the towns for meat." [44] Leicester added his plea to Sherley's. "For God's sake and for all your poor countrymen's here," he wrote, "send with all haste if but £10,000 to keep their lendings and the poor men in life." [45]

From time to time reforms were instituted which the officers did not really want, however much the Queen, the Dutch, and the soldiers did. In March 1587 an order went out to the army that since Her Majesty was acquainted with "sundry abuses by the captains toward the poor soldiers in converting to their own proper uses such sums of money as have been delivered unto them . . . ," henceforth wages were "to be paid to the soldier by the pole." [46] This was to be done by the Treasurer at War or his deputies in the presence of the muster master or his deputies. Thereafter the muster master counted the men, deducted the difference between a full-strength company and the actual strength, and upon his certificate the Treasurer at War paid the captain for the number of men certified. There was a startling increase in the strength of the companies, but within two months the Queen learned that these new orders were "impugned by some of the captains in a kind of mutinous and disordered sort, by threatening the muster master and casting out libels against him." [47] As a matter of fact, Leicester himself disregarded the order. The muster master, Sir Thomas Digges, complained that after he and his men had "by great travail discovered many frauds and abuses," whereby he had heaped upon himself the great hatred of many captains, these commanders had appealed to Leicester, who "did mitigate or pardon the checks [i.e. the deductions for men not present]" and ordered that the cavalry troops, including his own, should be passed without checks, so that whereas the savings made by the muster master ought to have amounted to £13,000 they only amounted to £3,000.[48] Three months after the new orders went into effect the captains had succeeded in breaking down Her Majesty's regulations so thoroughly that, although the cavalry squadrons were exceptionally weak, the captains were drawing pay for squadrons at full strength.

A year later there was a second reform. Not only was the Treasurer at War to pay the captains just for the number of men certified by the muster master, but this was to be done in the open, in the presence of the corporals, or sergeants, or six of the longest-service soldiers.[49] The additional stipulation makes it evident that some in high places suspected collusion between the Treasurer at War and the captains. The attempted reforms had one effect at least. They made the muster master the most unpopular Englishman in the Netherlands. He was particularly unpopular with Sir Thomas Sherley, for Sir Thomas could make no payments without a certificate from Thomas Digges, which proved confining. Sherley had not been in office two months when an observer wrote, "I fear me that Sir Thomas

Sherley shall have something to do with the muster master . . . for they run a violent course." [50] Later Digges pleaded with Burghley for his pay, "so long forborn after others by whom Her Majesty has been damaged are fully paid, or overpaid, whereas I, that never increased her charge one penny, saved many thousand, am yet unsatisfied by £1,000." His brother, James Digges, commissioner for musters, he said, also remained unpaid, "through Sir Thomas Sherley's malice towards him, whereof I have also had some taste for doing my duty faithfully." [51] A few months later, writing to Willoughby, Thomas Digges referred to the "maimed abbreviates of Mr. Treasurer's [Sherley's] accounts," and noted that "for the £142/17/6 alleged to be paid me, he never paid me one penny for which he has not good warrant, and he has one from the Earl of Leicester to pay me £400 more than I ever could get of him. . . . As for the £561/1/0 averred to be paid to Captain Isley . . . he never paid that sum for him. . . . Whatsoever I see, I will not meddle with more than concerns myself, being now no officer, but happily disburdened of that thankless place, where, for my faithful services I have got so many enemies, and have been lately threatened by Mr. Treasurer that if I be one of the combiners against him, he will so use the matter, as that although he have as many thousands of Her Majesty's treasure as is supposed, there shall be little found due to me; well knowing nevertheless that there is nigh £1,000 due to me. . . ." [52]

While their father was occupied with these great but vexing matters, Captain Thomas and Captain Anthony were close to the dirty business of war. As has been indicated, the military career of young Thomas was largely confined to one engagement at which his cavalry squadron was present but he was not. In January 1588 his troop was ordered to Zwolle, a walled city in the province of Overyssel, east of the Zuyder Zee. Sherley's lieutenant in command of the company reported to Lord Willoughby that he had arrived at Zwolle on a Friday afternoon. He showed the city fathers his patent or order to be stationed in their city, but the burgers showed little appreciation for the company's proffered protection, especially since there were already garrison companies in the town. The authorities of Zwolle explained that the year previously they had had the honour to entertain the Count de Meurs's company. Unfortunately the Count's men had been short of funds. The burgers had extended them credit, and in fact were still doing so for the simple reason that there was no way to make them pay. Although reluctant to take in Sherley's men, the burgers provided them with bread and cheese, and oats for their horses. The English troopers were allowed to pass in and out of the town and some of the soldiers took the opportunity to have their saddles and gear repaired, a bit of housekeeping that immobilized the company. Meanwhile Sherley's lieutenant continued his endeavors to have the company accepted as part of the garrison. The authorities procrastinated, but promised to answer him later, "which answer," reported the lieutenant, "I had on Saturday towards the evening to this effect, alleging that horsemen could do no service there, and that considered, they would take no horsemen in, which allegation is known to be contrary and that there is no place in these seventeen provinces more fit for horse than that, and where a company may annoy the enemy at their pleasure." [53] The lieutenant being obviously indignant, the burgers placated him by promising that if they were relieved of one of the companies already stationed in the town, they would take in Sherley's horse. Leaving the company under the command of the cornet, evidently a young and inexperienced officer, the lieutenant left to seek to obtain from Willoughby an order for the transfer of one of the companies already in Zwolle. "I departed from the Company," the lieutenant wrote Willoughby, "on the fourth day, being Sunday, to procure Your Honor's letters to that effect hoping at my return to get the company in, leaving such direction with the officers that if, being followed, the company had not been overthrown. . . ." He had commanded, the lieutenant declared, that the men were to sleep in their arms, with their horses ready saddled and a good watch kept. Unfortunately no watch was kept and although the soldiers slept, it was not in their arms. In fact, in Lord Willoughby's judgment, Sunday was spent drinking and sleeping before the gates of Zwolle. Hugh Ashen, trum-

Spring Valley Library
Colorado Mountain College
3000 County Road 114
Glenwood Springs, CO 81601

peter, who lost his horse and trumpet in the eventual disaster, declared that on Saturday the company had intelligence that the enemy, 300 foot, eight mounted men, and four mounted pages, were within one Dutch mile of them, but Sunday night the English were so totally unaware of the actual position of the enemy company that when between 11 P.M. and midnight the latter pounced on them, Sherley's men were taken completely by surprise. There was a meadow nearby, the trumpeter said, and if the English could have reached it (which they did not) they might have saved themselves since they were attacked only by infantry. Sixty-three horses and about thirty men were lost, twenty men were unaccounted for, and only twenty horses and thirty men were saved. The cornet, who was killed, was blamed for the disaster. "I, hearing of this news," the lieutenant reported to Willoughby, "came again to Zwolle to make provision for the burying of our men, and saying that I was sorry for the death of the Cornet, the rest of the Company that was there made answer and said that if I loved him I might be glad that he was slain for if he had lived he would have lived in disgrace of the world for that night's service, considering that the soldiers were willing to do anything and their commander so amazed that he could not perform anything."

Other survivors beside the trumpeter were questioned as to what had actually happened. James Wright, gentleman, had heard that the lieutenant had been offered money to depart. Robert Gremes, gentleman, declared that the burgers of Zwolle commanded the company to depart the day before they were surprised. The day after the disaster, Gremes declared, he went into the town and charged the burgers with having betrayed Sherley's company, whereupon, "he was then wished by the quartermaster to hold his peace for that they had offered him [the lieutenant? them?] 400 guilders."

William Armeshow declared that after being taken prisoner, his captor, Count Harman, had told him that Sherley's company were betrayed by the burgers of Zwolle and that they (the burgers) had sent a hostage, a burger disguised as a farmer, to the Spanish force and this hostage remained with the enemy until the return of their men from their attack upon the English company. Five other members of the company also claimed to have heard the enemy captain, Count Harman, say that a burger was sent to him disguised as a peasant and that he kept this burger until he had proof that the information given him by the townsman was accurate, and these facts were also affirmed by other survivors.

Although he could not question those said to be responsible for the dastardly deed, namely the dead cornet, the burgers of Zwolle, and the enemy, Lord Willoughby reviewed such information as was available and came to the grim conclusion that "it were better for Her Majesty to turn bad captains of horse into good captains of foot." [54]

Yet having lost his troop through negligence, young Thomas was treated with that excessive consideration which may be remarked on later occasions. The Privy Council instructed Lord Willoughby that he "should . . . forbear to alter the company of Captain Sherley, and that allowance be made unto him of four months' checks [the pay of men killed, taken prisoner, or missing] toward the new repairing of such of his said band of horse as were lately lost and the redeeming of the prisoners taken by the enemy." [55] Willoughby was outraged. He addressed a letter to Burghley, signed by himself and two other officials. They thought as well of young Sherley as his years allowed them to, but they feared the precedent might prove very chargeable to Her Majesty, "when other noble and experimented leaders (who have lost many horses and men in notable services) shall hereby be drawn to sue for the like favor; which, if refused, will make great discontentment, to see such bounty bestowed where the loss grew by negligence." [56] Eighteen months later Willoughby was still fuming. He asked that "I may have allowance for my horses lost in honorable service as Sherley had for his which were negligently cast away whilst they were drinking and sleeping at Zwolle portes." [57] The skirmish put a temporary end to the career of Thomas in the Low Countries. Two months later his squadron was given to his brother Anthony.[58] Far from returning to England in disgrace, Thomas was sent to Ireland, and there on 26 October 1589 was knighted by the Lord Deputy, Sir William Fitzwilliam. He came home, not a broken soldier, but a shining knight. Being temporarily done with war, he repaired to the court of Queen Elizabeth and there solaced himself with that other knightly preoccupation, love.

His brother Anthony Sherley was a captain of infantry and first saw service at Brielle, commanding a garrison company with a bad reputation. His men were undisciplined and robbed the neighboring farms, and punishment was no deterrent. When he was first appointed commander the men refused to accept him. Lord Burgh, commander at Brielle, transferred them from the garrison to the field force, but they mutinied and refused to leave. Lord Burgh executed four of them, whereupon the others went quietly.[59] The company behaved no better in the field. Less than three months after Lord Burgh executed the mutineers Lord Willoughby reported to Leicester "certain abuses in Mr. Sherley's company." [60] Anthony must have felt a certain amount of relief when he gave up the company to take command of his brother's troop of horse which had been badly mauled in the disastrous skirmish at Zwolle. At the time he took over, his brother's cavalry was stationed at Utrecht, but the Dutch had long importuned Lord Willoughby to garrison that city with infantry companies, and Willoughby cast about for a billet for Sherley's cavalry. He suggested Zwolle, but that city had refused the troop when commanded by Thomas and now refused it when commanded by Anthony. Willoughby next thought of Arnhem, but the city fathers there had previously quarreled with Anthony. Having received His Lordship's patent directing them to take in Captain Sherley's troop, they thanked Lord Willoughby for his care of their safety, but they knew not how to support a whole troop. They begged that instead of Sherley's horse, His Lordship would send thirty, or at most forty, of his own troop. To their prayer that they be spared the presence of Anthony's horse was added that of their Stadholder.[61] "Your Lordship's patent had been accepted and obeyed here," wrote an English officer from Arnhem, "if it had been for any other than Captain Sherley whom they will by no means have . . . and it is to be feared that if he were here he should not walk the streets without danger of his life." [62] For lack of some place to go the troopers remained at Utrecht. Officially they were not wanted,[63] but it was reported to Willoughby that, "there is much secret practising, and great odds laid that Captain Blount's company will not be removed, nor Captain Sherley's either, unless his private debts are paid." [64]

Later Lord Willoughby found several towns willing to have Sherley's and Blount's cavalry but those commanders found the towns distasteful. Taking advantage of Willoughby's absence at Ostend, Sherley and Blount contrived to have their troops sent to Rheinberg.[65] They were there in June 1588, but the journey had been arduous and they had not as yet "attempted anything against the enemy," Anthony reported, "their march having been so long, their companies so wearied and their intelligence too small to hazard their credits." [66] Though the English were nonbelligerents the enemy was not so quiescent. A month after Anthony wrote, Rheinberg was besieged, and two weeks later it seemed likely both town and troops would be lost.[67] "Since they first entered the town I have not by letter or otherwise heard from them," Willoughby reported to the Privy Council, "I cannot yet advise what means may be had to relieve them." [68] Fortunately Willoughby found means and they were extricated. He again had the problem of finding a place for them. The Stadholder of Utrecht hastily asked that no orders for their readmission into that city be given before he had an opportunity to talk to Willoughby.[69] Meanwhile, difficulties arose between Sherley and his commander. Anthony and four other captains complained to Willoughby that no funds were ever given them to replace horses, or to repair and replace equipment. They and their men were never paid in full, and the portion of their pay actually received was not enough to live on. Their position was so difficult, they declared, that if they did not receive help they would ask permission to resign.[70] In the same month in which Sherley's squadron had been gotten out of Rheinberg, Willoughby had consented to a Dutch request that the squadron be sent to Gelderland to serve with the Dutch forces there.[71] The following month Colonel Schenk, the commander in Gelderland, complained bitterly that although Anthony's cavalry had been promised they had not arrived.[72] Actually, instead of going to Gelderland they went to Gorcum in the opposite direction, for in October it was discovered that three troopers in Sherley's squadron were doing a thriving business in that town coining counterfeit double ducats and dollars.[73] Although they had been due in August, neither Sherley's company nor Blount's had arrived in Gelderland by December. The Council of State at The Hague remonstrated with Willoughby. They had heard from their deputies that Blount and Sherley refused to march, saying they had no money and were in debt. "It is very unfitting," the Council thought, "that such frivolous excuses should interfere with the service of the country." They prayed Willoughby to issue peremptory orders that Sherley and Blount march without delay.[74]

The next month Willoughby solved the problem of Anthony's cavalry troop. He solved it in the same way Lord Burgh had solved the problem of Anthony's infantry company, which is the way such army problems are often solved. He transferred it out of his command. In January 1589 England was preparing a massive attack on Portugal, the counterblow to the Invincible Armada sent against England the previous year. Willoughby drew up a list of companies to be sent on the expedition against Portugal, and Sherley's cavalry was on the list.[75] Actually it did not go to Portugal, for although its strength had always been given as one hundred lances it was found on arrival in England to be a mere remnant of a company and was demobilized.[76]

CHAPTER III

The Sherleys Lay Down Their Arms

IN 1589, then, both brothers were temporarily without commands and their military careers were suspended. How inspiring their father might have appeared to them at this time. Whereas they were *hors de combat,* he was at the height of his military success, a friend of the powerful and making money in more ways than they or any other captain had thought of. In addition and as a side operation, in this very same year the brilliant parent was on the point of getting into his hands all the lands belonging to Norwich Cathedral—a rich plum worth £2,000 per annum.

Sir Thomas the elder remained Treasurer at War until 1597. In the same period, 1589–1597, Anthony Sherley had many adventures, but the life of Sir Thomas the younger was comparatively uneventful. He resumed his military career eventually but not before he had dallied for some time at court—perhaps too long, since while tasting those pleasures he contracted a secret marriage, which put an end to the fun. The court was in progress and had reached Cowdray, the seat of Viscount Montagu in Sussex, when his matrimonial adventure came to light. The Queen with her retinue arrived at Cowdray on Saturday, 15 August 1591, and was welcomed in the usual way with speeches and entertainment. The next morning the party breakfasted on three oxen and 140 geese, and Sunday was spent pleasantly enough. The following day there were more speeches and entertainment. On Wednesday the court dined out of doors at a table 72 feet long.[1] It was a week of gaiety and pastoral charm, but before it was out, there were a number of miserable people, the Queen was out of temper, and young Sir Thomas was out of the court.

Some months previously, he had been powerfully attracted by a widow then at court, Frances, Lady Stourton, the sister-in-law of Robert Cecil and the sister of Lord Cobham. Young Sherley had, he said, "a desire to make her possessor of all my love and thoughts." [2] This desire pleased his father and was not unpleasing to the lady's relatives. Unfortunately young Sir Thomas was not steadfast in his affection, both because he was "shaken with the slanders she was subject unto," and because there was at court another lady even more fair and desirable than Lady Stourton. As a matter of fact, Sir Thomas saw, loved, and secretly married Frances Vavasour, the daughter of Sir Thomas Vavasour. But, although married to Frances Vavasour, he continued to assure Lord Cobham, his own father, and Lady Stourton that he remained true to Lady Stourton, pursuing this equivocal course, he said, "for fear of offending my father with my double dealing, neither durst I in outward show to him to seem to leave my first desires till I had found some good means to win [him] to like the second." [3] How his duplicity became known while the court was at Cowdray is not clear, but this was one of the rare occasions when Sir Robert Cecil showed signs of being outraged. He assured Sir Thomas the elder that he "could not be so simple as not to see the injury your son offered me, to pick me out only, and to the last hour, even at Cowdray, to abuse a lady and her friends whom I ought to regard, but when I saw that he forgot his duty to his father, I did determine to remember no longer his wrong to me." [4] The Queen also was furious. Few things infuriated her more than to have a lady of her court marry secretly.

There are obvious reasons why such actions displeased her. She stood *in loco parentis* to her maids, if not to all court ladies. As for her courtiers, she had a right to know what they were doing. Irregular conduct on the part of anyone was bad for the reputation of her court. These reasons are sufficient to explain displeasure. They do not quite explain why the marriages of others so enraged the Virgin Queen that she exiled or jailed offenders. Cecil wrote Sherley that "the Queen did command me to signify that her pleasure is, that you shall forthwith directly make it known by public act that for the act of such contempt to her court as well as for his wilful perjuries and unnatural disobedience to yourself, you cannot digest it." [5] Sir Thomas the elder was more than willing to obey Her Majesty but he did not know "by what other open act I can show my dislike, having forbidden him my house and abandoned him from me and out of my sight." [6] He besought Cecil that the Queen might be moved to consider that he himself had been wronged, "in having my son inveigled (for so I do conceive it) and in a sort stolen from me." [7] He was not convinced a child was on the way, for as concerned the lady, "neither do I know her to be with child nor do care whether she be or not." [8] "I do confess to your Lordship," he wrote Burghley, "that I am even weary come home and almost overcome with the great grief and trouble of my own private [affairs] in regard of the most unhappy wretched dealing of my unworthy boy, by which I stand vexed both in heart and soul." [9] The only person to take a sanguine view of the affair was Lady Paget, the culprit's aunt. Young Thomas' action, she felt, was the result of overpowering love. She had no doubt, she wrote the father, that in time the marriage would bring him true joy, and she was sure Her Majesty was well appeased.[10] In the latter assumption she was grievously mistaken, for a few days after she wrote, the Queen ordered young Sir Thomas to be confined in the Marshalsea prison. He was still there fourteen weeks later when he addressed a touching letter to Lord Burghley. "I prostrate myself most humbly," he wrote, "at Her Majesty's feet, and will not think any chastisement too much . . . yet . . . if Her Majesty shall please, of Her Gracious goodness, to esteem mine already straitened punishment sufficient . . . I will think and acknowledge that Her Majesty doth deal most graciously with me"; and he dated the letter from "the sorrowful Marshalsea." [11] Probably he did not remain in prison long after writing this letter, for although the Queen was quick to anger, she did not harbor grudges. There is one indication at least that Sir Thomas may have become a more sober and useful man after his marriage. In the Parliament of 1593 he sat as a member for Steyning, the

Sherley pocket borough, and possibly (though one may doubt it) he and his lady had a few years of domestic happiness.

By 1597 these quiet times were over, for in that year his father suffered a reversal of fortune and was relieved of his duties as Treasurer at War. It was reported that "young Sir Thomas Sherley dares not go abroad so far engaged is he for his father's debts." [12] A few months later the Privy Council granted him a protection "to pass quietly without arrest or impeachment for the space of forty days." [13] Still evincing that tender regard which has been noted, the Council secured for him the captaincy of the infantry company in the Low Countries which his father had commanded. In writing to Sir Robert Sidney in the Netherlands the Privy Council passed lightly over Sherley's record and reminded Sidney that Sir Thomas "having (as you know) already served as a captain in those Provinces we hold him very able and worthy of that charge. . . . We do heartily pray you to let him have the commandment of the company as captain . . . to continue until you shall receive order to the contrary from Her Majesty, whereunto we doubt not you will be inclined in compassion towards the gentleman, the rather to gratify us, which shall not be forgotten." [14] Although the request came from the Privy Council, Cecil was probably behind the action, for less than three weeks after he had gotten the company young Sherley wrote Cecil asking for help in keeping it. He reported that his father's successor, Sir Thomas Fludd, "did yesterday write to my Lord governor that the Queen's Majesty had promised him the leading of that company . . . as without it he was not able to occupy his place of paymaster and he (thirsting still for it) is like to get it out of my hands" if Cecil did not cross him in the pursuit thereof.[15] Cecil came to his rescue and he retained the command.

About two months later this company was one of ten withdrawn from the Low Countries to accompany the Earl of Essex on The Islands Voyage,[16] the sergeant major of the land forces on that adventure being his brother Anthony. The expedition set sail in July, was driven back into the port by a storm, and sailed again on 17 August. It was a frustrated and fruitless expedition, and it was over before the end of October. In the months following (November and December 1597) Sherley's company was at Dartmouth, and in January 1598 he no longer commanded the company.[17] His career as a soldier was ended. Henceforth he sought fame and fortune at sea, as his brother Anthony had decided to do a few years earlier.

Whereas after 1589 there was a long hiatus in the adventures of Sir Thomas the younger, there was, as has been said, little time for inactivity in the life of Anthony. It will be remembered that in 1589 his company was shipped home from the Netherlands to take part in the raid on Portugal, but, being a mere remnant of a cavalry troop, it had been broken up. He could not have been idle more than a few months, for in the summer of 1589 he took part in an expedition to France. In that summer, Henry III was assassinated and the Huguenot Henry of Navarre was proclaimed king of France as Henry IV. France was torn by religious wars, and Queen Elizabeth aided Henry IV and the Huguenots in their war with the Catholic League. In October Willoughby, with a force of 4,000 men, was sent across the Channel. Anthony Sherley was with the force, and in the three months' campaign that followed he distinguished himself. La Noue, a famous Huguenot soldier, singled out Sherley for special commendation, describing him as a "gentil cavallero."[18] Although the English force fought gallantly, it was woefully cut up. Of the 4,000 men probably not more than a thousand returned to England in January 1590, and in the same year a new danger loomed. A Spanish force of 3,000 men under Don Juan de Aguila had landed at Saint-Nazaire and together with forces of the Catholic League had fortified Blavet.[19] The enemy landing acted like an electric shock to Elizabeth and her ministers, even though it had been a probability for some time. The Queen wanted the Spanish out of Brittany. She agreed to send troops to the aid of Henry IV provided she was repaid her expenses and was given one or two good Breton ports. Henry agreed to everything. He promised that the French forces in Brittany would be at all times twice the size of the English, which they never were. He promised to repay Elizabeth for her help, which he never did. He evaded the question of ports as long as possible, finally promised, and gave up Paimpol when there was no way out.

The English expeditionary force consisted of three regiments: one commanded by Sir John Norris, the commander-in-chief, the second by his brother, Sir Henry Norris, and the third, perhaps in recognition of his distinguished service with Willoughby's French expedition, by Anthony Sherley. Some troops were drawn from the Low Countries, and others from England. There were difficulties and delays, but on 11 April 1591 it was recorded that "this morning, being Sunday, my lord general with Sir Henry Norris [and] Captain Anthony Sherley . . . took post horses at London to ride to Southampton."[20] Sailing from that port the English contingent was met off Jersey by the troops from the Low Countries, and the whole force, numbering, not 3,000 as had been planned, but 2,400, continued to Paimpol on the Northwest tip of Brittany, where they debarked in the first days of May. On the march southward the cavalry was led by Anthony. Passing beyond Guingamp they encountered an enemy force which Sherley and his cavalry put to flight in a brilliant action, though on a small scale.

In fact the whole campaign in Brittany was on a small scale. The French royalists did not quite trust their English allies, and the aims of their opponents, the French Catholic League and the Spanish, were also in some degree divergent. Neither side was strong enough to gain a decisive victory or bold enough to try. Though this was a minor war of skirmishes, raids, and indecisive battles, the very lack of definite battle lines made it a ferocious one, and since this was a religious war—that is to say an ideological one—both sides felt justified in wreaking slightly more cruelty on their opponents than might have been admissible in a simple struggle for trade or prestige. One chronicler noted that his village had been pillaged forty times by one side or another. The English and French royalists were discouraged by their inability to win a decision. As a result of a council of war, Sir Henry Norris was sent home in February 1592 to ask either that the troops should be reinforced or deployed elsewhere. Not only did Sir Henry go home, but nearly everyone else did, for Sir John Norris, Colonel Sherley, and a number of other high officers departed for England the following month, leaving the English troops to the care of the sergeant major, Arthur Wingfield.[21] The English were now down to 1,200 men.[22] Their reduced numbers and the departure of the leaders heartened the opposition. In May the Anglo-French troops were disastrously defeated at Craon, and the remnant of the English force was later caught at Ambrières near Mayenne and wiped out.[23] If not a case of too little and too late, at least the expedition was too little. The news of the disaster at Craon brought fresh requests for help from the French, and Queen Elizabeth took advantage of their need to press once more her old demand for a French port. A new treaty was signed in June 1592, and new forces were sent to France. The English and French were each to supply 4,000 men for the Brittany campaign, and Henry IV agreed to hand over a Breton port to the Queen. Consequently in November 1592 Sir John Norris, with Anthony Sherley and the troops, returned to Brittany. Concerning the port, the French agreed to hand over Paimpol and the isle of Brehac.[24] Norris assigned to Sherley the responsibility of fortifying Paimpol, and the latter returned to England with a detailed list of smiths, masons, carpenters, and materials which he would need to carry out his task.[25] His mission proved unnecessary. While he was away, the Catholic League captured Paimpol. Although it was later won back by the French royalists, Henry IV, reasoning perhaps that the English seemed incapable of holding it, refused to give it back to them.[26]

About a year later, Anthony was employed on a more agreeable mission. He accompanied Sir Robert Sidney on a special embassy to the French court and while there was knighted by the King.[27] True enough it was not an important honor. He was made a knight of Saint Michael, an order which in former ages had been prestigious, but which by the reign of Henry IV had been conferred on so many and fallen so low in esteem as to be known in France as "the dog collar to fit all dogs." In conferring the order Henry IV was merely making a friendly gesture, but unfortunately the conferring of titles on her subjects was another one of the many things which aroused Elizabeth's fury. Returning home, Anthony found himself where he and members of his family were so often to find themselves—in jail. He was questioned by the Lord Keeper, Sir John Puckering, and by Lord Buckhurst as to the oath he had taken, the crucial point being whether in receiving the order he had sworn allegiance to Henry IV or promised to defend the Roman Catholic faith.[28] His answers proved a little vague and he was committed to the Fleet prison. A few days later Sir George Carew had a go at questioning him. He was asked "what oath he took at the receiving of the Order of Saint Michael, and the manner thereof." Anthony declared "that oath I took none . . . the effect of the King's demand was that I should promise in his hands never to bear arms against him for . . . any Christian prince but my sovereign." [29] This answer was also unsatisfactory, and he was returned to prison. More than a month later at least two attempts were made to have him forswear and disclaim the knighthood. "We had Mr. Sherley before us," reported the Lord Keeper, Sir John Puckering, and Lord Buckhurst to Sir Robert Cecil, "and from Her Majesty expressly commanded that he should sign the enclosed, and further acknowledge by submission in writing his great contempt in not doing the same at the first offer thereof as he was then commanded. . . . Wherein, albeit we did, in the most earnest and sharpest course that we might, urge the performance of Her Majesty's said commandment, he would by no means yield, and notwithstanding our often sharp reprehensions, and our strict urging him in duty thereunto, yet this was his final and resolute answer. For the first, that this matter concerned his reputation, more dear to him than his life; his life and all that he had was at Her Majesty's commandment and that he had rather lose his life than lose his reputation, desiring rather to die than live with disgrace, which he accounted the yielding up of this would bring upon him. . . . And for the second, he thought it . . . not any contempt to seek to preserve his reputation, and so in like manner, refused the same. For which his most contemptuous dealings, we, after due and just reprehensions, returned him to the Fleet, with strait commandment to the Warden to continue his strait and close imprisonment, as formerly we had given in charge." [30] In the end a compromise was reached. Anthony recanted on any oath he had taken and the insignia of the knightly order were sent back to Henry IV, but henceforth he was always referred to officially as Sir Anthony Sherley.[31]

Henry IV was vastly amused at the furore aroused by his giving Anthony the Order of Saint Michael. If, that merry monarch observed, Queen Elizabeth, as a friendly gesture, should declare a visiting Frenchman a knight of King Arthur's round table, and if thereupon he should become furious and insulted, one would have a comparable situation.

Anthony, now Sir Anthony, was freed from prison and resumed his rank of colonel of a regiment in Brittany, where he remained until 1595. He may well have been present at the final victorious action there, a grimly satisfying end to years of fruitless skirmishes, small victories, and bitter defeats. Don Juan de Aguila had constructed fortifications at Crozon with the intent of cutting off Brest from the sea. An expedition under Norris and Frobisher was dispatched to avert this new danger. On 7 November 1594 the English took Crozon, the 350 Spanish in the place being either put to the sword or perishing in the sea. After this exploit Norris returned home, and at the end of February 1595 the last of the English troops were taken off the Breton coast. There is no indication that during his service in France Anthony was anything other than a brave and dutiful soldier. Indeed, all surviving records show that he was one of the best and most valiant, serving throughout the campaign except for short visits to England, as when he came home to be jailed for being honored by the French.

Before the end of the campaign, Anthony secretly married Frances Vernon, a first cousin of the Earl of Essex. Like the Sherley brothers, the Vernon sisters had a penchant for secret marriages. Elizabeth, Frances' sister, secretly married the Earl of Southampton, and the Earl was exiled from the court as a result. Sir Anthony fared no better. In April 1595 he wrote, "I am here in the country and as far as I can judge, exiled from all hope of recovering such grace in the Court as my best endeavors have ever held their course for." [32] It was charged that Sir Thomas Sherley the elder had arranged the match for Sir Anthony in order to advance the fortunes of his family, a charge which the elder Sherley indignantly denied. Far from arranging it, he declared "the marriage was made and concluded by my son himself without my privity. The Earl [of Essex] was the first that brake it unto me when my son was in France and I had no reason to refuse to give my consent to the marriage . . . having no just cause of exception against the gentlewoman, though I had reason to have wished my son some match of wealth, though she had been of much meaner blood." [33] Regarding the Earl of Essex he observed that "neither do I use him in any cause of mine or find it reasonable for me to commit my fortune into the hands of a man that seemeth to have small regard of his own." [34]

Unfortunately after suffering so much for love, Sir Anthony was unhappy. Exiled from the court, he moved to Inglefield, a property in Tilehurst (now part of Reading) which Essex had sold him even though it is doubtful whether Essex owned it.[35] Sir Anthony was now thirty. He was not a court captain. He had been fighting since he was twenty, which would perhaps have ruined any tendency toward domesticity, if he had ever had such leanings. Moreover he was a younger son, seeking to make his way in the world, not the toilsome way of a city merchant, but some easy, brilliant road to fame and fortune such as his father appeared to be following. He turned as did so many Elizabethans to adventure at sea, planning an expedition against the Portuguese island of São Thomé off the African coast. For some time English privateers (although the term was not then used) had been making rich hauls by capturing Portuguese vessels coming from São Thomé laden with sugar. Sir Anthony was more ambitious. He planned to capture the source of supply. His father stood behind him and financed him. It was an adventure which promised rich pickings, such a one as old Sir Thomas might have thought of himself. Young Sherley looked forward to the beginning of action and the end of domesticity. He was well into his plans by November 1595.

"Sir Anthony Sherley goes forward on his voyage very well furnished," wrote Rowland Whyte to Sir Robert Sidney, "led by the strange fortune of his marriage to undertake any course that may occupy his mind, from thinking on her vainest words." [36]

The year 1589, which marked a temporary end to the military careers of both Sir Anthony Sherley and Sir Thomas the younger, was also a turning point in the life of their father. In that year his duties as Treasurer at War were enlarged and, perhaps because of that increased responsibility, he contracted with a group of merchants, headed by William Beecher, a prominent London merchant, who were to do part of his work for him. This was Sherley's undoing. If it had not been for the contract with Beecher, he might have gone on stealing the Queen's money with no more hazard than that encountered by others who were doing the same thing.

The first expansion of Sir Thomas' duties beyond the Low Countries occurred in 1589 when troops were withdrawn from the Netherlands for the raid on Portugal. Sir Thomas was given the task of paying and supplying these detachments. Later, when companies were sent to Brittany from the Low Countries, he paid and supplied them also. He hired ships, bought horses, wagons, and ammunition, and paid the troops when Essex commanded an army in Normandy in 1591, when two thousand troops were transferred from Brittany to Ireland in 1594, and when a little later two thousand men were sent into Picardy.

To comprehend how English troops came to be spread so far, one may recall the years when the Queen and her councilors debated whether to remain isolationist or become interventionist, whether to help the embattled Netherlanders or not. Sir Thomas himself had witnessed and even taken part in the debate on that question. He had sat in Parliament in 1572, 1576, and 1581 and listened to those advocating war (for that is what it came to) on high principles. There had been some shrewd councilors, one may not perhaps have the temerity to call them wise, who wished to base the decision for intervention or isolation on the low principle of the survival of their country. But the men of high principle triumphed and England became committed to the far-flung ideological war, a commitment to fight Catholicism and Spaniards wherever they might be found, the distinction between the two becoming obscured in the enthusiasm for the cause.

It is of some interest, if unimportant, to recall that there had been those, such as Sir Walter Mildmay, who had advocated armaments and all measures of warlike preparedness. The war machine once set in motion was difficult to stop. When the grave decision for war had to be made, Mildmay and other erstwhile bold spirits hung back, but war came, and spread as wars are apt to do. Sherley, if he remembered Mildmay's fine speeches in Parliament, must have done so with gratification, for it was the likes of Sir Walter Mildmay, bold in speech and timid in action, that gave the likes of Sir Thomas Sherley, quick, bold, and unscrupulous in action, such wonderful opportunities. Sir Thomas became the key figure in the logistics of the far-flung war, and the London merchants, principally Beecher, were his associates.

The contract between Sir Thomas and Beecher was designed to lighten the load of Sir Thomas' expanding activities and to provide at the same time a satisfactory profit to both parties. In explaining the agreement later, Sherley said that the merchants were unable to give him any security for the large sums of the Queen's money which he placed in their hands, "whereupon they did offer unto me gift and consideration of money in respect of my hazard and adventure with them. . . . They and I did agree upon a profit which I should have out of those industries of theirs, and I did receive of them divers sums of money upon the same agreement. I do assure myself that no man will think it reasonable that I being bound both in my body and in my lands to the Queen's Majesty for the answering of her treasure, should deliver the same so hazardously as to such a fellow as Beecher without some commodity and profit to myself to be yielded by him in respect of my hazard. . . . I ever took it that a man may with honesty accept a gratuity given; if a man may not also accept a gift proceeding in respect of a hazard, I must think it most wonderful and say, Lord have mercy upon me." [37]

The agreement was what in our day would be termed a defense contract. The entrepreneurs who now make such contracts in wartime take the wise precaution of making them on the basis of "cost plus 10 per cent." These Elizabethan merchants agreed to supply Flemish pounds, food, and clothing for fixed amounts. They were men of experience and it may be presumed that in fixing the prices at which they agreed to supply the items, they allowed themselves ample margin to take care of any foreseeable increase in the amount they themselves might have to pay for foodstuffs or Flemish pounds.

Unfortunately, a series of droughts and bad harvests in Italy, beginning in 1587, upset all their calculations. By 1590 it was said that the Italian poor were eating grass, and next year the famine was worse. The Dukes of Florence, Ferrara, and Urbino, and the Republic of Venice bought grain wherever they could find it. Since the Dutch were the great dealers in grain, which they got in the Baltic countries, the Italians were soon relying on the Dutch. News of the astounding profits to be made in Italy spread through the Netherlands, and the price of grain in the Low Countries shot upward. The impact on Beecher and his associates was almost immediate. In October 1590 they admitted that, because all the grain was going to Italy, they could not supply wheat to the garrisons at Flushing and Brielle. Grain was bought with Flemish pounds, now needed by the Italians, and the English merchants complained that they could not buy Flemish money at any reasonable rate.[38] In this impasse, in lieu of cash, the soldiers were paid in kind. The captains were soon bewailing the fact that they were receiving half their soldiers' pay in English cloth rather than Flemish pounds. The material was good warm stuff, but the soldiers could not eat it. Curiously, as the disbursement of raw cloth increased, the quality of the clothing furnished went down. The captains also protested that the clothing their men received was shoddy and not according to specifications.

The struggle to fulfill his contract proved too much for Beecher, and in December 1596 he went bankrupt. He immediately accused Sherley of withholding £43,000 of the Queen's money. "Sir Thomas Sherley hath been put to many troubles," remarked Rowland Whyte, the court postmaster, who was paid by Sir Robert Sidney to send him news and who therefore followed the case with avidity, "by the merchants breaking [going bankrupt] to borrow money, plate, jewels of all his friends, sons and daughters; land he offers to sell but everybody afraid to purchase it, because he is an accountant [is responsible] to the Queen." [39] By March, Sherley was himself bankrupt. "I fear Sir Thomas Sherley will out," wrote Whyte, "for he accepts no bills of exchange, keeps his house and can hold up his credit no longer." [40] Later he reported, "Now I may boldly write unto you that he is fallen. . . . Sir Thomas Sherley's suit is that Her Majesty may suffer him to sell his lands for her satisfaction . . . and seems resolute that his debt to the Queen is small; but the world thinks otherwise." [41] Still avidly interested, Whyte reported in a few days that "the Queen is greatly incensed and disquieted with Sir Thomas Sherley's doings, for he made at first £4,000 the cause of his breaking and now every day the sum increases to five, six and seven thousand pounds." [42]

It was evident that Sir Thomas' enigmatic bookkeeping was causing trouble, for later Whyte reported, "This afternoon the Lords were at my Lord Treasurer's about the accounts of Sir T. Sherley; it is said he owes the Queen more than he is worth." [43] The Lords of the Treasury and the accountants were to change their minds many times as they puzzled over Sherley's books, but these peculiar books had long been a puzzle. Nearly a decade earlier the Privy Council had been confused by one of Sherley's accountings; it ran to twenty-two pages and remarkably showed more money paid out than had been received, a puzzle that one acute examiner resolved when he discovered that the accounting began immediately after the date on which Sherley had received a large sum of the Queen's cash. Although his balance sheets invariably itemized numerous receipts and disbursements, there were always some expenditures for which no amount was given.

The Queen's officials were both puzzled and unhappy. "We have conferred divers times with Sir Thomas Sherley," Sir John Fortescue wrote to Sir Robert Cecil, "and have at last brought him to yield to assure all his lands to my Lord Keeper, my Lord Treasurer, my Lord of Buckhurst, and myself to the use of satisfaction of Her Majesty's debt; which being paid they remain to himself and his heirs . . . we have gotten good cause of seizure of his lands and goods." [44] Sir Thomas was also unhappy. "I am offered," he complained to Sir Robert Cecil, "a strange and most extraordinary course of handling, and such as I never heard to be offered to any man in this world, which is that before my accounts be determined, or any certain debt known upon me, I should make over all my lands . . . to be returned to me when the Queen's Majesty is satisfied; and in the meantime no provision of livelihood for me, my wife, and children. Now, Sir, what haste there will be made either to do the one or the other when all my land is thus put out of my possession and others possessed therewith, God doth know; but I have cause to think that it will be doomsday first." [45]

In April, Sherley was insisting that he owed the Queen no more than £8,000, but the Queen's auditors were insisting that he owed her £19,000. It also seemed clear that Beecher had given him more than £15,000, "by gift or allowance . . . for part of his gain in respect of hazard." [46] In that same month Beecher and Sherley had an altercation before the Privy Council which ended in Sherley's being sent to the Fleet, and six commissioners were appointed to determine the truth of their conflicting statements. Sherley assured the commissioners, among other things, that in the last year before he went bankrupt he had borrowed less than £1,800 from Beecher, but he admitted to Burghley that he had left the troops unpaid in the Low Countries by more than £5,000. In August the commissioners completed their examination and concluded that Beecher owed Sherley slightly more than £18,000. Sherley seized on the finding with joy. "Beecher in the presence of your Lordship and others, and to my face," he recalled to Burghley gleefully, "did most impudently affirm that if he did not make good proof that I was above £30,000 in his debt, he would be hanged at the Court gate. Whereunto it pleased your Lordship to say that if he did not make good proof of it, I should be delivered from my imprisonment and he should be in my place." [47] Sherley's glee was premature, for whereas the auditors found that Beecher owed him, they also found that he owed the Queen £23,000 odd. Beecher was sent to the Fleet, but Sherley was not released. In October he prayed that he be given liberty. "I speak nothing of the decay of my health," he averred, "because I esteem least of that, being more willing to die than live in this declination of my fortune . . . ," [48] but he had numerous affairs and lawsuits and needed his freedom to attend to them. In December he was given leave to attend to his affairs during the day provided he returned to prison at night. He was probably released in January 1598, a poor man certainly but not a broken one, for he was soon involved in a number of ingenious projects.

CHAPTER IV

The Sherleys Take to the Sea

WHEN Sir Francis Drake returned home with a hold full of Spanish treasure, said one of his compatriots, he "enflamed the whole country with a desire to venture unto the seas, in hope of the like good success, [so] that a great number prepared ships, mariners, and soldiers, and travelled every place where any profit might be had." [1] Of this multitude that ventured on robbery at sea, Sir Anthony was one. As has been noted, in 1595 he planned to loot the island of São Thomé. At the end of that year, his father purchased nine ships for him from Thomas Heaton of Southampton—the *Gallion, Constance, George, George Noble, Archangel, Mermaid, Swan,* a half share in the *Black Wolf,* and an unspecified share in the *Beavis.*[2] In April of the following year a galley and a pinnace were added to the Sherley fleet. Heaton had made money by sea raiding for a decade, but just before selling his ships to the Sherleys, he had lost in the same way, a circumstance which might have given pause to men less intrepid than Sir Thomas and his son Sir Anthony. The Sherleys not only bought the fleet of eleven ships and manned and provisioned it, but also recruited a private army of 1,500 men. It has been reckoned that the cost of the expedition was between fifteen and twenty thousand pounds, nearer the latter than the former. If he captured São Thomé, Sir Anthony stood to gain much, but he would have to gather in loot worth 20,000 pounds in order to break even. If he failed, he lost considerably, and the chances for failure, as an expert in this field, K. R. Andrews, has estimated, were about nine to one. It is remarkable that the Treasurer at War, burdened with the task of feeding and paying a number of overseas armies, had the energy and funds to collaborate on fitting out the expedition.

In the spring of 1596, the fleet was ready to sail except for one trifling matter: Sir Anthony had no plausible excuse for putting to sea—no cloak of legality for the intended raid. There were various methods whereby a show of legality might be obtained. Sir Anthony might procure a letter of reprisal, as his brother did later, or he might buy a license from the Court of the Lord High Admiral, or for a suitably valuable gift to the Admiral obtain a letter from him directly. Sir Anthony chose, perhaps in the interests of economy, to circumvent the High Admiral and obtain a commission from Queen Elizabeth, a course which, as subsequent events showed, was perhaps more expensive in the end. He set about obtaining a commission in the good old Elizabethan way. He wrote to his friend Anthony Bacon, who was Essex' secretary in charge of the Earl's network of spies at home and abroad. Sherley asked Bacon to intercede for him with Essex to obtain a commission or letters patent from the Queen. He did not neglect, of course, to send along to Bacon a suitable present when he made his request. Bacon graciously acknowledged having received the "honorable rich token" which Sherley had sent and assured him that "this day I have remembered and recommended the expedition." [3] Sherley in reply expressed his pleasure that the nobility of Bacon's mind had persuaded him to accept the token, and thanked him for "remembering me to my Lord Essex, to whom I have written about that commission which I hope and have need to receive presently."

Unfortunately Essex was himself preoccupied with the task of preparing a fleet designed to defend his country and to enrich himself. The Queen had sealed a commission authorizing Essex and Lord Admiral Howard to raise 5,000 soldiers and to engage an equal number of mariners for an expedition against Spain, for it was rumored that Spain planned to attack England. Essex and Howard were charged to destroy Spanish ships, lay waste Spanish towns, and gather as much booty as possible. Actually, this enterprise developed into the expedition to Cadiz, probably the most successful Elizabethan raid on Spain. Essex and the Lord Admiral were in the opposite predicament to Sherley. They had a commission to perform the voyage, but they were struggling to find ships and men. The Lord Admiral, for example, excused himself from coming to court because he, Ralegh, and Lord Thomas Howard, who were also taking part in the expedition, were busy every day from early till late, up and down the river looking for seamen. As Ralegh put it, he went dragging in the mud from one alehouse to another, hunting runaway sailors.[4] Being so pressed with his own problems, Essex neglected the matter of Sir Anthony's commission, but at length obtained it. When Sherley received the commission, he was bitterly disappointed. He needed, he complained to Bacon, authority "to govern this heap of confused people, which I have here gathered together." Essex, he felt, had slighted and neglected him. "I have cried out to my Lord," he wrote to Bacon, "I have implored his letters, and I have not received one so much as unto myself, but only this poor commission, which doth but diminish the reputation of what I am." [5] His complaint was heeded, and he received a new commission. It would perhaps have been better if he had been satisfied with the first one. In their efforts to procure land forces for their expedition, Essex and the Lord Admiral issued subcommissions to trusted officers to recruit companies. Sherley's new commission was actually one of these subcommissions. In accepting it, he became nominally part of the expedition of the Admiral and Essex, and they were his superior officers. Sherley was by this commission empowered to levy, muster, and arm volunteers for Her Majesty's service to the number of 1,500 men, and to command all ships set forth at the charge of himself and Sir Thomas Sherley, Treasurer at War.[6] In line with his new status, Sir Anthony moved his squadron from Southampton to Plymouth, the rendezvous for the fleet of Essex and the Lord Admiral. He arrived there with nine ships and 1,400 men, exceedingly well armed. He was now ready to sail, and asked the permission of Howard and Essex to do so. "But no way to release me could be possibly imagined nor thought of," he wrote to Bacon, "except I would deliver 500 men armed, and four ships victualed for four months, for this journey [Essex' expedition to Cadiz], which I did as frankly condescend unto, as a man would, that had no way left to escape apparent ruin, but that miserable one, yet better than none at all." [7] In return for his four ships and 500 men Sherley asked that he might have two men out of each ship of the Essex expedition to make up the lack in his own crews. Howard and Essex readily agreed, but Sherley never got the men. Indeed, Sir Anthony remarked, being still at Plymouth, that if ships could be moved by promises, he would have enjoyed such favorable gales that "I had been by this time past the Canaries." [8] Essex later helped him with money, but Sherley remained bitter toward the Lord Admiral, although his reasons for being so were not the best. He had avoided rendering the Admiral his due emoluments, but the latter had ended in getting more from Sherley than he would have gotten had he sold Sir Anthony a license. A curious consequence of Sherley's having a commission in the expedition that sacked Cadiz was that thirty years later a story was current in Spain that he had been with Essex on that occasion.

Sherley finally sailed on 20 May 1596 with five ships, the *Beavis, Gallion, George, George Noble, Wolf,* and in addition a galley and a pinnace. Off Cape Verde he fell so ill that he was "hopeless of life," and the crews were "all dismayed and comfortless through that his exceeding extremity." [9] Because of contrary winds the plan to sack São Thomé had to be abandoned. Casting about for something worth looting, the squadron headed for the Cape Verde Islands, where a landing was made at Praia, on the island of São Tiago, but nothing was found there worth taking. The anonymous chronicler of the voyage records that feeling frustrated, "divers of our company were very importunate with our general, that he would go to the city of Santiago [the city of São Tiago on the island of São Tiago], being six miles off." Sherley yielded and led his 280 men toward São Tiago, but "that night we lost our way," says the chronicler, "and lay under a hedge." The English finally arrived at São Tiago but found that the strength and situation of the place were "sufficient to have daunted a man of very good courage, for it standeth between two steep cliffs strongly housed, and three exceeding good forts commanding the whole." Only one narrow path led into the town. It was obvious to all, including Sir Anthony, that the Portuguese meant to lure the invaders along the path and trap them in the town; but Sherley, records his admiring chronicler, "with an excellent resolution (like unto himself) cried out, 'All courage my hearts . . .' " and led his men into the city, where "we presently by the General's direction (whose skill, spirit, and diligence can never have sufficient commendation) barricaded up all the streets, and brought ourselves into a very convenient strength." The Portuguese then counterattacked. In the first assault, Sherley lost 80 of his original 280 men, and the Portuguese "still prosecuted their assault, not giving us time either to sleep or eat, so that we were in exceeding extremity." [10] Finally, "scarce able to defend any one assault more," Sherley withdrew his men to his ships under cover of night, and sailed for the West Indies. The total booty taken in the Cape Verde Islands was one small ship laden with cloth and wine, a sad contrast to the intended capture of the island of São Thomé.

On the Atlantic crossing, Hakluyt's informant said, "our men fell generally down [sick] . . . the disease was so vile that men grew loathsome unto themselves, frantic and desperately raving, among whom our good General's part was not the least; for his disease was vehement, the grief of his mind, the lamentation of his men, and the loss of those whom he loved were to him torments more than durable; all which with patience and humility in prayer he humbled himself unto. But had not his mind been invincible and his desires above the ordinary course of men, it had been impossible that life should now have rested in him." [11] After minor adventures, during the course of which the ship *Wolf* deserted the expedition, Sherley arrived off the Jamaica coast where Kingston is now situated. The Englishmen found Jamaica a marvelous, fertile island, a garden and a store house. "During the time that we remained in this isle," says the account in Hakluyt, "the captain of the isle came often aboard us, we having pledges for the security of their promise. They were in fine at our general's devotion . . . so that now we were as one people and in one peace together." [12] This account by Sherley's anonymous chronicler and admirer is a touch different from the Spanish version of what happened during Sherley's visit to Santiago de la Vega (Spanishtown). In the descriptions of these events by the villagers whose houses were sacked, the aura of brotherly love is lacking. When Sherley's men came ashore, the townspeople fled to the woods and camped there. According to the inhabitants, the English looted the empty town and burned a few houses. Through Indians, Sherley got into communication with the town officials camped in the woods and demanded a thousand arrobas of meat and four thousand cargas of cassava as ransom for the city. The Spanish at first refused the ransom demanded, whereupon the English rode over the countryside flushing out townspeople wherever they found them. Francisco Gallego, a citizen, testified later that "the men came ashore and entered into this town. They looted and sacked the country . . . did much damage, burning about sixty houses." [13] Francisco Arnaldo, treasurer general and official judge of the island, declared that he and some others were sent "to talk with the English general by order of the said governor [of the island] and to tell him that he should be mindful of the damage and ruin the English had perpetrated in the country; that he should not permit women and children to suffer in the wilds; and that he should order his men to re-embark, for they had looted the houses outside the town of the most of the wealth of the country and had perpetrated many other harmful acts." [14] Captain Francisco Bejarano deposed that he knew "the English went by bands through the wild places and overran and laid them waste." After sacking the camp of the abbot, for example, the English bore down on the camp of Captain Bejarano, so that he, his family, and others were forced to flee. Bejarano returned to the camp and saw the English "breaking and opening boxes from which they took more than 3,000 pesos." Don Francisco, Marqués de Villalobos, the abbot of the monastery, stated that he "and the fathers of the Convent of Saint Dominic . . . fled to the wilds. A guide showed them [Sherley's men] the way to the camp of the Fathers; the Fathers and Abbot had to flee, leaving behind their clothes, money, jewels and other things which the English stole." Fray Pedro de Ulloque, who was camped with the abbot, declared that he saw that "a numerous band of the English all armed . . . came to the said abbot's place, . . . and all the . . . people with him were forced to take to flight. . . . So the said abbot, this witness, and the other friars went to the plantation of the accountant general, Pedro de Castillo, where this witness knows and saw that since the said abbot had escaped quite naked, the said governor gave him a jacket and a cloth pair of breeches with which he dressed himself." [15]

Shortly after Sherley had departed, a Spanish ship came into port. The captain, Don Fernando Melgarejo de Cordova, testified that he had arrived at Jamaica the first of March and learned that on the fourth of February an English fleet had come into the port. The English had looted the town and asked as ransom "one thousand arrobas of meat and four hundred loads of cassava. . . . They began to set fire to some huts. Accordingly, it was decided to give them what they asked, whereupon they returned to their ships." [16] Actually before the Spanish vessel arrived and before Sherley departed, two English ships under Captain William Parker arrived in port, and they were joined by a pinnace commanded by Michael (later Sir Michael) Geare. Sherley, Parker, and Geare agreed to sail in consort for the Bay of Honduras and sack the town of Truxillo. Parker, a daring and experienced captain, was a successful raider before and after, but unfortunately not during, his association with Sherley. Arriving in the Bay of Honduras and finding Truxillo too strong, the English took the town of Puerto de Cavallos, "the most poor and miserable place of all India." After this disappointment, relates Sherley's chronicler, "our hopes were all frustrate. . . . Our general reserving unto himself his silent inward impatience, labored to do some memorable thing." The memorable thing that Sherley and Parker concocted was to make their way up one of the rivers flowing into the Gulf of Honduras to its headwaters; then to carry a boat in sections to a stream flowing into the Pacific. Putting the boat together, they planned to make their way downstream to the ocean. They actually got thirty leagues up river, but found nothing worth looting, nor any connecting stream. Since many of their men were ill, they turned back and embarked on their ships, which were waiting for them in the Bay of Honduras.

The adventure had failed and Parker and Sherley parted. Parker sailed alone into the Gulf of Mexico, where he captured the town of Campeche and a frigate laden with silver and other valuable goods. A few years later, he accomplished the remarkable feat of capturing Portobelo and made another rich haul. After leaving Parker, Sherley, "whose restless spirit continually labored to avoid the frowns of fortune," conceived a second extraordinary plan. He in the *Beavis* and accompanied by the *Gallion* would go to Newfoundland, take on provisions there, return southward, rejoin the rest of the fleet, and the reunited squadron would then sail into the Pacific by way of the Straits of Magellan. "Being thwart Havana," says the historian of the voyage, "by what chance I know not, but all his ships forsook him the 13 of May, and here in a desperate place he was left desperately alone." [17] If the chronicler could not adduce at least one reason why Sir Anthony was deserted, he was less skilled in elementary arithmetic, obviously, than were his shipmates. To go to Newfoundland, return, and sail round the Horn, and then reach England by crossing the Pacific was at least a voyage of 40,000 miles. Elizabethan sea-dogs went down to the sea in ships not in search of colorful adventures, nor to add a glorious page to English maritime history. Their motive, curiously like that of modern entrepreneurs, was mainly profit. These particular seamen had been at sea a year without profit. The deserters were simply engaged in the familiar operation of cutting their losses. Actually not all Sherley's ships had deserted since he himself had sent the *George* home with letters, but now the *Beavis* made its solitary way to Newfoundland, arriving there "without an hour's victuals to spare." Sherley sailed from Newfoundland for England on 27 June, but news of his adventures had preceded him. The *Wolf,* which had deserted him in February, arrived home in March "with no news [other] than of the misery of their voyage." A rumor ran for two days, said Rowland Whyte, "that he [Anthony] had gotten a frigate richly laden, but it doth not continue for good." [18]

Sir Thomas the elder must have longed for it to be true. At this time he was deep in his financial troubles, and the return of Anthony with rich prizes could have meant freedom and affluence to him. "Though I take little hope of the news brought of my son Anthony," he wrote, "yet am I advised by some friends of mine to send an express messenger to Plymouth." [19] The flickering hope was soon extinguished. When Anthony reached England in June there were, of course, no prizes, and of that fleet which had cost nearly £20,000 only one ship remained. For the father, the son's homecoming was bitter, but it was no less so for the son. Sir Thomas' bankruptcy, removal from office, and imprisonment had all occurred during Sir Anthony's absence. "I am weather beaten home . . ." wrote the latter, "and met with the bitterest discomfort of my father's troubles, . . . but I will endeavor . . . to comfort his age and relieve my own wants, and though I be broken in pieces with all manner of mishaps, yet will I follow this mine service to see how God will please to bless me." [20]

Although he meant to comfort his father in his advanced years, he was able to devote only a modicum of time to filial affection, for by following his service Sir Anthony evidently meant continuing to seek his fortune at sea. Luckily at that moment there was an opportunity of doing so. Sir Robert Cecil noted a few weeks after his return that "poor Anthony Sherley is come home alive but poor, and goeth out with the Earl," [21] by which he meant that Sir Anthony was to take part in a new expedition of the Earl of Essex' which has since been known as The Islands Voyage.

In revenge for Essex' sack of Cadiz the previous year, the Spanish had prepared a fleet to invade England. A storm scattered the armada, and the surviving vessels in bad condition assembled in El Ferrol. The primary object of Essex' expedition was to destroy these Spanish ships. If the Spanish fleet had already left El Ferrol, it was to be destroyed at sea. After its destruction, Essex was free to look for plunder wherever it might be found. He was empowered to sail to the Azores to intercept the treasure fleet if he so decided.

Essex sailed on 10 July and had barely gotten to sea when his fleet was dispersed by a violent storm. John Donne, who was among the gentlemen volunteers, wrote:

> It rained more
> Than if the sun had drunk the sea before.
> Some coffin'd in their cabins lie, equally

Grieved that they are not dead, and yet must die,
And as sin burdened souls from graves will creep,
At the last day, some forth their cabins peep.[22]

The storm over, the expedition limped back to port. The provisions had been spoiled and lost in the tempest. The beer had gone bad in the casks, a real calamity since beer was the usual beverage on long voyages. Luckily (or unluckily), when the fleet had returned, a prize was brought into port laden with Canary wine, and the wine was appropriated by Essex to replace the spoiled beer.[23] Many ships had been damaged, and "this violent and dangerous tempest," wrote Sir Arthur Gorges, had so "cooled and battered the courages of a great many of our young gentlemen, who seeing that the boisterous winds and merciless seas had neither affinity with London delicacy, nor court bravery, as that discharging their high plumes, and embroidered cassocks, they secretly retired themselves home, forgetting either to bid their friends farewell, or to take leave of their General." [24] One of those too sick to continue was Sir Ferdinando Gorges, the Sergeant Major of the forces. Essex appointed Sir Anthony in his place, Sherley thus becoming one of the principal officers of the expedition.

Since ships had been damaged and many young gallants had gone into voluntary retirement, Essex consulted with his lieutenants on the best course to pursue. Eventually it was decided to discharge all of the soldiers except 1,000 Low Country veterans. Without an army, a large-scale attack on El Ferrol was out of the question. As an alternative, Essex proposed to lead a forlorn hope into the port, destroy the fleet, and, if possible, get out again. Sir Anthony was sent to London to inform the Queen and the Privy Council of the reduced size of the expedition and of the decisions taken by the council of war. This was Sir Anthony's first return to court since his exile following his secret marriage.

"I pray you . . . ," Essex wrote to Cecil on behalf of Sir Anthony, "do him with Her Majesty what favor you can, for, on my credit, he doth wonderfully deserve to be cherished," [25] and he wrote the Privy Council that he was sending the Sergeant

Major, Sir Anthony Sherley, since he was best acquainted with the state of the forces and had been a hearer "of all our opinions and disputations every way." [26] Sir Anthony was restored to the Queen's favor, for she received him graciously. "Sir Anthony Sherley, his instructions and letters," wrote Cecil to Essex, "were read by the Queen, and he himself presented by my Lord Ho:[ward] and me, used with great favor both in the privy and drawing chamber." [27]

By mid-August, the ships were repaired, the beer had been replaced with good Canary wine, Sherley had returned from court, and the Earl was ready for sea again. The Queen had refused to risk Essex and her ships, and had vetoed the plan of sending a forlorn hope into El Ferrol. As an alternative, it was planned that Sir Walter Ralegh, Rear Admiral of the expedition, would take fire ships into the harbor and burn the Spanish vessels. Actually when the English fleet arrived off El Ferrol, contrary winds made it impossible to get fire ships into the port. In this impasse the first objective of the expedition, the destruction of the enemy fleet, was abandoned. The English went cruising off the coast of Portugal in the hope of intercepting the treasure fleet on its way from Spanish America. Essex with three squadrons cruised between Cape Finisterre and Cape Roca, and Ralegh's squadron cruised southward of him. From a passing English privateer, Ralegh heard that the Spanish fleet had actually slipped out of El Ferrol, had evaded all three of Essex' squadrons and his own, and was on its way to the Azores to meet the treasure fleet. Ralegh believed the rumor. He communicated it to Essex, who also believed it, whereupon the whole English fleet, without verifying the information, sailed for the Azores in pursuit of the Spanish—who were safe and snug in El Ferrol. A Spanish fleet so close to England had been the incentive for mobilizing the Essex expedition, and the Earl's first objective had been to destroy the enemy ships. There was now no fleet between these Spanish vessels and England. It was a golden opportunity, and as soon as he could, the Spanish admiral, Don Martin de Padilla, took advantage of it. When his ships were ready he put to sea—objective, Falmouth. Unfortunately for this able admiral, as on the occasion of the Great Armada, the winds were on the side of the English. Padilla's fleet was scattered by a raging storm. For three days the gallant Spaniard grimly fought the elements, but at last was forced to give up and run for the Spanish coast. Contemplating this most fortunate dispersal of the Spanish ships, Sir William Monson remarked that "we must ascribe this victory to God for certainly the enemy's designs were perilous and not diverted by our force." [28]

As a matter of fact, the force alluded to had for some time been occupied with rather exciting adventures in the Azores. Sir William Monson commanded the *Rainbow* in Essex' expedition and has left an account of the voyage. While there were many distinguished noblemen and valiant soldiers commanding vessels on the occasion, Monson was an old experienced sea-dog and he was often consulted by Essex.

After watering at the Island of Flores in the Azores, Monson advised Essex to sail westward, with his fleet fanned out from north to south, and showed that if the treasure fleet followed its usual timetable (which indeed it did), the English were bound to intercept it, for it could not possibly be more than two hundred leagues from where Essex' squadrons were then anchored. In this Monson erred only in the particular that the treasure fleet, as it turned out, was actually only fifty leagues away. Essex was impressed by Monson's advice and resolved to follow it, but he was "diverted by divers gentlemen, who, coming principally for land-service, found themselves tired by the tediousness of the sea, so that they courted nothing more than to be on shore." [29]

As a result, Essex remained in the islands. But if he would not go to the treasure fleet, it eventually came to him. Some of his men, being ashore on the island of Graciosa, where Essex was then anchored, saw four sail far at sea, one of which seemed to be a Spanish carrack. Monson was sure this was part of the treasure fleet, and so was Essex. Monson admonished Essex to dispatch a squadron to head off the Spanish flota from reaching Angra on the island of Terceira, for which fortified harbor they were undoubtedly heading. Monson was then dispatched to keep in touch with the Spaniards, and Essex promised to send twelve ships to aid him. After Monson had sailed in pursuit of the Spanish, Essex was persuaded by a commander of a small bark that the ships Monson was chasing were not Spanish but actually part of Essex' own fleet. The Earl thereupon decided not to dispatch the twelve ships to aid Monson as he had promised and not to head off the fleet if it were indeed making for Terceira. Meanwhile Monson reached the treasure fleet. All night long he showed lights, burnt Greek fire, and shot off guns to attract the twelve ships which were coming to his aid, but, of course, to no avail.

At daylight the main body of the Spanish fleet was two miles ahead of Monson and a Spanish frigate and a galleon were behind him. The *Garland,* commanded by the Earl of Southampton, came up, but instead of giving chase to the fleet as Monson was doing, the Earl turned back to capture the frigate. While the Earl was looting the frigate, the *Mary Rose,* Sir Francis Vere, commander, and the *Dreadnought,* commanded by Sir William Brooke, hove in sight. The Spanish captives from the frigate persuaded the Earl of Southampton that the ships approaching (actually the *Mary Rose* and *Dreadnought*) were Spanish galleons. Southampton thereupon commanded Monson to abandon the chase of the treasure fleet and concentrate on capturing the approaching galleons. Monson argued that they were not galleons but English. When the vessels were close enough to identify as the *Mary Rose* and the *Dreadnought,* the treasure fleet was hopelessly out of reach. Carrying ten million pesos in bullion it reached safe anchorage under the guns of Angra.

The one memorable act of the English fleet was the capture of Fayal by Sir Walter Ralegh and his squadron. Essex had ordered Ralegh to rendezvous with him at that island, and although Essex was closer to Fayal than was Ralegh, the latter lay before the town of Horta for four days waiting for Essex. Ralegh hesitated to attack without permission of the commander-in-chief, but finally did so, capturing the town. The next day Essex arrived, angry and envious of the success Ralegh had achieved, and was on the point of court-martialing him. "All our proceedings in Fayall," explained Sir Arthur Gorges, who was with Ralegh, "were by Sir Guillie Merrick, at large related unto our

General [Essex] and . . . wrested into an evil sense by him, Sir Christopher Blount, Sir Anthony Sherley, and others, by putting my Lord [Essex] in the head that these parts were played by the Rear Admiral [Ralegh] only to steal honor and reputation from him . . . , which intimation of theirs was an exception that they knew our general was very apt of his own disposition to take hold of, being a man that did affect nothing in the world so much as fame." [30]

The advice and urgings of Sir Christopher Blount, Sir Anthony Sherley, and the others very nearly resulted in Sir Walter Ralegh's being beheaded long before he actually was, but Lord Thomas Howard mediated in the quarrel and at length Essex and Ralegh exchanged apologies. Essex eventually restored to rank all the officers he had broken for obeying Ralegh. The expedition sailed home, "full of discontent." All discipline was lost; "the fleet kept no order at all but every ship made the best haste they could." [31] The Islands Voyage was a typical Essex adventure; bold resolutions in one direction were succeeded by hesitation and bold resolutions in the opposite direction. Still, on this expedition there seem to have been more missed signals, misunderstood orders, countermanded instructions, ships wrongly identified, useless excursions, and lost opportunities than was usually the case. One remembers that the ships' spoiled beer had been replaced by the prize cargo of Canary wine which perhaps both induced failure and comforted the unsuccessful.

The official report on the voyage was signed by the chief officers of the expedition, including Sir Anthony Sherley. The signatories admitted they had come home empty-handed, but they hoped "Her Majesty will think our painful days, careful nights, evil diet, and many hazards deserve not now to be measured by the event." They also were aware that there were those, "others that have set warm at home and descant upon us," but such men, they knew, "lacked strength to perform more, and believe they lack courage to adventure so much." [32]

Sir Anthony was at the end of a second unsuccessful voyage, but his resilience was unimpaired. Having arrived home at the end of October, he was gone again in two months on an adventure which would lead him by way of the Netherlands to Italy and then Persia.

Sir Anthony departed on New Year's day, 1598, and in that same year Sir Thomas the younger, following the example of his younger brother, sought his fortune at sea.[33] He went on no royal or quasi-royal expedition but departed with a letter of mark or reprisal. Legally speaking such a letter empowered a merchant robbed at sea to recoup his losses by taking money or goods of equal value from any ship belonging to the nation that robbed him. There was no really effective way to establish the value of what the English merchant had lost. There were no means to determine whether the Spanish goods he captured as reprisal were of equal or greater value; or to prevent the wronged merchant from enlisting the help of another merchant, or sea captain, in helping him in the action of reprisal; or prohibiting him from selling his letter of mark to one more capable of exacting reprisal. There quickly sprang into existence whole fleets of vessels employed in the profitable business of taking reprisals. The ports of Weymouth and Southampton were very largely ports for fitting out privateers (as they were called in later centuries) and for marketing the prize goods captured. From 1585 until the end of the century, there were at least one hundred vessels employed at all times in privateering and sometimes as many as two hundred. "Voyages of purchase or reprisals," remarked Thomas Nashe in 1599, "are now grown a common traffic." [34]

Even before letters of mark were generally issued, the English had a bad reputation at sea and such letters increased it. In 1582 the Spanish ambassador presented at the English court a great number of complaints on the part of his compatriots against English pirates. The Danes called the English thieves at sea, and some Germans thought the Queen deliberately outfitted pirates; the French of Rouen hated the English who lived, they said, by despoiling their ships, and a Venetian official was firmly convinced that there was not an English sailor who was not a pirate.[35] "Nothing is thought to have enriched the English more," the Venetian ambassador to England remarked, ". . . as the wars with the Spaniards in the time of Queen Elizabeth. All were permitted to go privateering and they plundered not only the Spaniards but all others indifferently." [36]

By the time Sir Thomas the younger took to sea, privateering was a business for experts, with voyages usually being backed by merchants and executed by professional seamen. It was seldom that a country gentleman such as young Sir Thomas ventured to command a privateering cruise, and when he did so it was usually with such results as Sherley achieved.[37]

Sir Thomas ventured into these strange and, as it proved, shark-infested waters in 1598. In July of that year it was noted that he was "general of a fleet of ships," his armada including the *Golden Dragon, Saint George, Black Hogg, Primrose,* and *Pilgrim.* That Sir Thomas the elder, by now a bankrupt, and his son, who owned nothing in his own right, could have gotten control, however precarious, of six ships was a minor miracle of financing. The fatherly enterprise of old Sir Thomas is also worth remarking, for now he not only had put his sons in a way to learn the sundry devices of army captains but had guided them to the interesting trade of robbery by sea. He took this trouble when Anthony and Thomas were past thirty and when another parent might have been inclined to let them fend for themselves. Fitting out the privateering venture was not easy, for as young Sir Thomas confessed, "my poverty did wrap me in many inconveniences." [38] He borrowed £100 from Sir Robert Cecil, and in addition he, like other privateers, was probably backed by a merchant, for he was forced to transfer ownership of the *Golden Dragon* and the *Primrose* to one John Skinner. Sherley got so deep in debt to Skinner that the latter hired a man to watch over Sir Thomas' activities at Southampton while the latter prepared to put to sea. In the course of his preparations, Sherley made a journey from Southampton to Bristol. When he returned he found that during his absence Skinner's representative, Godfrey Markham, "that serpent-headed fellow," as Sherley characterized him, did "riotously spend above £300 (as he himself did gloriously give forth) amongst my people, and so won their hearts that at my return to Hampton, I had not five men left at my command." Markham even took the sails off Sir Thomas' ships to prevent them from leaving port, so that, says Sherley, "I was forced to go to sea with one ship which I did rather choose than the disgrace of being cozened of all." [39]

He was at sea by the middle of August, and by 10 September 1598 was back at Southampton, having captured four ships of Lübeck. Although citizens of Lübeck were neutrals and their vessels not lawful booty, Sherley sought Cecil's help in the probate of the prizes since, Sir Thomas claimed, "their Dutch [i.e. the Lübeckers'] cunning, in colouring Spanish goods will make that questionable which is clear." [40] Actually the cargos were salt and cork. For several centuries Dutch and Baltic ships had been hauling home cork for fish net floats, and salt to pickle herring. Salted fish was one of the mainstays of life, trade, and prosperity in northern Europe. It would be difficult to find cargos less suspect. The Queen was angry that Sherley had interfered with neutral vessels, and the latter was soon beseeching Cecil to intercede for him to obtain the Queen's pardon. He excused his actions by saying that the Lübeck vessels had resembled Spanish treasure ships, that "another reason was the unreverent words that they used against Her Highness," and his own opinion that although officially on friendly terms with England, the Lübeckers were not "well willers to Her Majesty." [41] The Privy Council found no cause for the four vessels being detained, and ordered them returned to their masters, but before the order could be carried out, Sir Thomas the elder intervened. He had reason to think, he informed Cecil, that great store of money and riches was hidden under the salt carried by the Lübeck ships, and prayed that at least one vessel be emptied and the ship searched. Thereupon the Privy Council reversed itself and ordered the mayor of Portsmouth to have a vessel unloaded. The mayor carried out the order, "not forbearing to rip up the very ceiling [inner lining] of the said ship," [42] but no Spanish treasure was found—only salt and cork.

Although the first voyage had ended without profit, Sir Thomas, being stout of heart, immediately embarked on another. On the second venture he captured "one small Brazilman and six great ships" laden with timber. "These ships," he said, "were not given me, and I am sure I have paid dear for the carriage of them." All went well until 20 December, when, being then in the Bay of Biscay homeward bound, he ran into a tempest. "I was so distressed in this storm," he says, "I was forced for the safeguard of my ship to cut my mainmast overboard, and in that instant I lost my foresail which was split in a thousand pieces. . . . I lost my rudder from my ship, and we drove like a wreck, being utterly unable to work for ourselves, being utterly destitute of all help but only from God." He wrote this description of his misfortune from the Isle de Ré, off the French coast in the Bay of Biscay, where, he said, "I remain until I can borrow some money upon my ship to bring me into England." [43] Since the letter was addressed to Cecil, obviously he hoped to borrow where he had borrowed before. He also wrote that one of his prizes was cast away on the Isle de Ré, but he hoped the others had reached England. Three of them actually did, for the High Court of the Admiralty later ordered that the *Rose* of Amsterdam laden with timber and other goods was to be returned to its owners, at the cost and charges of Sir Thomas Sherley, who had captured it. The *Three Kings* of Edam and the *Red Lion* of Amsterdam were likewise to be restored to their proprietors, along with their equipment and cargoes. Those who had bought or taken any parts of the cargo or fittings of the *Red Lion* were ordered by the court to return them to the vessel.[44] In his first six months as a privateer, Sherley had brought in seven ships, none of them lawful prizes. Indeed, far from showing a profit, he had been at some additional expense to restore the vessels to their owners.

In the summer of 1599, he turned away temporarily from privateering to command a ship in Her Majesty's navy during one of the strangest, though unimportant, episodes in English history. In that year, 1599, the English intelligence system was not at its best. The intelligence network organized by Walsingham had degenerated since his death, and Essex being then out of favor, the private spy system organized by him at his own expense was out of touch with government. The Queen's ministers were depending for foreign intelligence on tavern gossip, reports of sea captains and merchants, and letters from ambassadors.[45]

In the spring and early summer of 1599, news came in that the Spanish were collecting ships and galleys in La Coruña. Actually, as subsequently became apparent, this flotilla was intended to ward off a blow by a Dutch fleet, but in England rumors were rife that Ireland or England was about to be invaded. Alarmist reports, said Sir Robert Cecil, came in "with a whirlwind." The mobilization of both a fleet and an army were immediately ordered by the Queen and her Council. More than 25,000 horse and foot were ordered to assemble at designated stations between 10 and 16 August.[46] More than 10,000 men were to be concentrated in Kent, and in addition to its naval contribution, the city of London was asked to raise 6,000 men. The Earl of Cumberland was commanded to defend the city and undertook his task with zest. He ordered that a bridge of boats be thrown across the Thames to protect London from invasion, and vowed that with 1,500 musketeers he would defend the bridge or lose his life upon it. The bridge was begun at considerable expense to the citizens of London but never completed. The preparations to fight to the last ditch baffled the Londoners who could see no enemy on the horizon, much less at the door.

The fleet as well as the army was mobilized in haste. Lord Thomas Howard was named admiral and Ralegh, Fulke Greville, and Monson were among the captains. Sir Thomas Sherley was given command of the *Foresight,* an old ship of 300 tons and 37 guns which was broken up five years later. "Sure I am," wrote the doughty seaman, Sir William Monson, "the preparation was on both sides very great, as if the one expected an invasion from the other." [47] Admiral Howard was to have a council consisting of Ralegh, Greville, and Sir Henry Palmer, which was to be consulted on all matters. The Admiral was also instructed not to engage his ships "in any fight or in any port in such sort but that you may come off from them again from the danger of either firing, boarding or sinking." [48] This admonition to give battle only when it could be done without damage to property proved easy to follow since there were no Spanish ships in sight. But although Howard could see no Spanish vessels, his landlocked superiors could. They were not less gifted than Tilburnia in Sheridan's *The Critic,* who though snug and safe at home imagined the menace of a Spanish fleet so vividly as to exclaim:

> I see their decks
> Are cleared!—I see the Signal made!
> The line is formed!—a cable's length asunder!
> I see the frigates stationed in the rear;
> And now, I hear the thunder of the guns!

Lord Howard and his fleet, including Sherley in the *Foresight,* cruised in the Downs for three or four weeks, but never a Spanish Armada did they see. "There was never greater expectation of war with less performance," remarked Monson.[49] Londoners, seamen, even foreign observers were baffled by the occurrences. "There is much talk here," wrote a resident of Brussels, "of the groundless alarms taken in England about six galleys. Men wonder that so wise a Council was not more provident than to put the Queen and realm to excessive charge in time of peace upon a false alarm, drawing ships together and assembling men in great numbers."[50] The Spanish fleet in La Coruña gave chase to a Dutch squadron, as the Spanish had all along intended to do. The English ships returned to their ports, and Sir Thomas to the sad problems of a privateer.

Those difficulties were the usual ones of a lack of cash and an accumulation of debts, and the special problem caused by the fact that his vessel the *Golden Dragon,* was really not his, but Thomas Skinner's. Sir Thomas begged Sir Robert Cecil for another hundred-pound loan, promising to repay it as punctually as would the Lord Mayor of London, but £100 could not save him.[51] Two of his wrathful creditors had young Sherley jailed for debt. His father appealed to Cecil, explaining that unless some means could be found to satisfy the two creditors, his son would be utterly undone, for he had exhausted the help of all of his friends. Cecil issued an order that young Sir Thomas should be free from arrest, but the creditors treated the order with contempt and young Sherley remained in jail. Means were found to satisfy the two creditors and Sherley was released, but in another appeal to Cecil, old Sir Thomas predicted that unless an order was issued instructing the sheriff of Kent to accept no more suits against his son, young Sherley would be back in prison.[52]

Cecil probably so instructed the sheriff, for it was now Skinner's turn to complain to him that the Sherleys, father and son, had forcibly possessed his ship and now held it without danger of arrest. Skinner implored Cecil's pity. His estate, he declared, had been grievously impaired by the privateering adventures of the two Sir Thomas Sherleys. He prayed that they should be summoned before Cecil to answer his charges.[53] His pleas were unavailing. Young Sir Thomas put to sea with two ships, the *Golden Dragon* and the *George*. As in his previous voyages, his cruise was a short one, for he was back in port by April 1600, and he sent Cecil the news that "it hath pleased God to send me two prizes." [54] Young Sherley was himself far from well. "I never saw poor gentleman in a more miserable estate," reported Sir Ferdinando Gorges, the commander of the fortress at Plymouth, "being afflicted with extremity of sickness, nearly destitute of honest and trusty servants, and matched with an unruly rout of mariners." [55]

One of the two prizes, the Hamburg ship *Saint Michael,* was laden partly with enemy (Portuguese) goods and partly with neutral goods. "Since our strangers [foreigners] in London," Sherley wrote Cecil from Southampton, "are very apt to give men impediment where they have any hope . . . to benefit themselves, I am bold humbly to beseech Your Honor . . . that I may have my right with as much favor as may be." [56] He also informed Cecil that "I have besought my cousin Gorges I might have had some place with him to have laid in such goods as I desire to have retained for a time . . . but I find him very loath to yield . . . I most humbly beseech Your Lordship that you will be pleased to pretend some cause to write unto him . . . to require him unto it." [57] The fortress commander, Gorges, also wrote Cecil. "I have been entreated by Sir Thomas Sherley," he declared, "to take into my custody some things of his, because as it seemeth by him he is in doubt it may be liable unto his debts . . . but because I do not know how it may be taken if complaint should be thereof made unto Your Lordship, I have forborn to yield." [58]

Actually the situation was otherwise. "We are informed," wrote the Privy Council to Gorges some weeks later, "that Sir Thomas Sherley has caused the better sort of the merchandise to be unladen and put into the fort under your charge. . . . This shall be to require you to cause all the goods, merchandise and other things . . . bestowed again in the ship and so sent up hither, whereof we require you not to fail as you will answer the contrary. . . . We marvel that you would receive any goods into the fort without a perfect inventory taken of the same." [59] Later the Council learned that in addition to the part of the cargo placed in the fort, other portions of it were scattered about in warehouses and cellars in the town. The port officials were commanded to gather up all the goods, relade the ship, and send the vessel to London.[60] When it arrived there the Hamburger owners complained that two-thirds of the goods had been embezzled by Sherley. The remainder of the goods were, they said, impounded and "for the most part perish." [61] Nearly five months later Sir Julius Caesar, judge of the High Court of the Admiralty, urged that Sherley's old creditors be satisfied out of that portion of the cargo which was fair prize. "The residue of that complement will not be worth their travail who labor for the same," he declared. "The sugars run out upon the ground, where they lie so plentifully that grievous it is to behold it, and the spoil made of the merchants' goods, which are not prize, is so great that . . . if good order be not taken the good prize will not satisfy half the same." [62] Sherley's claim to the ship, Sir Julius decided, was founded only on violence, "and is unlawful and of no effect, and therefore is in law void; and we adjudge that the said Sir Thomas Sherley junior, knight, and his companions ought to be removed and expelled from their said forcible possession, and by these presents we so remove and expell them accordingly." [63] Caesar thereupon restored the ship to its German owners.[64] There is no record whether or not the other prizes, the West Indiaman taken by Sherley and three ships captured by his consort, the *George,* were judged fair prizes.

The following year, 1601, there was a lull in Sherley's piratical activities. He was returned as member of Parliament for

Bramber, but having also the opportunity to serve for Hastings, he chose the latter. Actually he was occupied with affairs which were more important to him than Parliament.

The Queen was now aged, and old loyalties were fraying out. The Essex conspiracy in which that rash Earl had attempted to take over the government by force and had been made shorter by a head for his pains had just taken place. Not only Essex, but many others had become bored by the Queen's long reign, "for things of long continuance though never so good are tedious." There was a "credulous desire of novelty and change, hoping for better times, despising the present and forgetting favors past." [65] Essex, or at least those of his party, had been in correspondence with James VI of Scotland since 1589. Sir Robert Cecil kept in touch with King James from 1601. It is not surprising that the Sherleys did also. In a letter written to James I long after, Sir Thomas recalled to the King what had happened at the time of the Essex conspiracy in February 1601. He declared that he and his father had conferred at that time and on a number of occasions with the Earl of Mar and Edward Bruce, Lord of Kinloss, the ambassadors whom James, then King of Scotland, had sent to England, and with Sir David Foulis, who accompanied them. These men, he said, "in one conference amongst divers others with my father and me did greatly wish some good means to be found to furnish Your Majesty with a round sum of money. Many debates there were to that purpose and no likely way could be thought of, till I offered to hazard my life and estate to attempt to take from the Turk . . . his treasure and lay it down (being taken) at Your Majesty's feet. This project was allowed and liked; whereupon I rode post to Florence and put myself into the service of that Duke, for the better countenance of my business and to have a rendezvous where to refresh myself and my men. At my return from thence I met Sir Thomas Erskine, now Lord Fenton, at Paris and by express command from Your Majesty I made relation unto him of mine expedition in this business who did well allow of it. At his return into Scotland at that time he passed through England and was at my father's house in the Blackfriars and did (at both times) spur on this enterprise." [66] Such is Sir Thomas' account of how he happened to go to sea again in 1602. In that year for the first time since 1598 he had gotten a respectable fleet together, four ships and two pinnaces. He declared that these ships and the expenses of his two subsequent voyages cost his father £14,000. Indeed, certainly to get even a precarious hold on six ships and to put to sea twice must have involved enormous expense. In preparing for the first cruise, young Sir Thomas found himself, as usual, short of money, and, as usual, turned to Cecil. "I am a humble suitor to your Honor . . ." he wrote, "now at my very last cast to adventure £100 with me . . . I assure Your Honor . . . within two days after the receipt of this money (if you shall send it me) I shall be put to sea." [67] Others put money into the venture, including the mayor of Southampton, and Sherley made plans for his voyage, but meanwhile the Privy Council was planning otherwise. Perhaps because they knew of his relationships with James VI of Scotland, or simply because they feared he would head for the Mediterranean, which the Council had forbidden to privateers, they tried to stop him. Sherley's letter to Privy Councilor Cecil indicating he was ready for sea was written on 19 March, but the Council did not order him held at Southampton until 6 April and by then it was too late, Sir Thomas having sailed with his six ships and 900 soldiers, in addition to mariners, on 27 March or 1 April. Perhaps the Privy Council was not very anxious to hold him in port and in any event he did not get far. One of his pinnaces, the *Nan,* departed without leave four days after the fleet put to sea. Three days later, running into a storm, the *Virgin* lost her rudder, and the *Dragon* sprang a leak. The following day Sir Thomas put in at Falmouth. On the ninth of April his vice-admiral, the *Lion,* commanded by one also called Thomas Sherley, reached Falmouth. Resolved to enter in style, the *Lion* fired a salute with the unfortunate result that the cannon burst, killing two men, wounding a number of others, tearing up the deck and breaking the mainyard. Toward the end of April, being still in Falmouth, Sir Thomas was faced with a mutiny, or perhaps a mass resignation. Led by four of their captains, four hundred of his soldiers forsook the expedition, whereupon it was reported, Sherley "abridged his voyage, selling four of his ships to furnish two and so begins on a new reckoning." [68] He sailed from Falmouth on 2 May. Eleven days later, on May 13, he made a midnight landing on the Portuguese coast near the mouth of the Mondego River, about twenty miles from Coimbra. Sherley's men easily captured the town or village of Buarcos, but about 9 o'clock the following morning, relates the anonymous chronicler of the voyage who was with the landing party, "one of the captains . . . possessed the companies of such a fear (I know not upon what vain imagination) that they retired from the town some half mile so that our admiral had much to do with many persuasions to cause them to return, whereby they of the town had gained sufficient time to carry and convey away their best goods." Having captured Buarcos and found little, the invaders took a nearby castle which yielded less, and then conquered the village of Taverede, where they found stores of wheat, wine, and fish. It having been a long hard day, and having reduced two villages and a castle, the English retired to their ships. The next day they landed again, overcame a priory, conquered another village, Figueira da Faz, and appropriated the fish, wine, and wheat previously discovered at Taverede. The Portuguese now sent a flag of truce to Sherley, begging him not to set the villages afire. Sir Thomas demanded, as the price of his forbearance, twenty hostages who were to be held until the villages were ransomed. No hostages were forthcoming. Sir Thomas held the man who came to him with the flag of truce, but that Portuguese was able to convince Sir Thomas that as an ambassador or negotiator he had the right of diplomatic immunity, so Sir Thomas set him free. This was the second day of the English raid, and the countryside was now aroused. There was some skirmishing with the inhabitants, and Sir Thomas was forced to withdraw to his ships and sail away southward. On 21 May the fleet doubled Cape Saint Vincent and the following day was "spent in laboring to prevent many disorders" among the crews. Sir Thomas had now decided to take Garachico on the island of Tenerife in the Canaries, but he gave up this plan and decided to capture Ayamonte on the south coast of Spain instead. He arrived off Ayamonte on 30 May, but the *Lion* anchored so far off shore that it was impossible to row the landing party to the beach before daylight, and the *Virgin* got stuck on the bar at the entrance to the bay. It being now impossible to surprise Ayamonte, Sherley decided to capture Algusero, which was not far away, and made a landing near that town on 2 June. Algusero was found to be very strong so that after divers skirmishes in which one man was lost and another hurt, the attempt to capture the town was given up. Sherley next resolved to sail for the island of Graciosa in the Azores, but a few days later changed his mind. He hoped to sail for the isle of Bayon, but gave up the plan. Three-quarters of his men being now extremely ill, he decided to head for home, a decision to which he held with commendable resolution. He arrived in Southampton on 20 June. "Sir Thomas Sherley is returned with his navy royal," wrote that inveterate gossip John Chamberlain, "and yesterday he with his Lieutenant General Colonel Sims, posted to the court, as though they had brought tidings of the taking of Seville or some such town, whereas God knows, they have but sacked two poor hamlets . . . in Portugal, the pillage whereof he gave to his army, reserving to himself only two or three peasants to ransom, of whom when he saw he could raise nothing he would not bring them away for shame." [69]

His success being something less than spectacular, Sir Thomas was soon organizing a fifth voyage. In August he began to sell shares (bills of adventure) in the proposed cruise as he had done before. The mayor of Southampton again had a share. The town clerk ventured £5, and many others followed his example. There were now stricter regulations governing voyages of reprisal, and Andrew Studley, a former mayor of Southampton, was Sherley's surety for abiding by the Lord Admiral's regulations.[70] The conditions imposed upon Sherley probably included the proviso that he keep out of the Mediterranean, but when he sailed in the first part of October with three ships, the *Dragon, George,* and *Virgin,* he headed straight for the forbidden waters and a series of adventures which kept him away from England for years.

According to young Sir Thomas he went to sea in 1601 to get money for his future sovereign, James VI and I. In that same year Father Persons wrote from Rome that his brother Anthony "complaineth of much mal treating done his brother by Sir R[obert] C[ecil] in taking away his wife and keeping her openly, whereupon he hath taken ship and gone out of England with full purpose never to return." [71] Some two years later Francis Michell wrote to Cecil. In his recent journey in Holland, he related, he had met Sir Calisthenes Brooke, who "recounted sundry passages in our converse . . . not forgetting the friends of his lady's fortune, and how she lost those that then were and still are able to do most for her. We remembered Your Honor to be the only procurer of the pension she now liveth on, but (as it seemed by him) her ladyship had made an evil requital, by being too busy about a libelous 'lost letter' concerning you and the lady Shurlye. And hereupon (which is the cause of my now writing) it was by you (as he delivered unto me) imagined, or by some of her friends, or self, in excuse of her wrong doing, fathered, that I, living then with her as trencher companion, must needs be either the deviser, contriver, or publisher of that letter." [72] It may be that, as well as intriguing for James of Scotland, Sherley was eager to get away from a wife who was having an affair with Cecil or someone else, but it is also undoubtedly true that he was suffering from a chronic Sherley complaint, lack of cash and many debts, and that was reason enough for adventuring to sea.

CHAPTER V

Sir Anthony and Robert Sherley, Their Journey to Persia

WHEN Essex and his brave, proud, admiring captains came home from The Islands Voyage, it was to an icy welcome from the Queen. The futility, if not the folly, of the expedition was apparent. Contemplating the fact that the enormously expensive expedition had accomplished nothing, the Queen vowed that she would never again send her ships out of the Channel. In the first days after the Essex expedition had limped home, the coterie of captains surrounding Essex noted the welcome and seethed with anger. Their resentment was heightened when they learned that a few days before their return the Queen had raised Lord Admiral Howard to an earldom. On that occasion, Howard had been called not only the conqueror of the Invincible Armada, but the hero of Cadiz. He was an old man, past sixty, a threat to no one and well deserving recognition, but all the world knew, and Essex' friends knew, that the hero of Cadiz was not Howard but Essex. To bestow the title on another, the hotheads surrounding Essex reasoned, could only have been done to affront their patron. Filled with "dangerous discontentments" Essex left London and sulked at Wanstead. How fleeting, he must have at least realized, was military glory. In 1596 he had returned from Cadiz a hero, and now a year later he was obviously regarded as an incompetent. It may well have been that he was in a mood to strive for that civil or "domesticall" greatness which Francis Bacon had advised him was the wisest course. If this indeed was his mood then events transpiring in the city of Ferrara seemed to offer a golden opportunity to achieve a brilliant diplomatic, rather than a military, victory. The city had been held by the Este family as Dukes of Ferrara, and their court was, and had been for two centuries, one of the most brilliant in Europe. It was famous not only for its elegance and luxury but for the host of artists, men of letters, and savants who found patrons in the Este family. The court of Alfonso d'Este II, Duke of Ferrara, who reigned during the last decades of the sixteenth century, was no less gay and glittering than that of his predecessors. Alfonso II was the patron of Torquato Tasso (whom he later imprisoned) and of Giovanni Guarini, the dour author of a wonderfully light but penetrating drama, the *Pastor Fido*. Other things for which Ferrara was famous under Alfonso II were intolerably tyrannical government, unbearably heavy taxes, and unbelievably corrupt officials. At the end of October 1597, only a few days, in fact, after the return of Essex from The Islands Voyage, Alfonso II died, suffering great pain from kidney stones, his body covered with pustules of a certain type. Alfonso II had bequeathed Ferrara to his nephew, Cesare d'Este. The Papal See had old quarrels with the house of Este and now claimed, which was not proven, that Cesare was illegitimate, and by that fact debarred from holding the Dukedom of Ferrara. Pope Clement VIII himself now claimed Ferrara as a fief of the Holy See. Cesare d'Este seized the city and sent emissaries to the courts of Europe to plead his cause and to enlist support.

Probably Essex received news of what was transpiring in Ferrara sooner, and in more complete detail, than anyone else in England. His private spy network which was directed by Anthony Bacon was excellent for France and Italy, although practically nonexistent for Spain, Germany, and the Low Countries.[1] At this time Spain held Milan as well as the Kingdoms of Naples and Sicily and was powerful in shaping the policies of the Holy See. Essex' whole foreign policy, insofar as he had one, was simply implacable enmity for Spain. At the moment, although France was wavering and weakening, England and France were allies, and at war with Spain. Ferrara for a century and a half had been the faithful ally of France. Alfonso I had fought on the side of the French at the battle of Ravenna (1512). His son, Ercole II, married Renée, daughter of Louis XII of France, and had been an ally of France in fighting the

Spanish. In any contest, then, the French might be expected to support their traditional allies, the Estes. The claim of Cesare was also supported by his brother-in-law, Ferdinand, Archduke of Tuscany, who showed a sturdy independence of Spain as well as of the Pope. Except for relatively short intervals the Estes had long been enemies of the Papacy. Venice, also, had long struggled with the Holy See and feared the ever-increasing influence and power of Spain in Italy.

It would appear then, and this may well indeed have been the way the situation appeared to Essex, that in the conflict developing between Pope Clement VIII and Cesare d'Este the latter would be supported by France, Tuscany, and Venice, and the former by Spain. In the months of November and December 1597, while Essex brooded at Wanstead and mulled over the news coming in from Italy, affairs had by no means stood still elsewhere in Europe. Reports reached England from Spain that there was to be a fourth armada and that Philip II planned to invade England in the spring of 1598. It was also clear that Spain, on the verge of bankruptcy, wanted peace with France in order to have a free hand against England. "How fortunate," remarked the Venetian, Francesco Contarini, "is the conjunction for France, for the Spanish in their desire for peace will condescend to terms they would not otherwise have accepted, and the Queen of England and the States of Holland in their suspicion of French diplomacy are forced to make offers of help to his majesty [Henry IV]." [2]

All these facts were known to Elizabeth and her court as well as to Essex sulking in his stately tent at Wanstead. At this juncture the Queen needed Essex and, as always, he needed success and glory. Suddenly toward the end of December the Earl appeared at court and there was a happy reconciliation between him and the Queen. On 28 December Elizabeth named Essex Earl Marshal, and at least outwardly their personal relationship was as close as it ever had been.

One can surmise that it was in these last days of December that Essex proposed his plan to fan the contest for the Duchy of Ferrara into a conflagration. If all Italy could be involved in war, Spain would be so occupied defending her interests there that there would be no energy left for hostilities against England. There was to be no openly acknowledged English intervention in Italy, no grandiose expedition in the old Essex style. A handful of courageous, experienced captains would go to Ferrara armed with ample funds with which to bribe and corrupt judiciously. Essex evidently felt he had the man for the job in that former colonel of horse under Sir John Norris, and his own Sergeant Major of the forces on his recent voyage, Sir Anthony Sherley. An additional qualification may have been that the Sherleys were quite evidently well connected in Italy. Sir Anthony's younger brother Robert was at the court of Ferdinand, Archduke of Tuscany, and had been for five years; and a few years later his elder brother also visited the Florentine court. Sir Anthony was given a pass by Essex, who, Sherley said, "was at that time in estate to have given it to any manner of condition and [in any?] manner." [3] He avowed that "neither did I go without Her Majesty's knowledge, nor in my opinion license." [4] Essex was said to have provided him with £8,000,[5] a sum so large that more than four years later Sir Anthony wrote that "I am not yet out of wonder at his unlimited liberality." [6] Before departing, Sherley conferred several times with Sir John Stanhope, the Treasurer of the Chamber, a functionary of the royal household, and it is possible that more illustrious and financially able interests had decided to risk a few thousand pounds on an adventure which, if successful, would be worth a hundred times what it had cost.

Sir Anthony probably left London on New Year's eve, 1598, and the manner of his going was related by his father, who had probably just been released from the Fleet prison. "It may please your Honor," he wrote Cecil, "I am driven most against my will to complain to your Honor of the most unnatural or rather cruel dealing of Anthony Sherley towards me: the case is this. There were two jewels of his pawned for his own debt for £551, whereof he did exceedingly urge me to procure means to redeem them promising most faithfully to see the money satisfied again within ten days. I made means for it even of such friends as give me means to live and without whom I have no means to eat. He hath repaid only £120 and upon Monday last he promised to pay the other £431 and bound his promise with an oath upon his salvation. Monday in the evening my man came to him according to his appointment. He told him it was not then ready but did assure him to have it the next morning, being yesterday, and when my man came to the place where he lived, it was told him that he was gone out of the town, and upon better and further enquiry I do understand that he is gone out of the town with purpose to go beyond the seas, but whether with licence of the Queen's Majesty or to what place I do not know, only I know that I am most vilely handled by him. He first wounded my estate by his voyage and now hath more undone me, being in the desperate case that I am in, by this cozening of me of the money which I am no ways able to repay where it was promised. He cannot be far gone for he was seen in London after nine of the clock yesterday. . . . If he be gone without the licence of the Queen's Majesty, then Your Honor will know best what is best to be done, but if he be gone by Your Honor's leave, I truly trust that he may be stayed until he make delivery either of the jewels or of the money. This is wickedness to lay affliction upon affliction upon his poor aged parents." [7] Sir Anthony and his companions sailed from Southwold for the Netherlands on New Year's day and debarked at Flushing, a gay place in summer, but then, as always, a dreary place in winter. Sir Robert Sidney, the English governor there, though obviously baffled by their mission, received his countrymen courteously and entertained them. From Flushing the party walked to Middelburg, which was not more than a pleasant walk. There they took a hoy across the eastern Scheldt and passed through Brielle, where Sir Anthony's first mutinous command had been stationed. At The Hague, Sherley and his companions were met by George Gilpin, Queen Elizabeth's agent in the Low Countries. "Sir Anthony Sherley is come . . . ," wrote Gilpin to Sir Robert Sidney at Flushing, "marvelling much he comes with such a train, and this time of the year when passages are so difficult," and added the intriguing remark, "I am of Your Lordship's opinion touching Sir Anthony Sherley's coming over, and will, if occasion be offered, touch a word of that he reports so largely to serve for a *caveat,* if he will so take it." [8] Sherley was cordially received by Prince Maurits and by the States General. The latter presented the distinguished travelers with fifteen great flagons of wine, and Prince Maurits provided them with an escort of horse, 25 troopers of Sir Nicholas Parker's squadron. The troop turned back at Cologne, and Sir Anthony, ever the generous spender, gave the men a handsome present.

Meanwhile time had not stood still in Italy. Cesare d'Este had made haste to send his best men to plead his cause at foreign courts. They could have been used more advantageously at home, for Pope Clement VIII moved with decision to rescue Ferrara from the usurper. He appointed Cardinal Aldobrandini his commander, and the Cardinal pushed forward the task of raising an army with energy.

There were some elements in the situation which had been overlooked by Essex, Sherley, and those associated with them in the enterprise, if anyone was. Henry IV of France was a new Catholic and he wished to give proof to the world that he was a devout one. Other things being equal, he would doubtless have remembered the loyalty of the house of Este to France, but at the moment it was important that he should demonstrate his sincere Roman Catholicity. He assured the Pope that he would send an army across the Alps to help fight for the Papal rights in Ferrara, and if necessary lead the army himself. Venice, Florence, and other Italian states which had shown signs of coming to the aid of Cesare d'Este would doubtless have continued to extend to him their warm sympathy, but at the mention of a French army crossing the Alps it was apparent that cordiality might be very expensive, and their interest in Cesare evaporated.

Sir Anthony had regarded the Este family as "having through their just condition of ruling woven themselves into the sincere affection of that people." [9] Actually, as Cardinal Aldobrandini approached Ferrara with a Papal army, that sincere affection was not evident. Cesare d'Este was indecisive, and his ablest advisors and administrators had been sent to foreign courts. While he debated what to do, the citizenry of Ferrara, happily contemplating the possibility of lower taxes, went about the task of preparing a gala welcome for the approaching Papal forces. Finally Cesare rode out of his city in tears, and his aunt signed for him a convention giving up to the Pope all claims to the Duchy.

News of the collapse of Cesare, and consequently the collapse of the hope for a big general war, reached Sir Anthony at Augsburg. Sherley's reason for going to Italy had vanished in the smoke of the bonfires which welcomed the Papal army in Ferrara. But Augsburg was not far from Venice, the mecca for men of affairs and gentlemen of pleasure. The Piazza de San Marco, the inveterate traveler Thomas Coryate declared, "is worthy to be celebrated for that famous concourse and meeting of so many distinct and sundry nations. . . . There you may see many Polonians, Slavonians, Persians, Grecians, Turks, Jews, Christians, of all the famousest regions of Christendom." To divert these merchants drawn there by weighty affairs, there were so many courtesans, says Coryate, "it is thought there are of them in the whole city and other adjacent places . . . at the least twenty thousand, whereof many are esteemed so loose, that they are said to open their quivers to every arrow." [10] What band of experienced captains being close to a city so rich in cultural advantages would not have longed to see it? Besides, Sherley had £8,000. He went on to Venice, where, says one of his companions, "we did solace ourselves almost three months," and where, another comrade declared, they saw everything worth seeing, "to Sir Anthony's no small cost for in his rewards he was there and elsewhere most royal." [11]

A score of young foreign experienced captains spending freely was bound to attract attention, even in the highest circles. The Doge entertained Sir Anthony, "with all princely compliment," reported one of his companions, "sending him to his lodging a royal banquet of all kind of confected sweetmeats and wine in great abundance." [12] Sir Anthony was on intimate terms with other patricians and sent a messenger to the court of the archduke at Florence to have his younger brother, Robert, join him.

An observant reporter wrote a Frankfurt merchant that "there is a gentleman here named Sherley. He has been in

France and was a captain of the English light horse there, nevertheless he speaks very bad French. . . . He has come through Holland but nevertheless he does not speak well of the gentlemen of the Estates, but on the contrary he infinitely exalts the grandeur of Spain, and even more that of the Pope, and says that Spain and the Pope have made him great offers, and that if he does not find better elsewhere, he shall see what he can do. . . . If he were really wise, he would talk less and there would be more to fear . . . but he is a spendthrift who consumes all he has . . . it is said here he comes on what he has borrowed, and it is not believed he is sent by Essex." [13]

Actually Sir Anthony was by no means giving himself up entirely to pleasure. He cast about for a new enterprise, being anxious "to do some good and extraordinary thing before I returned back, and to make him [Essex] as a good factor, either a return of good satisfaction or of honors for his money." [14] The difficulty was that the possibility of war at Ferrara had attracted *condottiere* from all over Europe, so that as one of them put it there were in Italy more unemployed captains than soldiers.[15] Eventually the Venetians found work for Sir Anthony and his idle captains to do.

The prospects of Venice at this time were not bright. Traditionally the basis of Venetian prosperity was traffic in oriental merchandise. The ancient overland trade route from the East ran through the Euphrates valley and across the desert (or alternately by the Red Sea and the Isthmus of Suez) to the Mediterranean, where the silk, precious stones, spices, and drugs were gathered by the Venetians and sold throughout Europe. But the Portuguese had opened the sea route from the Orient to Europe around the Cape of Good Hope. Worse, they had built a strong fortress and base at Ormuz on the Persian Gulf, where they could shut off the route to the Mediterranean by the Euphrates valley, and, in time, control the Red Sea also. The Venetians, contemplating their dwindling reserves and empty warehouses, were hopeful that the English would oust the Spanish and Portuguese from the oriental trade, and also from their base on the Gulf of Persia. Not many months before Sir Anthony arrived in Venice, the Venetian ambassador in

Spain had reported to the Doge and Senate that a messenger had been sent from Madrid to the Portuguese fortress of Ormuz. "He bore letters to the Viceroy," the Venetian reported, "calling his attention to the progress of English commerce in those parts, and charging him to hinder it by all means in his power. These orders are thought difficult to execute; for the English will not readily abandon that trade." [16] The English had long been interested in trade with Persia and the Orient generally. English traders had reached Persia through Russia decades before Anthony's sojourn in Venice. In 1592 the Levant Company had been enlarged and virtually amalgamated with the Venice Company, so that there were probably Englishmen in Venice at the time Sherley was there who were well acquainted with Venetian trading problems and sympathized with them. What was more to the point, Sir Anthony obviously knew that his patron Essex had before this moved to ascertain the strength and disposition of the Spanish and Portuguese forces in the Orient and the volume of their trade there. By an arrangement between Essex and the Dutch merchant prince Balthasar de Moucheron, Essex had sent John Davis, the famous navigator, as a pilot on the Dutch voyage to the East Indies under Cornelis de Houtman; and Tompkins, another of Essex' men, also went with Houtman. Davis reported to Essex upon his return that, "according to those directions which your Lordship gave me in charge at my departure; I will make farther known to your Lordship . . . of the King of Portugual his places of trade and strengths." [17] In another letter Davis wrote Essex that, "according to your Lordship's command and directions, I have to my farthest best, discovered the trades, passages, and Spanish forces of East India." [18]

Part of the time that Sherley was at Venice, Davis was on this voyage for Essex. Since both Essex and the Venetians were interested in oriental trade and well aware of the difficulty posed by the Portuguese ensconced on the Persian Gulf, it was almost inevitable that the topic would arise in conversations between the Venetians and Sherley. It cannot be pretended that hitherto Sir Anthony himself had evinced any interest in the flow of oriental trade, but he had undeniably shown a lively desire to plunder Spanish and Portuguese. It was not too difficult for the Venetians to propose that Sir Anthony and his unemployed captains should strike a blow against their enemy and his, the Portuguese established on the Persian coast. The Doge "urged it as a matter most necessary and of weighty consequences, promising to signify his allowance and opinion thereof to my Lord Marshal [Essex]." [19] Giacomo Foscarini, one of Venice's most skillful and experienced statesmen, also pressed Sherley to undertake the exploit, affirming it to be "beneficial to all Christendom and in particular to Venice, which by the traffic overland from thence was mightily enriched before the Portugals were lords of those parts. . . . To prove that it stood with the grounds of Christianity he [Foscarini] used many reasons, as the transporting of the war far from our homes, as it were, into another world, the overwhelming of ambition and dispersing of those wares and merchandise to all traffickers, which to the impoverishing of all estates are now only made private to the Spaniard." [20] By an accident (perhaps arranged by the Venetians), it happened, says Manwaring, one of Sherley's companions, that "in that time we lay in Venice, Sir Anthony did fall into some conversation with a Persian merchant, which did traffic in Venice for the King of Persia. . . . This merchant told Sir Anthony of the royalty of the Sophi, his king, which pleased Sir Anthony very well." By an odd coincidence, Sherley was also put in touch with a certain traveler, "newly come to Venice from the Sophi's court whose name was Angelo, born in Turkey, but a good Christian, who had traveled sixteen years and did speak twenty-four kind of languages. This Angelo did likewise acquaint Sir Anthony of the worthiness of the King of Persia, that he was a gallant soldier, very bountiful and liberal to strangers." Angelo, whose full name was Angelo Corrai, assured Sir Anthony that if he would go to Persia, "it would be greatly to his advancement," and with unbelievable generosity promised that he, Angelo, "would be his guide and attend on him thither." [21]

Such were the Venetian proposals, and Sir Anthony was irresistibly attracted by them and so resolved that the extraordinary thing he would do for his patron as a return for his money would be to strike a blow at Spain through Persia. Some time later he declared that Essex "proposed unto me (after a small relation which I wrote unto him from Venice) the voyage to Persia," but his friend Thomas Chaloner averred that Sherley undertook the "journey toward the Levant without especial order, and perhaps disagreeing from some letters received at Venice." [22] Sherley later wrote that the desire to give some return to Essex "made me undertake this matter of Persia in which I proceeded in the beginning of it with the King [the Shah of Persia]; and in the language of it, a true . . . subject to Her Majesty and like a gentleman. . . . My first motions to the King were against Spain as my letters to my Lord of Essex and to Mr. Anthony Bacon and Mr. Secretary, which are yet extant do testify, inciting him by all sorts of persuasions against Ormuz." [23] Such were Anthony's reasons, as he gave them, for going to Persia. One might have an inclination at first not to believe him. One might think that surely this was not his only reason for going, that he hoped for something more lucrative than a diplomatic victory. After all he was an Elizabethan. Actually, although Sir Anthony throughout his life needed, spent, and owed large sums of money, and often neglected the distinction between *meum* and *teum,* his adventures were as often as not undertaken for "that unseen thing called honor." It is quite possible, then, that in going to Persia he had no other objective than to endeavor to break the Persian-Spanish accord, and do damage if possible to the Portuguese established at Ormuz.

Sir Anthony's entourage, as he prepared for his journey to the Orient, included not only those who had accompanied him from England, but Robert Sherley, Angelo Corrai, the volunteer guide and interpreter, and Abel Pinçon, a Frenchman who had studied in England, had "run some wild courses in his youth," and in his later years was employed by Cecil as a secret agent. Altogether twenty-six or twenty-seven persons in Sherley's party embarked on the voyage, six of whom were classed as gentlemen; the others, including a few Persians, were servants. Three of Sherley's companions, Abel Pinçon, George Manwaring, and William Parry, have left accounts of the journey to Persia, and Sir Anthony wrote one himself, fifteen years after the event. Sherley's account is not a detailed narrative of the journey, since as he explains, "I did not behold with the eyes of a common pilgrim or merchant which . . . make their judgment upon the superficial appearance of what they see, but as a gentleman bred up in such experience, which hath made me somewhat capable to penetrate into the perfection and imperfection of the form of the state." [24] The party embarked at Malamocco, a small port near Venice, on 24 May 1598.

The first part of the journey would bring them to the island of Zante, usually a ten-day journey, but on this occasion it took twenty-two or twenty-four days. Sherley and his men ran out of food. They attempted to beg or borrow provisions from the Italian passengers but were refused. Fortunately a party of Persians, "though Pagans by profession," fed them. The refusal of the Italians to help them did nothing to increase the friendly feeling of the English for the Italians. What friendliness existed disappeared when an Italian allegedly made a scurrilous remark about Queen Elizabeth. None of the English heard the remark. Sir Anthony learned about it two days later from a servant. Thereupon he ordered one of his meanest servants to beat the man said to have cast aspersions on the Queen. The Italian was beaten so soundly, said Sherley's companion, William Parry, "it is impossible he should ever recover," and until, added George Manwaring, "he [the beaten man] burst both his arms." The crew and most of the passengers were outraged at Sherley's action. The captain demanded to know how, on a ship he commanded, the English had dared do such a thing, whereupon Robert Sherley gave the captain "a sound box," the first appearance of the youngest Sherley in action. The English drew their swords although they were twenty-four against sixty according to Parry, or twenty-one to two hundred fifty by Manwaring's count. The Italians also were ready to fight, but three Armenian merchants entreated both sides to make peace, "which the Italians did first consent unto," whereupon Sherley and his companions also put up their swords. The conflagration was extinguished, but the captain continued to smolder. When the ship anchored in the harbor of Zante and the Sherley party put off for shore to seek provisions, the skipper sent their baggage after them, trained his guns on their boat, and threatened that if they attempted to return aboard he would sink them.

Temporarily at leisure in Zante, Sherley dispatched a letter to Henry Lello, the English ambassador at Constantinople, in which, according to Lello, Sherley declared "how he was sent by Her Highness towards the Red Sea to meet with a fleet of Hollanders that are gone thither under color of traffic, requiring me . . . to send him the Grand Signor his commandment or pass, through his Dominions, which accordingly I have done." [25] Sir Anthony had given Lello the same explanation for his journey which he later offered the English merchants at Aleppo, namely, that his enterprise was connected with the Houtman voyage and Essex' interest in it. Sherley hired a boat to take the party from Zante to Crete, but the vessel was so old and leaky "that in eleven days (in which time we passed from Zante to Candia [Crete]) continually during all that time four men had as much toil as they could endure to lave water out of this rotten boat." In Crete the Englishmen were entertained not only by the governor but also by gentlewomen "who often times did make us banquets in their garden with music and dancing." From Crete Sherley and his companions were nine days getting to Cyprus, where they put in at Paphos, which despite its exotic and stirring history, Sir Anthony found a disappointment. There was, he said, "no show of splendor nor habitation of men in a fashion." From this point onward the three accounts of the voyage differ, after the manner of eye-witness accounts. For example, the travelers encountered the Italian ship on which they had voyaged from Venice to Zante—at Tripoli says Manwaring, at Cyprus say Sherley and Parry. The Italians on the ship got their revenge, says Parry, by informing the Cyprian governor that they were English pirates, whereupon the governor held them for two days and only released them upon payment of a huge sum. The revenge was wreaked at Tripoli, says Manwaring. The master of the Italian vessel went to the governor there, "and did counsel the governor to hang us all, which he consented unto." Thereupon, continues Manwaring, Sir Anthony sent the interpreter Angelo Corrai to the governor to explain that they were in fact Englishmen on their way to the court of the Sultan, but the governor would not listen to Angelo and put him in chains. Finally upon the intercession of some Armenian merchants, the governor agreed to take ransom for Angelo, "to Sir Anthony's great cost." Sherley's story is much better. It has a villain, heroes, and a moral, and is replete with human interest. It seems there was aboard the ship a Portuguese, one Hugo de Potso. He urged the governor of Cyprus to rob Sherley and his companions, saying they were pirates but very rich. This evil conversation was overheard by certain Armenians who were so "moved with the enormity of so vile an act (that Christians should sell and betray Christians to Turks, and that upon no cause of offence)," that they hired a vessel, supplied it with victuals, and coming to Sherley and his men "beseeched us, with tears in their eyes, to fly from thence," [26] which they did, thus escaping the evil governor and the vengeful de Potso. Weeks afterward, when Sherley and the party had reached Aleppo, de Potso learned that they were there. Still pursuing his evil ways, de Potso set out for Aleppo to persecute the Englishmen but when within four miles of the city he dropped dead on the road. The death of the evil Portuguese showed, observed Sir Anthony, "how much it pleaseth God to favor good intentions [which he always had] . . . no question, good intentions have such a sympathy with God's own disposition, that he will both assist them which have them, for their better encouragement and for others example, being one of the chief means by which he instructeth the world."

Sherley and his companions had arrived at Aleppo only after further hardships and harrowing experiences. Of Aleppo a contemporary Englishman wrote that "this is the greatest place of traffic for a dry [inland] town that is in all these parts, for hither resort Jews, Tartarians, Persians, Armenians, Egyptians, Indians, and many sorts of Christians, and enjoy freedom of their consciences and bring thither many kinds of rich merchandises." [27] It was one of the more important trading points of the English Levant Company. There were fourteen merchants there in addition to the consul, Richard Colthurst.[28] The merchants at Aleppo, like all members of the Levant Company, looked hopefully to a revival of trade by the overland route no less than did the Venetians and, also no less than the Venetians, longed to see the Persian coast cleared of the Portuguese. Sherley was very hospitably received by these English merchants because, as one of them, William Clark, put it, "his [Sir Anthony's] voyage as we well perceive is to meet Captain Davis with certain Flemish ships in the East Indies to take some hold of the Spaniards there, but he keepeth all very secret." [29] Clark also noted that "his worship will continue here yet some twenty or thirty days and take his voyage to Bilong [Baghdad]." [30] About a month after noting the arrival of the Sherley party, Clark reported that "he [Sir Anthony] hath here taken up of the whole company 3,000 dollars to be repaid the treasurer [of the Levant Company] in England by the Earl of Essex, whereof we have no doubt but good payment will be made, yet for my own part was not over willing to give my consent." [31]

The travelers remained six weeks in Aleppo, and they were so well taken care of by the English consul, Colthurst, and by the merchants that Sherley long after retained the fondest memories of them, declaring that from the consul, "and from all the merchants there abiding, I received such an entertainment, with so careful, so kind, and so honorable a respect, as I must needs say, they were the only gentlemen, or the most benign gentlemen that ever I met withal, for my company being so great, that it was no light burthen unto them." [32] Yet in spite of the kindness of his compatriots, the stay in Aleppo was, he admitted, a wearisome time, and for other members of the party who were maltreated by the Turks, it was a painful, unpleasant time. Having already obtained, through Lello at Constantinople, a passport from the Sultan, Anthony also obtained from the Pasha of Aleppo a pass empowering him to proceed through the country on his journey to Persia. To obtain the pass, Sherley declared to the Pasha that he was an English merchant. Finally he and his party departed for Baghdad. Their journey and their sojourn in Aleppo had been noted in far-away London. "We hear," wrote John Chamberlain to Dudley Carleton, "that Sir Anthony Sherley hath been at Constantinople, and there wrung out of our merchants £400, and from thence he went to Aleppo and there scraped together £500 more, wherewith he hath charged the Lord of Essex by his bills, and so is gone on, God knows whither, to seek his fortune." [33]

Before setting out Sir Anthony bought cloth and jeweled ornaments in order, he says, "to carry the fashion of a merchant." The party left Aleppo on asses, mules, and horses on 2 September 1598. They were now on a trade route which had been traveled for centuries by Europeans as well as Orientals. From Aleppo, the route ran overland to Bīra, the head of navigation on the Euphrates. At that point the way was by boat to Al Falluja, where camels and asses were again hired for the short overland journey to Baghdad. Sherley and his party were accompanied as far as Bīra by four English merchants, two Turkish officials (a Cadi and a Deftarder), a company of Janissaries, and other travelers who took advantage of the presence of the soldiers to make the journey. Traveling only at night, they reached Bīra on the fifth day, passing through a rich and fertile country which had been ravaged by Arab marauders. They remained at Bīra a few days and purchased there provisions and a boat. On 10 September 1598, in company with twelve other boatloads of Turkish, Jewish, and Venetian merchants, and Turkish officials, they set off down river for Baghdad.

At Rakka the party stopped, perhaps were forcibly stopped, to pay court to one Abu Risha, the paramount chief of a tribal group based at Ana. Sir Anthony described Abu Risha as "a poor king with ten or twelve thousand beggarly subjects living in tents of black hair cloth." Both Manwaring and Pinçon noted that he had a stud of several thousand camels, and Pinçon adds that "he also keeps many small horses and birds of prey, and leopards with which to catch gazelles." Sir Anthony had an audience with Abu Risha, and Manwaring relates that the King tendered them a banquet consisting largely of fruit, melons, radishes, and rice, which, he adds, was not free. As Parry put it, Abu Risha "borrowed (without a privy seal or bill of his hand) some thirty yards of cloth of silver until our return." Like all travelers from classical times on, the Englishmen were struck by the bubbling asphalt and crude oil at the town of Hit. The Arabs were using asphalt to waterproof their boats, and both

Arabs and Persians had petroleum lamps. Sherley and those companions who chronicled the journey are silent on an incident which occurred within the party. "Sir Anthony Sherley being within eight days journey of Babylon [Baghdad] upon the river Euphrates," wrote William Clark at Aleppo, "it so happened that some discontent came betwixt some of his company, whereupon he put two of them ashore who passed the desert in great misery and danger, being robbed and stripped naked by the Arabs, and forced to go so two days journey without any food. So five days past they came into Aleppo in miserable case, God knoweth. They remain at our counsel's until the coming of the [ship] *Angel.*" [34] The two men were named Browne and Kydman. Sir Anthony sent a letter to Colthurst, the English consul at Aleppo, charging him with the safe, close, and discreet keeping of the two men, who, said Sherley, not only had the horrible intention to deny Christ, but were contriving treason against Her Majesty, and plotting against some of the most prominent men in England. He promised to send his brother back to Aleppo with a full statement of their crimes, signed by six men of the party, but in the meantime "a trifle of it I will tell you, as poisoning four of the best in England." Sir Anthony professed himself "ashamed that any of mine should be tainted with so detestable crimes, but since I am charged with the knowledge of it, I am bound in my duty to God, my prince and the world . . . for the returning of them unto the hands which have power to make satisfaction for such enormities." [35] He never sent back his brother Robert with the statement, signed by six members of the party, as he had promised, but Browne and Kydman were sent to England and imprisoned. The latter in 1598 speaks of being incarcerated upon the accusation of Sir Anthony Sherley, but was then free on bail. He declared that he was the victim of malice, and since he had been cleared of suspicion and charges of treachery he asked Sir Robert Cecil that he should be given unconditional freedom. Unhappily, in 1599 he was back in jail. "My imprisonment is very grievous unto me," he wrote Cecil. "I do understand Robert Browne is come into England who is accused of the same fact as I am. . . . My only request is that it will please Your Honor to respect the cause how maliciously we are dealt withal by Sir Anthony Sherley, or whosoever wrote that letter against us. . . . If I ever meddled with matters of state or practiced any villany against my prince, I wish that I may have such punishment laid upon me as a traitor do deserve." [36]

After expelling Kydman and Browne the party continued to Al Falluja, where the voyage down the Euphrates ended, and the travelers hired camels and asses for the short journey to Baghdad. Before arriving in the city the Cadi, in whose company they had traveled from Aleppo, warned Sir Anthony that the Pasha of Baghdad might confiscate his goods. The Cadi offered, for a small charge, to declare to the Pasha's officers that part of Sir Anthony's goods actually belonged to him. Sherley accepted the bargain, which turned out to be a good one, for immediately the party entered Baghdad, the Pasha took all of Sherley's merchandise, paying him half of what it was worth, "which," says Parry, "was good pay for so ill a debtor." Probably because the amount of his merchandise was inadequate to justify so large a party, if indeed he were a merchant, as he claimed to be, "I gave out," says Sir Anthony, "I had more goods coming with the caravan by land." This falsehood had the unfortunate result that he was forbidden to leave Baghdad, the Pasha doubtless looking forward to another shipment of merchandise at half price. This Pasha, an unpleasant type, threatened to send Sherley in chains to Constantinople and to cut off the heads of his followers. Sir Anthony replied, says Manwaring, "that as for his own life, he did not respect it, but for his followers; and he desired to endure any torments himself so that his company might pass quietly without hurt." Far from being cowed by the Pasha, says Manwaring, "Sir Anthony carrying a gallant mind, as he ever did, would not do any obedience unto him." The party remained in enforced idleness a month in the city. Sir Anthony was without money and, as often happened in times of stress, he was ill. "I had my brother with me," he related. "I had also five and twenty other. . . . I had no means to give them sustenance to live." [37] To make matters worse, says Parry, they heard that letters were on their way from Aleppo ordering Sherley and his men be held in Baghdad, as indeed they already were. Sir Anthony related that relief came suddenly, munificently, and from an unexpected quarter. A Florentine merchant whom he had known on the journey from Aleppo to Baghdad came to him, "and as a man moved in his very soul with anguish . . . beseeched me, not to cover myself longer from him, who did truly wish me well, not so much for my person (which he could know little) but because his conceit was, that I would not have hazarded myself in such a journey, but for some great end, which he did believe well of . . . and taking me by the hand, beseeched me again to believe him. . . . He had already hired horses, camels, and mules for me . . . and then opening his gown, he delivered me a bag of chequins, with these very words, 'The God of Heaven bless you, and your whole company, and your enterprise, which I will no further desire to know, than in my hope, which persuadeth me that it is good; myself am going to China, whence if I return, I shall little need the repayment of this courtesy, which I have done you with a most free heart; if I die by the way, I shall less need it.' "[38] The amiable Florentine's generosity was not ended, for he also devised a stratagem whereby the Sherley entourage was gone five days before their departure was discovered by the Pasha. In reflecting on this almost miraculous occurrence, Sir Anthony observed that although God had chosen him to be an example of affliction, yet he was permitted this stroke of fortune because God wished to show his pleasure in his having "fastened my mind to that good purpose."[39]

Concerning their departure from Baghdad, Manwaring's account differs somewhat from Sherley's. Manwaring declared that permission for them to leave was obtained by one of the Pasha's officers, an Armenian named Magevalo, who also arranged for Sherley to obtain 800 crowns from certain Venetian merchants in Baghdad. Clark, the English factor in Aleppo, to some extent corroborates Manwaring for he noted that Sir Anthony had been ill at Baghdad and without money, and that he had borrowed 800 dollars from a Venetian, giving him a draft on the English merchants at Aleppo. The English at Aleppo had decided not to honor Sir Anthony's draft until they had heard from England whether or not Essex had repaid the

Levant Company the 3,000 dollars Sherley had previously obtained from them. "It was reported at his being here," recalled Clark, "that he was sent upon Her Majesty's affairs. If it be so no doubt but good payment will be made, but some think he goeth upon his own business, which I fear will prove too true." [40] Whatever the source of the money he obtained, Sir Anthony declared that it was "not only sufficient to give us abundant means for that time, but to clothe us all in rich apparel, fit to present ourselves before the presence of any prince, and to spend extraordinarily in gifts." [41] Parry's account of how the party left Baghdad says nothing about money, only that on hearing that orders for their arrest were on the way, they stole silently out of the city in the dead of night. In any event, either through a stratagem devised by the Florentine, or because they were befriended by a favorite of the Pasha, or simply because they stole silently away, the party continued overland to Persia. They were amply supplied with funds which either had been given them by the generous Florentine, or obtained by an arrangement made by the Pasha's Armenian official with Venetian merchants, or by Sherley's signing a draft on the Levant merchants. Leaving Baghdad on 4 November 1598, Sir Anthony and his companions experienced more remarkable adventures and beheld more wonderful sights.

After they had been five or six days on the road they asked the Persians with whom they were traveling if they would be forced to pass the residences of any more Turkish governors, and they were told that they would have to pass a very powerful governor, Qubad Beg, "at which answer," says Parry, "it had been an easy matter to have found a company of poor hearts near their master's mouths," but the travelers managed to evade Qubad Beg. They were struck by the ruins of ancient towns which they passed and all the chroniclers remarked the passage through the land of the Kurdish tribesmen. Manwaring notes that the Kurds lived in tents, moved from place to place, rode on bulls and cows, and "except we did look well unto them, they would filch and steal anything they could lay their hand upon" (or, as Parry put it, they were "addicted to thieving not much unlike the wild Irish").

On 1 December 1598 Sherley and his companions reached Qazvin in Persia, a city, says Pinçon, "a little smaller than London in England and the same length, but it is very badly built of baked earth, and the houses on the interior are of chalk." They waited there a month for the return of the ruler of Persia, Shah Abbas, who was away chastizing the Uzbegs.

CHAPTER VI

The Persia of the Sherleys

THE frontier of sixteenth-century Persia changed during the periodic wars with the Turks and Uzbegs, but generally speaking the northernmost province on the west frontier, in the Caucasus, was the Persian segment of Georgia. South and east of Georgia was Azerbaijan, with its capital of Tabriz, and Persian Armenia was part of Azerbaijan. South of Azerbaijan was Kurdistan, where the nomadic tribes had aroused the wonder and curiosity of the Sherleys and their companions; south of Kurdistan was the province of Kirmanshah, which the Sherleys had also traversed on their way to Qazvin. To the east of Kurdistan and Kirmanshah lay the central provinces, and southeast of Kirmanshah was the mountain province of Luristan. Adjoining Luristan on the southeast was Arabistan or Khuzistan. In the eastern part of this province dwelt the Bachtiari, a tribe which was not conquered until 1930, the reason being, as a member of the tribe remarked, that the land has always been so impoverished and desolate that it has not been worth conquering. The great province of Fars, also Pars, was known to the Greeks as Persis, from which was derived the later name of Persia. It extended some distance along the Persian Gulf and its capital was Shiraz. East of Fars lay the province of Kirman, the Carmania of the ancients, and southeast of Kirman was Makran. The hold of the Shah over the latter province was tenuous and sometimes nonexistent. Baluchistan, which lay along the coast, was even less likely to acknowledge Persian suzerainty. The great province of Khurasan lay on the northeast borders of the country. The present boundary between Afghanistan and Persia cuts through Khurasan. Along the coast of the Caspian were the provinces of Mazandaran and Gilan, the latter being the great silk-producing region. This is by no means a catalogue of all the

Persian provinces, but these were the lands visited by and best known to the Sherleys.[1]

The peoples of Persia were of various races and modes of life. Except for the low-lying plains along the Caspian shore and the Persian Gulf, the country is mountainous where it is not desert. Arable land lies in pockets and oases, so that there always has been a mixture of sedentary and nomadic people. Of the latter the majority were descendants of Iranian tribes who had moved to the plateau many centuries earlier. There were also large numbers of Turkish, Turkoman, Arab, Baluchi, Brahui, Afghan, Georgian, Armenian, and Jewish people.

Religions were almost as various as the races. The Georgians were orthodox Christians; the Armenians were Gregorian Christians, and while the bulk of them were in Persian Armenia, there was a great colony of them settled in Ispahan, as well as in other towns. In the Kurdish mountains there remained a small number of Nestorian Christians. Along the shores of the Persian Gulf, despite the official hatred for their sect, were a number of Sunnite Moslem tribes. The Jews lived mostly in Ispahan, but there were also colonies in Hamadan and Kashan. The adherents of Persia's ancient religion, the Zoroastrians, had a quarter in Ispahan. Languages were also numerous, including, in addition to Persian, various Turkish dialects, Kurdish, Arabic, Georgian, Armenian, and Pashtu.[2]

The character of the people, as reported by travelers, was as varied as the races encountered, and accounts differed with the characters of the observers. The Persians, Herbert thought, were "generally of a very gentle, obliging nature, facetious, harmless in discourse, and little inquisitive about exotic news; seldom exceeding this demand: if such and such a country have good wine, fair women, serviceable horses, and well tempered swords." [3] Manwaring found the Persians courteous and friendly to strangers, as did his companion William Parry, but their fellow tourist Abel Pinçon thought them very dangerous, extremely greedy for money, liars, wantons, blackguards, drunkards, and cheats.

On one point Persians, foreigners, and all the world agreed, and still do agree—the Persians were a nation of poets. Omar

Khayyám, as presented by FitzGerald, is known to all English readers, and although Persian scholars would agree that FitzGerald's quatrains are not always Omar's, they are nevertheless Persian in origin. Hafiz also is widely known, and it is said that this poet even had the power to charm the terrible Tamerlane. Hafiz once wrote:

> If that fair maiden of Shiraz would accept my love
> I would give for the dark mole that adorns her cheek,
> Samarkand and Bokhara.

When Tamerlane captured Shiraz, he sent for Hafiz. "I have subdued with the sword, the greater part of the earth," he said, "I have depopulated a vast number of cities and provinces in order to increase the glory and wealth of Samarkand and Bokhara, the ordinary places of my residence and the seat of my empire; yet thou, an insignificant individual, has pretended to give away both Samarkand and Bokhara, as the price of a little black mole setting off the features of a pretty face." Hafiz bowed to the ground. "Alas! O Prince," he said, "it is this prodigality which is the cause of the misery in which you see me." [4] Regardless of whether or not they were poets, all literate Persians wrote verses on the slightest provocation. Curiously enough, although there were hordes of verse writers, and perhaps because the Shi'ah theologians insisted on rigid religious conformity, poetry which had been the glory of Persia had become mediocre in the later sixteenth century. There were brilliant Persian poets, migrants from Persia, at the court of the Great Moghul in India, but they found no generous patrons in their own country.

Although poetry was not at its best, other arts flourished. The architecture of the age was inspiring, and the practice of covering buildings with tiles reached its zenith in this period. Over a blue or white glaze the tilemakers painted a second glaze made of finely ground metal alloys in suspension. The gold, silver, and copper of the alloys turned in the baking process to ruby red, turquoise, blue, brown, and gold. In other ceramic arts the Persians also surpassed, the pots, bowls, and vases of the period being remarkably beautiful. The metal work of the time also reached a high state of perfection, and rugs, of course, were of great beauty.[5]

Persians had also less intellectual interests and diversions which were not unlike those of their English contemporaries. The nobility, the verse-writing set, were very fond of hawking, hunting, and polo. The people amused themselves with wrestling matches, bear baiting, bull baiting, and fights between rams, all of which were familiar in merry England, but Persians arranged what could not be seen in London, fights between two camels or two antelope. As for less salubrious amusements, Persia was a country of vineyards and vintners, and Persians, generally speaking, took less kindly than did other Moslems to the injunction in the Koran to abstain from alcohol. Europeans often remarked on the relatively small number of prostitutes in Persia. Since their religion permitted Persians to have a number of wives, and numberless concubines, there must have been little effective demand, to use the economists' phrase, for prostitutes; but pederasty was a popular diversion. One aspect of Persian life frequently remarked by foreigners was the constant horseback riding. A Persian gentleman, Cartwright averred, never walked, and a slave or humble man never rode. A gentleman would mount and ride even the most trifling distance. Persians fought on horseback, transacted public and private affairs on horseback, bought and sold on horseback, and conversed with their friends on horseback.

There were many famous cities, the names of which at least were known throughout sixteenth-century Europe. The capital at this time was Ispahan or Isfahan, whose stately buildings struck sixteenth- and seventeenth-century travelers as magnificent. That magnificence is still evident in the twentieth century.[6] The Persians with pardonable pride and provinciality referred to their capital as "half the world." A ride around the huge walls of the city, said an English traveler, was an easy day's journey on horseback. An Italian traveler of the period, Pietro della Valle, stated that the area within the walls of Ispahan was nearly as large as Naples, but the Persian capital had suburbs without, so that actually in size it would surpass Rome or Constantinople.[7] The maydan, or great central square of the city, was so spacious that it was used as a polo field, and around the maydan were shops in arcades. The noble avenue of Chahar Bagh was two miles long and as broad as Holborn, said one Englishman. It led to the bridge of Allah Verdi Khan, which ranks with the great bridges of the world, being 388 yards in length with a paved roadway thirty feet wide and three thoroughfares on three separate levels.[8] Since the King's court was at Ispahan, said the English traveler John Cartwright, "all matters of importance have recourse to this place, all ambassadors of princes and agents of cities make their repair thither and such as aspire and thirst after office and preferments run thither amain with emulation and disdain of others." [9]

The city was noted, as were most Persian cities, for its beautiful gardens, which were so numerous that "at a little distance from the city you would judge a forest, it is so large; but withal so sweet and verdant that you may call it another Paradise." [10] Another English traveler reported that, of all gardens, the Shah's was the most delightful. It was, he says, "all flourishing and beautiful, replenished with a thousand sundry kinds of grafts, trees, and sweet smelling plants, among which [were] the lily, the hyacinth, the gilly flower, the rose, [and] the violet. . . . There are a thousand fountains and a thousand brooks; among them all, as the father of them all, a pretty river which with his mild course and delightsome noise doth divide the garden from the King's palace." [11]

Qazvin, the first city known to the Sherleys, had been the capital of Persia under Shah Tahmasp and served as the base in the Shah's wars against the Turks. Sir Thomas Herbert thought it in grandeur equal to any city in Persia with the exception of Ispahan. "I saw growing there," he reported, "grapes, oranges, limes, lemons, pomecitrons, musk and water melons, plums, cherries, peaches, apricots, figs, gooseberries, pears, apples, pistachios, filberts, hazelnuts, walnuts, almonds, and excellent pomegranates." Another observer of the period described the city as being very wealthy, "by reason of the king's palace and the great concourse of merchants which resort thither." It was situated, the same traveler observes, in a fertile plain, three or four days' journey in length, in which were some two thousand villages, but he thought the city "evil builded, and for the most part all of bricks not hardened with fire but only dried in the sun as are most parts of the buildings of all Persia." He was struck by the central square or maydan, which he judged to be very nearly a mile in circumference and where such varied items were sold and exchanged as horses, mules, camels, pearls, diamonds, gold, silver, and Spanish dollars. The money lenders to be found there, Cartwright avowed, would "lend upon any pawn and that with as great interest as our devilish brokers and scriveners take in London." [12]

About two-thirds of the journey from Qazvin to Ispahan was Kashan. "There is not made in any place of Persia," said the traveler Sir John Chardin, "more satin, velvet, tabby, plain tissue, and with flowers of silk, or of silk mingled with gold and silver than is made in this city." [13] Sir Thomas Herbert wrote, "It is a city both great and lovely, and ancient too, abundantly peopled, overtopped by no hill, unseasoned by no marshes. . . . This noble city is in compass not less than York or Norwich . . . here are full manufactures of silks, satins, and cloth of gold curiously wrought and colored." [14] Cartwright was "persuaded that in one year there is more silk brought into the city of Kashan than is of broadcloth brought into the city of London." He was sure that "the city aboundeth with all necessaries whatsoever consisting altogether in merchandise and the best trade of all the land is there being greatly frequented with all sorts of merchants, especially out of India." [15]

The three cities which have been noted were in the western part of Persia. In Fars, and its capital, was the city of Shiraz, "the seat of knowledge," the city of Hafiz and of other famous poets, but famous not only for poets but for its wine.

South and east of Shiraz, at the head of the Gulf of Oman, were two other places which loom large in the lives of the Sherleys—the port of Gombroon on the mainland and the fortress of Ormuz on an island in the gulf, both of which were Portuguese possessions. "If all the world were a ring," ran a Persian proverb, "Ormuz would be the jewel in the ring." In the first decades of the sixteenth century the rulers of Ormuz paid tribute to Shah Ismail, but the town was captured by the Portuguese in 1507–1515 under Affonso d'Albuquerque, and thereafter the Portuguese refused to pay tribute. It became one of Portugal's richest trading points, and the Portuguese called it "the brightest jewel in the crown of Portugal." The Portuguese built there an awe-inspiring fortress which was described by Sir Percy Sykes, a professional soldier, who visited it in the present century. The fortress "consisted of a square . . . round which were barracks and store houses, built into the massive forty-foot wall which had a parapet eighteen feet wide. A steep rise led to the inner work in which [was] . . . a superb reservoir, an oval forty feet high and fifty feet long with a passage encircling it about twenty feet above the bottom. . . . A final rise brought us to the summit of the fort, some sixty feet above the ground level. There, overlooking the ruined city, was all that was left of a sumptuous palace, while numerous cannon lying about bore mute witness to the stormy past." [16]

At the time of the Sherleys' arrival in Persia, one of the country's greatest rulers, Shah Abbas of the Sufavi dynasty, was on the throne. Persia as the Sherleys knew it was really the creation of Shah Abbas' great-grandfather, Shah Ismail (1499–1524), who had reformed and re-established the nation. He had accomplished the task by forcibly imposing the Moslem Shi'ah creed on all Persia, although at the time the Sunnis were in a majority in Tabriz and numerous in other cities. By imposing the Shi'ah doctrines, Ismail separated the Persians from the Sunni Moslem world on the west, namely the Ottoman Turks, a separation which incidentally exacerbated the chronic Turko-Persian wars. In his struggle to unify the country, Ismail had the support of seven warlike Turkish tribes, and as a consequence, as late as the time of Shah Abbas, the language of the court was not Persian but a Turkish dialect.

Throughout the period of the Sufavi monarchy and indeed both before and after that era, Persia was beset by Turkish invasions. The lands of eastern Europe suffered the same misfortune, and the idea of an alliance between Persia and the Christian countries of Europe constantly recurred. Between 1285 and 1291 Arghun, the Mongol ruler of Iran, sent letters and embassies to the Pope, and to the kings of England and France, calling for a mutual effort against the Mamlukes based in Egypt. Much later the Emperor Charles V corresponded with Shah Ismail on how best to coordinate the efforts of Persia and the Empire against the Turk. Soon after his accession to the throne in 1524, Ismail's son, Shah Tahmasp, dispatched envoys to the Emperor asking for help, and in the following year (1525) the Emperor Charles proposed that the Turks should be struck simultaneously by the Persians on the one side and the Christians on the other. Shah Tahmasp reigned for fifty-two years, and on five different occasions during his reign the northwestern provinces of Azerbaijan and Georgia were invaded by Turkish forces; Baghdad and most of Mesopotamia passed into the power of the Turkish Sultan, Suleiman the Magnificent. The struggles of Shah Tahmasp with the Turk are referred to by Milton in *Paradise Lost:*

> As when the Tartar from his Russian foe,
> By Astracan, over the snowy plains,
> Retires, or Bactrian Sophi, from the horns
> Of Turkish crescent, leaves all waste beyond
> The realm of Aladule, in his retreat
> To Tauris or Casbeen. [Book X, lines 431–436]

Through the reign of Tahmasp, during which both Christians and Persians suffered at the hands of the Turks, the idea of a Perso-Christian alliance persisted. When Shah Tahmasp was an old man, the Republic of Venice sent an envoy to his court to persuade him to attack the Turks. The envoy reported that the Turks were about to seize Cyprus, and after they had attained that goal, the Venetian prophesied, Persia would be the next victim. Following the victory of Lepanto, the idea of an alliance was taken up by the Pope, who wrote Shah Tahmasp, pointing out that their common enemy was now beaten and demoralized. "A strong army should be mobilized by you," the Pope wrote, "and the enemy [Turkey] invaded . . . while the Christian allies will lead against him from Europe, by sea and by land, powerful and valorous forces." [17]

Actually the Turks had been only half of Shah Tahmasp's problem, the western half. On the east he was equally bedeviled, as had been his father, Shah Ismail, by the Uzbegs. By 1510 these tribes had overrun Khurasan. In that year in a swift campaign Shah Ismail routed them, but one of the first campaigns of Shah Tahmasp, in 1527, was against the Uzbegs, who were again overrunning Khurasan. Tahmasp died in 1576, and there then ensued eleven years of rebellion, murder, intrigue, and disorder, during which time the various factions fought for power and the throne was occupied by a series of weak rulers. The Uzbegs inevitably took advantage of the chaotic conditions in Persia to invade Khurasan, and the Turks, also seeing their opportunity, invaded the western provinces. In a few years Georgia and all of the lands south of the Caucasus, namely Mingrelia and much of Armenia, passed under the control of the Turkish Sultan, Murad III.[18] Tabriz, where the caravan routes from east and west met, one of the most important Persian commercial cities, was also captured by the enemy. Philip II of Spain, seeing Persia sorely beset, followed the example of his father, the Emperor Charles V, and sent an emissary to Shah Muhammad Khuda Banda, who was then on the throne, proposing a Perso-Spanish league against Turkey, but there is no record of a reply from the Shah. Shah Abbas, the grandson of Tahmasp, ascended the throne in 1587, and inherited a sea of troubles. The Uzbegs, now at the height of their power under a strong leader, Abdullah II, were firmly established in Khurasan, and on the west, as has been said, the Turks had taken Tabriz and occupied the western provinces. The great Moghul ruled Kandahar, and a number of provinces had virtually become independent. Abbas was only sixteen when he ascended the throne, but he had able advisors and generals. He began his reign by sternly suppressing the petty potentates who had set themselves up in Gilan, Mazandaran, and Luristan. In order to have a free hand to deal with the Uzbegs in Khurasan, Abbas made a costly peace with the Turks, ceding to them his western provinces. In 1592, seven years before the arrival of the Sherleys, Pope Clement VIII sent a proposal to Shah Abbas that he and the Christian princes should combine in a league against the Turk, but Abbas was still occupied with the Uzbegs and was not yet ready to deal with the enemy on the west. In his campaign against the Uzbegs he was at first unsuccessful, but at the time the Sherleys arrived in Qazvin he had finally triumphed over the Tartar horde; he was also contemplating sending an envoy to the Emperor, the Pope, and other Christian princes as his grandfather and great-grandfather had done, with a proposal such as the Pope had made to him, that Persians and Christians should form an alliance against the Turks.

Contact between Persia and the West, by the time the Sherleys arrived there, was obviously no new thing, and European travelers to the country had become common. Venetian merchants and diplomats had been making the journey to Persia for over a century, and quite a number of Englishmen had preceded the Sherleys. The English had either arrived by way of Russia as representatives of the Muscovy Company, or they had come overland from Aleppo by the desert route, often as representatives of the Levant Company. One of the earliest Englishmen, if not the earliest, in Persia was Anthony Jenkinson of the Muscovy Company. He made the journey down the Volga, crossed the Caspian, and arrived in Qazvin by caravan in November 1561. He was given short shrift by Shah Tahmasp, who indeed had the generous impulse to send a gift to the Turkish Sultan consisting of Jenkinson's head. Neither discouraged nor frightened, Jenkinson arranged a second trading expedition of the Muscovy Company which was sent down the Volga to Persia in 1564, and a third trading venture followed in 1565. As the result of fresh quarrels, the Turks threatened to close the border to Persian silk. In Persia, silk was a royal monopoly. The Shah was the chief merchant of his country, and the sale of silk yielded an important part of his revenue. In the serious situation threatened by the Turks, Shah Tahmasp was eager to establish trade with England by way of Russia, and granted the Muscovy Company generous trading privileges and safe passage for their merchants throughout his dominions. The trade via Russia at first appeared to be successful, but the anarchy into which Persia fell after Tahmasp's death (1576), and the dangers from pirates and storms on the Caspian Sea, finally convinced the Muscovy Company that the losses and risks were too great, and as a result the trade was given up after the sixth voyage in 1581.

The other overland route into Persia, the one taken by the Sherleys, had been previously traveled by John Newberry and other Englishmen. In 1579 Newberry, as a private traveler, had visited Tripoli in Syria, Jaffa, and Jerusalem, and the year following he took ship to Tripoli, made his way to Aleppo, and from there, following the centuries-old route, crossed overland to Bīr, and thence journeyed down the Euphrates and made his way overland to Tabriz, where to his great surprise he learned that the year previously English merchants had been in that city selling cloth. As an employee of two merchants, Edward Osborne and Richard Staper, and of the Levant Company, he made the same journey in 1583. On this occasion he went overland from Aleppo to Bīr, voyaged down the Euphrates to Al Falluja and from there crossed overland to Baghdad, precisely as the Sherleys were to do some fifteen years later. It was said that Newberry was the first Englishman to visit Ispahan, Shiraz, and southern Persia. On this third journey he was accompanied by the almost fabulous traveler Ralph Fitch, by John Eldred, England's pioneer in India, and by other merchants. It is a banality to say that trade routes are traveled by merchants, but it is worth remembering that traders are not writers and their names are not recorded in the annals of diplomacy. They are frequently careful that their goings and trafficking, their routes, ventures, markets, and associates should not be publicized. It is probable that other English merchants visited Persia but left no record.

When the Sherleys first arrived at Qazvin, Shah Abbas being absent on his expedition against the Uzbegs, the Shah's high steward came with a great train to the house where Sherley and his companions were lodged. "This much you shall receive every day for your provision beside other commodities," that official said, laying twenty pounds of gold at Sir Anthony's feet, "this do I of myself, until we hear from our King, who, I am sure, will treble it at his return." [19] Sir Anthony, having, as one of his companions observed, a princely mind, merely turned the money over with his foot. "Know this, brave Persian," he replied, "I come not abegging to thy king, but hearing of his great fame and worthiness thought I could not spend my time better than come to see him." Upon hearing these words, the same companion reported, the high steward was overcome with respect. "Now I see," he exclaimed, "thou art a prince thyself." [20] No sooner had the high steward departed than the governor of Qazvin called upon Sherley, and from then on the two dignitaries sought to outdo each other in showing hospitality to the Englishmen.

When the Shah returned to Qazvin, he camped some distance from the city to prepare a triumphal entry. He sent word that the English were to ride out to meet him in Persian costume, which they did. Sir Anthony for the occasion wore a turban worth two thousand dollars, and a jeweled scimitar swung at his side. Robert Sherley was attired in cloth of gold, Angelo Corrai's garments were of silver cloth, and all of the others wore silk and velvet. As the two parties approached each other, the Shah was accompanied by a band of courtesans, "riding astride in disorder, and shouting and crying in every direction as if they had lost their senses," their cries being such "as the wild Irish make." [21] Persian troops also accompanied the Shah, carrying the heads of slain Uzbegs on their lances. Some said there were twenty thousand heads on the lance tips, but others counted only twelve hundred. Shah Abbas at this time was about twenty-seven, a short, dark, wiry man, a valiant soldier and tireless hunter. When Sir Anthony and his men reached the royal party, Sherley dismounted and kissed the Shah's foot. "My speech was short unto him," he said later, "the time being fit for no other." He informed the Shah that "the fame of his royal virtues had brought me from a far country." He begged Abbas to consider "the danger and the expense of my voyage, only to see him, of whom I had received such magnificent and glorious relations." [22] The Shah kissed Sir Anthony and Robert three or four times and swore a great oath that Sir Anthony would be henceforth as his brother. A magnificent banquet was held in the Sherleys' honor at which were served pears, melons, quinces, pomegranates, oranges, lemons, pistachios, almonds, grapes, sweets, and wine. "There we drank joyously with His Majesty," related Abel Pinçon, "who gave us a very good welcome, showing us by word and by deed that our arrival was highly agreeable to him." The English were entertained with music and dancing girls, of whom it was said by a later traveler that "each limb . . . seems to emulate—yea to contend which can express the most motion, their hands, eyes, and bums gesticulating severally and after each other, swimming round and now and then conforming themselves to a Doric stillness." [23] When the banquet was ended, "the king arose, taking Sir Anthony by the arm and so they walked arm in arm in every street of the city, the twenty women [dancing girls] going before, singing and dancing, and his noblemen coming after, with each of them one of our company by the hand . . . and thus for the space of eight days and nights did we spend the time in sporting and banqueting with all the pomps they could devise." [24] In these first days at Qazvin the Shah also ennobled Sir Anthony, making him a mirza, a title given originally only to princes but later extended to men of good birth, "which made the people much to admire . . . that he vouchsafed that high favor to a stranger without desert or experience of his worth." [25]

Shah Abbas invited Sir Anthony and his companions to accompany him to Ispahan. They accepted the invitation, and there was an exchange of gifts before all departed for that city. The accounts of the gifts vary so widely that one is apt to get the erroneous impression that Sir Anthony and his companions received gifts on more than one occasion. As Sir Anthony remembered later, he was given sixteen thousand ducats, forty horses, two with exceedingly rich saddles plated with gold and set with rubies and turquoises, the saddles for the other horses being either plated with silver or of gilt and embroidered velvet. He also received sixteen mules and twelve camels laden with tents and necessary travel gear. Earlier he had only remembered being given thirty horses and four gold-plated saddles, which accords with Robert's memory of the gift. Other members of the party had different recollections; Pinçon recalled distinctly that the Shah gave Sir Anthony thirty horses, that two of the saddles were enriched with turquoises and rubies but the latter were of inferior quality. There were a few good horses, Pinçon remarks, but the rest were old hacks, badly saddled and bridled. He remembered that Sherley was also given twelve camels, five mules, carpets, and a number of tents, but actually received only 150 Spanish dollars in cash.

Sir Anthony presented the Shah with a magnificent gift which he himself described: "Six pairs of pendants of exceeding fair emeralds, and marvelous artificially cut, and two other jewels of topazes, excellent well cut also." He also gave the Shah a gold enameled cup, a salt container, and "a very fair ewer of crystal covered with a kind of cutwork of silver and gilt . . . (all of which I had of that noble Florentine.)" [26] The gift is also described by Pinçon, in whose account the "six pair of pendants of exceeding fair emeralds" become "an emerald pendant shaped like a grape," and the topazes, cup, salt container, and ewer are not mentioned at all. "Monsieur Sherley," Pinçon relates, "presented to the King a number of girdles and pistols which he had brought from Aleppo. . . . The matchlocks of the pistols were inlaid with mother of pearl, but this present was not of much value." [27]

On the road to Ispahan, the English diverted themselves by hawking and hunting, and paid never a penny for their food. After being ten days on the road they arrived at Kashan, where they were summoned to meet the Shah in the maydan, "a fair place, like unto Smithfield." Here there was feasting and entertainment, after which the whole party continued on to Ispahan, where there was more feasting and pleasure, for the Persians were "the merriest men alive; no people in the world have better stomachs, drink more freely, or more affect voracity, yet are harmlessly merry, a mixture of meat and mirth excellently becoming them." [28]

Sir Anthony remained less than six months in Persia, from 1 December 1599 until early May 1600. The most notable characteristics of the stay were the number of exploits he was subsequently said to have performed in Persia and the remarkable way in which his reasons for going changed after he had gotten there. As to his exploits, there has always been a tradition that Sir Anthony wrought great things for the Persian army. Of his less than six months in Persia, about three months were spent at Qazvin or in travel. Of the remaining three months, two weeks were passed in Ispahan before Sir Anthony broached the subject of a Perso-Christian alliance, and then a month was spent in debating that momentous question. During the discussions on his proposal by the Shah's advisers, Sir Anthony was quite ill, and that illness continued after the debate was ended. There followed a final month of merrymaking and feasting. The time available for army reform to be effected by a man who never knew Persian or the Turkish dialect of the court was negligible. Sir Anthony was given, he says, 25,000 foot and 5,000 horse to train according to the rules and customs of the English militia. He was also commanded to reform and retrain the Shah's artillery. It has sometimes been said that Sherley introduced cannon into the Shah's army, but this cannot be true. Sherley's commission was to retrain the artillery, which must therefore have already existed, and Don Juan of Persia, prior to the Sherleys' arrival, took part in the siege of Tabriz at which the Persians employed cannon. Also, Corrai related that when the Sherleys arrived, the Persians had many cannon, having captured them from the Tartars, and that "moreover there is no lack of masters to manufacture new ones, these masters have turned against the Turk and have come to serve the King of Persia." It was probably true, as Herbert remarked, that the Persians "detest the trouble of cannon and such pieces as require carriage," [29] and as a result did not use guns properly. Don Juan says, in fact, that the artillery was commonly held in reserve, a misuse of the weapon from which the Persians suffered a number of times, but a device which they had copied from the Turks. Infantry, while used in considerable numbers, was also likely to be held in reserve. It has sometimes been intimated that the Sherleys taught the Persians the use of muskets but this also is untrue, since Persian infantry carried firearms in Don Juan's day. Manwaring thought the Persians "very expert in their pieces or muskets," and added, "I did never see better barrels of muskets than I did see there." [30] Sir Anthony observed that the infantry carried "long pieces, half a foot longer than our muskets . . . which they use well." [31] It may have been that Sir Anthony was able to demonstrate how infantry and artillery could be used more effectively, and that he did indeed introduce the idea of militia. Pietro della Valle, who spent some years at the Shah's court, said that in 1618 the Shah's army contained fusileers, a recent innovation, similar to militia which had been formed at the suggestion of Sir Anthony Sherley. By the time della Valle arrived in Persia, Robert Sherley and others left behind by Sir Anthony had lived in Persia for years, knew Persian, and had served in the army. Their influence was probably greater than Sir Anthony's, whose sojourn in the Shah's country was so brief.

The way in which Sherley changed his reason for traveling to Persia is most curious. The Venetian statesmen had persuaded him that a journey to that country to break the Perso-Spanish alliance would benefit Christianity generally. Ambassador Henry Lello secured him a passport through Turkey because Sherley had represented that he was journeying to Persia to link up with Davis and Cornelis de Houtman, and intended to smite the Portuguese. The English merchants at Aleppo furnished Sir Anthony with three thousand dollars since they also understood that he intended to attempt something against the Portuguese. From Persia, Sherley wrote a letter to Anthony Bacon, of unusual interest since it marks a transitional stage between what Sherley up until then had said he intended to do and what he subsequently declared had been his objective. He begins the letter by saying that "some days after the New Year [i.e. after Easter] a gentleman from the King [the Shah] shall be dispatched with one of mine to all Christian princes with presents and letters of persuadement to peace with protestation against those that will be obstinate, which I have done only with this intent, that since the King's father and himself have by great ceremonies and oathes strengthened the league first made with the Spaniard, if the King of Spain shall be found only faulty in the not satisfying of his demand he shall be the utter and more honourable cause of breach, which upon my life shall be done." Sherley goes on to say that he has also been in touch with the King of Lahore and Cambara [the Great Moghul of India] and if he could be assured that the Earl of Essex desired it, "I will hazard to light more fire upon a sudden than will be quenched in many years." [32] After his return from Persia, Sherley maintained that he had gone there for the purpose of forming an anti-Turkish Perso-Christian league. Thus the Turks, whose passport Sir Anthony had accepted and with whom both the Venetians and the English merchants at Aleppo were anxious to maintain friendly relations, by a strange reversal became the enemy that Sherley was bent upon destroying. The reversal of objectives had in all probability been brought about by Shah Abbas, who, at the time he first met the Sherleys, was already intent on winning back his western provinces from the Turks. Part of his plan for the forthcoming war was, as Don Juan of Persia states, an alliance with the Christian princes. How fortunate it must have appeared to Shah Abbas that there should be ready and waiting at Qazvin upon his return a group of well-connected, experienced European soldiers who were anxious to serve him. Yet in his account of his stay in Persia Sir Anthony appropriates the idea of a Perso-Christian league, and he was apparently happily oblivious of the long history of the efforts to form such an alliance.

He began, he says, by proposing the alliance to the King's great general, Ali Verdi Khan, who advised him that "since you have begun in so happy an hour, to break the ice of so great and so good an enterprise, follow it without fear, since God will prosper your good intention in it." [33] Still, Sir Anthony proceeded with caution, studying Shah Abbas, "to make myself learned in the purpose of his actions, by his nature, and inclination; . . . to get first a kind of possession in his own affection." Meanwhile he said nothing to the sovereign "of that which was the main purpose of my coming," since, as he explained, "it was too great a business to expose, without such an occasion as might help my good intention, with the goodness of itself." [34]

Fourteen days after his arrival in Ispahan Sir Anthony finally resolved "to try the uttermost of my fortune, in bringing to a resolution, that enterprise; the imagination of which, had cost me so much time, and so much danger; and was the chief moving cause at the first, and now the only moving cause, of coming thither." [35] Being so resolved, he proposed the Perso-Christian alliance to the Shah. He thereby set off a stormy debate among the ruler's chief advisers which lasted for a month and so filled

Sir Anthony with anxiety and perplexity, he relates, "that I fell into a very dangerous sickness, in which the king never failed daily to visit me himself." [36] A résumé of the debate takes up thirty-three pages of Sir Anthony's account of his Persian travels, but in writing that narrative his object was not to describe countries or chronicle events but simply to trace the history of this proposal. "I speak only," as he put it, "of a good intention, tossed with the tempests; first of many desperate calamities; then with many potent oppositions." [37] Certain diplomatic events conspired in Sir Anthony's favor and the Shah finally decided to seek an alliance with the European countries and to send an ambassador to the Christian princes. Looking back later on those stirring days, Sir Anthony reflected that though he had been bitten by the viper of malice, it was "impossible that malice itself, much less the infusion of it in wicked spirits can take from me, the true knowledge to this time, and memory to posterity, that I was a zealous author of so Christian-like a purpose." [38]

The Shah had another problem; his plan for fighting the Turk was complicated, as his grandfather Tahmasp's had been, by the need to find additional outlets for the silk which normally passed through Turkey to European markets. He turned, as had Shah Tahmasp, to the possibility of sending silk through Russia, although the Muscovy Company had long since found that scheme commercially impractical. Sir Anthony relates that he persuaded Shah Abbas to consent not only to the Perso-Christian alliance but to free trade, without customs or excise charges, for all European merchants, but in view of the sovereign's needs, he was probably persuaded with a minimum of effort. Sir Anthony also persuaded the King to tolerate Christian worship in his domains, but since those dominions already harbored Nestorian, Orthodox, Armenian, and Roman Catholic Christians, and since the Shah was sometimes more tolerant toward Christians than they were to one another, that concession also probably required no great persuasive effort.

Having decided to send an embassy to Europe, the Shah selected Sir Anthony to be his ambassador, or at least one of his ambassadors. Before leaving Persia on his mission, Sir Anthony corresponded with old friends. In April he wrote the Earl of Essex, informing him that he had a pension of 30,000 crowns per year from the Shah. "I will confess," he added, "my vice was borrowing not robbing, and now it hath pleased God to give me means, so hath he bestowed a will upon me to satisfy the wants; wherein if men use my name with patience for awhile till I can send over I will pay all that I owe." [39] He also wrote to his old friends the English merchants at Aleppo, asking them to repay a thousand dollars which he had borrowed in Persia, but these erstwhile hospitable gentlemen had no enthusiasm for the transaction. "I think he may burn his bill," said the merchant Clark, "for here there will be no repayment," and added that it would "be a warning to some of us; to know how we trust such slippery gentlemen." [40]

CHAPTER VII

The Persian Embassy to the Courts of Europe

THE story of the embassage which Shah Abbas sent to Europe is sometimes befogged because readers have certain preconceptions of the dignity of an ambassador which the Persian monarch never had. The word "ambassador" suggests a prestigious person to whom all members of the party or embassage are subordinate. In the view of Shah Abbas the honors attached to an embassy were scanty and he was inclined to distribute them among the participants. In the group which left Persia for the courts of Europe there was a venerable Persian, Husein Ali Beg, and a Dominican friar, Nicolão de Melo, both of whom, in addition to Sir Anthony, may have had ambassadorial status. A European would assume that the question as to who was the leader of the embassy could be settled by examining the letters of credence, but the letters sent by Shah Abbas are not much help and probably were not intended to be. In Sir Anthony's letter of credence to the Emperor, the Shah stated in substance that "valorous Sir Anthony Sherley came to Persia from Frankland. He has enjoyed the highest rank in our service; you must know that he has made a place for love of you in our hearts, and I desire to make a league with all you princes of Frankland. An honored subject of ours goes with him as Ambassador to the sovereigns. We desire that you shall treat with the said Sir Anthony and consider him as our supreme commissioner." [1] Other letters to other monarchs read: "Anthony Sherley has arrived at our Court, and during his residence has shown his most pure and faithful affection toward us, and now as he is returning to his own land, by his means we have sent as our ambassador our highly esteemed Husein Ali Beg in company with the aforesaid little Lord." [2] A European monarch had the choice, then, of treating with the Shah's supreme commissioner, Sir Anthony Sherley, or his ambassador, Husein Ali Beg. The Dominican, Nicolão de Melo, the third candidate for ambassadorial status, had arrived in Ispahan with a Franciscan. De Melo claimed to be the brother of the late king of Portugal and said that he had been sent abroad by Philip II of Spain as Procurator General of all the Indies. His companion swore that de Melo was Bishop of Ormuz. De Melo "would fain, by the King's commission, have been an agent in the present action wherein Sir Anthony was principally employed," says Parry, "and likely he was to have been one with universal consent, but that the writings and all other things thereunto incident were before perfected and finished." [3] Sir Anthony had secured de Melo an audience with the Shah, and "there in my own presence," says Sherley, "he desired the King to put no confidence in me." At the conclusion of the audience, Sir Anthony told him "that he had not truly understood my purpose which was the general service of all Christendom," and despite de Melo's most despicable behavior Sir Anthony, ever the true Christian, procured for the friar "a particular letter both to the Pope and King of Spain in which he should have equal authority with me." [4]

The Shah sent, then, three ambassadors, or maybe two, or one, but since for the Persian monarch an ambassador was partly a messenger, partly a propaganda agent who played upon the European concept of an ambassador, the number was not too important. In the Near East of the seventeenth century an ambassador whose mission was displeasing to a foreign court was apt to have his beard cut off and returned to the court from which the envoy came. In the case of particularly unpleasing missions the complete head might accompany the beard. Like other eastern potentates, Shah Abbas was accustomed to employ in this office men of little prestige or those who were no longer useful at home. When on one occasion a courtier asked to be sent as an ambassador to Europe, the Shah expressed his astonishment that a nobleman of high rank should make such a request. When some years after Sir Anthony had been sent to Europe, the Shah was asked why he sent so many ambassadors there, he replied that the Pope and the Christian princes had promised him help in the war against the Turk, and by sending a stream of importunate messengers he hoped eventually to prevail upon them to perform what they had promised.

Sir Anthony, Husein Ali Beg, and Nicolão de Melo were not the only ministers dispatched at this time. Assad Beg, one of the Shah's merchant factors, was sent to Italy, and there he let it be known confidentially that he was actually an ambassador. Angelo Corrai, who had come to Persia with Sherley, returned overland to Italy alone, carrying letters not only from the Shah and Sherley but also from de Melo to the Pope, the King of Spain, Don Cristóbal de Moura, and others; a priest, Francisco da Costa, who passed through Ispahan about two months after Sherley had left, was also entrusted by the Shah with messages to the Pope. In addition, an ambassador, Pir Quli Beg, was sent to the Czar of Russia to pave the way for the passage of the Sherley party through that country.

The selection of both Sir Anthony and Husein Ali Beg as ambassadors appears to have been a trifle casual. It will be remembered that in the spring of 1599 Sherley had written Anthony Bacon that shortly after the New Year (i.e. after 8 April 1599) the Shah intended to dispatch an envoy to the courts of Europe "with one of mine." [5] Sherley wrote before the event took place. After the embassy reached Europe, one of his companions wrote that the Shah's original intention had been to send Robert Sherley, but another member of the party averred that the Shah had no other intent but that Sir Anthony should be his ambassador with "a great man of the Persians to accompany him in those businesses, but the whole burden thereof to lie upon Sir Anthony, who undertook the same accordingly." [6] At least it appears to be true that for a time in the spring it was undecided which Englishman should be sent and there was also some question about the selection of a suitable Persian. A very prominent and noble gentleman was selected but almost at the last moment he was unable to go. Husein Ali Beg, Sherley related, was in disgrace for "some ill part that he had played." The Persian begged Sherley to include him in the European embassy. Sherley, yielding to his entreaties, asked the Shah's permission to take Husein Ali Beg with him, "in the form only of a testimony, though honored with some good words in the letters, for the better reputation of the business; which the king was exceeding backward in consenting unto, desiring me either to go alone, or better accompanied." [7]

The ambiguous embassy left Ispahan early in May 1599. It numbered at least twenty-four persons exclusive of servants. Manwaring, Parry, and Pinçon, all of whom have left accounts, were in the party, and of course there were the two friars and Husein Ali Beg with his own retinue of Persians including a secretary, Uruch Beg, who later turned Christian and as "Don Juan of Persia" also left an account of the embassage. Fifteen Englishmen, including Robert Sherley, were left behind, the latter, the chroniclers agree, as a hostage to insure the return of Sir Anthony. Since the object of the embassy was to form a Perso-Christian alliance against the Turk, the party wisely went by way of Russia. Also, as Pinçon remarks, Sherley in going through Turkey to Persia had passed himself off as a merchant, but while he was in Persia the Turkish agents there had learned that he was something quite different, and he would have been a marked man in Turkey. Shah Abbas wished to send silk to Europe through Russia and perhaps desired to familiarize his people with that country, an additional reason for taking the Russian route. The party went from Ispahan to the shores of the Caspian and there took ship. The vessels plying that sea were crude but "if these ships are badly constructed," remarked Pinçon, "the sailors are even worse, and ill-versed in their trade, for they understand as much about the stars as pigs do about spices, and they never use the compass; that is the reason why they always keep close inshore, not daring to venture into the open sea." The vessel bearing the embassy cautiously followed the coastline around the Caspian but even within sight of land the storms terrified the passengers. During one particularly devilish tempest, said Pinçon "one heard a dreadful medley of voices and prayers. We of the Religion prayed in one way; there were some Portuguese monks who threw figures of the Agnus Dei into the sea to appease it, and . . . the Mohammedans invoked 'Ali Ali, Mahommet.' " [8] Eventually, after two months at sea, the ship reached the estuary of the Volga, where the travelers were met by a party of soldiers, each man carrying an oar and an arquebus, which latter, says Pinçon, "they handle about as dexterously as an ox would a flute." The soldiers rowed the party up stream to Astrakhan in a day and a half, where "they asked us whence we came, what we wanted, and whither we were going, and put many other questions to us in the square, the which they wrote down, together with our replies and took to the governor. . . . Then the governor gave us one of his Cargoli [*karaul,* guard] for an attendant, and this man never went further from us than the threshold of our door. They generally give them to strangers, chiefly in order to spy what they are doing, and to see that no one of the country has intercourse with them and that they never go out to reconnoiter the fortifications of the towns." [9] The party stayed a fortnight in Astrakhan, for, it was said, "travelers arriving at this gateway to Russia can go neither forward or back until the governor of Astrakhan sends a messenger to Moscow advising the Czar of the arrival of the party and asking for instructions as to how to treat them." At Astrakhan the party overtook the ambassador Pir Quli Beg dispatched by the Shah to Boris Godunov, and the combined parties proceeded together on the long journey up the Volga. They were accompanied by a detachment of troops and were given food and transportation, "for so is the custom of that country to all travelers of that nature, having withal a guard set over them; so that they are little better than prisoners as long as they are within the limits of his [the Czar's] territory." [10] Above Kazan at Cheboksary the river was frozen, and the party proceeded by sled to Nizhni Novgorod, and thence by sled to Moscow. As inevitably happened on these long treks from Persia to Europe the members of the party quarreled along the way.

At the beginning of the journey, Sir Anthony had dined each evening with Nicolão de Melo, but the good fellowship vanished before the embassy left Persia. As a matter of fact it transpired that the Dominican was not all he might have been. While still in Ispahan, "this Friar had each night a Persian courtesan to lie with him," and while still journeying through

Persia, de Melo confessed that he was a simple friar and not the Procurator General of the Indies. In gamesome vein he confessed "how he would bring men's wives after he had shriven them to his bent as taking advantage of their confessed faults." [11] After he had quarreled with de Melo, Sir Anthony declared that "for male and female of all sorts I think under heaven there lives not such a villain." [12] De Melo also quarreled with his companion the Franciscan, Father Alfonso, who declared that de Melo had spent his life most lewdly in the Indies, and added that the real reason for de Melo's return to Spain was that he had been recalled by the King because he was doing more harm than good where he was. At Astrakhan, the two having completely fallen out, Sherley made de Melo a prisoner, which he did, he explained, "with good confidence because I was in a country [Russia] in league with my Mistress [Queen Elizabeth]." [13] Later it was said that Sherley tried to drown de Melo. The Persian members of the party declared that Sherley threatened to kill the friar simply because the latter had asked for repayment of a thousand crowns he had loaned Sir Anthony and for the return of ninety diamonds he had entrusted to Sherley for safe keeping. The English also quarreled with the Persians, "insomuch that had we not had a guard in our company, one of us had killed another." [14] So the embassy journeyed on, the Persians quarreling with the English, and the English with the Dominican, and the Dominican with the Franciscan, until in January 1600 the party reached Moscow, where Sir Anthony quarreled with Pinçon and had new quarrels with the Persians and de Melo.

The Moscow of the sixteenth century, some travelers declared, was bigger than Paris or London. The city walls were of stone; there were fine stone churches, a cathedral, a palace, unpaved streets, filth, log huts, slaves, and magnificent nobles. The court of Czar Boris was there, a czar who had so recently been Boris Godunov, a powerful boyer and regent of the kingdom. The only heir to the throne, Prince Dmitry, had been murdered, and Godunov was the natural successor. He could have seized the throne, but he felt the need for a popular demonstration in his favor. Led by the patriarch, an immense religious procession had knelt and moaned that Boris should be czar. Those who did not moan sufficiently loud were beaten to stimulate their enthusiasm. Godunov could only bow to the people's will and become Czar Boris. He was able, suspicious, and afraid, and fear spread through Moscow, seeping from the palace into barracks, churches, law courts, counting houses, and hovels. Boris' spies and informers were everywhere, for he distrusted Moscow and the city mistrusted him "for faults of conscience, unseen but felt." The winter of 1600 was not a propitious season for tourists to Moscow.[15] Sherley and his companions "were entertained in the best sort they could, with a crew of aqua-vitae-bellied fellows, clad in coats of cloth of gold." The show being ended, they were shut up in prison for ten days, and later the Czar "daily sent his great dukes to examine Sir Anthony upon divers frivolous particularities to prove if they thereby might grope out some matter of advantage against him." [16] Friar Nicolão, supported by Pir Quli Beg, the Persian ambassador to Czar Boris, denounced Sir Anthony to the Czar's officials, charging that Sherley had gone to Persia and was returning to Europe not for the good of Persia or of Christendom, as he pretended, but for his own ends. Unfortunately Sherley's letter of credence to the Czar recommended him to the monarch's favor only as a traveler on his way to Europe, which tended to bear out the friar's charge. Sir Anthony was then summoned before commissioners, where, after de Melo made in his presence further accusations against him, "Sir Anthony, whose blood already boiled with excess of his choler's heat . . . and being by that graceless and ungrateful friar further provoked, he, not able, though instantly he should have died for it, to suppress his heat, gave the fat friar such a sound box on the face, his double cause of choler redoubling his might, desire of revenge withal augmenting the same, that down falls the friar as if he had been struck with a thunderbolt." [17] This show of spirit on Sir Anthony's part impressed the Russians and gained Sir Anthony and his campanions better treatment, as Sherley's courageous conduct in Baghdad before the Pasha had bettered their condition. Sherley subsequently had his revenge on the friar for the latter had secretly celebrated the Roman Catholic mass for some of his faith who lived in Moscow. Roman Catholicism was detested in Moscow as the religion of the Poles, who were also detested. Though the Dutch and English protestant merchants were allowed to worship publicly, Roman Catholics were forbidden even to follow their religion in their homes.[18] Sir Anthony reported to the Czar's officers that Friar Nicolão had been ministering to his coreligionists, whereupon the friar was banished to a monastery on the White Sea, or on the island of Salcastei or Saliskot, although later he returned to Astrakhan.

The Shah's emissaries wintered in Moscow, "expecting every day . . . some mischief to be done unto us, or to be sent into some part of his [the Czar's] country to be kept where we should not have heard from our friends in haste, which we feared worse than death." Sir Anthony complained that he had arrived in Russia in September, "and now it is February and am yet held prisoner . . . and that which is most of all none of my countrymen suffered to come unto me." [19] Don Juan of Persia says that "on any occasion when we might wish to go forth to view the city of Moscow, it was due from us to send to the Captain of the Citadel for his license, and he would then give us four soldiers to walk with us as a guard." Don Juan also notes that even the Russians did not have complete freedom. "No one under pain of death might leave Muscovy to go into any foreign country lest he should get into communication with other folk and learn better." [20]

While immured in Russia's capital Sherley wrote to his friend Anthony Bacon. He was, he said, "exceeding faint," and in a state of indecision, "for that unseen thing called honor is so hourly before the eyes of my mind." There in Moscow in that winter of his discontent, he confessed to Bacon that honor was one thing he knew not how to attain. "By Jesus," he wrote, "I am far worse . . . and I divided from myself by not knowing what to determine upon." He avowed that "I am and ever will be Her Majesty's true and faithful subject," and he outlined a plan whereby there might be prepared "a mighty blow to the King of Spain." The plan was for a son of Don Antonio, the Prior of Crato, to go to India and there, in conjunction with the Moghul of India and disaffected Portuguese, to seize the Portuguese possessions. Sir Anthony claimed to have received a letter from the Moghul outlining the plot.[21] Possibly this was the same scheme he had in mind when he had assured Essex that he was in touch with the Grand Moghul of India and that on a word from Essex he would light such a fire as could not be quenched in many a year.

It was shortly after Easter that the party was allowed to proceed on its way. His experience in Moscow rankled with Sir Anthony, for more than twenty years later he was to write of the Russians that "these people are false, lawless, and without honor; malicious, suspicious, and so much given to drinking that from nine in the morning until the following day it is impossible to deal with them; they are liars and extremely cruel." [22] Leaving Moscow the embassy proceeded overland through Pereyaslavl to Yaroslavl, where there was a house or factory of the English Muscovy Company.[23] From there the party ascended the Volga about fifty miles to Rybinsk, from where they voyaged up a tributary and portaged to the Sukhona, and so on through Totma and Veliki Ustyuk and down the Dwina to Kholmogory and Archangel, where the Muscovy Company had been ensconced for nearly half a century. Archangel as an English port had had its beginning in 1553, when a group of London merchants sent Hugh Willoughby and Richard Chancellor on a voyage of "discovery of the northern part of the world." After many adventures and hardships, Chancellor was received in Moscow and given trading privileges, which resulted in the formation of the Muscovy Company. The Company constructed a factory at Kholmogory, a flourishing and ancient town on an island near the mouth of the Dwina. Each spring when the ships arrived from England the island was covered first with violets, and then with wild roses, and so the merchants called it Rose Island.[24] By 1557 the Muscovy Company had a rope factory on Rose Island, and a decade later there were well-built homes and warehouses. In 1591 the factory was moved down river, about forty miles, to Archangel. Each year the Company sent a fleet laden with goods to the port, and although by the time the Persian embassy reached there English trade at Archangel had passed its peak, a number of ships of the Muscovy Company still arrived each spring. During the month the party were in Archangel, Parry wrote, "we were divers times invited aboard English ships, where we were royally banqueted at the agents' charge and the merchants'." [25]

At Archangel began the affair of the Shah's presents which, as Don Juan of Persia says, "it will be well not to pass over in silence." Don Juan begins his account of these gifts intended for the European monarchs by remarking that "Sir Anthony was a man of great parts, although short of stature, and he was much given to ostentation, in spite of the fact that fortune had not dowered him with wealth." The Shah had ordered that in foreign countries the Persians were to follow Sir Anthony's advice in business matters. Here at Archangel Anthony explained that, since the ship they intended to take to Stade in Germany was old, if storms were encountered cargo would probably be thrown overboard to lighten the vessel. It would therefore be prudent to send the thirty-two cases of presents from the Shah to the princes of Europe by a different vessel. By great good fortune he had a friend who commanded a fine stout ship then in port on which the gifts could be transported with the utmost safety and confidence. The cases were put aboard the fine ship and that was the last the Persians ever saw of them. Husein Ali Beg, Don Juan, and their compatriots maintained that these goods of great price were sold by Sherley to his friend the captain of the merchantman, "for afterwards we had notice how our pieces of brocade and cloths had afterwards all been publicly sold by the English merchants in Muscovy." [26] Sir Anthony maintained that upon opening the cases he found that the intended gifts, far from being worth three or four hundred thousand crowns, were actually worth only about a hundredth part of that amount. Rather than give such unsuitable presents, Sir Anthony said that he pretended to send the gifts to England, but actually sent them by merchants back to Persia.[27]

Embarking at Archangel, the embassage voyaged round the North Cape to Stade at the mouth of the Elbe, a port which owed its commercial development to English merchants. Until 1597 it had been the trading center for the Company of Merchant Adventurers. In that year, because of the jealousy of the Hansa merchants, the Company was expelled from Stade, but many independent English traders remained, and were there when the Persian embassy arrived. (Incidentally, Lionel Cranfield, who later as Earl of Middlesex loomed large in the life of Thomas Sherley the younger, transacted a great deal of business in Stade in his days as a merchant.) It is evident that the Persian embassy had been helped on its way to a considerable extent by English traders. They had been assisted and entertained by the servants of the Muscovy Company in Moscow. They had gone on to Yaroslavl, where there was an English factory, from thence to Archangel and more merchant hospitality, and following the lanes of commerce, they had arrived at Stade. The secret of success of more than one famous pioneer, pathfinder, or traveler has been that he stuck close to the well-established routes of trade.

When on the voyage homeward the ship arrived off the coast of Holland, William Parry transferred to a passing merchantman bound for England, carrying with him Sir Anthony's letters which had been written at Archangel. When he arrived home, Parry was made much of, wrote and talked of his travels, and was embalmed, as were so many others, in the verses of Sir John Davies of Hereford. Leaving the ship at Stade, the rest of the travelers took galleys to Emden and made their leisurely way through Germany, being entertained by the German princes through whose domains they passed, until they reached the court of the Emperor Rudolph II at Prague on 20 October 1600. Here they were given a sumptuous and splendid welcome, being met outside the walls by the Lord Chamberlain, von Schönberg, with a train of fifteen coaches and an escort of three hundred horsemen. As they entered the city, crowds, which in his excitement Don Juan estimated at 10,000 people, gathered to stare at the exotic and impressive cavalcade. It is said the Emperor Rudolph watched from a window, an indication of the tendency in him which worsened as the years went by to withdraw from, and to suspect, all society. The Emperor loved to dabble in alchemy, astronomy, and astrology. Persuaded that he would be murdered by one of his own blood, he eventually refused to see foreign ambassadors, or even his own ministers. Covered galleries, in his later years, connected his apartments with his stables so that he might pass from one to the other without being assassinated by those whom he was sure lay in wait for him.[28]

Though the Persian embassy was welcomed royally, both the Emperor and his ministers were puzzled and cautious. Was not Queen Elizabeth the ally of the Turk? And was not this professed ambassador from the Turk's enemy an English knight? There was obviously more here than met the eye. The Emperor's ministers endeavored to persuade both Sherley and Husein Ali Beg to return to Persia, volunteering to deliver for them the Shah's letters to the Christian princes. When neither would consent to return, the Austrians attempted to separate them and to attach an ambassador of their own to Husein Ali Beg. Sherley also refused to agree to this arrangement. Yet despite their suspicions, the anti-Turkish league of Persians and Christians attracted the Emperor's ministers. Some of them at least must have been familiar with previous attempts to form a Perso-Christian league. This might be the occasion when the effort would be crowned with success. An emissary was dispatched to Persia with the Emperor's promise to fight the Turks with all his might.[29]

Foreign diplomats at Prague were more puzzled and wary than the Emperor's advisers. The Spanish ambassador suspected that the Persians were seeking to trade directly with Germany, England, and the Low Countries without the mediation of Spain, Portugal, Venice, or Turkey, and in this, of course, he was right.[30] The Venetian ambassador at Prague, though at first puzzled, finally wrote triumphantly to his government that he had detected the secret design. The Englishman, though ostensibly accredited at the Emperor's court, was really negotiating there with the Spanish ambassador to purchase from Spain the right to take over a port at the mouth of the Red Sea, to buy there all the goods destined to pass overland to Europe, to divert the merchandise to the Russian route, and to sell it in English and northern European markets.[31]

Meanwhile news of the Persian mission and its object spread over the rest of Europe. Perhaps the first news received in England of Sir Anthony's return came from Aleppo, where Angelo

Corrai, hurrying overland, had met Richard Colthurst, the English consul and Sherley's erstwhile friend. Colthurst wrote home that Sir Anthony was returning home via Russia. He "hath had wonderful great entertainment of the King [Shah] with many exceeding rich gifts from the King and 8,000 ducats towards his charges," wrote Colthurst. "His brother remaineth in Persia till his return. God grant his voyage turn us to good, but yet he turneth us no money." [32] Later Parry arrived in England and delivered Sir Anthony's letters for Sir Robert Cecil, James VI of Scotland, the Earl of Essex, Queen Elizabeth, and his parents. In his letter to James VI, Sherley declared himself to be the true servant of the Scottish king. He avowed that the favor of James had given him courage not to yield "under the burthens of such misfortunes as have been almost intolerably tossed over me." Well aware of the zealous Protestantism of the Scottish King, he explained that he was devoting himself to the work of the Lord, and that it had so far pleased God Almighty to bless the efforts of his humble servant. Taking credit for what had been done by Shah Ismail more than three-quarters of a century earlier, he declared that he had succeeded in separating the Persians from the main body of the Moslems, but he had done even more. He had persuaded Shah Abbas to unite with the Christian princes against the great enemy of God and man, the Sultan of Turkey.[33]

Though he was, as he had declared, the true servant of the King of Scotland, and though the favor of that monarch was his mainstay and guide, yet it was also true apparently that the light in the eyes of Queen Elizabeth was for him "the fairest light in the world," and the objective of all his adventures had been "to do some extraordinary thing which might honor Her Majesty's most excellent person." He had "only used the favor and love of the King of Persia for her glory." [34] He confided to Sir Robert Cecil that he looked upon Cecil as the "patron of me and of my actions." [35] Still this regard for Cecil did not preclude esteem for Essex. "If I be so happy as this letter may present itself before Your Lordship's eyes," he wrote the noble Earl, "you shall see in it the constancy and say [see?] the fullness of my affection signed with that hand which no thing nor cause between heaven and earth shall ever alter . . . the last words Your Lordship spoke unto me were the star which guided me, so great strength had your excellent virtue in my mind . . . I am so much beside myself that if I were not a little contained by one assured confidence that so rare and excellent virtue and worthy, as Your Lordship's, can but receive a momentary eclipse, I protest before God I know I should come from myself and that little reason I have." Although Sherley protested that always "did I love you [not] for your fortune but for yourself, though I confess freely that I would and will at any time spend my life to make your fortune worthy of yourself," [36] still this protestation did not nullify the fact, as he declared to Cecil, that his sole desire was to lay his life and fortune before "the most excellent royal feet" of Queen Elizabeth.[37]

In his letter to his father, Sir Anthony declared that "if I might write unto you as I would I should tell you a large discourse of a number of strange and diverse fortunes which I have passed since my fortune forced me the way which I took from you, but since my unhappiness is such that I have more to say for the disculping myself from my fault to you than I can . . . I must set aside those discourses. . . . Sir, where men are, there are ever faults, which either confessed or amended or both mollify the rigor of the severest justice . . . but in my fault to you I am so truly faulty that I can not show myself to myself without unmeasurable shame . . . even now do I cry out unto you for your favor without which I utterly renounce any feeling of happiness in anything my travels or fortune can give me . . . receive discourse by this gentleman, my friend [Parry] who is a true witness of my whole pilgrimage." [38] He had previously written to his father, and his father had replied to him addressing the letter to him in Persia, but since the letter is now in the Cecil Papers, it had probably been intercepted as had many another. "I have your four letters of yours which do import your filial regard to me and also your remorse towards me," old Sir Thomas wrote, "whereof I take much comfort; so does your mother . . . [who] with myself have been long comfortless, as you knoweth. . . . If you mean any good to your parents do it speedily or else it will not do the good which otherwise it would." [39] In addition to his letters from Persia and Archangel, Sherley had written the Queen from Emden, asking for permission to return to England. Elizabeth denied the request and had called upon Sir Anthony's friends to reprove him for his vanity and folly in meddling with a mission so dangerous to her amicable relations with the Porte.[40]

In France the arrival of Sir Anthony and his party at Prague did not, of course, cause the stir that it did in England, although Sir Anthony's presence at the Imperial court did not go unnoted. Henry IV may have remembered how he had tried to honor this colonel of the English forces and thereby for his pains brought down upon himself the extreme displeasure of Queen Elizabeth. "It cannot be believed," he wrote, "that this Englishman has undertaken the negotiations without the knowledge of his sovereign." [41] The French ambassador at Constantinople echoed the suspicion of his King that Sherley was the secret agent of Elizabeth. He confided to his colleague, the Venetian ambassador, that the Englishman at the Emperor's court had been sent to Persia by Queen Elizabeth to persuade the Shah to cut off supplies going into Spain's fortress of Ormuz, and to promise Shah Abbas that England would send a fleet to harass the Spanish and Portuguese vessels in the Persian Gulf.[42]

In Italy, news of the arrival of the Persian embassy caused more excitement and alarm than it did anywhere else, for those other messengers from Persia, Angelo Corrai, da Costa, and Assad Beg, had arrived before the embassy. The first was Corrai, who reached Venice in November 1599, some eighteen months before Sherley. "This morning," runs an account in the Venetian archives, "there appeared at the door of the most Excellent College a man of small stature with a black beard, of olive complexion, robed in a black camlet, of about forty years; this man said that he was an agent of the King of Persia, and that he wished to enter the most Excellent College in order to present certain letters to His Excellency. The Excellent College, having learnt of this, ordered me, the Secretary, Pellegrini, to conduct him with proper respect to the ante-chamber and there to see and find out exactly who he was, whence he came, and what he wanted. I followed these instructions. He told me his name was

Michael Angelo Corrai of Aleppo, that he came from the King of Persia, sent by the Englishman Antonio Sherley, who had lately spent some months in this city, and was now in Persia, held in great esteem by that king; that his letters were in the Italian language and had been given to him for His Excellency by Signor Sherley, with other letters for the High Pontiff, the King of France, of Spain, the Emperor, the Grand Duke of Tuscany, Cardinal Aldobrandini, and the Queen of England; that the said Signor Sherley was to have left Persia a few days after him with letters from the King, and with gifts for all these princes; and the said King, intent on his purpose, yet knowing that the journey of the said Antonio to all these princes would necessarily be fraught with great danger or at least much delay, had desired the said Michael Angelo to go privately to Italy by the Constantinople route with letters from Signor Sherley, so that his will should be known in any event."

Corrai appeared before the College and the letters from Sir Anthony were opened and read. "For the sake of security," Sir Anthony wrote, "this man will supplement the brevity of my letters." By questioning Corrai, the College learned that the Shah intended to declare war on Turkey, that he loved Christians, and probably also that Sir Anthony's mission was to unite the Christians and Persians in an alliance against the Turks. This mission was so different from Sir Anthony's purpose when he left Venice as to be almost diametrically opposed to it. Corrai was told by "the Excellent Savj [Councilors] that he was not to make himself known to anyone, and I [the secretary, Pellegrini] repeated this to him by order of Their Excellencies, and he replied that it was well, he would not speak further with anyone." Questioned as to how many people he had with him, Angelo replied that he had brought three companions. "It was said to him," the report of Pellegrini continues, "that it would be well for him to advise them not to speak of this affair to anyone, to which he answered that they could not speak Italian. After this I conducted him outside the Most Excellent College, and he departed." [43]

Even if Corrai did not speak to anyone, and supposing his attendants could not gossip with other servants, Corrai delivered to the Pope the letters from the Friar de Melo which had been entrusted to him, so that the Pope knew almost as soon as did the Signory of Venice that a Persian ambassador was on his way, bringing a proposal for a Perso-Christian league against the Turk and the glad, if erroneous, tidings that Persia was ripe for conversion to Christianity.[44] The Pope had been disheartened because the Christian forces fighting the Turks in Europe had suffered severe defeats and because the Turks were on the verge of establishing relations with the protestants of central Austria.[45] He was greatly encouraged by the news Corrai brought, and a month or so later he sent subsidies to the Emperor and attempted to form a coalition against the Turks, an attempt that, with the exception of Venice naturally, was received sympathetically by the Italian cities. About a year after Corrai's arrival, that is toward the end of 1600 (about the time Sir Anthony was arriving in Prague), the Augustinian priest, Francisco da Costa, who had passed through Ispahan, arrived in Rome. He, too, reported to the Pontiff that the Sherley–Husein Ali Beg embassy was on its way with a proposal for a Perso-Christian alliance, and he also reported that "what generally speaking can be said of the King [Shah] is that he shows himself well disposed towards Christians and desires extremely to have priests and Christians in his realms." [46]

About the time da Costa arrived, Assad Beg, the Shah's merchant factor, came to Italy. He carried letters from the Shah to the Signory of Venice, and like a number of Persians who preceded and succeeded him, he was commissioned to sell silk and to buy such items as the Shah required, but he had also been charged by the Persian ruler to provide for the wants of the Sherley embassage and to observe how the ambassadors were received by the Christian princes.[47] Assad Beg was recognized at Venice by a number of Portuguese who had known him at Ormuz where he had also transacted business for the Shah. One of these was Don Diego de Miranda, who had left Goa for the homeward journey with the priest, Francisco da Costa. Don Diego now became Assad Beg's special friend and introduced the Persian to Francisco da Costa, Father Antonio Abioso, and the brother of the latter, the Bishop of Pistoia, who was greatly interested in the Indies.[48] Assad Beg became well acquainted with the Bishop of Pistoia, who took a great liking to him. The Persian assured the Bishop confidentially that he was really not only a merchant but an ambassador from the Shah and that the latter wished to turn Christian and desired that Christian missionaries be sent to Persia. The Bishop received these confidential disclosures with great joy. He longed to have a part in the great work of Christianizing Persia, and he sent his brother (Father Antonio Abioso), Don Diego de Miranda, Assad Beg, and Francisco da Costa to Rome with the glad tidings which had been imparted to him.[49] The Pope received joyfully this confirmation of the news he had first gotten from de Melo's letter and immediately dispatched Costa and Miranda to Persia with letters to the Shah, preparing the Shah for the imminent arrival of Christian missionaries in his country.[50] This embassy was sent at the end of February 1601. Consequently, before the Husein Ali Beg–Sherley party arrived in Italy, two things had happened: Venice had decided that the mission was dangerous and likely to damage the Turkish trade; and the Pope, having heard a good deal about the proposals and glad tidings to be brought by the embassy, looked forward eagerly to its arrival.

Meanwhile, largely oblivious of the commotion they were causing in the world, the Persian embassage enjoyed life in Prague. "For the next three months," says Don Juan of Persia, "we took our ease resting at the Imperial Court, during all which time they entertained us sumptuously." [51] Sherley lived so royally that by Christmas 1600 he owed 46,000 thalers, and his creditors were becoming impatient.[52] Since life showed signs of becoming less enjoyable anyway, Sir Anthony, Husein Ali Beg, their servants and dependents finally left Prague on 5 February 1601 for the journey to Italy. "In view of the great expense which the Englishman incurred," wrote the Venetian ambassador, "the Emperor has given him two thousand florins, and another seven hundred for the journey. Between these two ambassadors they have received a present of two thousand thalers' worth of silver, very little compared with their hopes, though they cost his Majesty one hundred and twenty thalers a day all the time they were here." [53] When he left Prague,

Anthony took with him the cup-bearer to the Papal Nuncio, the Cavalier Pagliarini of Ancona, a knight of the order of Saint Lazarus, who was to have considerable influence in his life.

Going by way of the Brenner Pass, Sherley and Husein Ali Beg proceeded to Mantua and to Verona, where, says Don Juan of Persia, they awaited the return of an emissary sent to Venice requesting permission for the embassy to enter the city. "The Venetians, however, now sent for answer that as a Turkish ambassador was at that very time with them treating of important matters of state, it would not be convenient for them to receive us," which discourtesy, says Don Juan, so affronted Hussein Ali Beg that he "gave answer, that he cared not a jot for the Turkish ambassador, nor would pass comment on this discourtesy of the Signory of Venice."[54] The mission proceeded to Ferrara and Florence, where the party arrived on the morning of 16 March 1601, while the Grand Duke was in Pisa. The travelers were lodged in the Pitti Palace, and Sir Anthony, being considered more important than Husein Ali Beg, was given the better rooms. The latter and his Persian entourage caused some comment by taking their meals while sitting on the floor, and Sir Anthony was also observed critically. Enea Vaini wrote to the Grand Duke, who was then at Pisa, that "this Englishman doesn't appear bodily hale and sound to me; I know nothing about his soul. His face does not strike my fancy. I feel that if we were to go to an inn together for dinner, I would end up with the bill. He speaks with much kindness and humility in an almost unintelligible mixture of Spanish and Italian."[55] Three days after his arrival in Florence, Sir Anthony and others attached to the embassy went to Ambrogiano and on the following day visited the Grand Duke at Pisa. They were shown Genoa, returned to Florence on 28 March, and left for Siena two days later. In the latter city Husein Ali Beg quarreled with Sir Anthony over the missing gifts from the Shah to the Christian princes. Husein charged that Sir Anthony had not only sold the Shah's presents, but had taken the valuable gifts given himself in Moscow, that Sherley had even taken his money and spent it as he pleased. The quarrel was composed by a Cardinal sent by the Pope to conduct the emissaries to Rome, but the journey toward the holy city was not a happy one. "They arrived in such a state of hostility over precedence," reported the Spanish ambassador, the Duque de Sessa, "each claiming to be the principal ambassador, that they came to blows in Verberbo, forty miles from here, and the Englishman left one of the Persians who came with the other, the ambassador, badly wounded." [56]

The embassage was met outside the city by the Prior of Rome, the son of Juan Francisco Aldobrandini, then a boy about eleven years old, who was accompanied by the secular nobility. At the meeting Sir Anthony and the Persian renewed their quarrel, "and it took more than a little effort to calm them down." [57] The entry of the embassage into Rome surpassed the pageantry of the entrance into Prague. Drums rolled and trumpets blared, and as darkness approached the way was lit by torches. As the procession of Persians, English, and Italians neared the Castle Sant' Angelo, a salvo was fired in their honor, and when they reached the Palazzio de la Rovere, where they were to be lodged, salvos were again fired.[58] Unfortunately, upon entering the palace Anthony and Husein Ali Beg scuffled on the staircase over who should have the better apartment. "Perhaps someone may be found," the Cardinal D'Ossat, the French ambassador, wrote his sovereign, King Henry IV of France, "who shall tell them that since they being but two and sent by the same prince on the same mission cannot agree between themselves, they will find it difficult to bring about a union of so many Christian princes and others in order to ruin the empire of the Turk." [59] Husein and Sir Anthony both claiming to be the principal ambassador, some days were spent in passing messages, demands, replies, and ripostes between the Papal officers and the rival claimants. Despairing of finding out the truth, the Pope resolved to grant separate audiences, Sir Anthony being received on one day and the Persian on the day following. In the opinion of some members of the diplomatic corps, but not of others, this implied that Sherley was the principal ambassador. Both emissaries informed the Pontiff of the Shah's plan for a Perso-Christian league and his desire to have Catholic missionaries and Christian churches in Persia and to do everything necessary for the advancement of Christianity. Sir Anthony added that God had so touched the heart of the Shah that the whole kingdom might be converted, a piece of misinformation which gave the Pope infinite comfort. The official messages were a small part of what the two men had to say, most of their eloquence being reserved for the denigration of each other. Sir Anthony, Husein charged, had taken advantage of his knowledge of the language to usurp the Persian's place as ambassador. He labeled Sir Anthony a man of low character, who in Persia had professed to be a Moslem. He made it clear that the letters to the Pope and the Christian princes had been entrusted to him, and that Sir Anthony's place in the embassy was actually equivalent to that of a secretary.[60] Husein Ali Beg had particularly interesting information for the Venetian ambassador at Rome, whom he informed that, although the embassy had been forbidden to go to Venice, Sir Anthony had sent a secret agent there. This agent, the Persian warned, was not to be trusted and above all he should not be given presents for Sir Anthony was now so crushed with debt that the sole object of himself and this agent was to extract money from princes.[61] Sir Anthony had, as a matter of fact, sent the erstwhile cup-bearer to the Papal Nuncio, the Cavalier Pagliarini, to Venice. Pagliarini was to forward to Sir Anthony such letters as were sent to him from Persia. The information given the Venetians by Husein Ali Beg proved quite useful. The Venetians got in touch with Pagliarini in Venice, and so arranged matters with Sherley's man that they received copies of such letters as were forwarded to Pagliarini from Persia for Sir Anthony.

In Rome the complaints of Husein about Sir Anthony were matched by the latter's complaints about the Persian. Sherley complained that the Persian, knowing the English were a suspect nation at Rome, had been emboldened to think that any charge he made against Sir Anthony would be accepted. "It has been amusing," the Spanish ambassador wrote, "that as if it were something important, this whole court from the men of rank to the cobblers and the very servants of the Pope are divided, some favoring the Englishman and others the Moor, who has seemed more reliable because he has always spoken consistently. The Englishman is doubtless a liar and unreliable though a great talker and well informed." [62] Surely, despite what he himself said, Sir Anthony was exempt from the general suspicion of Englishmen for he was now a Roman Catholic, having been reconciled either at Prague or on his first arrival in Italy in 1598.[63] This change in faith was to mean a great deal to him in a material sense, but there is little indication that he was deeply affected by his new religion.

The most remarkable news about Sir Anthony during these first days in Rome was that communicated by the Duque de Sessa, the Spanish ambassador, to his King five days after Sherley's arrival. "The Englishman was very much bound to the Count of Essex," Sessa reported, "and since the latter's imprisonment and death, he is completely without hope of ever again being admitted to the presence of the Queen . . . [so that] he is determined to serve Your Majesty if Your Majesty should so desire. He is a practical man and a good soldier on sea and on land. He has been to the Portuguese Indies and knows much about them. He has been to Persia and other places and he offers Your Majesty important information." [64] About two weeks after his arrival in Rome, in conversations with the Duque de Sessa and Father Persons, Sherley declared that all the best soldiers in England realized the superior military advantage Spain would gain by maintaining a fleet of twenty-five or thirty ships in the Scheldt. He gave it as his opinion that with an enemy fleet stationed there, the English would find it impossible to defend all the vulnerable points on their coast and a landing could be made easily. The best places to land were Sandwich, Ipswich, Harwich, Hull, and Hartlepool, but of these Sandwich offered the best chance of success. Sir Anthony judged that in one day a landing party could make Sandwich strong and in a few days impregnable. From that port a landing force could easily strike at London, which he estimated could be taken by twelve or fifteen hundred men. Once London were taken, the enterprise against England would have been accomplished, for "it is common knowledge that the city of London is extremely alienated from the Queen, because of the death of the Count of Essex." [65] To take London, as Sir Anthony put it, would be to strike at the heart, while to attack elsewhere would be only a sting. When asked about Plymouth and the ports on the Irish and St. George's channels, he declared that although landings could be made and ports taken there would be little strategic advantage in such an operation. Similarly, although a landing in Ireland could be troublesome for the English it could never be a mortal wound. The Spanish ambassador noted that "this gentleman repeats with many exaggerations and arguments that the attack on London will achieve greater results more easily and more quickly than would an attack anywhere else." [66] In later conversations, Sir Anthony warned the Spanish embassy that the English had the intention of combining with the Dutch to damage Spanish-Portuguese trade in the Orient, and also that in England there was much discussion about taking Jamaica and Santo Domingo. Here certainly were two subjects on which he had had first-hand information. In the report of these conversations forwarded to Spain, it was recommended that although Sherley professed himself a zealous Catholic and desirous of serving Philip III of Spain, his opinions and information ought to be received with caution, for his conversion was still green. No agreement had been made with Sir Anthony, the report continued, only gratitude expressed for his devotion, the matter being left that when he returned from Persia the following year he would enter the service of the Spanish king.[67]

Sir Anthony also had interesting conversations with the French ambassador at Rome, the Cardinal D'Ossat. "He told me," related the Cardinal, "that he was the good servant of the King [Henry IV of France], and had served him in past wars; that he wished to be my servant also, and came to declare himself as such." The Cardinal was cautious, and shrewdly conjectured what the probable situation was from the facts he had in hand. "I know very well," he wrote, "that he was in conference with the English Jesuit, Father Personio [Persons], and with the Spanish ambassador," and he thought that "it may be that he, being far from his own country and in need of money, will accept a post from the Spaniards." [68]

Sir Anthony left Rome at the end of May, "suddenly and unexpectedly," said the Venetian ambassador. Actually he was now more nearly the servant of the Pope than a Persian ambassador and was ostensibly returning as the Pontiff's emissary to Shah Abbas. Concerning the lack of success of his embassy, he wrote that "I can attribute such effects but to sickness of the time, which have their power chiefly dominant over my fortunes. . . . I have taken with me only four gentlemen, and am gone in that sort that, except the Pope himself, no man knoweth whither I am gone; having been forced for that purpose to disperse my company into divers parts; which as I was most sorry to do, so I know when they shall understand the cause, they will be contented I have done so." [69]

His instructions from the Papacy were to proceed secretly through Turkish territory. At the Pope's request, the Spanish ambassador furnished Sir Anthony with letters to the Spanish viceroy in the Indies and the Captain at Arms there. The letters were of dubious value to Sherley, for the Spanish officials in Rome knew all about Sir Anthony's raids on the Azores and Jamaica and his depredations elsewhere in Spanish America. "It seemed best to me," the Spanish ambassador blandly explained, "to inform them [i.e. the Spanish-Portuguese authorities in the Orient] that the Englishman had been a heretic and a corsair in Indian waters. . . . I sent this word because if the facts were glossed over, and if by chance the officers in the Indies already knew these things, they would know that he had dissembled and fooled the Pope and myself. They would be suspicious and perhaps he might be in bodily danger." Sir Anthony, he added, had agreed to include this information in the letters.[70]

On departing from Rome, Sherley left behind a number of unhappy people. "He has done many out of much money," wrote the Venetian ambassador, "and loud are the lamentations." [71] The French ambassador reported that Sherley "has deserted his following to whom he owed money, and he deceived them with false hopes and promises that they would be paid by a certain Englishman in Rome, with whom he said he had deposited the necessary money, whereas he left nothing at all." [72] One of Sir Anthony's former servants related that, in the Sherley household at Rome, one day there would be plenty of money and the next day none, that Sir Anthony's servants had left him, "and daily comes of idle sorts to him." [73] Sir Anthony was himself discontented at the time of his departure. The Pope had given him one thousand escudos for the journey which he thought too little. Cardinal Aldobrandini had added another four hundred, but he remained unhappy. He went first to Ancona and then to Ragusa, where he came to the notice of the Conde de Lemos (Spanish viceroy) at Naples, whose reports to Madrid echoed an enterprise first outlined in Anthony's letters from Russia, and hints of which crop up elsewhere in letters and reports. "Inquiries were made," wrote Lemos, "to ascertain his intentions and it was understood that he was waiting for a son of the Prior of Crato [the pretender to the Portuguese throne] . . . and that they were planning to go to Alexandria and from there to the Portuguese Indies by way of the Red Sea, where they had contacts with certain Portuguese and Dutch who had left Holland to carry out business in India." [74] The Conde de Lemos went on to say that he had sent an agent to arrest Sherley. About six weeks later the Count relayed to Madrid a report received from his agent in Ragusa. Sherley was in that city, and had waited there for Don Manuel, the son of the Prior of Crato. Their plan had been to go overland to India, and with the help of a Dutch fleet presumably headed there and of certain renegade Portuguese already in India, to capture the Portuguese possessions there.[75] The plan had not come off, since Don Manuel instead of going to Ragusa had gone to Holland. Subsequently the agent and the Conde de Lemos reported to Madrid that they had failed in their plan to arrest Sir Anthony.[76] A servant of Sherley's, probably Pagliarini, had come from Venice and talked to his master. Subsequently the two had left Ragusa for Venice, planning to return to Persia by way of Moscow. While in Rome a servant had robbed Sherley of copies of the Shah's letters to the Emperor, and the Emperor's to the Pope. The thief had sold the letters in Constantinople to the Turkish government. This may have been the news that Pagliarini brought to Sherley in Ragusa, but if Pagliarini was not the source then there is evidence that others brought him this news. The Turks had long known about Sir Anthony's activities, but Sir Anthony now knew that they knew. One might conclude that he changed his plans because of this knowledge, had there not been a rumor current among the Persians in Rome before Sherley left there that he had no intention of going farther than Ragusa in any event. It is certainly doubtful whether, after the affair of the Shah's gifts to the Christian princes and his quarrel with Husein Ali Beg, it would have been wise for Sherley to return to Persia.

Actually there were few places where Sir Anthony could go. Queen Elizabeth had forbidden him to return to England. The Cardinal D'Ossat had made it clear that an emissary (or ex-emissary) of the Shah of Persia would not be welcome in France. Regarding Spain, Antonio Gouvea, an Augustinian friar who had been in Persia, declared that Sir Anthony had no desire to go there, "because he knew in his conscience the offences he had committed against the crown of Spain in various places, and thinking that the Spanish crown would not be unaware of the real reason why he had undertaken that voyage to Persia he separated from the Persian ambassador." [77] One realm where his activities were viewed with sympathy was Scotland. James VI addressed a letter to Shah Abbas in which he praised the ability and diligence of Sir Anthony, and he advised Sir Anthony for the time being to remain quiet and consider himself an exile.[78] But Scotland was not a real possibility as a place of refuge. While some places were really dangerous for Sir Anthony, others would be merely uncomfortable. Venice was one of these. He had left Venice with the avowed purpose of splitting the Perso-Spanish accord, a break which the Venetians desired. He had returned with the objective of forming, directly contrary to Venetian interests, a Perso-Christian alliance against the Turk. As the Shah's emissary and on such a mission he was unwelcome in Venice, but he had not been forbidden to enter the city, and so he went there.[79]

Husein Ali Beg, Sherley's erstwhile companion, lingered in Rome about a week after Sherley's departure. He predicted that Sir Anthony would not actually return to Persia, that he would go to Ancona and from there to Ragusa and no farther. Husein was himself determined to go to Spain, deliver the Shah's letter to Philip III, and take ship from Portugal to Ormuz. This intention, he declared, proved his honesty, for once he had arrived at Ormuz it would be easy for the Spanish-Portuguese officials, before allowing him to proceed into Persian territory, to determine whether or not he was a genuine ambassador of the Shah. Actually he did go on to Spain. Before he left Rome, three members of his entourage were converted to Catholicism, and in Spain three more were converted, including that Uruch Beg who became Don Juan of Persia. The wholesale conversions impelled Husein to depart for Persia as soon as he possibly could, but he died on the way home.

CHAPTER VIII

Sir Anthony as a Secret Agent

SIR ANTHONY arrived in Venice in late August or early September 1601. Many years later he said that when he arrived there he was a Spanish agent, possibly dating his service from the spring of 1601, when he had advised the Spanish on the best way to invade England.[1] In the intervening months, of course, the Spanish authorities had tried to arrest him at Ragusa. Perhaps Sir Anthony's secretary, Pagliarini, was more accurate than his master when he said some years later that Sherley had eaten the bread of the Catholic King since 1602.[2] Inasmuch as Sherley had been given one thousand escudos by the Pope and four hundred by Cardinal Aldobrandini before leaving Rome for the journey to Persia, he was probably in no hurry to eat anyone's bread before the time mentioned by Pagliarini.

Sir Anthony was also a Scottish secret agent, but the date when he became one is even more difficult to fix than the time at which he entered the Spanish service. Essex and his brother-in-law and sister, Lord and Lady Rich, were in communication with the Scottish King as early as 1589.[3] The involvement of his patron did not necessarily commit Sherley, but a number of facts lead one to suppose that Sir Anthony was in touch with James before he left for Persia. One indication is the statement of Don Juan of Persia that when Sir Anthony arrived in his country he announced that he had come from Scotland; Sherley's suggestion to Shah Abbas that his ambassador should be accredited to James VI and the fact that Sir Anthony wrote to the Scottish King from Archangel also point to an early connection with the King of Scots. Certainly Sir Anthony corresponded with the Scottish court when at Rome in the spring of 1601. At that time Lord Henry Howard, acting for Sir Robert Cecil, advised Edward Bruce, King James's agent, not to trust

Sherley, "who doth only watch to set his compass as the reasons and respects of state embolden him." [4] In reply Bruce reminded Howard that Sherley was first introduced to the service of King James by Anthony Bacon, "as I believe by your privity." Bruce went on to say: "as to any messenger from him, only Captain Eliot excepted, we had never none, the Duke of Mercoeur having recommended that gentleman to the King, he brought here a letter from Sir Anthony bearing the image of his own fortune and what disasters had happened unto him in his journey, but of the state of England or Spain we never had advertisement from him in his time. King James had never so much account of him as you suppose, and whatsoever he hath undertaken to the Spanish ambassador for him, he is not bestand [in haste] to acquit him of such a charge." [5]

Whenever he began to do so, Sherley was certainly working for both Scotland and Spain in the spring of 1602. His chief task for his Spanish employers was the promotion of Anglo-Spanish amity. What he did for the Scots is not clear. "I dare pawn my life that if His Majesty [King James] vouchsafe to be confident of me and soundly," he wrote eloquently and vaguely, "I will not only prevent all the purposes which are and shall be complotted against His Majesty in these parts, but also procure him both strong friends and that means which he wanteth most which is money abundantly." [6] Meanwhile, in lieu of money King James received copious amounts of advice, often that he ought to cultivate the friendship of Spain, but on one occasion upon the best means of obtaining the English throne. The King of Scots should, Sir Anthony advised, work for the impoverishment and weakening of England, since this would lead to discontent with the government and make the people receptive to change. As an effective means to this end, he recommended that "His Majesty must be pleased to fomentate the wars of Ireland." [7] Since Spain had invaded Ireland the year previously, this advice to James of Scotland fitted nicely with the Scottish-Spanish amity which Sherley advocated. Sir Anthony's devotion was such, he assured King James, that "though my good heart have thrown me into a multitude of dangers, yet I will never cease my true loyal efforts living, and it shall be true honor for me to die a martyr for such so great and so excellent a prince as Your Majesty." [8] As proof of his devotion he sniffed out hidden dangers, as when he reports that "I have heard the voice of a practicer which I cannot yet penetrate into, but the fashion of this gentleman maketh me fear him much." [9] His assignments were such that "I have scaped hardly with my life many times since Mr. Keith's departure, also as the danger of a harquebus and an arrow shot in at my window and missed me most narrowly." [10] But aside from the notion that the service he rendered was dangerous, that he protected the King from shadowy enemies and sought to procure him undefined riches, one gets no clear idea of what Sir Anthony was doing, proof perhaps that insofar as ability to keep one's activities hidden was a criterion he was a good secret agent.

Sprinkled through Sir Anthony's letters are indications that his undefined duties are poorly rewarded. At times he felt assured that King James would not forget his faithful and diligent servants in Italy, whom "Your Majesty well knoweth in their several conditions and will not leave destitute." [11] At other times he felt less confident and warned James that, "if you please not to have a gracious consideration of me, I shall be precipitated to utter ruin." [12] He suggested the propriety of the King's furnishing him with an "effective letter of credit in the Great Duke and Duchy [of Tuscany] to give me credit, the well using of which His Majesty shall need not doubt of," [13] and he passed along for the Scottish monarch to ponder a remark of the French ambassador at Venice. "I marvel Monsieur Sherley," that diplomat had exclaimed, "that after all the great good fortune you have enjoyed, you have chosen to play such a hungry part." [14]

Cecil had at least two agents, Simon Fox and Thomas Wilson, keeping Sherley under surveillance. These two were probably the most experienced spies on Cecil's payroll. There is at least the possibility that Simon Fox may have been Simeon Foxe or Fox, the youngest son of the author of the *Book of Martyrs;* Simeon Foxe had been a soldier in the Low Countries and Ireland, and later went to Padua where he took a medical degree, returning to England in 1603.[15]

Wilson, later Sir Thomas Wilson, had the checkered career which one would expect a secret agent to have. Previous to serving as Cecil's spy in Italy he had traveled in Europe, knew Spanish as well as Italian, and had translated Jorge de Montemayor's romance "Diana," a story from which parts of Shakespeare's *Two Gentlemen of Verona* are drawn. After his service in Venice he was consul in Spain, and years later he was used to draw from Sir Walter Ralegh sufficient admissions to justify his execution. Cecil quite probably would have excepted Wilson from his sweeping judgment on the spies in his employ that "I consider that those I use are but the sons of Adam." [16]

In his days in Venice Wilson was often in Sir Anthony's company. Being spies with antagonistic assignments, they were keenly interested in each other's activities. According to Wilson, Sherley was inclined to have his assignment appear more harrowing than it actually was. Concerning Sir Anthony's story that he had been the target for both an arrow and an arquebus shot, for example, Wilson declared that "he [Sherley] being one time in my chamber (as before I estranged myself quite from him upon the knowledge of his treachery, I could never be rid of him) there was shot into the window by a little boy an earthen bullet, out of a wooden crossbow such as boys use here, which hitting upon the wall and the noise making us look about, we found in the wall the print of a bullet which haply had been there many years, yet at first we thought it had been done at that time, till looking well about, we found the broken earthen bullet, and after I understood how it was shot. And this was that goodly matter." [17] Wilson reported to Cecil that "he [Sherley] hath also very lately sent a messenger unto the King of Scots, to show him the plots which he understands are wrought against him in England, and how he hath no way to obtain his purpose there, but by joining himself with Spain." [18] Sherley, knowing his activities were being reported, sent a messenger to Chief Justice John Popham. "I have given this gentleman a letter to Your Lordship," he wrote, "because by him Your Lordship may inform yourself of me against the vile false bruits which have so wrongfully and scandalously been made of me." [19] At one point Wilson notified Cecil that "I am forced at this present, to change my lodging, and live very retired, and make it be given out that I am gone out of town, only to shun his [Sherley's] impudent company, which intrudes himself every day by force, only to spy by me, whether I know of his practices."[20] Sir Anthony, no less resourceful in disparagement, referred to Wilson as "a fellow of a vile occupation, one Wilson, an intelligencer, who hath said and writ that he hath letters of that violence against me from the Queen and Council that no Englishman must either converse with me or any of mine."[21]

"I remember one thing now, which I have not written before," Wilson recalled, "when he [Sir Anthony] thought, that I thought myself greatest in his books, he discoursed to me the danger and trouble which must needs come after the death of Her Majesty. . . . I believe he is persuaded by the viper at Rome [Father Persons], to work the conjunction of the King of Scots and Spain . . . and saith that his treating with the ministers of Spain, was only to break his neck and do his country service—a fair tale."[22] On this subject Sir Anthony advised King James that "Wilson . . . continueth by himself and his instruments, those practices and voices which I wrote to Your Majesty . . . and hath added this new device to spread, that Your Majesty is now joining yourself with the Spaniard."[23]

The only extant report of that other agent of Cecil's, Simon Fox, is of an attack on Sherley, an incident of which there are several divergent accounts. One night in May near midnight, wrote Fox, Sir Anthony was assaulted and "one of his company was sorely hurt; himself, happily escaping the blow, was born over a bridge in the water."[24] Another account of the incident has it that the attempt on Sherley's life occurred about eight o'clock as he was walking with two friends, a Scotchman and an Englishman. The trio were set upon by six assassins whereupon the Englishman fled, the Scot was badly wounded, and Sir Anthony falling, or being thrown, into the canal became entangled in his cloak and almost drowned.[25] Wilson got an account of the incident directly from Sherley. "He saith he was set upon with partisans and albards [halberds], his gentleman which is now gone to Scotland hurt, himself thrown into the channel, etc., which, after, he told me he assured himself, was done by the Spaniard's procurement . . . but I have heard since . . . it was by the procurement of a fellow which had let him have for 40 or 50 ducats in wine, and finding no means to get his money vowed to have his blood." [26]

In August Sir James Lindsay, a brother of the Earl of Crawford, arrived in Venice on his way to Scotland with messages for King James from the Pope. "This man and the rest coming hither went presently to seek out Sir Anthony Sherley," Wilson related, "with him they are all in all, the one inviting the other continually, and participating their counsels, and devices together. . . . Sir James Lindsay sweateth and sweareth by no beggars that King of Scots must be king of England; that there were 2,000 English gentlemen vowed to stand for King of Scots though there were many that they knew did nothing but plot and work against him whereof, he said, of any that lives abroad he knew me to be one of the chiefest and dangerousest, nay more than that, that I was one of the chiefest plotters of the death of King of Scots . . . a heinous accusation and I know Sherley is the author hereof." [27]

It might have surprised Wilson to know that Sherley disapproved of Sir James Lindsay almost as much as he did of Wilson. Sir Anthony assured Lindsay of his firm affection and professed admiration for the true nobleness of his heart and his noble and excellent good parts, but he wrote to King James that "my honor and duty command me to say plainly to your Majesty, that I do infinitely dislike his [Lindsay's] diffidence [distrust] of Your Majesty; his fear to offend particular men known to be your mortal enemies at home; his plenty of money; having received no arrearages from the Spaniard, and the liberality of the Pope could bear no proportion with his expense." [28] It appeared preposterous to Sherley that Lindsay could have suspected that "I should have set Mr. Craig as a spy upon him which must needs arise from the guiltiness of his own mind." Sir Athony felt obliged to tell King James that Lindsay "feareth to hazard the favor and opinion of some foreign princes. . . . I know his company to have been dangerously chosen by him in these parts." [29] Lindsay left Venice for Scotland towards the end of 1602. He carried letters to both James and his Queen from the Pope and was well received. There is nothing to indicate that the King of Scots took Sherley's hint not to receive Sir James while alone and unprotected.

During 1602 Sir Anthony kept in touch not only with Scotland and Spain but with England also. In March he assured Sir Robert Cecil that in departing from England he had left Her Majesty's gracious presence but not her service and reassured him later of "my constant disposition to Her Majesty's service and honor and good of my country, and to pursue for good heart to yourself." [30] "I have suffered indigence itself and even heavy scandals and defamations," he wrote the Countess of Cumberland, "all these cannot move me from the duty I owe Her Majesty, natural respect to my country, and regard to my first and last reputation." [31] About the same time he declared to Chief Justice Popham that it was strange he should be persecuted by those from whom he might have expected comfort. He desired "nothing but such an opinion as shall be proportionate to a gentleman's merits," and he would "ever study to magnify the honor of my Queen and Country." [32] There was no basis, he assured the Chief Justice, for the false stories that he was an agent of Spain. If he were in the employ of Spain, he pointed out, he would not be in actual physical want which was his condition at the moment. In Persia, he declared, "I tried to influence the King of Persia to break with Spain." In Rome the Spanish had tried to murder him. Formerly, he observed to the Countess of Cumberland, "if the error of anyone's judgment carried him to the King of Spain's service, they would with all good means labor to apply him to his country and . . . not by . . . rejecting his humility, his patience, his beseeching . . . force him from himself and his Prince and his country." He felt that a combination of malice and ill fortune had multiplied misery upon him. "Let me know," he begged the Countess, "how I am, for I know what I am." [33]

Although Sir Anthony received some stipend, present, or emolument from both the Spanish and Scottish courts, these were inadequate to his needs and he supplemented his income in other ways. In the summer of 1602 he fell in with an alchemist and apparently interested a number of his fellow countrymen in the schemes of his new friend. He borrowed money from these compatriots and thus was able to live for a few months in a large house with a numerous following.[34] He also got some money from Aurelian Townsend, whom Cecil had added to those already keeping Sherley under surveillance, although Townsend was not an efficient spy. He was Cecil's steward, and a young poet who enjoyed the friendship of both Ben Jonson and Edward Herbert. Later, during the reign of Charles I, he had a great literary reputation and wrote the court masques. His talents and the polite world in which he moved did not equip him to cope with Sir Anthony. "I have several times informed you," wrote Townsend to Cecil, ". . . of the loss I have sustained by lending two hundred scudi to Sir Anthony Sherley; and to my discontent at the lack of this money is now added the fear that your Honor should be angered with me for having been free with your money . . . but if you knew how cunningly he laid the net in which finally I was entangled, you would not wonder that a young man like me was not strong enough to resist the affection, the consideration, and the promises of Sir Anthony. . . . If I had not and did not still think him a most attached friend to our country and to yourself, all my affection for him would not have conquered my sense of duty as a subject and as your servant." [35]

In March 1603 two dramatic events, one good, one bad, occurred in Sherley's life. His patron, James VI of Scotland, became King of England, and he himself was arrested by the Venetian government. Dread of Spain and the Turks were the two spectres which haunted the Venetian republic for decades. Spain not only possessed Milan to the north and Sicily and Naples to the south, but enjoyed the support of the Papacy, between which and Venice there was an ever-widening rift. There were also ample Spanish funds with which to bribe officials in Venice so that the menace of this foreign power pervaded the city itself. The fact that Sir Anthony was in regular correspondence with the Spaniards was enough to frighten the Venetians, but at the beginning of 1603 a Persian merchant arrived in Venice, and Sherley immediately got into touch with him.

Fearing that in addition to his efforts on behalf of Spain he was about to renew his pro-Persian, anti-Turkish activities, the Venetian authorities immediately began an investigation which lasted more than two months, involved the College, the Ducal or minor council, and the Senate, and resulted in the arrest and imprisonment of Sir Anthony.[36] The affair began on 3 March when the College (the administrative body which prepared and presented public business for the consideration of the Senate, the Ducal council, and the Council of Ten), noting that the day previously a Persian merchant had arrived in the city, instructed their dragoman, Giacomo Nores, to visit the Persian. He was to conceal the fact that he was acting for the College and find out what he could about the visitor. Subsequently Nores reported to the College that the Persian was named Fetchi Beg and that he was a merchant factor of the Shah, who had sent him to Venice to sell 139 bales of silk and to buy certain goods desired by the Persian sovereign. Incidentally this merchant factor of the Shah also became imbedded in Venetian history, or at least in one Venetian history, as a Persian ambassador.[37] When Nores had called on the Persian at his house, he had found a number of people there, among them a young Venetian of a well-known family, Angelo Gradenigo, who had been to Persia. When the other guests had left, Nores reported, Fetchi Beg locked the door and asked Nores if he knew a certain Anthony, an Englishmen. "I, pretending not to know anything about him, answered 'No,' " said Nores, "and asked him the reason for his question." Fetchi Beg answered that he had known Sir Anthony slightly in Persia, there being no close association since Sherley was a nobleman and he a merchant. On the previous day when he had arrived in Venice, Fetchi Beg related, he had been met by the servants of Sir Anthony, who invited him to stay at the house of their master. Fetchi Beg had replied that his agent in Venice, Cristoforo Suriano, had already engaged a house for him and he proceeded to the house Suriano had rented. Incidentally this Cristoforo Suriano was probably not the distinguished Venetian who was employed abroad on diplomatic missions in these years. Fetchi Beg had only been in the house a few hours when Sir Anthony called with six or seven followers. Sherley was indignant, Fetchi Beg said, that his hospitality had been refused and even became unpleasant and threatening, so that the Persian had felt constrained to spend his first night in Venice in Sherley's house, but returned to his own house in the morning.

Two weeks later, on 19 March, Fetchi Beg, who by now knew that Nores was in the pay of the Venetian government, begged Nores to report to the College that he continued to be annoyed by the Englishman, Anthony, who constantly sent Jews and others with proposals to sell his silks advantageously but never indicated any specific buyer. Only the day before, the Persian merchant complained, Sir Anthony with about twelve armed men had endeavored to get into his house by force, and not being able to, returned later with more armed men, threatening and insulting both the Persian and Cristoforo Suriano, his agent, so that the latter dared not walk the streets. Since it was obvious that Sherley wished to get possession of his silks, Fetchi Beg agreed that Sir Anthony might have them for 100,000 sequins cash.

The morning after Fetchi Beg had complained to the dragoman Nores, two Levantine Jews knocked at the door of Fetchi Beg's house before dawn, saying that they wanted to speak to the Persian on behalf of Sir Anthony, that they were Sherley's agents and intended to bring the 100,000 sequins for the silk that very morning. Without opening the door a servant told them that Fetchi Beg was sleeping and that it was no time to transact business. The Jews insisted vehemently on seeing the Persian; the servant thereupon opened the door and when the Jews entered, so did Sherley. Once inside the house, Sir Anthony demanded that the silk storage rooms should be unlocked, and that he should be allowed to see the silk. Fetchi Beg retorted that he would rather have his head cut off than allow Sherley or his agents to touch the goods without first receiving payment. While they argued, armed men entered the house one or two at a time. A servant of Cristoforo Suriano who had slept that night at Fetchi Beg's house slipped out to warn his master. Fetchi Beg subsequently told the dragoman Nores what had occurred, and Nores reported the occurrence to his employers, the Venetian authorities.

The College at this point turned over the information they had gathered to the Doge and the Ducal Council, and that body voted unanimously that one of the captains should arrest Sherley wherever he might be found. Captain Battista Moretto arrested Sir Anthony "as the bell tolled," said Moretto, in his own house in the quarter Santo Angelo, and took him to prison. The minor council ordered Moretto to return immediately to Sherley's house, search it, confiscate all papers he could find, and to get all the information possible on those living in the house. Moretto found that the Sherley menage consisted of eleven persons including Sir Anthony. In addition to servants there were Julio Sartor and his wife from Milan; Sherley's secretary, the Cavalier Pagliarini; two Englishmen whose names are given as Simon Misisi and Tomas Leton [Leighton?]; Roberto Goro [Gore?] and George Craig, Scots. The captain gathered up what papers he could find and brought them to the minor council.

After the arrest of Sherley and the search of his house the Doge directed the College to continue to gather evidence, and they secured the testimony of the Cavalier Pietro Duodo, who had been Venetian ambassador at Prague when Anthony first arrived there from Persia. Duodo said that he had known the Cavalier Pagliarini at Prague, where the latter was the cupbearer to the Papal Nuncio. Pagliarini had within the last few days asked one of Duodo's servants if Sherley had been arrested for reasons of state, since if that were so, he intended to move out of the house. Pagliarini had also informed the servant that Sherley received a pension from the King of Spain.

The College also questioned Angelo Gradenigo, the young Venetian who had been to Persia and who frequented Fetchi Beg's house. Gradenigo's testimony on the predawn visit of Sherley and his brokers ran as follows: "The Persian asked me to sleep there that night both because it was New Year's eve for him [the Persian year begins with the vernal equinox] and also because of what the Englishman might do, so I went home to get my arms and I returned to the Persian at three o'clock at night to sleep there. When morning came there was a knock on the door. I went to answer it, and Zanetto, the servant of Messer Cristoforo, shouted out of the upstairs window, 'Is this the time to go knocking at doors?' The two men at the door were the Jew brokers. I told them that the Persian was in bed and to come back later. They answered in Spanish that they had brought the money. In a few moments there was another knock at the door and this time it was the Englishman and his men."

A member of the College then asked: "How many men were with the Englishman?"

Answer by Gradenigo: "About ten men all with swords."

Question: "That Zanetto whom you mention, what did he do?"

Answer: "He went out saying that he was going to call his master."

Question: "Why did he want to call him?"

Answer: "I don't know, he went along the shore."

Question: "This Persian, did he complain about the Englishman?"

Answer: "Yes, most illustrious sir."

Question: "Why? Was he afraid? Had he been threatened?"

Answer: "Threatened no, but he was lamenting that in this land no one could feel safe."

The College also questioned Cristoforo Suriano, who was first asked if a certain Englishman frequented the house of his Persian client, to which Suriano answered, "I have only seen this Englishman in the house of the Persian once, the first night of his arrival in Venice."

Question by the College: "Did the Persian frequently complain about the Englishman?"

Answer by Suriano: "At first he was only surprised by his kindness, but later he complained, because it was said by many that the Englishman intended to deceive him in some way."

Question: "Why would one think that the Englishman intended to deceive him?"

Answer: "It has been said that the Englishman is swamped

with debts; that he wanted the Persian to lodge with him so that he could handle his affairs."

Question: "Did he give the Persian occasion to suspect him?"

Answer: "His many offers made the Persian suspect him."

Question: "Has the Englishman been to the Persian's house since the first evening?"

Answer: "Sir, I do not know, but I do know that he often sent Armenians, Jews, and others to say that he wished to buy the Persian's silks."

Question: "Didn't he once go to see the Persian early in the morning?"

Answer: "Yes, most illustrious sir."

Question: "What happened?"

Answer: "The day after Saint Gzeppo's day, myself and the merchant went to check the weight of the silk I had sold the previous day. On the way I met my assistant, Zanetto, who said the Englishman, together with some Jews and armed men, was at the house of the Persian. I started toward the house, but I was warned by some brokers . . . not to go any further for the court yard was full of armed men. I then went immediately to the palace to inform the Avogadore [the magistrate] or some senator."

On March 24 the Senate confirmed the arrest of Sherley made by the Ducal Council and appointed a commission to try Sir Anthony, the commission being apparently drawn from members of the College. Six days later, four letters found by Captain Moretto in Sherley's house were thought important enough to read in the Senate. One was from Francisco Peña, the celebrated Spanish auditor, or judge, in the *Rota,* a papal court of law and arbitration. Peña was devoted to the Spanish ambassador at Rome, the Duque de Sessa, and worked indefatigably for Spanish interests. Peña's letter to Sherley was dated from Rome in February 1603, and in it Peña expressed satisfaction that Sir Anthony showed himself a fervent Catholic; he referred to previous correspondence, was extremely satisfied with the progress of their common affairs, and he assured Sherley that he would hear from Martino Alfonso Mixia, secretary to His Catholic Majesty.

The second letter was from Mixia, who also was pleased with the progress of the affairs in which they were mutually engaged. "I shall not fail to provide you warmly with means to assist you," Mixia promised Sherley, "as your most illustrious lordship will learn in detail from Ludovico Lopez." The other two letters were from Gaspar de Garnica at Rome, who informed Sir Anthony that the Spanish ambassador, the Duque de Sessa, was also very pleased with the progress of events. After hearing the letters the Senate voted that Sherley should be tried on the charge of insulting the Persian and in the meantime they would deliberate what ultimately ought to be done about the letters and about Sir Anthony.

The trial opened on 2 April. "There appeared before the Commission appointed by the most excellent Senate," the trial proceedings run, "a man of medium height with a red beard. Judging from his appearance he could be about 36 years of age [he was, in fact, 37 or 38]. He was asked to state his name, fatherland and profession, and he answered: Most illustrious sirs, my name is Anthony Sherley, an Englishman, and a soldier."

Question: "A soldier of whom?"

Answer: "I have been around the world several times always with an appointment of general in the service of the Queen."

Question: "Do you know a merchant who has come to this city from Persia?"

Answer: "Yes, most illustrious sirs."

Question: "On what occasion did you meet him?"

Answer: "In December I received a letter from my brother who is at the court of the King of Persia, informing me that a certain Mehemet Essin [Mehemet Essin had visited Venice sometime previously], who was a friend of mine in Persia, was coming here, and that in deference to the Persian King I was to show him as much honor as possible."

Question: "This merchant, [i.e. Fetchi Beg] has he lodged in your house?"

Answer: "He lodged in my house the first night."

Question: "Has he brought merchandise to this city?"

Answer: "They say so; they say he has brought 200 bales of silk."

Question: "Have you ever told the merchant that you would help him sell his silks?"

Answer: "Yes, most illustrious sir."

Question: "Have you sent other people to negotiate?"

Answer: "Yes sir, a certain Moise, a Levantine Jew, and my secretary the Cavalier Pagliarini named Giovanni Tomaso who is of the order of the Duke of Savoy."

Question: "Have other people beside these gone with you to the Persian's House?"

Answer: "No sir, with the exception of two pages and a Scottish gentleman, a friend of mine and a very noble person, Mr. George Craig, and my interpreter."

Question: "Have you ever concluded an arrangement for the sale of the silk?"

Answer: "Mr. Pietro Michiel [his interpreter] promised me that no one would see the silks before myself, because the Persian merchant had told him so."

Question: "You are asked if you have ever concluded an arrangement for the sale of the silks."

Answer: "No, most illustrious sir."

Question: "Have armed men ever gone with you to the house of the Persian?"

Answer: "No sir, never, not even I carried arms."

Question: "To your knowledge, has the Persian ever been threatened in order to make him open his silk storage rooms?"

Answer: "No, most illustrious sir, never."

Question: "Have you ever been in the house of this Persian at night?"

Answer: "No, most illustrious sir."

Question: "Try to remember well if on the 19th of the past month at night before dawn, that is between the 19th and 20th, you were at the house of the Persian."

Answer: "I was there but not at night, between 11 and 12 o'clock, called there by the Persian."

Question: "Who was with you?"

Answer: "Battista Moretino, a broker, Mr. George Craig, two pages, the Cavalier Pagliarini, who also brought two merchants from San Benetto, and the rest of my people who were waiting for me in the street, since it was advisable to be well protected."

Question: "Who were the people waiting in the street?"

Answer: "Mr. Simon Smifiz, an English nobleman, Captain Lass, an Englishman; the servant of Mr. Craig; no one else."

Question: "Did you send someone to knock on the door before you yourself approached it?"

Answer: "Yes, most illustrious sir, but since the Persian did not want to open the door to anyone but myself, I went to the door."

Question: "Try to remember well if you sent two Jews to knock at the door before you yourself approached it."

Answer: "Yes sir, one was the interpreter, Moise, and the other was his companion. They went together with Moretino and the Cavalier Pagliarini."

Question: "Why go there so early in the morning?"

Answer: "Because the day before I had been authorized by an Armenian to buy the silk at 55 grossi while others had only offered 54."

Question: "Who promised to pay 55 grossi?"

Answer: "Myself through Moretino."

Question: "Did you intend to buy the silk for yourself?"

Answer: "No sir, but I intended to buy it in my name in order that the Shah might know I had done this service for him."

Question: "For whom did you really want it?"

Answer: "I don't know. Moretino told me that there were merchants who would give 55."

Question: "Did the Persian merchant tell you that if you wanted his merchandise you were to give him first 100,000 sequins on deposit?"

Answer: "No, most illustrious sir, but I told the Persian that I would not take even a thread of silk that had not been paid for in cash, and I would prefer to leave with him, 1,500 ducats as a down payment for the silk not yet sold and paid for."

Question: "So that no promise was made to the merchant to bring him 100,000 sequins?"

Answer: "No, most illustrious sir, but with regard to what the Persian merchant says in this regard, a bag of 50,000 or 60,000 ducats had been prepared and the remainder would have been provided from time to time even if the amount required was 200,000 and they also added that they [the merchants from San Benetto brought by Pagliarini] could drown him in money."

Question: "Was the Persian ever asked to open the storage rooms?"

Answer: "No, most illustrious sir. I asked to see only a single bale of silk in order to see what sort of silk it was, but the Persian said this was not possible because the silk had been sealed by this Court. I said immediately, 'since you had already sold the silk you did wrong to send for me. You will not deceive me anymore. Good Morning,' and I went away."

Question: "Try to remember whether you asked to have the storage rooms opened and if the Persian merchant replied that he had no intention of opening them since the 100,000 sequins had not been brought as was promised."

Answer: "Most illustrious sir, if it will please your most illustrious lordship, I will speak the truth. The Persian said, 'I do not refuse to show the silk but I don't see the money'; and I said, 'Why are you interested in money if as you say the sale is concluded and the silk sealed by order of the court?' Actually, the merchants present told the Persian that the money was ready, but I do not know these merchants apart from the fact that they are from San Benetto."

Question: "It is strange that in a free city where Justice is administered, a man may go to the house of a foreign merchant with armed followers at strange hours, and by using threatening language and other unlawful means, try to get his merchandise away from him. This court wants the truth on this affair."

Answer: "Most illustrious sir. It is only just that the truth should be known. It is a thing worthy of this most liberal government which administers justice to everyone. I will give in a few words what happened. On 20 December, I received letters from my brother, and on 15 January, an Armenian, named Mergevali, came to see me. Both asked me to lodge in my house one Mehemet Essin, which I did, and since then Mehemet has died. Now I was asked to lodge this other Persian. I said I would, although they are barbarians. . . . Informed of his arrival I went to look for his boat. I sent him refreshments . . . I prepared my house for him . . . I decided to go and tell him I had prepared my house for him as requested by Mergevali and my brother. . . . I asked the Persian whether he wanted to lodge in my house. He answered he would come after eating. . . . In the morning this Cristoforo [Suriano] called to him at the window and the Persian left without thanking me or saying anything. I, being a servant of the Shah, informed him through Mr. Pietro Michiel that he should not let himself be deceived by brokers and that he should show his merchandise to me before showing it to anyone else. He sent for me through an Armenian. I went to his house but the brokers slammed the door on my face and I almost got hurt, which angered me. After lunch, the broker Moretino came to me and said, 'I think that these brokers have agreed on 54 grossi, but I can sell at least 40 bales at 55 grossi.' I told him about the insult I had suffered and that if it were not for the respect I owed to the Shah, I would have nothing more to do with the matter. After all, I am a gentleman and not a merchant. But if Moretino could get 55 grossi, I would make another effort, simply to show that I honored my service to the Shah. . . . So through my interpreter, I informed the Persian that if he had not sold the silk, I could sell it at 55, and he sent for me several times through the Armenian and my interpreter. I exerted no other pressure."

Having given his testimony, Sherley was asked to sign a transcript of it, which he did. He was then returned to prison. His evidence was given on the second of April. Nearly three weeks later (on 21 April) the commission before whom he testified brought to the Senate a petition from Sherley in which he said that he was quite ill, and upon the recommendation of the commission the Senate voted that he should be allowed a servant and moved to one of the newer prisons where he would have a better opportunity to recover his health. A week later (29 April), the Senate having heard that Sir Anthony was a brother of the famous pirate Sir Thomas Sherley who had plundered Venetian vessels with great damage to their area of trade, it was voted by the Senate that the commission which had heard Sir Anthony's testimony again question him and attempt to find out whether he had any correspondence with Thomas. Accordingly on 5 May Sir Anthony was again brought before the commission, where he declared that for seven years he had neither heard from Sir Thomas nor received letters from him. He had known that Sir Thomas had been in the Mediterranean and that he had held a privateering commission from the Grand Duke of Tuscany. He also knew that at the moment he was a prisoner of the Turks, having been kept in touch with events by the English merchants at Venice. His further testimony ran as follows:

Question: "Did you know about his departure from England?"

Answer: "No, most illustrious sir, for seven years I have known nothing."

Question: "When did you receive your last letter from him?"

Answer: "I have known nothing about him for seven years. My brother married against my wishes. His wife has persecuted me. I have often fought duels with her brother, Thomas Vavasour, and both of us have been injured in the fighting. I heard recently that a relative of this woman, named Charles, has arrived in Venice. He intends to harm me in order that the property may go to the children of that woman and not to me. [Frances Vavasour Sherley had died, and all hands were evidently counting on Sir Thomas' early demise in a Turkish prison.] These matters are the reason for my leaving England; my brother was supported by Secretary Cecil and I by the Earl of Essex."

Sir Anthony then begged that his case should be settled soon since he had been in prison nearly two months, and on 10 May the Senate voted that he should be released from prison with the proviso that he should leave the city within eight days and that he be prohibited from ever returning. Four days later Sir Anthony petitioned for an extension of the time he might remain in Venice to three months in order that he might pay his debts and cure himself of the stone, and he submitted a medical certificate to the effect that he was suffering from a disease of the kidneys and renal pains and that he was undergoing a cure. As a consequence, on the seventeenth he received permission to remain in Venice twenty days more.[38]

While he was in prison, that second momentous event affecting his life had occurred which has been already mentioned. On 24 March Queen Elizabeth died and James VI of Scotland became also James I of England. It was an event for which many had been preparing for some time. Thus, although in 1600 the activities of Sir Anthony aroused the indignation of Sir Robert Cecil, in 1602, when Cecil himself was in touch with King James and knew that Sherley was, he wrote to Sir Anthony expressing his good opinion of him.[39] After James secured the throne Sherley's status changed from that of a man of ill repute to that of a royal favorite. An indication of the new esteem accorded the name of Sherley is that in 1604 Sir Henry Wotton, whose status had also markedly improved, being that of King James's ambassador at Venice, wrote the Duke of Tuscany to say that "I have never been able to doubt the goodness of your highness toward me; princes are born to do good to men of good will, of which I am one. Perhaps it would not be too much vanity in me to hope that on some occasion I might be of such service to your great name as a Thomas or an Anthony Sherley."[40] Letters between Sir Anthony and King James were frequent and cordial. On 9 May 1603, the day before he was released from prison, Sherley replied to a letter from the King, who "had been pleased to command Mr. Keith to give me so gracious comfort." He assured James that the Spanish ambassador would not have worked for his release if his imprisonment had not been a manifest act of persecution. The proof of this fact was that the Senate, which was only concerned with matters of state, had handled the affair. That body never concerned itself with cases involving such a charge as was brought against himself. The remainder of his letter to the sovereign is devoted to his favorite subject, the wisdom of Anglo-Spanish amity, a topic which, he says, he has been urged to lay before King James both by the Duque de Sessa at Rome and the Spanish ambassador at Venice. Noting that King James had sent word by Mr.

Keith that he would be pleased to see trouble fomented for France as long as it was not apparent that the King of England connived at it, Sherley drew attention to the fact that the power of France was constantly increasing. That country had recently made treaties with Switzerland, the German princes, the Pope, the Grand Duke of Tuscany, and Venice. The growing preponderance of France, he argued, could only be offset by a reconciliation between Spain and England. Sherley did not maintain that England should trust Spain, but only that where their interests coincided much was to be gained by friendship and collaboration; even a show of amity could avert war.[41]

His erstwhile jailers, the Venetians, were soon aware of Sherley's new status. Not long after he had been given his liberty and before the news had reached England, the Venetian ambassador at London, Giovanni Carlo Scaramelli, had a pleasant talk with a gentleman of King James's court. The English monarch, this gentleman of the court said, held Sir Anthony in the highest esteem. Sherley had always been of the King's party, and the only reason he had not returned to England was that as a relative and dependent of Essex' he would have been persecuted. Sir Anthony was not the bad subject he was said to be, nor had Sherley ever been, the King's gentleman averred, a dependent of the King of Spain, except so far as the services of King James required him to be. His Majesty therefore begged the Doge, unless Sherley had committed crimes against Venice, which could not possibly be the case, to release Sir Anthony and hand him over to King James, who would have the greatest pleasure in seeing him again and rewarding him. King James also begged that the Doge would instruct the Venetian ambassador at Constantinople to do nothing hostile to Sir Thomas the younger, who was a prisoner there.[42] About two months later Scaramelli reported that "the King asked me about the Sherleys, and what had become of Thomas, who was in Turkey. I replied that I did not know, but that as far as Anthony was concerned, I knew he was free to come home if he chose, for Your Serenity had dismissed him from your states, with orders never to return. The King said, 'If they have done anything amiss I do not wish to say a word for them, but if Anthony has not conspired against the State of Venice, I wish him to be able to come home as a gentleman.' " [43]

About a week later Cecil urged Scaramelli to give the King an account of the Venetian charges against Sir Anthony, and finally in order to please James, the Venetian Senate revoked the order expelling Sir Anthony and ruled that he might stay in Venice at his pleasure. On hearing the news King James remarked, "I am very well pleased; Sir Anthony's father is a very honest gentleman," which was a bit off the mark, and not quite a commendation of Sir Anthony. A few months later King James issued a license authorizing Sir Anthony to remain overseas and recommending him to foreign princes, thus legalizing his departure from England.[44]

Sir Anthony's efforts to convince the English court that the great enemy of England was no longer Spain but France involved him in the affairs of Edmund Thornhill, Canon of Vicenza, who believed that the calling of the Jesuits to France meant that the secret dispatch of Jesuits to England was now to be controlled from that country. Thornhill, after graduating from the English College at Rome, had elected, rather than risk his life in England as did his fellow seminarians, to remain in Italy, where he found a snug berth and diligently accumulated academic degrees.[45] He had unsuccessfully sought permission to return to England in 1602, and in February 1604 with Sherley's help he tried again. Sir Anthony wrote to Cecil, the King, and his father on the Canon's behalf, indicating that the priest had information of the greatest importance for the English government. "I judge that this new calling of the Jesuits into France is a main point of that which he will treat of," [46] he wrote. He assured King James that "the overture I made of his [Thornhill's] repairing into England proceeded from a good purpose in me," [47] and he said to Cecil that he had "with a good heart applied myself unto you," [48] but it is not apparent that Thornhill's information when he did impart it to the court was of startling importance.

Actually, in the spring of 1604 Sir Anthony's efforts on behalf of Thornhill were only of peripheral interest to him, for he had become a secret agent of the Emperor. In February he assured the Imperial ambassador at Venice of his most loyal feelings for the sacred person of the Emperor,[49] and for nearly eighteen months thereafter he regularly furnished that sovereign reports on the Turkish army and on Turkey, with whom the Emperor was at war—reports which he just as regularly received from the English ambassador at Constantinople. In June 1604 he warned the Emperor that two Turkish armies were ready to move, one into Hungary and the other against the Persians, and he was able to say that "the little that I hear from the English ambassador is enough to convince me of the extreme weakness of Turkey." [50] Three weeks later, on the basis of more recent information, he reported that the two Turkish armies he had previously mentioned numbered 60,000, but only about a third of that number were combatants.[51] Both enemy armies, his source reported, were more hopeful of making peace than bent on making war. Turkey was torn with dissension, the treasury empty, and the government corrupt, "so to quote the actual words of the [English] ambassador," he wrote, "Your Majesty can gather the fortune that God has prepared for your sacred person." [52] Assuring the Emperor of his personal affection, Sherley declared that "I work still for your Majesty and am ready for any sacrifice for your cause. If my life and my blood can play the smallest part they shall be given with the same readiness as heretofore." [53] In September, the information received from the English ambassador at the Porte and forwarded to the Emperor was that the Turks were considering withdrawing the forces operating against the Emperor in Hungary and turning them against the Persians.[54] The following month, rather than extracting information, Sherley forwarded a copy of the English ambassador's letter, drawing the Emperor's attention to the fact that Turkey was afflicted with plague, famine, tumults, and civil war.[55]

It is improbable that the Venetians were unaware that Sherley was passing information from Constantinople to Prague. As has been said, they lived in fear of the Turks. It is not surprising that on 1 December 1604 the Council of Ten resolved, for important public reasons, to order Sir Anthony to leave Venice within forty-eight hours, never to return under pain of death.[56] This time there was no plea from Sherley for an extension of time, no protest from the English court on his behalf. He left Venice immediately. "It calls itself a republic," he later wrote of Venice, "and under the guise of liberty is the most tyrannical state that ever existed." [57]

Henceforth he forwarded his reports to the Emperor from Ferrara. The Turks have been disastrously defeated by the Persians, his January report ran. They are dreadfully short of money, "thus writes the English ambassador at Constantinople in his letter of 20th of December." [58] The following month he was able to forward to the Emperor not only a copy of the most recent letter of the English ambassador at the Porte but also information from the English consul at Aleppo.[59]

Sherley's correspondence with the Austrian court was sometimes concerned with a Persian ambassador who had arrived at Prague in July 1604 as a result of an Austrian emissary's having previously been sent from Prague to Persia. In the spring of 1605 Sir Anthony was called to Prague to assist in negotiations with the Persian envoy. "Sir Anthony Sherley came to Prague the 2nd of June by post from Messina," an English report from Prague ran, "where he did remain a pensioner to the King of Spain. It is said the Emperor sent for him." [60] The report was accurate. For an undiscovered reason he had gone to Prague by way of Sicily.

The negotiations with the Persian ambassador evidently proceeded satisfactorily, for that emissary left for home in October. Before the Persian's departure, in fact only six or seven weeks after his arrival, Sir Anthony also left Prague. He had again achieved the status of an ambassador and was on his way to Morocco, the joint representative of James I, Philip III, and the Emperor. Since he was an ambassador, and no longer a spy, his visit to Prague may be considered as entirely satisfactory except for an incident of little importance that happened at Linz, on his way to the Imperial court. On the strength of being called to Prague by the Emperor, he borrowed 100 gulden from the Imperial agent at Linz. Since the agent issued the money without a warrant and since Sherley neglected to repay it, the agent himself was forced to repay the money to his government.[61]

During these years Sir Anthony kept in touch sporadically with his brother Robert in Persia, with Sir Thomas the younger (then languishing in a Turkish prison), and with his parents. Writing to his father in February 1604, he called upon him "to remember my brother, the injury of whose case calls upon you for as speedy remedy as it is possible. I labor what I can in the meantime to comfort him, and with the Duke of Florence his ministers, but besides that the Duke is a good prince and loveth money more than his servant, there is so great a unity between him and the French, that he will not move against the deed of any of the French ministers. . . . I would to God this did not show in my brother's sufferings and all those who love him for his sake. I can but pray to God (besides what, Sir, I do otherwise) to comfort him and you." [62]

William Burton, a friend of Sir Thomas the younger who labored to secure his freedom, went with Sir Anthony to Prague. "I pray you use Mr. Burton with that respect that his love to me doth deserve which (you see) is exceeding great," [63] wrote Sir Thomas to Sir Anthony, while to Burton Sir Thomas wrote, "I can be no gladder of your favor withall with my brother than I am that you find so good entertainment at his hands of which I never made so much as one scruple of a doubt. . . . I am much comforted that my brother hath undergone a weary journey to Prague for me for without that or some other money from Christendom, all hopes here are as dead as you left them." [64]

Robert in Persia was almost as unhappy as Sir Thomas in a Turkish prison, and he wrote a number of letters to Sir Anthony dwelling on his misery.

CHAPTER IX

What Befell Robert in Persia, His Brother Sir Thomas in Turkey, and Sir Thomas the Elder in England

AMONG the first Europeans to see Robert Sherley after Sir Anthony left him in Persia were John Cartwright, an English clergyman, and John Mildenhall, a merchant. A servant of Richard Staper, one of the founders of the Levant Company, Mildenhall had come out to the Levant "about my merchandise" and some months after his arrival in Constantinople set out for Persia with John Cartwright, who had gone to the Orient out of curiosity. The travelers, having rested two months in Aleppo, took a route somewhat different from that which the Sherleys had taken. They arrived in Qazvin, where Robert then was, in the first days of September 1600. Robert's house was "the only harbor and receipt for all poor Christians that travel into those parts," said Cartwright, and he and Mildenhall remained a month in the city before resuming their travels.[1] The only mention of this visit, other than what Cartwright himself says about it, is found in an anonymous narrative, probably Augustinian and also probably Spanish, in the Vatican library. Robert Sherley, this report declares, "favored the heretics who went to Persia, such as an English clergyman who stayed four months in his house, and John Mildenhall, also an English heretic, sent previously by the Queen to the King of the Moguls to obtain from him certain sea ports in the East Indies. . . . He, Sherley, presented him to the King of Persia both on his going out and on his return."[2]

Some two years after the visit of Mildenhall and Cartwright, Robert Sherley encountered those emissaries, Father Francisco da Costa and Diego de Miranda, whom the Pope had so optimistically dispatched to the Shah with the glad tidings that missionaries would soon arrive to Christianize Persia. The two harbingers of holy men had quarreled along the way and Father Francisco da Costa had so far strayed from his Savior's precepts as to steal Miranda's belongings. When they reached Persia, Miranda was almost naked, and an English captain, one of Robert Sherley's companions, compelled da Costa to give Miranda back his clothing. Later Miranda quarreled with Sherley, and in fact behaved so badly that Shah Abbas dubbed him "The Fool." [3] In September 1602, while these emissaries were still there, the first Catholic missionaries actually to settle in Persia arrived. These were the Augustinian fathers Jeronomo da Cruz, Cristoforo do Spiritu Santo, and Antonio Gouvea, who had been sent by the viceroy of the Portuguese Indies from Goa on the orders of Philip III. The Shah was then encamped at Mached, returning to Ispahan after another campaign in Khurasan. "As we entered the city of Mached, Friday, 4 September 1602," Gouvea wrote, "the King of Persia sent nearly all of the most distinguished men of his court, captains, governors, officers of his household, and a great number of cavaliers to meet us. . . . A little before the others rode a young Englishman about twenty years of age named Robert Sherley." [4] Gouvea explains that Robert had been left as a hostage by his brother and that he was a favorite of the King, who generously gave him everything he needed. "His riding ahead of the rest," says the Friar, "was an indication of the desire he had to have news of his brother, a desire which we were little able to satisfy." [5] Robert was a young man of good character, although infected with errors due to his upbringing, says Gouvea, and by the grace of God (aided, Gouvea implies, by his own eloquence) Sherley was converted to Catholicism.

Subsequently Robert had cause not to love the Augustinians, or they him. A report rendered later by one of the order described him as "a man of medium height, fair and beardless, aged about thirty years. He wears in one ear a small ring with a tiny diamond. He is a man of sagacity but a boaster, pretender, and conceited." [6] Another report, also probably Augustinian, relates that Robert remained in Persia as a hostage for his brother, that he was converted when the Augustinian fathers first arrived, and underwent a renewal of faith with the coming of the Carmelites. "In Persia he had gained the goodwill of the King and of the nobles, by whom he is liked," the account runs, "because he renders service to all and sundry, and gives trouble to nobody; besides which he conformed to their habits and customs in things that were not contrary to [our] religion, even though far from edifying. For the rest, he did not set much of a good example, because he got drunk . . . and favored the heretics who went to Persia." [7]

In 1603, the year following his first meeting with the Augustinian fathers, Robert met in Gilan the embassy which the Emperor Rudolph II had dispatched to Persia as a result of the proposals conveyed by Sir Anthony. The ambassador, Etienne Kakasch de Zalonkenemeny, died soon after Sherley met the travelers. Under the leadership of two of the party, Georges Tectander and George Agelastes, and guided by Sherley, the embassy resumed its journey on 26 October 1603. Tectander related that Robert had been left behind as hostage for his brother. Sherley led the party as far as Qazvin and there turned the group over to a Persian who guided them to Ispahan.[8] Henry Lello, the English ambassador at the Porte who had been intercepting Robert's letters to Sir Anthony, informed Cecil that at that time Robert was an overseer of the Shah's customs.[9] Since Sherley knew both English and Italian, and by this time had also learned Persian, he might have proved a very useful customs official. It seems quite probable that he also served as a soldier in the campaigns against the Turk. When Robert eventually returned to Europe, Anthony Nixon printed a number of stories of his heroism as a great captain in the Persian forces, fantastic tales, but with perhaps a basis of fact. On one occasion, for example, the Turks outnumbered the Persians ten to one, which put fear into the hearts of the Persian soldiers; Robert Sherley made a speech to them, promising to be the first man in battle, then catching up a strong staff, pulling down his beaver, and putting spurs to his horse, he furiously rushed upon the enemy with such a desperate resolution that the Turks were amazed at his valor, for he ran without stop through the Turkish troops and like a lion massacred those he met.[10] In any event it is quite certain that Sherley accompanied the Shah on his campaigns, and this being so, it could reasonably be concluded that he had some part in the fighting. In a letter to Cecil on behalf of Thomas Powell, one of Sherley's companions, the Persian sovereign remarks that Powell "hath been in the company of the worthy gentleman Robert Sherley in all the actions, sieges, and battles that we have had against the Turk, and hath done us in those wars great service." [11]

Robert's life in Persia through 1603, if not enjoyable, at least was tolerable, but afterward it became much less so. Cartwright says of him and his companions that they "at the first were very kindly treated by the king, and received large allowances; but after two years were fully expired, and no news of that great and important embassy . . . he began to frown on the English, notwithstanding Master Sherley through his good desert, soon gained the King's gracious favor again." [12] In a letter to Sir Anthony, intercepted by Henry Lello, Robert declares that "I am so besides myself with the travailes and wants I am in, and the little hope I have of your return or of any man from you, that I am almost distracted from the thought of any help for my delivery out of this country . . . in the time of your being here . . . he [Shah Abbas] entrapped us with deceit and flattery, his intention being only to serve his own turn, for believe me in all his actions, he publisheth to the world the hatred he bears to the name of Christians, for every day he maketh slaves of the poor Armenians, which are daily brought like sheep into every market, burning and pulling down all Churches. . . . As for myself I cannot deny but he giveth me still the same means he was wont; but God knows it is in such a scurvy fashion that I cannot possibly maintain myself with it, and it is every year da mal in peggio [from bad to worse]. . . . I would long since have solicited my friends in England for my delivery, but that I know you have extolled the King's name and my usage here, even unto the skies, and my dearest love toward you hath ever been such, that I would rather choose to die cooped up in my miseries, than make a contrary report . . . the next year, God willing, I am resolved to take my license, as I have already written unto you by divers ways, and if perchance, I be enforced to seek my passage from hence by some means that haply will be unliking unto you at the first appearance, yet I know I do it to avoid an evident danger, which I will manifest unto you hereafter." [13] In a second letter to Sir Anthony, written more than a year later, Robert confessed that "I rest mightily confused, insomuch as I can have no true advice from you; and although the long time of our partings, and distance of place hath haply withdrawn your wanted affection from me; yet methinks the conscience you owe to honor should bind you to give satisfaction to that king who so confidently has credited you with his secretest purposes. Your often promising to send presents, artificers, and Signor Angelo [Corrai] and I know not how many else, hath made me be esteemed a common liar; brother, for God's sake, either perform, or not promise anything, because in this fashion you make me discredit myself, by reporting things which you care not to effect. . . . I thought now you had left off dissembling compliments; there is no more friendship nor brotherhood; truth, honor, and conscience being banished from the earth; dear brother pardon me if I be plain with you, the losers have free liberty to speak what they list, by which I am authorized, having lost my time, and am in hazard to lose myself also." [14] Robert enclosed with his letter one from the Shah to Sir Anthony together with his translation of the King's words, "because haply in those places you live in, you shall find few, or none at all to translate them unto you." The Shah complained that "it is seven years since he sent you into Christendom, he knows not where you are, nor what you have done in his service, nor the reason why you return not unto him." [15]

At the time he wrote (the fall of 1607) Robert was at Qazvin. A few months later he met there a group of Carmelites bent upon establishing a Persian mission. "There was residing in the city of Qazvin," wrote the Carmelite, Father Paul Simon, "an English gentleman, Robert Sherley. . . . For about ten years this gentleman had been in Persia in the service of the King. . . . He invited us to dine, and we showed him great confidence, knowing the harm that he could do us if he were opposed to us, although at that time he was not in much favor with the King. He told us that every day the King and some of the nobles were badgering him to turn renegade, making him great promises. The pay which the King had formerly been accustomed to give him was coming in with difficulty, and only partially. When he had asked permission to depart the Shah had refused, saying that he and his brother had eaten his [the Shah's] bread for so long." [16]

At this time the Shah was in a bad humor with Europeans generally and with Catholic clergy particularly. The Emperor Rudolph II was by now so withdrawn from the world that he was incapable of ruling, and chaos was evident in various parts of his empire. He surrendered much of his power to his brother, Matthias, who concluded a twenty-year peace with the sultan of Turkey. The promise to fight the Turks with all his might, which Rudolph II had dispatched to Shah Abbas at the time of Sir Anthony's first arrival in Prague, was now void. The whole burden of the Turkish war was left to Shah Abbas. The Augustinian fathers had aggravated the Persian monarch by maintaining that the Armenians in Persia should be placed under the jurisdiction of the Roman Catholic church, a proposal which was not only distasteful to the sovereign but distressing to the Armenian patriarch. In this hostile atmosphere Robert saved the newly arrived Carmelites from many an error. He assured the Shah that these clergy had no intention of interfering with the religion of the Armenians, and succeeded eventually in securing an audience for the Carmelites at which the Shah showed himself friendly and generous. The friars had decided meanwhile that one of their number ought to return to Rome and report the true conditions existing in Persia. Robert begged the friars that they would intercede for him and obtain the Shah's permission for him to return to Europe also. Father Paul Simon, the superior of the Carmelites, declared to the monarch that the Pope had specifically asked that Robert Sherley should be returned, a deception which the Father felt justifiable under the circumstances.[17] This account given by Father Paul is substantiated by a letter of the Shah to the Pope, in which he says he is sending Robert Sherley as his emissary, because the Emperor and the Pope had asked that he should do so; otherwise he would have sent one of his own subjects.[18] There are other explanations of why Robert was dispatched as the Shah's ambassador to the courts of Europe. The Spanish suspected that Sherley was sent to their country with attractive offers of trade in order to forestall a possible attack on Persia by the Portuguese at Ormuz.[19] The Shah was too often warring with the Turks in the west to keep a vigilant eye on his Iberian neighbors on the east.

One of the Shah's motives, perhaps his principal motive in dispatching an envoy, was precisely that suspected by the Spanish, but this fact is not at variance with Father Paul Simon's statement. Shah Abbas having already decided to send an emissary, the Carmelite probably influenced the sovereign to select Sherley rather than one of his own subjects. As has been said, the person selected to carry his proposals was not of major concern to the Shah.

Before leaving Persia Robert married, in February 1608, Sampsonia, the daughter of a Circassian chieftain, she being then about nineteen, some ten years younger than her husband. She was baptized by the Carmelites and given the name of Teresa. Subsequently this oriental wife of an English gentleman caused something of a stir in Spain, England, and Italy. Her story is imbedded in many books and her portrait by Van Dyke is preserved at Petworth.

For a number of years the unhappiness of Robert in Persia was exceeded by the distress of his brother Sir Thomas in Turkey. As has already been indicated, immediately after returning from his fourth privateering voyage Sir Thomas organized a fifth expedition. He sailed with three ships, the *Saint George,* the *Dragon,* and the *Virgin,* probably at the beginning of October 1602, for the forbidden Mediterranean. He returned to the court of the Grand Duke of Tuscany, where "he carried himself in that honourable post as became both a soldier and a courtier."[20] The Grand Duke "did honorably furnish him with such necessaries, as for his purposed employment did fully satisfy his longing expectation." One of the necessities furnished Sir Thomas on this occasion, as it had been on a previous occasion, was a license to raid Turkish shipping and settlements.

Sherley put to sea and "lay hovering to, and again a long time upon the straits of Gibraltar, in a continual expectation of some purchase or other, to satisfy the desires both of himself, and of his company, in whom of late he found a strange alteration, both in their countenances, and behaviors towards him, savoring of discontent." At last a merchant vessel hove into view which appeared to be what Sir Thomas had been waiting for, "and having cause given," he fought her a long time before he could board her. Once aboard, he and his men were forced to fight another eight hours before they could take her. In the battle Sir Thomas had a hundred killed with many wounded, "and when all the cards were told, he found that the gain did not answer the loss he had sustained." His men were again discontented, and the very night following the fight the *Saint George,* commanded by William Piers, deserted him. With his two remaining ships he put back to Leghorn where he stayed eight days, replenishing his supplies and recruiting fresh crews. He got thirty Greeks and Italians from the galleys and twelve or fourteen shipwrecked English sailors, together with their sailing master, one Peacocke. An English resident at Leghorn wrote home that Sir Thomas was sailing under the flag of the Grand Duke and that his activities would probably damage the Levant trade. This or other reports brought a protest to Cecil from the Levant merchants. Sherley, they said, intended to raid Turkish possessions, "whereupon will follow the overthrow of all English intercourse in the dominions of Turkey." The merchants prayed that their lordships, the Privy Council, would "prevent the common danger that this private attempt may bring upon the whole nation." The traders at Leghorn, the English traders apparently, were also aroused for they "corrupted his [Sherley's] men and made them mutinous, alleging that the course he took was indirect, and dangerous, his plots shallow and unlikely to succeed, and that he failed of warrant and authority for his proceedings." Sir Thomas was able to put to sea with his two ships only with much difficulty and discomfort. On the third night of the voyage when off Sicily, Peacocke, the master he had taken aboard at Leghorn, made off with his second ship, and the following morning the crew of his own vessel mutinied. "They plainly told him that they would be no longer under his command . . . alleging with unkind words . . . that their hopes and expectations were deceived of him." The ship's officers took their commander's part and together they persuaded the men to return to their duty. Foul weather, declared Sir Thomas, drove him to Zea (Kea), where they found a Venetian ship in port. The crew wanted to plunder it; Sir Thomas endeavored to dissuade them, and the mutiny flared up again. To divert their attention, according to Anthony Nixon, who may have gotten the story from Sherley, Sir Thomas proposed that they should plunder a village on the island, which although a Turkish possession was populated by Greeks. On 15 January 1603, Sherley landed a hundred men in two companies, his lieutenant in command of the leading detachment and himself bringing up the rear with the other. The villagers fled with their valuables, and while the English vainly searched the houses for loot, the natives, armed with sticks and stones, counterattacked. Sir Thomas ordered a retreat. The lieutenant's company straggled down the hill at a trot. Sir Thomas's company fought a rear-guard action, killing two of the inhabitants, but reaching the level ground near the coast and perceiving that their comrades were in flight, they also broke and ran. Sir Thomas and two others, unable to make their escape, were assailed by ten Greeks.

Generally speaking the English had a very bad reputation among the Turks. Turkish vessels and cargoes were seized repeatedly, sometimes in the very harbors, as Sherley's men had wanted to seize the Venetian vessel. The wretched inhabitants of the archipelago were continually plundered for provisions and whatever else of value could be found, as Sir Thomas had attempted to do. Sherley consequently could hardly have expected to receive tender care. He did not. He and his men were beaten down, disarmed, and made prisoners. Nine of the ten who had effected the capture were for killing Sir Thomas and his companions on the spot, but the tenth man prevented them. The natives stripped Sherley, binding his hands with one of his

Count Anthony Sherley, the second son of Sir Thomas, from an engraving made in 1601, after he had arrived in Prague as ambassador from Persia. In spite of being in the service of Shah Abbas of Persia, he soon entered the pay also of Philip III of Spain and James VI of Scotland, and later of the Austrian Emperor Rudolph II. (From *General Biography* [London, 1818], Vol. XX, facing p. 133; reproduced by permission of The Huntington Library, San Marino, California.)

Count Robert Sherley, Sir Thomas' third son, from the portrait by Sir Anthonie Van Dyck at Petworth House. Like his brother Anthony, he also served as an ambassador from the Shah of Persia to the courts of Europe. In this role Count Robert usually dressed as a Persian. (From the Petworth Collection; reproduced by permission of Petworth House.)

Countess Teresa Sherley, Robert's Circassian wife, from the portrait by Sir Anthonie Van Dyck at Petworth House. Count Robert married her during his lengthy stay in Persia, and she accompanied him on many of his travels. (From the Petworth Collection; reproduced by permission of Petworth House.)

Inscription on a marble slab in the floor of the church of Santa Maria della Scala, in Rome, marking the last resting place of Countess Teresa Sherley and the bones of Count Robert. The slab, about three feet by seven feet, bears the inscription on its upper half; on the lower part are heraldic designs of inlaid marble. The memorial is set in the nave at the right, near the rear of the church. A translation of the inscription reads:

D.O.M.

Robert Sherley, most noble Englishman, Emperor Rudolph's Count, his knight entitled to wear ornaments of gold. Ambassador of Shah Abbas, King of Persia. At the behest of the Roman Pontiff, renowned orator to the Emperor, to the Kings of Spain, England, Poland, Muscovy, Morocco, and to other European Princes.

Theresia Sampsonia, native of the region of the Amazons, daughter of Samphuffus, Prince of Circassia.

For her most beloved husband, the resting place of herself and the bones of her husband who died in Persia and whose bones were brought to this city by herself in her twenty-ninth year.

1668

(The photograph was secured with the assistance and permission of the Carmelite priests of Santa Maria della Scala.)

On the wall to the left of the main altar a second marble plaque commemorates the gift to the church by Countess Teresa Sherley of a number of flambeaux to be lit on the anniversary of the festival of Saint Bacchus.

garters. Barefooted and naked he was led back to the town, buffeted by Greeks along the way.

News of the battle of Zea soon got to the interested governments. The captain of a Venetian vessel, probably commanding the very ship Sir Thomas's crew wanted to plunder, forwarded the news to Zante, and the Venetian governor there sent it on to his superiors at Venice. "I took my cargo on board at Zea," the captain wrote, "an English privateer arrived. The captain landed his men to go and seize the Cadi [the chief magistrate] because he would not give them bread. A riot ensued and two of the inhabitants were killed. Three Englishmen were captured, the commander being one of them. They say he is a great personage and is called Tomaso Seler." [21] As has been noted, the Venetians almost immediately identified the English pirate as the brother of Sir Anthony, whom they had in prison. Robert Cecil received the news of Sherley's capture from Ambassador Lello at the Porte, who concluded his account by saying that Sir Thomas and his companions were still prisoners on the island since the inhabitants feared "lest the ship [the *Dragon*] should recover them in their transporting hither [i.e. to Constantinople], at his coming, when any [of] his sinister designs shall be discovered unto these [the Grand Seignor] it will go hard with him and the rest, and what I shall allege in excuse thereof I know will not easily be accepted." [22] Actually the Greeks of Zea had no cause for fear. Sherley's vessel remained in port three days after the skirmish, neither attempting to treat for Sir Thomas and his fellows nor to rescue them by force. The *Dragon* then sailed away, bent on piracy. As a prisoner, incidentally, Sir Thomas achieved a fame he never attained at sea, for his three ships, cruising separately, committed piracy far and wide. The news of their exploits traveling faster than the report of his capture, Sherley's name became the terror of the seas. The very model of the fearless buccaneer, he would apparently plunder a village one day and strike like lightning at a settlement a hundred miles away the next.

Sir Thomas was later transferred in an open boat to Negropont (Euboea), where he arrived about 20 March. From here he appealed to the English consul at Petriaes, who failed to answer his letter, whereupon he was chained to a slave and the two were placed in a dungeon on bread and water. From Negropont he also appealed to Lord Burghley, Cecil's elder brother. "I have travailed to get my living by my sword, and the labor of my hands," he declared to Burghley, "in handling which course I have thrust into the Straits with two ships which are wholly mine own. I have done nothing prejudicial to any of Her Majesty's friends, only sought to make my voyage upon the Spaniards, in which pretenses whilst I did labor, my ship sprang a great leak, so I was forced to put into Gio [Zea]." [23]

Someone at Constantinople informed the Pasha admiral that Sherley could pay a ransom of 50,000 chequins, whereupon the Pasha sent four guards to fetch Sir Thomas to Constantinople. The Turks were apt to regard all Europeans who entered Turkish territory as wandering sheep to be shorn. Captured pirate captains were especially welcome as promising a good clip. On 23 July 1603, Sherley and his guards were ferried to the mainland and began the 500-mile overland journey to Constantinople. Sherley was in chains, on mule back, often with his legs tied under the mule's belly. If the party stopped overnight in a town he was placed in stocks; if darkness overtook the party on the road, his legs were chained and his hands manacled. At Constantinople, after some haggling, the Pasha finally declared that he would have 50,000 chequins or Sherley's head. Sir Thomas refusing to pay ransom, his feet were put in stocks, his body stretched over a boulder placed in the small of his back, and his hands tied in front of him. Bowed backward, he "continued in this estate, from Saturday the 23 of August, 1603, until the Tuesday following, in which time, he was suffered to rise but four times in twenty-four hours." [24] Subsequent to his ordeal the Pasha again asked for 50,000 chequins ransom. When Sir Thomas declared he was unable to pay such a sum the Pasha ordered him beheaded, and he was returned to prison to await execution. There a friendly Jew visited him who suggested that he should agree to pay the fifty thousand and then find excuses for delay in paying. In the meantime one of a number of things might happen: King James might intercede for him, or the Pasha, not getting the fifty thousand, might be satisfied to take less, or, Turkish public office being a precarious vocation, the Pasha might be replaced. Sherley followed his friend's advice, promising to pay the Pasha 40,000 chequins if he might pay over a period of time and if meanwhile he might have a servant, good food, and good quarters, all of which the Pasha agreed to. Subsequently Ambassador Lello advised Sir Thomas that he had made a mistake in making such a promise, whereupon Sherley revoked the bargain and was returned to prison. Shortly afterward, as Sherley's Jewish friend predicted might happen, the Pasha, rather than Sherley, was beheaded. Ambassador Lello began negotiations for Sherley's release all over again when a new Pasha Vizier was appointed. On one occasion he secured an order for Sherley's release but the Sultan later revoked it. Soon afterwards the Sultan died. "I doubt not," said Nixon, commenting on the demise of that potentate, "but Sir Thomas, together with the pleasure that he now conceives in the remembrance of his forepassed miseries, doth not forget in his daily prayers . . . that divine power that . . . delivered him so happily, even from the very gate, and gulf of death and danger." [25]

Probably Sir Thomas' first year in prison was his worst. In December 1603 he and the two prisoners captured with him at Zea were placed in a shed two yards square, "having neither clothes, bed, fire, nor any good meat." [26] It was cold and frosty with snow on the ground. In the first two weeks in these quarters, one of Sherley's companions froze to death. Sir Thomas continued in these miserable conditions until April 1604, when, receiving money from his father, he was able to purchase a chamber and hire a servant. Though he was still a prisoner, life became at least bearable. Meanwhile he continued to dispatch letters appealing for help, and many of his compatriots tried to aid him. As has been noted, King James asked that Venice should have its ambassador at Constantinople work for Sherley's release. Sir Thomas' father besought Cecil to instruct the English ambassador at the Porte to secure his son's liberty, "for it doth please his highness [King James] to afford his gracious favor to me and mine." [27]

Young Sir Thomas appealed directly to Cecil, averring that

"I have ever found more true comfort from you than from all England besides," [28] and he wrote to King James that, "without Your Majesty's express letters to the Grand Turk for my liberty, I am like to end my miserable life in most wretched servitude." [29] He also appealed to his brother Anthony, to his friend William Burton, who had accompanied Sir Anthony to Prague, and to Thomas Glover, the flamboyant, resolute, able servant of the Levant Company who succeeded Henry Lello as ambassador in 1606. Although his relatives and friends did what they could, Sir Thomas' release actually depended on negotiations initiated by Ambassador Lello. Despite good evidence to the contrary, Sherley believed that the ambassador had no real intention of helping him. "When he [Lello] receiveth a fresh letter from the king or any councilor," Sir Thomas wrote to Sir Anthony, "then he rampeth like a bear for two or three days, and then, as Sir Dru Drurie was wont to say, finger in mouth and no more news." [30] Sir Thomas' release was finally secured on 6 December 1605, by a direct appeal from King James to the Sultan conveyed by Lello. "Not withstanding this man's fault," the Sultan declared to Lello, "I present him to the King of England." [31] At the same time his surviving companion, captured with him by the villagers of Zea, was also freed. Upon his release Sir Thomas, being very sick, lived for a time in Ambassador Lello's house and did not leave Constantinople until 15 February 1606, more than two months after gaining his freedom. During this period he met the Venetian ambassador at Constantinople, who was greatly disturbed, as was his government, with the depredations of English pirates. "This Thomas Sherley is a man of high spirit as I gathered from his conversation," the Venetian reported to his government, "he has great schemes in his head to induce his sovereign to abandon the Turkish alliance." [32] These great schemes and his friendship with the Venetian ambassador were soon to cause trouble for Sherley.

On leaving Constantinople Sir Thomas proceeded slowly by way of Corfu, Otranto, and Ascoli to Naples, where he arrived on 22 May. He wrote to Cecil from there a few days later that "I am forced to stay for want of money, until my brother his servant has received his half year's pension, which is promised within a few days." [33] Captain Alexander Hepburn, a Scottish expatriate, helped Sir Thomas out of his difficulty by loaning him money. Tobie Matthew, the Catholic son of the Archbishop of York, later knighted "for what service God knows," who was then living in Florence, wrote in August that "Sir Thomas Sherley hath long since shaken off his fetters and lives in Naples like a gallant." [34]

Sherley had informed King James that "I intend to visit many courts, and will seek to enable mine understanding with all things fit for your royal service." [35] Accordingly he proceeded homeward at a leisurely pace, stopping for a time in Venice and at the Florentine court, renewing there his friendship with the Grand Duke, who gave him a letter to King James. There lived in Florence at the time, Sir Robert Dudley, self-styled Duke of Warwick. Sherley and Dudley were apparently friends, despite the awkward fact that Sir Thomas' wife had been Dudley's mistress. The affair was explained by Anthony Standen, a most colorful patriot, traitorous papist, wily agent, gallant diplomat, or devout Christian depending on the point in history from which he is viewed. "I will tell you, my dear sir," Standen wrote to Belisario Vinta from Rome, "about an illegal marriage which took place here a short time ago between the Duke of Warwick [Robert Dudley] and a young gentlewoman, the daughter of the Admiral of England and a cousin in the third degree of the Duke. This noble had a wife in England of very noble family and no less beautiful than she was noble. She and the Duke were married many years and had three [actually four] children. But the noble Duke claimed to have been previously married to the wife of the noble Thomas Sherley who came a little while ago from Turkey. On the death of this woman [Lady Sherley], although there was no legal proof that he was ever really married to her, he [Warwick] abandoned the mother of his sons, claiming to be now free and not legally married to her, and took this third lady, the daughter of the Admiral. The Pope gave him a dispensation on account of the blood relationship only, not taking into account the previous intrigues, since these were unknown to the Pope. As for the cavalier himself, I love him, and his courage and great abilities, especially in naval matters deserve all praise and consideration, and would to heaven this misfortune had not befallen him." [36] The much married cavalier, as has been noted, was Sir Robert Dudley, who had assumed the title of Warwick. "He was a person of stature, tall and comely," says Sir William Dugdale, "also strong, valiant, famous at the exercise of tilting, singularly skilled in all mathematick learning, but chiefly in navigation and architecture, a rare chemist and of great knowledge of physic." Anthony à Wood described him as "a compleat gentleman in all suitable employments, an exact seaman, a good navigator, an excellent architect, mathematician, physican, chemist, and what not. He was a handsome, personable man, tall of stature, red hair'd and of admirable comport, and above all noted for riding the great horse, for tilting, and for being the first of all that taught a dog to sit [i.e. set] in order to catch partridges." [37]

Dudley had in fact married a sister or a cousin of Thomas Cavendish, the navigator. Apparently this wife soon died; Sir Thomas Sherley's wife became Dudley's mistress, and then in 1596 or 1597 he married Alice Leigh. It was this lady whom he deserted in 1605 in order to run off to Florence with his second cousin Elizabeth Southwell, she being disguised as a page. Sir Robert was at that time thirty-seven and Miss Southwell nineteen. In 1605 or 1606, not long before Sir Thomas arrived in Florence, Sir Robert wished to show that he had never been legally married to Alice Leigh, so that he might marry Elizabeth. He declared that he had married Lady Sherley in 1591, the year in which she had in fact married Sir Thomas. At that time, 1605 or 1606, he produced as evidence the Latin translation of an English document purporting to have been drawn in 1592. In this curious instrument two friends of Sir Robert Dudley testified that to their memory Sir Robert had legally married Frances Vavasour sometime about the year 1591, although there had been no public ceremony. Since, as has been said, their testimony was given in 1592 and they could come no closer to fixing the date of the alleged marriage than "about 1591," they were remarkably vague witnesses. For a number of reasons it is obvious that the document is a forgery,[38] but that need not obscure the fact that the heartless young gallant, Sir Thomas Sherley, who had long years before at Cowdray falsely deceived and jilted Lady Stourton had been himself discarded for another.

Sir Thomas arrived in London in the first half of December 1606. In the July following he was at the court in London, and from there wrote a great number of letters to his friends in Italy and elsewhere, most of which in the light of subsequent events it would have been better not to have written. He wrote to the Grand Duke of Tuscany vowing, "I shall never cease to be willing to put my life in danger to serve you." [39] He also wrote to Sir Robert Dudley at Florence, whom he addressed as the Earl of Warwick. "As my service was wholly devoted to my Lord your father in his life," he informed Dudley, "so I am and ever will be desirous to do your service as any poor kinsman you have." He besought Dudley "to hold me in the Duke's good opinion," and argued that "it can no way be ill for you to have me in those parts, because I am so much yours truly." [40] A letter to his brother Anthony at Naples informed him that "I have not yet gotten my suit, but am fairly promised." [41] He was probably referring to a scheme he then had in hand for bringing a group of Levantine Jews into the British Isles. He had promised the Jews, doubtless for a consideration, to intercede for them with King James. His Jewish clients desired to settle in England, to enjoy freedom of religion, and to be allowed to build synagogues. Sir Thomas assured the King that the Jews would be willing to pay an ample annual tribute of so much per head for these privileges. Failing to gain these rights, which James viewed with disfavor, the Jews wished to settle in Ireland, again provided they might enjoy religious freedom. They were willing to pay two ducats per head for the privilege. In urging that his clients be allowed to settle in Ireland, Sir Thomas explained that they were mostly experienced merchants. They could quickly develop a trade with Spain in such Irish commodities as salted salmon, corn, hides, wool, and tallow. The trade would bring a great deal of bullion into the country and the customs and excise taxes on the commodities would pour gold into James's coffers. If the King were unwilling to grant the

Jews the right to settle in Ireland, then Sir Thomas knew that his clients could be made to pay at a high rate for the simple privilege of being allowed to trade in English ports.

There would be a great advantage, Sherley pointed out, in simply having the Jews within easy reach. They would always be good for a loan, more or less forced, and whereas it was difficult to get even ten thousand pounds out of the London merchants, his Jews would be good for a million. He illustrated the truth of his assertion by pointing out that the dominions of the Duke of Mantua were among the least prosperous of the Italian states, yet the Duke got a good revenue from his Jews, who had the right to conduct trade but no right to establish synagogues. Concerning the shrewd Duke of Mantua, Sherley observed that "once in three years he picks 300,000 or 400,000 crowns out of his Jews." Sherley felt sure that once these Levantine immigrants were in James's dominions, it would be found that they could be made profitable on numerous occasions and in many ways, but he warned that "at the first they must be tenderly used for there is great difference in alluring birds and handling them when they are caught; and your agent that treats with them must be a man of credit and acquaintance amongst them [e.g. Sir Thomas] who must know how to manage them, because they are very subtile [sharp] people." [42]

Sherley had a fateful correspondence with Giovanni Basadonna at Venice, the nephew of the Venetian ambassador who had aided him in Constantinople. "I make no doubt but to shake the foundation of the trade of the English in those parts [the Levant]," he boasted to Basadonna, and assured the Venetian that "your letter to me has been a great engine to better [batter] that business withal." [43] All of Sherley's foreign correspondence passed under the scrutiny of the Earl of Salisbury or his agents, and when enough evidence had accumulated, in the first week in September, he was clapped in the Tower. He had achieved English imprisonment in less than nine months after arriving home from his Turkish imprisonment.

"Some say," Rowland Whyte wrote to the Earl of Shrewsbury, "it was for overbusying himself with the traffic of Constantinople, to have brought it [the Levant trade] into Venice and to the Florentine territories." [44] The Venetian ambassador in London also heard that Sir Thomas was arrested for attempting to divert the Levant commerce from England to Venice, and that the English ambassador at Venice had intercepted letters proving his complicity in such an attempt.[45]

From the Tower, Sir Thomas confessed to the Earl of Salisbury that "I wished to have his Majesty mislike all trade with Turks, in which I respected not the merchants but my own desires." The meaning of "engines to batter," he explained to Salisbury, "was all the forcible arguments I could use to distaste the State here from continuing the used trade with the Turk . . . plainly declaring the manifold abuses and indignities daily offered to his Majesty's imperial diadem and dignity by the English in those Eastern parts . . . , so vehemently did my desires burn to see a disposition in his Majesty to break with the Turks." [46]

In the Tower five questions were put to Sir Thomas: (1) How had he first entered into the plot? (2) Who induced him to take part? (3) With whom had he conferred either orally or by letter? (4) How far had he proceeded with the plot? and (5) What was the full scope and purpose of the plot? [47] Sir Thomas, while not admitting that there had been a plot, chose to answer the first two questions as one. While a prisoner in Turkey, he declared, he became aware "that all Christians there did exclaim against the English for furnishing the Turks with powder, shot, musket barrels, brimstone, cordage, and other kinds of munitions, and because our English rovers did make their rendezvous in Turkish harbors, selling both the goods and persons of Christians to the infidels." The English merchants at Constantinople were quite frank to admit that they sold munitions to the Turks. In fact they even sold the guns out of their ships. Sir Thomas had assumed, he declared, that if the facts were generally known there would be a reformation in the Levant trade. He thereupon gathered all the information he could about the practices of the English traders and subsequently wrote a book on the subject which was at the time of his arrest in the hands of "a grave, wise, learned, honorable person."

In answer to the third question, he replied that he had only discussed the matter with the Venetian ambassador in Constantinople. While he was visiting that diplomat on one occasion, they had talked of English trade practices. "Lord God," Sir Thomas reported the Venetian as saying, "that any Christian prince should so far forget himself as to arm or suffer his people to arm the Turks. In our state if any be known to send but a dagger blade to sell, he forfeiteth all the goods he hath laded, that ship where such weapon is carried; and his body is condemned to the galley for certain years, and it is so with the French also." Sir Thomas had assured the Venetian on that occasion that the practices of his compatriots were obviously unknown to King James and his privy councilors, otherwise they would have been stopped. "And so I took my leave of him," he says, "with promise to remember each other by letters. . . . At my coming to Venice, Bashadoni delivered me a kind of letter from the said ambassador (who is uncle to Bashadoni) and told me that his uncle had commanded him to do me all the kindnesses he could during my abode in Venice. . . . After my coming home I did tell your Lordships of certain abuses (as I took it) offered to His Majesty by the English merchants in Turkey, whereof some Your Lordships condemned in the merchants, some you regarded not, and so I let this matter sleep till Bashadoni wrote that letter to me which I showed to Your Lordships and answered to your order."

To the fourth question, how far he had proceeded in the plot, he replied that what he had already said covered "all that I have done in this matter, as I hope to be saved by Jesus Christ; neither do I think that the merchants my prosecutors can anyway be damnified by this or undone unless they hold it an undoing to them to have their amisses known, for Bashadoni and I be but two private men, unable to do good or harm to any—he being a meaner man in Venice than I am here."

In answer to the fifth question Sir Thomas declared that "the full purpose, hope and intent of this project was no more than I have already declared which I hold to be Godly and honest." Having made this statement, he implored Cecil's clemency. "It may please your good Lordship I have sent your Lordship the whole of that matter for which it was your Lordship pleased, with the rest of the Lords, to send me to the Tower. Neither have I hid one jot or scruple of anything; . . . and now I do in all humility beseech your Lordship that sith you have (like a counselor) stretched out your arm to punish me, you will now (as a friend, as you have ever in your goodness pleased to be to me), withdraw the hand of justice, and be a means to His Majesty for mine enlargement." [48]

Actually he was released sometime during the first half of 1608. His treatise on the Levant trade has never come to light, but his *Discourse on the Turkes* [49] may actually be the work in question or a watered-down version of it. There is a good deal in the *Discourse* about the shameful English trade with Turkey in munitions and Christian slaves. As might be expected, the Turks gain nothing by being described by Sir Thomas, and actually nearly half the book is an account of places visited on his return from Constantinople. As a final note on Sherley's Turkish adventure, on 20 December 1607 a license was issued for Sir John Ferne, William Massam, and Lionel Cranfield, merchants, to sell the ship *Dragon* formerly belonging to Sir Thomas Sherley.

When young Sir Thomas came home he found his father struggling with a burden of debt. After his release from prison in 1598, Sir Thomas the elder had tried in various ways to recoup his fortunes. The first of these schemes had its beginning during the years he was with the English forces in the Low Countries and concerned the lands of Norwich Cathedral. The lands of the church had formerly been those of a monastery. In the time of Henry VIII such lands were forfeited to the crown as were the lands of the colleges and chantries in the reign of Edward VI. Because of the difficulty of knowing where all land titles rested, unquestionably much property which ought to have been forfeited was concealed and not surrendered. From the time of Philip and Mary the officers of the Exchequer made strenuous efforts to discover lands which ought to have been forfeited but had not been. There sprang into existence a whole class of persons who made a business of examining titles with the hope of discovering flaws in them. When one of them declared to the officers of the Exchequer that he had discovered concealed lands, the Exchequer appointed commissioners to hold an enquiry. Such hearings were held in the absence of the person whose title was in question, and the judgment of the commissioners was almost invariably the same. The commissioners decided that the lands had indeed been concealed and did in fact belong to the crown. Thereupon the title-hunter obtained from the crown, for a price, a grant by patent to the lands in question. As soon as he received his grant he suggested to the owner that the latter should buy his interest. If the owner refused, a suit was commenced, and if the title-hunter won the suit he either obtained the lands at a rent or in fee. These grants were called "fishing grants," and a great many estates in England during the reigns of Elizabeth, James, and Charles were granted to such fishermen.[50]

On the basis of a fishing grant to Lord Wentworth, two title-hunters who succeeded him in the patent, Theophilus and Robert Adams, were granted in 1583 the lands of the Cathedral Church of Norwich as concealed lands.[51] In the same year the grant made to these men was passed, doubtless for a consideration, to Henry Rice, one of the Queen's gentlemen ushers. Sir Thomas Sherley the elder and a group associated with him purchased the patent from Rice. The lands of the Cathedral were worth £2,000 per annum,[52] and it was alleged by the Dean and Chapter of the Cathedral that Sir Thomas paid only £300 for the patent. From 1586 onward, when Sherley was with the army, he was also contesting for the ownership of these lands, being aided to some extent by Burghley and Lord Buckhurst.[53] At one point (in 1587) a compromise agreement was reached between Sir Thomas and the Dean of Norwich, but when the agreement was engrossed and sent to the Dean for signature, he found that it did not, in fact, embody the points which he and Sherley had agreed upon. As drawn the document provided that Sir Thomas and his partners should have a lease from the crown of the church's lands for 99 years, after which they were to revert to the Dean and Chapter.[54] The Dean refused to sign, and more than a year later still refused, remarking that he had always "found Sir Thomas a very strange man to deal withal; promising much, but of a contrary mind to perform nothing; but seeking the perpetual overthrow of their church and posterity." [55]

In this impasse between the Dean and Sherley, Attorney-General Popham gave it as his opinion that all concerned, Sherley, his associates, the Dean, and the Chapter, should surrender their rights to the crown, and that the lands should then be granted to Thomas Fanshaw, the King's Remembrancer of the Exchequer, and Peter Osborne, the Lord Treasurer's Remembrancer of the Exchequer, who were to make an equitable arrangement with both concealers and churchmen.[56] Accordingly in 1591 the litigants surrendered their titles into the hands of the crown. The lands were then granted to Fanshaw and Osborne with instructions to offer the ancient tenants (the church) a lease on the lands at a reasonable rental payable to the Queen. If the Dean and Chapter refused the lease, it was to be offered to Sherley and his partners. The case dragged on for a decade. When Sir Thomas was released from jail in 1598 it was still unsettled. The Dean and Chapter refused to take back a lease on their lands on the terms offered them. By 1600 Osborne had died and Fanshaw, proceeding according to instructions, offered the lease to Sherley and his partners. Unfortunately when they had the church's lands in their grasp, Sir Thomas and his associates could not agree on their several rights and shares, and so the prize slipped from them.[57] During the contest, incidentally, the church lands fell into a chaotic condition. "About the year 1582, and after," says Strype, "divers parcels of that church's lands were sold away forever, and money taken for them; others violently entered upon, without payment of rent, or farm. Some tenants had paid no rent for some years. So that the church at last had not a parcel of land, no, not the houses within the cathedral church, but they had been offered to sale; or else money taken beforehand for long leases." [58]

In this same year, 1600, in which the opportunity to secure the cathedral lands had slipped from his grasp, Sherley interested himself in the scheme of a certain merchant of Lübeck, Casper Van Zenden. In return for his having procured the release of eighty-nine Englishmen held prisoner in Spain and Portugal, the Queen granted Van Zenden a license which provided, their masters being willing, to seize, transport, and sell in Spain and Portugal such negroes as he could find in England.[59] Unfortunately, no English masters were willing to turn over their negroes to Van Zenden. Sherley, then, on behalf of the Lübeck merchant, forwarded a petition to Cecil in which Van Zenden asked that he be allowed to carry off the negroes whether or not their masters were willing, "seeing that all the blackamoors in England are regarded but only for the strangeness of their nation, and not for service to the Queen." [60] Sherley at least three times urged Lord Salisbury to grant Van Zenden's petition since he would derive some benefit from it, but Cecil was unwilling that the negroes should be taken forcibly, and consequently the patent proved unprofitable to both Van Zenden and Sherley.[61]

Sir Thomas subsequently endured two or three lean years, but soon after the coming of King James he became involved in a number of interesting activities. In February 1604, he was elected to Parliament from his own pocket borough of Steyning. Parliament was to open on 22 March, but on 15 March as the King went through London, and Sir Thomas rode attendance on him, a creditor took advantage of the occasion to have Sherley arrested for debt. Freedom from arrest, except for treason, felony, and breach of the peace, had long been an important privilege of members of Parliament, and on the first day of the session the attention of the House was drawn to the fact that the rights of one of its members had been violated. A writ of habeas corpus was issued and a few days later the warden of the Fleet appeared at the bar of the House with his prisoner. The warden refused to release Sir Thomas, holding that if he did so he would be responsible for Sherley's debt. A bill was then passed through both houses and sent to the King, rendering the warden harmless if he should release Sherley. This bill was read for the third time on 21 April, sent to the Lords, and read for the third time and passed there on 30 April. By that date the House of Commons had had second thoughts. The bill had invoked the aid of the King and the Lord Chancellor. It was felt that such language might be interpreted as meaning that Sherley was released through the intervention of the Lord Chancellor, the King, or both, thus tacitly surrendering, if not Parliament's privilege, at least the right to enforce it. The House therefore issued a writ ordering the warden to release the prisoner, but he refused to do so until the bill rendering him harmless had received the assent of the King. Thereupon on the order of the House the warden was sent to the Tower. The serjeant-at-arms of the House was sent to the Fleet to release Sir Thomas, but the warden's wife refused to free the prisoner. Parliament thereupon passed a new bill which differed from the first in that it omitted any appeal to either King or Chancellor. On 14 May Sherley was still in the Fleet prison, and the warden of the Fleet was still a prisoner in the Tower. On that day or the day following, the warden weakened and offered to release his prisoner, and shortly afterward Sir Thomas took his seat. The triumph of Parliament was complete and it cannot be denied that Sir Thomas had played an essential part in the famous victory.[62]

King James showed himself gracious and generous to Sherley as he did to his sons. The month following his release from the Fleet, that is in June 1604, an arrangement was reached whereby the manors and lands of the Sherleys would be restored to them and at the same time a certain amount of income secured to King James.[63] As has already been explained, Queen Elizabeth had required that Sir Thomas should place his lands in the hands of trustees until the income from the properties repaid the debt due the crown. In August 1602 the status of the lands had undergone a significant change, and one which would appear to have nullified any subsequent legal claim of the Sherleys to them. At that time Sir Thomas had conveyed his properties to Edward Coke, the Attorney-General, and to Thomas Fleming, the Solicitor-General, and to their heirs, who in turn were to grant them to Sir Thomas' three relatives, Edward Onslowe, John Shurley, and Anthony Sherley, a brother of Sir Thomas the elder, on condition that these three would pay Sir Thomas' debt to the Queen, which amounted at that time to £12,472 odd. At the time King James had come into the kingdom the three relatives had failed to pay off the debt, and the lands were again bestowed on the crown. On 22 June 1604, Sherley received from King James, "parsonages, impropriate tithes, lay prebends, chantries, free chapels, and colleges" in fee farm at an annual rental value of £1,002 odd. The rent was to be paid out of the income accruing from the Sherley manors and lands which were also granted to him in fee farm, also at a rent of £1,002 odd annually. In simpler language, for an annual rent of £2,004, Sir Thomas received both his ancestral lands and church properties belonging to the crown worth of themselves annually £1,002. By providing that the annual rent on one item (parsonages, etc.) was to be paid from the profits of the second (Sherley ancestral lands), the two properties were tied in one package. Sherley, for example, could not sell the lease on his lands without violating his agreement with regard to the church properties, nor could he sell his lease on the church properties without remaining liable for an annual payment of £1,002 from the profits of his land. There was in the agreement an additional stipulation to the effect that the debt due the crown from Queen Elizabeth's time was to be paid off at the rate of £400 per year for thirty-three years.

In the matter of leasing tithes and parsonages from the crown, it ought to be said in Sir Thomas' defense, if he needs any, that such leases were a recognized form of business enterprise. In the reign of Elizabeth the chief contractors for tithes were Tipper and Daw, who received 253 grants; Downing and Aston got 99 grants; Downing and Dodding, 74; Downing and Rant, 44; Adams and Butler, 67; and 40 grants went to John Farnham. In the reign of King James the combine of Morrice and Philips received the tithes of 451 parishes, and Philips and Moore, 93. In addition to their sale to the highest bidder, noblemen and favorites received tithes. Charles Brandon had the grant of the tithes of 87 parishes; the Duke of Norfolk, 40; Henry Wriothesley, Earl of Southampton, 30; Lord Audley, 22; and the Earl of Oxford, 17.[64] In receiving the income originally intended for the church, Sir Thomas was in good company. Normally the lay recipient of church income would be expected to provide a vicar, but this was not always so. There were seven parishes in Sherley's county of Sussex in which there had been no preaching since 1580.[65] In other cases the amount paid the clergyman was a negligible percentage of the income of the parish. For example, the lay holder of a living with an annual income of £300 paid only four or five pounds to the rector.[66] Two west-country vicars declared that whereas they each received less than £30 apiece their lay rectors received £400 apiece, and it was said that in the East Riding of Yorkshire in 1605 there were impropriations worth £100 to £400 apiece, where the minister had only eight pounds and "with much ado ten more were obtained for a preacher." [67]

Unfortunately tithes and parsonages did not prove as profitable as Sir Thomas had hoped. Within a year from the time he received them, he complained that they yielded so little benefit that he was utterly without means to pay either the £1,002 annual rent or the £400 annual payment on his old debt. Saint Saviour's in Southwark had promised to be a very profitable parsonage, but John Elphinstone wanted it and had elicited the support of both the Queen and the Lord Treasurer. "He will content himself with no other thing but only with this," complained Sherley, "which he would draw as it were out of my throat." [68] Sir Thomas tried to get Long Bennington, a profitable parish in Lincolnshire, but Mr. Roger Manners [the Earl of Rutland?] had solicited the King for it, and so apparently Sherley was not to have it.[69] About two years later he begged for £200 of additional impropriations, although he said, "I know the choice will be very bare after so great cutting as of late has been, having myself lately holpen some friends with the best of that kind that I know in all England." [70] A few months later he was still asking the Earl of Salisbury, the latest title Robert Cecil had acquired, for the £200 worth of additional parsonages. "If it please you to favor me herein," he wrote the Earl, "I shall hold myself most bound to Your Lordship forever, for thereby Your Lordship shall keep me out of a great mischief, even out of the lion's mouth. I assure your Lordship that the condition of these impropriations is much altered now after so long and divers gleanings. Nevertheless I shall hold myself in as great an obligation to Your Lordship as if they were of as rich quality as ever they were when they were at best and greatest plenty." [71]

In the same year, 1604, in which he got the impropriate tithes and parsonages, Sir Thomas obtained another means of augmenting his income. He was granted a patent to collect various small debts owed the crown, among which were all moneys received of recusants but not paid in, and all debts due to his Majesty which had been collected by sheriffs but not paid in.[72] Since he had been both a sheriff and a commissioner for recusancy, Sir Thomas may have had a good idea what sums were owed and even who owed them. Still, even if he received a generous commission on the bad debts collected his profits could not have been large. He secured a new patent a few years later which promised more satisfactory returns. The king granted him in 1607 the right to discover by any lawful means cases where real property had changed hands but had not been legally registered or recorded; "and whereof no license of alienation hath been sold forth nor any pardon hath been found for such alienation with[out] license," Sir Thomas, in collaboration with a deputy of the Lord Treasurer, was empowered to compound with any person who had been a party to such a transaction for any fines, fees, or penalties which should have, but had not, been paid to the crown. Of all sums which were recovered Sir Thomas was to have two-thirds and the crown one-third, and for this patent he was to pay £400 per year.[73] Unhappily this scheme was not profitable, either, since having procured the patents in 1607, he was probably already in arrears on the rent by 1608.

Yet in spite of his trials and tribulations, the lot of old Sir Thomas was not too miserable. At the time young Sir Thomas arrived home from Turkey, and Robert was about to start home from Persia, their father was still in precarious possession of his lands and manors and living at Wiston. When he pleased, he sat as member of Parliament for Steyning, and when in London he stayed as always at his house in Blackfriars. Considering the calamities which had befallen him, it was remarkable how little his life seemed to have changed.

CHAPTER X

Sir Anthony, Diplomat, Admiral, and Count Palatine

SIR ANTHONY had been called to the Imperial court at Prague in the spring of 1605, that is, before the Emperor Rudolph's insanity became so pronounced that his family resolved that Archduke Matthias, his younger brother, should take over his duties. Sherley left Prague for Morocco in July 1605 as the emissary of Emperor Rudolph, Philip III of Spain, James I of England, and a group of Austrian horse breeders. Morocco was an independent state, owing allegiance neither to the Turks nor to any European power. Elizabethans and their French, Dutch, and Spanish contemporaries knew that Morocco was a good place for trade. Englishmen had been trading there, in fact, since the middle of the sixteenth century. From that country one could obtain gold, "copper of the reddist and best for artillery than is found anywhere, sugar, dates, gum arabic for clothiers, amber, wax, skins dressed for wearing, and horses better than in Spain." [1] Contemporary Englishmen knew that Morocco, or Barbary (the terms were synonymous), was important for another reason. It provided a safe base from which to harry Spanish shipping. A Barbary pirate was usually an Englishman based at El 'Arîsch who patriotically, and profitably, was engaged in singeing the beard of the Spaniard. Sir John Ferne, who later was closely associated with Robert Sherley and also with Sir Anthony, had been one of these Barbary pirates.

From 1578 until 1603 Morocco was ruled by Ahmed IV, El Mansour (the victorious). Queen Elizabeth had exchanged both letters and envoys with Ahmed IV, whom the Elizabethans knew as Muley Hamet. Upon the death of this sovereign in 1603, control of his kingdom was immediately contested by his three sons, Moulay Zidan, Moulay ech-Cheikh, and Moulay Abou Fares. For seven years following the death of their father the three sons played a tragic game of hide and seek, two brothers allying themselves against the third and continually changing partners. At one time the Spanish would be called to the aid of one of the brothers, which would be the signal for the others to ask for Turkish help. At the time the Emperor and the kings of England and Spain conceived the idea of sending Sherley to Morocco, Moulay ech-Cheikh, having ousted his brother Moulay Zidan, ruled at Fez, and Moulay Abou Fares reigned at Marrakesh. The last-named, fat, pusillanimous, and sickly, lived in daily fear of being attacked by his brother ech-Cheikh at Fez.

These troubled waters promised good fishing. By offering help to one brother in eliminating the others, considerable advantage might be gained. Sherley's duty on behalf of the Emperor Rudolph was to offer aid to one of the contestants and to foment war between Turkey and Morocco, thus diverting the Turks' attention from the war in Hungary. His mission for Philip III of Spain was to offer one of the Moroccan rulers Spanish naval aid on condition that he would fight the Turk and also cede to Spain a strip of Moroccan coast, or at least a few good ports. Sir Anthony's task for the Austrian horse breeders was to buy horses. What James I hoped to gain by participating in Sherley's mission is not clear, except that a union of Christian princes against the Turks was frequently regarded in this period as both an act of piety and a panacea for Europe's ills. James, counting himself among the most pious, may have joined the consortium simply for the general welfare and the good of Christianity, even if on this occasion the issue was a bit beclouded by including in the anti-Turkish alliance a heathen king of Morocco. The English monarch's own son-in-law later spoke bitterly of the money and effort spent by James in antagonizing the Turks in the interests of Spain, but in this instance, at least, the criticism was not justified. King James was the only one of Sherley's four employers who did not pay cash, and indeed he did not pay at all for participation in this impressive if nebulous scheme. He passed his share of Sherley's expenses on to the English merchants. Charles Cornwallis, the

English ambassador in Madrid, wrote that Sir Anthony "hath showed an unexampled manner of license or passport from the King, my master, desiring all princes to give him passage through their countries, to assist and supply him in all necessities that might occur, which he would accept as a favor to himself, and concluding that what he desired of foreign princes, he straightly commanded to his own subjects." [2]

Sherley left the Imperial court in July 1605 with this unlimited letter of credit on English merchants and funds from his other three employers. He was more amply supplied with money than he had been since he had spent Essex' £8,000. He had with him an entourage of thirteen, including a number of interpreters and Sir Edwin Rich, the brother of Lord Rich. The party traveled to Genoa and embarked there for Morocco, but the ship was damaged in a storm and had to put in at Alicante for repairs. From Alicante, Sherley and his companions went overland to Cadiz, where they took ship for Safi, arriving at that Moroccan port on 2 October 1605. The three sovereigns, backing the wrong horse, had accredited Sherley to Moulay Abou Fares at Marrakesh.

By custom, Christian ambassadors remained in the port of debarkation for a period of purification before proceeding to the Sharifian court. Sherley stayed five months in Safi and became the sensation of Morocco. He dressed magnificently, wearing not only the order of Saint Michael which Henry IV had given him, but the regalia of the orders of the Holy Ghost and of the Golden Fleece which no one had given him. All Christian merchants of whatever nationality were invited daily to have both dinner and supper with him. Once during a meal he casually bought from a merchant guest both his ship and its cargo, paying partly in cash and partly in promissory notes redeemable after Sherley had gotten to Marrakesh. At the end of February 1606, his spiritual quarantine being ended, Abou Fares sent five hundred soldiers to conduct Sherley and his party to his court. Count Anthony presented each man in the escort with a new turban, and after his arrival in Marrakesh he continued to be fabulously generous. There was no one in the city with whom he had any dealings, declared the French agent,

Arnoult de Lisle, who did not receive a present.[3] "He had an apprehending and admirable wit to conceive the disposition of any people with whom he shall converse," wrote the author of *Muley Hamet's Rise,* "whilst he was among them [the Moroccans] he behaved himself very well toward the better sort, winning credit with them, and gaining the love of the poorer sort exceedingly by his largess, for if a Moor or a slave gave him a dish of dates, he should receive a reward as from an Emperor, and howsoever some may hold this a vice, counting him a lavisher, yet by this means he came to the knowledge of that which otherwise he never should have attained unto." [4] Sherley confided to a gentleman in the entourage of the French agent that he had forty thousand eçus to spend, and he told others that the King of Spain was willing to spend millions. Such was his charm and generosity that two Spanish merchants vied with one another in lending him money. The Sharif, Abou Fares, received him with grand éclat and lodged him in a magnificent house. While others in Marrakesh knew him for his generosity, the Sharif was given a demonstration of his pride and fearlessness. Two days after his arrival, on his way to an audience with Abou Fares, Sherley rode his horse across the *mechouar,* where the Sharif might ride but which even his sons dared not traverse except on foot. Sherley was received with great pomp and courtesy, but when he returned for a second audience, five days later, the entrance to the *mechouar* was barred by a chain. Furious, he turned and rode back to his house. The insult, he declared, had been offered not to himself, but to the Emperor, who would know how to avenge it. Poor Abou Fares was terrified. He sent three caids to assure Sherley that the insult was the fault of the porter who took care of the *mechouar.* That unfortunate domestic was beaten and thrown into prison, and thereafter Sir Anthony rode into the sacred place as before.

Although he maintained his own standard of living and the dignity of the Emperor, Sherley's mission did not prosper. Abou Fares, far from wishing to fight the Turkish Sultan, sought him as an ally and sent him a magnificent present of 300,000 ounces of gold. The attempt to obtain a stretch of Moroccan coast for Spain fared no better. Sherley encountered not only a current preference for the Turks as allies, but the opposition of both France and the Low Countries. France did a considerable trade with Morocco in cloth, spices, ironware, and other articles. France also sold considerable quantities of wheat in Spain and feared the possibility that with Moroccan ports in Spanish hands Spain might begin buying Moroccan wheat and encourage there the extension of wheat growing. The French agent, Arnoult de Lisle, felt confident that he could frustrate the designs of Sir Anthony and prevent such an unseemly development. "The extensive knowledge which I have of this country, and particularly of this prince and those in government," he wrote, "will provide me with sufficient arguments to dissuade them from this new alliance." [5] De Lisle did not overestimate his own abilities; much, if not all, of what Sherley had to say to both Abou Fares and ech-Cheikh was subsequently repeated to De Lisle. The Netherlands agent, P. M. Coy, also had a far better knowledge of the labyrinth of Moroccan politics than Sherley possessed. He was seeking permission to base Dutch warships in Moroccan ports to prosecute the war against Spain. His objective was thus almost diametrically opposed to Sir Anthony's. Considering the abilities of his rivals and the instability of Moroccan politics, it is no wonder that Sir Anthony failed to accomplish anything. Though he spent his friends' money, there is no record that he even bought horses for the Austrian horse breeders. It was apparent in May 1606 that nothing could be done, but Sherley lingered on in Morocco until August, being so deeply in debt that his departure was difficult. According to Coy, he owed 250,000 florins to the Jewish merchants and he freed himself from their clutches by leaving behind two of his party as hostages. Sherley also had difficulty with the Christian merchants in Morocco, to whom he owed sixty or seventy thousand florins. According to the Netherlands agent, Coy, he extricated himself from this situation by denouncing the merchants to whom he owed money as persons who were defrauding Abou Fares of customs duties, a charge that ruined many of them.[6]

In his last days in Marrakesh, Sir Anthony, desperately in need of cash, became involved in the sale of a remarkable ruby, said to have been stolen from the church at Saint Denis during the religious wars in France. The Frenchman possessing, if not owning, the stone was persuaded to entrust it to Sir Anthony to sell, the latter arguing that as an ambassador he had access to persons wealthy enough to buy it. Subsequently, although the details are not clear, Sherley apparently gave the stone to Abou Fares as ransom for thirty Spanish and two noble Portuguese prisoners. The prisoners signed promissory notes to repay Sherley on their arrival in Portugal. By this arrangement, of course, the Frenchman who originally had the ruby got nothing.[7]

On his return to Safi from Marrakesh, Sir Anthony was accompanied by a guard of four hundred arquebusiers under the command of a Portuguese renegade, Abdullah Sinko, who for some time had longed to return to his native Portugal. Sir Anthony had two ships waiting for him in the harbor, one commanded by Sir Edwin Rich and the other by himself. Sinko was smuggled aboard Rich's vessel, which slipped away during the night. The flight of the Portuguese renegade was discovered by the officers of Abou Fares at a time when five of Sir Anthony's crew were ashore. These men were seized and held as hostages for Sinko. Sherley sailed away without them, but they were later ransomed by the English merchants of Marrakesh.[8]

Having thus extricated himself from several difficult situations, Sir Anthony took ship for Portugal, bent on reporting to the court at Madrid rather than that at Prague. Sherley and his entourage debarked at Lisbon in the first days of September 1606. The English consul in Portugal reported that "his carriage here is very honorable," and that "he hath brought with him divers Portingalls, that were captives there, whereof two men of good account which are to yield him near 50,000 crowns for their ransom." [9] From Lisbon, Sherley proceeded to Madrid, where he arrived about 25 October. Although Sir Anthony had been employed by Spain for some years, except for his passage overland from Alicante to Cadiz on his way to Morocco, this was his first visit to that country. He did not see it at its best. It had, in fact been going downhill, at least since Philip II's death in 1598, shortly before which the Cortes of Castile had reported that "no one has either money or credit, and the country is completely desolated. Any money that is made is hidden away and the owner lives poorly upon it until it is gone. Trade is killed by taxation. In the principal cities most of the houses are closed and deserted." [10] Later, conditions became startlingly worse.

"I fear they will rule him," the dying Philip II had said of the courtiers and his son Philip III. As a matter of fact, Philip III was ruled by only one courtier for twenty years. This arrangement allowed the monarch to devote his full attention to jousts, cane-tourneys, bullfights, religious processions, and the congeries of superstitions which passed with him for religion. Above all, the arrangement gave Philip III time for hunting. On one occasion he hunted fifteen days straight, beginning at 4 o'clock in the morning and not returning until eleven at night, a most extraordinary example of application and devotion.[11] The courtier who ruled Philip III was Francisco de Sandoval y Rojas, Marqués of Denia and later, among numerous other things, Duke of Lerma. Until the death of Philip II he had been distinguished only for his incapacity and the favor he enjoyed with the future Philip III. For twenty years from the death of Philip II in 1598 he enjoyed undisputed power, during which interval the finest army in Europe became a remnant, the fleet was shamefully neglected, and commerce and state finance were ruined beyond hope of recovery. It was a common saying of the time that "Lerma and the woods are King," for such time as Philip III could spare from hunting he devoted to fulfilling the wishes of Lerma.

The court under Lerma was one of the most extravagant and wasteful in history. Grandeeships and titles were created almost without limit, and Philip III created more knights in one year than his father had in ten. There were available 46 captain-generalships, more than 20 viceroyalties, 500 knight-commanderships, some worth 20,000 ducats a year, and numerous other offices. These were sold by Lerma or his favorites. The one profitable occupation was to be a servant of the King or a servant of the King's servant. Waste became a fashion that spread to the humblest circles of the court. It was said that "the smallest hidalgo [i.e. the son of 'somebody'] insisted upon his wife only going out in a carriage. . . . Not even a carpenter or a saddler or any other artisan was seen but he must be dressed in velvet or satin like a nobleman. He must needs wear his sword and his dagger and have a guitar hanging on the wall of his shop." [12] The country swarmed with adventurers from the King's Italian dominions come to seek their fortunes, and with Catholic exiles from Scotland, Ireland, and England, many of whom enjoyed pensions from the king. There were O'Donnels and O'Driscolls; the Earl of Bothwell and Colonel Semple from Scotland; Father Creswell, who headed the English Jesuit College at Vallodolid; Sir William Stanley, who had commanded in the Low Country wars; and hundreds of others.

The expenses of the court rose from 400,000 ducats a year under Philip II to 1,300,000 under Lerma. Silver and gold arrived in great quantities from the New World but it hardly got beyond Seville before disappearing, either paid to foreign merchants or hoarded by officials. The precious metals disappeared from circulation and the country was on a copper coinage which was easily counterfeited, so that the quantity increased enormously and its value decreased proportionately. Lerma's solution to the problem was to publish a decree doubling the value of the coins; this of course merely doubled the prices. The nominal revenues of the crown were enormous, but they were not paid. The clergy of Castile supposedly supported fifty galleys on the Mediterranean coast, but there were only eight; Naples paid for thirty galleys but there were sixteen; Sicily paid for twenty and there were ten.[13]

At their lowest point the royal finances were in such condition that officials were appointed to go from door to door, accompanied by a priest, to beg alms for the King in order that he might maintain the grandeur of his court. Meanwhile the common people were starving. The cloth-weaving industry was being strangled by the *alcabala,* a sales tax imposed each time an article changed hands, and the cost of living was increased by the "milliones," an excise tax on food. Early in the reign of Philip III the Cortes of Castile had complained that "Castile is depopulated . . . the people in the villages being now insufficient for the urgently necessary agricultural work, and an infinite number of places formerly possessing a hundred households are now reduced to ten, and many to none at all."[14] Conditions were especially desperate in old Castile, and Lerma's brilliant solution to that problem was to move the court early in 1601 to Valladolid, the King issuing the decree one day and setting out the next like a fugitive fleeing before a powerful enemy. The change did nothing for northern Castile except to raise prices there and to ruin Madrid. Early in 1606 Madrid bribed the court to return. The King was offered 250,000 ducats and the sixth part of all house rents for ten years. Lerma was bribed with 100,000 ducats and a palace. Lerma's secretary, Don Pedro Franqueza, Conde de Villalonga, who a few years before had been a penniless Catalan adventurer, was bribed with 1,000 ducats, although later, when he was in disgrace, it was said that his bribe also had been 100,000 ducats. Don Rodrigo Calderón, Marqués de Siete Iglesias, Lerma's favorite, also got a handsome bribe.

When Sir Anthony rode into Madrid in October 1606, "with upwards of thirty persons all splendidly dressed,"[15] the court had been back in the city about six months. With some degree of plausibility Sir Anthony, in reporting to the Spanish government, attributed the failure of his Moroccan mission to the disturbed condition of the Imperial government which had sent him to Morocco and to the Imperial-Turkish peace. In April, while Sherley was still in Marrakesh, the insanity of the Emperor Rudolph worsened and it was at that time that his brothers resolved to wrest the power from him. In November, after his return, Archduke Matthias, as has been noted, made peace with Turkey. It would have been better for Sir Anthony's case if the peace had been made before he left Morocco rather than after, but even so it served his purpose. "I have described for you the moods of the Emperor and those of his statesmen," he wrote Villalonga, "and in the matter of the peace which they have concluded with the Turks, my estimate of the situation has proved to be correct." He went on to say that he thought the peace both dishonorable and unwise. It had been concluded at the moment when the Turks with slightly more effort might have been totally defeated. Peace had been made without consultation with either the Pope or Spain. It was injurious, Sherley declared, to both Christianity and the Empire. He had been sent to solicit aid in Morocco, with the assurance that the Emperor would never make peace with the Turk, but peace had been made. "If I had not been led by the hand of the Lord, if my aim had not simply been His glory, if I were still in Barbary," he declared to Villalonga, "Your Lordship can have no idea what my condition would be." [16]

Not only had the diplomatic mission been a failure, but Sir Anthony made no profit on the prisoners he had ransomed. He was especially disappointed with the two noble Portuguese. "I made myself even naked to deliver them to their friends and country," he complained to Lord Salisbury to whom he turned for help, "and now . . . they do not only deny to pay, but persecute me as much as they dare and can, with all the vile usage that can be devised." [17] He had no better luck with the ransomed Spanish than with the Portuguese. He took one of them, Juan Delgato, into his service. Delgato failed to pay his ransom, and Sherley failed to pay Delgato's wages, with the outrageous result, reported Sherley, that Delgato, "entered my house with an officer of the peace and others . . . they opened my chests, they reviled me, they searched the house, and they did not scruple to offer me the most extraordinary insults in the world." [18] The behavior of the ransomed men was so uniformly ungrateful that it appears likely they knew that they owed their freedom not so much to the generosity of Sherley, as to the sacrilegious greed of him who stole the ruby from the Church of Saint Denis. Correspondence with the Spanish court about the ransoms dragged on, but Sherley never came closer to getting the money he desperately needed. In addition, his creditors in Africa learned his whereabouts and made life unpleasant for him. Some four weeks after his arrival in Madrid, the Venetian ambassador wrote that "every day some new fraud comes to light. . . . He continues to live in great splendor though without money." [19] Under such circumstances splendid living was difficult even for Sherley. Later the Venetian envoy noted that "his debts compel him to live very quietly in his house and greatly diminish the repute he originally acquired by his splendor of living." [20] The English ambassador heard "by one that attended him in Barbary that he hath there played many parts of mountebankery which I fear some merchant factors in London will bitterly taste of; that those of Lisbon will hardly escape him, who hold him either in the account of a saint or a great sorcerer, so apt is the confused and promiscuous multitude to worship rather in Samaria than Jerusalem." [21]

The necessity of finding money increased daily, and Sherley proposed various schemes to the Spanish court whereby he might come by some of it. Among other proposals he offered, toward the end of 1606, to protect Naples and Sicily from the raids of Turks and pirates by providing a fleet of ten ships, which would maintain themselves by preying on enemy commerce. He intended to use English vessels and man them with English seamen, and he argued that they could not corrupt Philip III's subjects with their heretical doctrines since they would be fighting at sea. He also pointed out that for years the Grand Duke of Tuscany had used English ships and seamen to prey on Turkish shipping and certainly it was not inimical to the interests of Catholicism to use heretics to kill infidels and vice versa.[22]

In return for this service he asked to be given the title of general, appointed a member of the Collateral Council of Naples, and accorded the privilege of selling twenty thousand pieces of Dutch cloth in the Portuguese trading centers of Ormuz and Pernambuco, and at Cefalu in Sicily, free of the usual 30 per cent duty. He would, he stated, maintain his own factors in those places to carry on trade. Actually he intended, if the privilege were granted, to sell it to his friend Jeremias Baldmans, a Dutch merchant in Madrid, then on the verge of bankruptcy. He also called to the attention of the King's ministers the fact that the majority of the ships returning with cargoes of sugar from Brazil fell victim to Dutch pirates. In the previous September, he declared, these pirates had sold 4,000 cases of sugar in Plymouth alone, and in the previous May they had sold eight hundred cases in Safi; indeed, the Dutch corsairs supplied all the sugar that was needed in France, Germany, and parts of Italy. Sherley offered to supply ten or twelve ships which would sail in convoy, carrying all the merchandise the traders wished to send to Brazil and which would return with sugar cargoes. He would guarantee the merchants against all losses. In this way trade, which had been demoralized, would be restored; the royal revenues from customs would be increased; and the corsairs, no longer finding unarmed caravels on which to prey, would disappear from the shipping routes between Lisbon and Brazil.[23]

Another proposal concerned the importation of wheat. Nuremberg, he observed, largely maintained itself by buying wheat where it was plentiful and cheap and selling it where it was dear. Venice and Muscovy made great profits in the same way. In years of drought and crop failure foreigners in Spain sold wheat at exorbitant prices, and in so doing drained gold and silver out of the country. If His Majesty's government would calculate the amount of wheat imports needed each year and give Sherley a patent for five or seven years he would undertake to supply wheat at moderate prices for drought-stricken regions in Spain. Rather than take bullion out of the country he would take bills of exchange for the wheat on the places from which he had imported it. Still another proposition concerned the strategy of sea power. Sir Anthony observed that in order to be powerful at sea, His Catholic Majesty really needed fifty ships of war, divided into four squadrons, each designed to guard and protect a different stretch of sea. There was, he said, abundance of ship-building materials in Spain, and he offered to construct fifty ships there or, if His Majesty preferred, to supply fifty of the best ships to be found in Europe.

He proposed in addition a number of political reforms, which although they would not bring personal advantage to himself were put forward for the good of Spain. In line with his interest in sea power, he pointed out that the passage of the Strait of Gibraltar could be controlled by seizing two points in Morocco, Larache and Cafia.[24] He would undertake to do this for His Catholic Majesty with the aid of a renegade caid (possibly he had Abdulla Sinko in mind) and two thousand men. He further thought that it might be possible to induce Duke Charles of Sweden to harass Dutch shipping in the Sound, and he saw great advantage for Spain in arranging a marriage between Arabella Stuart, the next heir to the throne after James, and the Archduke Matthias, the brother of Rudolph II. Turning from European to world politics, he advised that the Straits of Singapore and Sunda should be fortified and that Saint Helena could also be made a useful strong point and way station on the route to the East Indies. As for the East Indies themselves, he considered the area too vast for a single government and advised that it be divided into two viceroyalties. Reforms were also needed in the West Indies, which he suggested should be divided into four trade areas centered at Cumaná, Santo Domingo, Cartagena, and Guatemala.[25] Except for the proposal for a fleet based in Sicily, the schemes were received by the King's councilors with a singular lack of enthusiasm. Their opinions in the form of a report or *consulta* were forwarded to Lerma.

Juan de Idiaquez, Comendador Mayor of Leon, who had served Philip II for decades before serving his incompetent son, confessed himself perplexed by Sherley's offers. "They seem paradoxical," he observed, "when one considers his past history. Although they say his father is rich, no one has the amount of money which is involved in carrying out the projects which he offers, and it is unlikely he could actually carry them through. It is evident from the record that wherever he goes, he sets great schemes in motion . . . he is a restless spirit and he knows too many things about this monarchy. He must be handled as one would handle an engineer who though no longer of much service is familiar with the innermost secrets of the great fortresses of the kingdom. One must consider carefully before sending him away scorned and despised. Being a foreigner and not having the obligation of vassalage, he could go wherever he saw the possibility of profit."

Sherley's offer to furnish a fleet of ten ships, based in Sicily, to war on the Turks and pirates was considered with especial care. The Marqués of Chinchón thought that although Don Antonio Sherley was by temperament extravagant and dangerous, his projects ought not to be scorned, since it was possible that one or another of them might turn out to be successful and worthwhile. As for basing a fleet in southern Italy, the dangers were that a great many foreigners would become familiar with Italy's seas and shores and that these foreigners would live by plunder, a mode of life that anywhere was only safe to accord to friends. Both the Constable of Castile, a distinguished diplomat, and the Count of Olivares took a pessimistic view. The former thought the scheme for a Sicilian fleet vain, badly planned, and dangerous. Difficulties would arise, he prophesied, and Sherley ought to be placated by offers which would fix his attention in a different direction. The Count of Olivares, who was to become the most powerful man in Spain, also felt that the best course would be to involve Sherley in duties which would deflect his attention from the proposed fleet. For one thing it was evident he would not be able to perform what he promised, and one could not be sure that granting him what he asked might not mean a break with England.[26] Don Gomez de Avila, who with Idiaquez and Don Cristóbal de Moura had been a member of the trusted personal council of Philip II, could not see how Sherley could employ English ships, sailors, and soldiers in Sicily without that fact being widely known. Certainly the English government would know it, and they could, if they chose, use these English mercenaries to launch an attack on Italy. Sherley, the Marqués observed, was a restless, dangerous person, wise in the ways of the world. It would be prudent to raise his salary and keep him in Spain. The Count of Miranda considered Sherley's genius extraordinary and dangerous, but he could see no disadvantage in granting him the right to base a fleet in Sicily. If he were given a patent to have such a fleet, it would soon be apparent whether he could perform what he claimed, and if he could not there would be no loss.[27]

When so many of the King's council were dubious about the proposed flotilla, it is curious that Sherley should have been granted the patent to provide a fleet for Sicily in return for the right to import cloth which he had requested. "Being well acquainted with you Don Antonio Sherley," the King's commission ran, "knowing you to be an experienced seaman, and trusting you to do your duty to God and to ourselves, we have chosen and named you as general of our galleons." Sir Anthony was given "license and authority to attack and take in the Mediterranean as many prizes as you are able of the ships and property belonging to our rebel subjects of Holland and Zeeland or belonging to Turks, Moors, or other enemies of Spain." All viceroys, captains-general, and other officers in Spanish ports were enjoined to honor Sir Anthony as general of the King's galleons, were to sell him all necessary supplies, and allow him to dispose of in those ports such ships and cargoes as he seized as prizes. Sherley was strictly warned that "no one under your command, foreigners or others, shall contravene in any way the laws and customs of these our kingdoms; if they do so they shall be punished without remission as would be our vassals and subjects." [28]

Unfortunately the plan was brought to a standstill because the Council of Portugal refused to allow Sherley's men to enter Portuguese possessions, even though in actual fact they would have been Baldmans' men. To make matters worse, in 1607 there were first rumors of a truce and then actually a brief truce between Holland and Spain. Trade relations gave promise of being easier, and Sherley's privilege to import cloth into Spanish and Portuguese possessions depreciated rapidly in value.

Sir Anthony continued to search for a way to make himself useful, and his movements were watched with suspicion by the English ambassador, Sir Charles Cornwallis. Concerning a proposed marriage between the French and Spanish royal houses he wrote, "Very lately is Sir Anthony Sherley (by what means I know not) made (as he saith) an instrument in the matter." He was more concerned when he detected Sherley meddling in English affairs. "Not to want occupation, very earnest he is become (as I hear) to intrude himself in the business for the conjunction with England, wherein, having perhaps by way of discourse from Villa Longa, gotten some taste, he pretends for the better shadowing himself with some smoke of trust or greatness, to be made a dealer." [29] Cornwallis also reported that Sherley might have a hand in a plot hatched by Father Cresswell and the Earl Bothwell for the invasion of Scotland, but he produced no definite information.[30]

By the beginning of March 1607, Sir Anthony's need for money was so great that he outlined to the Spanish ministers an alternative method by which he might exercise his commission as Admiral of the King's galleons. Gold from Timbuctu went overland through the desert to Morocco and was there traded for salt. In 1590 and 1591, a force of Spanish and Portuguese renegades in the service of Morocco had crossed the desert, destroyed the negro forces opposing them, and captured Timbuctu. They continued to forward gold over the desert to Morocco, and the camels returned laden with salt. Sir Anthony proposed that Spain should transport salt by ship from the Isle of Maye in the Cape Verde group to the mouth of the Senegal River on the mainland coast and trade it there for Timbuctu gold. This route, so much shorter and easier than the long three months' trek over the Sahara, would divert the gold from Morocco to Spain. Sherley's role would be to harass and make prizes of the Dutch ships which went every year to load salt in the Isle of Maye, to protect the Spanish ships transporting salt, and to thwart a similar Dutch design to trade salt for gold in the port of Arguin. This scheme, or variations on it, was not original with Sherley, and was in fact very old. The royal council considered Sherley overzealous in making the proposal and evaded answering him,[31] but in recognition of his past services to Spain, Philip III awarded him the cross of the Order of Santiago. It was not, indeed, the full regalia of the order, but it was a mark of recognition.[32]

Sir Anthony's condition was becoming desperate. "The Spanish policy is directed to feeding him with fair promises," wrote the Venetian ambassador. "They now tell him he is destined for a post in the Levant. He has neither money or credit." [33] Some weeks earlier Cornwallis had noted that Sir Anthony "offereth to sell some of his grants, at a very reasonable rate, but cannot arrive as I hear to at the half of what he requireth." He added that "this moveth him to a fast in the College of the Jesuits; and his attendants as I hear, to the like at home, not having yesternight a sixpence to pay for their suppers." [34] When Cornwallis wrote, Sherley's fortunes were at their lowest ebb. Within a few days all had changed. "Although he was embarged [sequestered] in his own house for debts which he owed," wrote a correspondent of Sherley's old enemy Thomas Wilson, "yet such way he found . . . that the day following . . . he departed the town in great bravery, notwithstanding divers great debts which he left unsatisfied . . . he purposeth to send Sir Edwin Rich (who is in his company) before to Naples, and himself to go directly to Prague, there to give account to the Emperor of his embassage into Barbary." [35]

The fact was that he had managed to sell his patent to import cloth into Portuguese possessions, or more precisely, he had traded it to Jeremias Baldmans, now bankrupt, for one hundred cannon which Baldmans' firm had at Bilbao, and then sold the guns to the Spanish crown.[36] Instead of going to Prague, he went to Naples. "My first intention," he wrote the King from the latter city, "was to go to Germany to perform the services which you wished me to carry out in those parts, but having heard by the account of Ensign Torres who had newly returned from Persia, that the Shah was disgruntled with the peace which had been made between the Emperor and the Turk. . . . It seemed more logical to stop here to discuss Levant affairs with the Count of Benavente, lieutenant of Your Majesty in this Kingdom, since there were matters calling for promptness in decision and execution, before I left to carry out the other negotiations." [37] Although Sir Anthony goes on to speak of things he had discussed before, the settling of the silk trade at Ormuz and the fortifying of Saint Helena and the Sabao Strait, it is not quite clear what service he performed for the Count of Benavente.

He remained at Naples until the latter part of August, when he took passage on the Duke of Savoy's galleys for Livorno. From there he made his way to Florence, but got a bleak welcome. "It seems the Grand Duke is somewhat distasted with him," wrote Anthony Tracy, who was at Florence at the time, "for besides he would by no means see him, he at first made some difficulty to grant him passage through his State. He was very well attended, richly jewelled, and as it was told me, well furnished with crowns and better with credit." [38] Another Englishman reported from Livorno that "Sir Anthony Sherley, going to Florence was kept at the gates above an hour before he could enter, and his Highness would not receive him. He came into Florence at 17 hours and departed at 21 hours." [39] Continuing on his journey, Sir Anthony reached Ferrara early in September, and Prague in October, where he was very well received and given an audience with the Emperor. He carried instructions from Philip III to the Spanish ambassador, who reported to Madrid that he had endeavored to execute the various tasks entrusted to him but had not as yet suggested that the title of count be conferred upon Sir Anthony.[40] Later the Emperor did confer the title of Count Palatine on Sherley "in recognition of his great travels and his extraordinary services to Christianity in embroiling the Turks in a war with Persia." At this time, except in the case of the Palatinate of the Rhine, the title of Count Palatine had lost all importance and was retained by old families who possessed other titles only as an indication of the ancient splendor of their houses. There is no record that Sherley was ever a Count of the Empire.[41]

Probably Count Sherley's chief task at Prague was to induce the Emperor to contribute to the cost of the fleet which was to be based in Sicily. He argued that it would be a weapon against the Turks, but failed to convince the Emperor. He also pressed for repayment of 100,000 escudos, which he contended was the sum he and his brother had spent in the service of the Emperor at the court of Shah, but in this effort he also failed. In the spring Sir Anthony left Prague and went to Ratisbon. The Imperial Diet was then gathered there, and he became acquainted with the Archduke Ferdinand. Pleading that as admiral of a Spanish squadron he was in great need of provisions, he obtained from Ferdinand the promise of 70,000 staras or estarnas of wheat worth 30,000 thalers. Subsequently Sherley made valiant efforts to obtain the grain but the Archduke never fulfilled his promise. Possibly as a substitute for the wheat, Ferdinand appointed Count Anthony governor of all his Adriatic ports, but the office carried no stipend, and according to what the Spanish ambassador could learn at the Imperial court, it was an empty honor.[42]

In April, Sherley reached Ferrara on his return journey to Spain. From there, much to the annoyance of Sir Henry Wotton, the English ambassador at Venice, Sir Anthony sent some of his entourage to Venice. Wotton had his secretary call on the Venetian College, or cabinet, to note that Sherley "amuses himself by keeping certain people in this city, for what purpose he could not say." [43] In all probability Wotton knew quite well why Sherley's men were in the city, for another Englishman reported that through agents in Venice Sherley was "busied to draw from thence as many English mariners and sea masters as with money and words he can persuade." [44] Sherley also sent his secretary, the Cavalier Tomas Pagliarini, to the Spanish ambassador at Venice with proposals for peace between Spain and the Turks, and the ambassador, Alfonso de la Cueva, Marqués of Bedmar, relayed the information to Madrid.

"Anthony Sherley has sent his secretary from Ferrara," Cueva reported, "to hand me proposals for peace between Your Majesty and the Turk, with a statement that the proposals were obtained through one of his agents . . . the provisions would appear to be so advantageous to Your Majesty and injurious to the Turk that I am doubtful about the reliability of the information. . . . I will endeavor to discover the sources of the conversations and anything else I can concerning the proposal and advise Your Majesty of what I hear." [45] The Spanish ambassador soon obtained reliable information. Sherley and the Cavalier Pagliarini, who had been in Sir Anthony's entourage since the latter had first arrived in Prague from Persia, had a falling out. When Sherley moved on to Milan, Pagliarini left him and went to Venice, a fact which worried Anthony considerably. "Before God," he wrote to his sister Anne, "I dare commit nothing to paper, and now less than ever, that villain Pagliarini . . . being run from me with all my papers." [46] In Venice, Pagliarini sent word to Cueva that he wished to speak to him. "After I had summoned him," reported Cueva, "he made a long statement against Don Antonio. . . . I asked him to send me a signed memorandum containing all that he told me which I would pass on to Your Majesty. This he has done . . . and I have sent the memorandum to Your Majesty with this letter." [47]

Pagliarini stated that he had been employed for eight years by Sherley and he prayed that such a pestiferous weed as Count

Anthony would be expelled from the company of illustrious men surrounding the King. "He left a brother in Persia as a slave," he declared, "he was afraid to return to Persia . . . Don Antonio is a man who comes running whenever there is an offer of money. He is fickle and corrupt and . . . mendacious by nature. . . . He lies awake all night devising schemes to extract money from princes. . . . He is overwhelmed by debt, owing money in every part of the world. His total debts amount to more than 200,000 escudos. Turks, Persians, Armenians, Moroccans, Jews, and many poor German merchants suffer because he does not pay them. . . . He manufactured a treaty between Your Catholic Majesty and the Turks, and presented it to Your Majesty as a new development. Don Antonio justified himself by saying that he was in Ferrara on the service of Your Catholic Majesty, that he did no harm in fabricating the peace proposals, and that he wanted to perform a famous deed. This affair is all smoke and vanity. . . . He seeks to cover up the fact that he has not armed and furnished a fleet as he promised Your Catholic Majesty. Don Antonio couldn't furnish and arm a rowboat. . . . He is a man who affects an air of mystery in everything." [48]

In May, Count Anthony left Italy for Spain, where he probably arrived about the beginning of August 1608, entering Madrid in great style with a retinue of twenty horse. He was later briefly in Valladolid with Sir William Stanley, who had betrayed the city of Deventer back in the days when both he and Anthony had been soldiers in the Netherlands. Count Anthony's main preoccupation was still to find some way of financing his proposed Sicilian fleet. He now proposed that this should be done by a tax on notaries and others in the kingdom of Sicily. The Spanish government, like others, was always interested in new and lucrative tax schemes. Sherley's plan was approved and in the spring of 1609 he set out for Sicily with official letters to the viceroy, the Duke of Escalona, which directed the Duke to levy the tax on Sherley's behalf.[49] Leaving Alicante in a small vessel, Sherley almost immediately met adventure. He encountered a storm and put in for repairs and fresh supplies at Majorca on 2 March. Quite voluntarily he rendered the King a favorable report on the conduct of affairs in that island. He reached Palermo before 20 March and was also pleased to report favorably from there on the conduct of the Viceroy, which he said was quite the contrary to that official's actions as they were described by his enemies at court.[50] "I have neither family ties with, or interest in, the Viceroy," he wrote to the King a little later, "but I speak the truth as a gentleman, and I know he [Escalona] pawned his own silver in Palermo for the service of Your Majesty and to take care of the needs of the soldiers of this Kingdom." [51] Unfortunately after so felicitous and harmonious a beginning, in less than a month Count Anthony was complaining bitterly to Madrid about conditions in Sicily. The soldiers who were to serve under him had been told evil things about himself and consequently they treated him with animosity. His commission did not give him sufficient authority to punish them. The port officials showed their ill will by maltreating his crews.[52]

Sherley's opinion of the Sicilians seemed to accord with that of his fellow countryman, George Sandys, who visited the island about this time. They were a people, reported Sandys, "standing much upon their honor, yet excessively given to idleness, talkative, busy-headed, quarrelsome, jealous, and revengeful." [53] The King's councilors considered Sherley's complaint and rendered an opinion, or *consulta,* in which it was observed that Sir Anthony, as a matter of fact, had not been given the powers usually accorded captains-general. It was recommended that he should be told that his commission was a novel one and that the King would look into the matter. Later he was given a commission in the form he desired.[54] Sherley regained his benevolent attitude soon after receiving this assurance, and his new commission. He praised the valor and prudence of the Viceroy, who had cleared away difficulties, despite the fact that a spirit of pure malignity was still evident in Palermo. He had, he reported, five ships in that port, another at Syracuse, and a seventh at Augusta, and these vessels would soon cleanse the seas of corsairs.[55] He endeavored to enlarge his squadron by recruiting a famous pirate, Dancer, or Danziger, who was promised pardon for past crimes if he agreed to serve under Sherley, but this effort was unsuccessful.[56]

Count Anthony was able to spare enough time from his duties to work out various schemes for the improvement of Sicily. The Armenians, he declared, made a great deal of money in the Levant by trading annually two millions of the Polish coins known as leonicos for chequins. The leonico, half silver and half alloy, was the coin most used in Turkey, while the chequins were gold. The exchange rate in western Europe was fifteen leonicos to the chequin, whereas in the Levant a chequin could be bought for twelve leonicos. He proposed that two mints should be established in Trapani. In the first mint, leonicos would be produced from Spanish silver. These leonicos would then be traded in the Levant for chequins which would then be recoined in the second mint into gold doubloons. The profits on the operation would be in the neighborhood of 20 per cent. The actual trading of leonicos for chequins would be carried on by forty or fifty families of Levantine Jews imported into Sicily for the purpose. Sherley further observed that the cloth-making arts were the most important in the world. The secret of England's strength was cloth manufacture and Holland's riches were due to cloth making and the dyeing of cloths purchased in England. Spain could quickly surpass the wealth of those countries by establishing the cloth industries in Sicily and Naples. Sherley offered to initiate cloth manufacture in Sicily, although, he warned, the industry would not prosper if foreign merchants, traveling to the island to buy cloth, were harassed by petty officials.

Escalona and his councilors gave Count Anthony's proposals careful consideration, and it appeared to them that the introduction of Hebrews into the viceroyalty might have grave consequences. In reply Sherley pointed out that the Jews of Rome, Avignon, Ancona, Florence, and Germany had not Judaized those places. As for the fear that Levantine Jews would act as Turkish spies, it appeared to him unlikely that moneylenders, being men of substance, would be attracted by the wages paid to spies.[57]

Amid the discussions on the numerous proposals for the reform of the kingdom, it may have been difficult for Escalona, as it certainly was for Sherley, to remember that Count Anthony had arrived in Sicily only some six weeks previously for the sole purpose of organizing a fleet to fight pirates and Turks. It began to appear that he aimed at nothing less than control of Sicily. As a consequence the project to equip a fleet languished for a few months. It was revived as a by-product of the deportation of the Moriscos, an event which has caused as much debate as the expulsion of the Jews or the revocation of the Edict of Nantes. It appeared to many Spanish at the beginning of the seventeenth century that someone must be to blame for the disastrous condition of the country, and the Moriscos were handy scapegoats. The hope that these Christians of Moorish descent would become sincere in their new religion, or even that they would give up their Moorish dress, had long since been abandoned by their Spanish neighbors. When peace was made between Spain and England in 1604, James I sent Philip III a number of letters he had found among Queen Elizabeth's papers which showed that the Moriscos of Valencia had plotted, or hoped to plot, an uprising with the help of the English and of the Swiss protestants. It is certain that the Moriscos intrigued with the Turks in the same way, but these people were so persecuted in a number of ways by their fellow countrymen that they were driven in desperation to look for help abroad. They were industrious, thrifty, and prosperous, characteristics which inspired in the Spanish both contempt and envy. They were essential to the cultivation of the land, a fact well known to the large landowners, some of whom tried to protect them. The Moriscos were most numerous in Valencia, and consequently that was where they were most hated. Lerma, a Valencian, shared the deep-rooted prejudice of his people. Some Spaniards had advised that the Moriscos be exterminated, others that they be transported to work in the mines in the Americas. Still others advised that they be deported to Africa. The all-powerful Lerma decided on the third course. The decision was made officially in 1608, and the actual planning for this most remarkable feat in mass transportation took place in the summer of 1609. All available shipping was to be mobilized. Naples and Sicily were to be denuded of vessels, and this detail of the plan soon became known to the Turks. Actual deportation began in September 1609, and from that date until the beginning of 1612, out of a total minimum population of 300,000 Moriscos, approximately 275,000 were exported to Africa.[58]

The Sicilian Viceroy, Escalona, got wind of Turkish plans to raid his coasts as soon as all the available vessels were dispatched to Spain. In this desperate situation he hurriedly asked Madrid for permission to revive Sherley's fleet. Count Anthony, he said, already had some ships in Sicily and had more on order. A reply reached him at the beginning of July. The home government had also learned of the Turkish plan. Escalona was authorized to take Sherley directly into the royal service and to do whatever else he thought necessary for the defense of the kingdom. The Viceroy immediately authorized Count Anthony to expend 56,000 ducats to arm and equip his ships, and he ordered 2,000 infantry to be ready to embark with the armada.[59] "Sr. Captain Peper will tell you," Count Anthony wrote his father, "in what a labyrinth of business I am, that I have not time to eat much less to write. I am going hence with 23 ships, 7,000 men to land, and 12 pieces of cannon. . . . The Turk is at Navarino as they say intending against Malta. What the King's purpose is I may judge . . . for my own part I know by God's grace that I will not fail to accomplish what I owe to my quality and your honor, and if I die, I will die well." [60]

He was indeed in such a welter of business that, to the distress of Escalona, he exceeded his budget and sometimes obtained ships without paying for them. An Englishman complained that by solemn oaths and fine promises Sherley had cozened him out of his vessel. One Anthony Carelson, skipper of Enkhuizen, putting in at Trapani, was offered seven thousand pieces of eight for his ship by Count Anthony. Carelson agreed to sell and turned over his ship to Sherley. More than four years later he was still trying to get his seven thousand pieces of eight.[61]

By October a fleet of eight vessels was ready, and Escalona ordered Sherley to put to sea. His orders directed him to divert Turkish forces from the coasts of the Kingdoms of Naples and Sicily and to clear the seas of pirates. He was forbidden to land on the Barbary coast, Myliti, Cyprus, Metallus, Dardinellos, Zio, or any other place in Turkish territory unless he felt assured of good results, for His Catholic Majesty was unwilling that men and ships should be lost on unimportant raids or those promising little chance of victory. From Palermo Sherley was to sail to Trapani and there embark two companies of infantry. From Trapani he was to go to Messina and embark more troops and then proceed to Syracuse for the rest of the infantry. He would then sail from Syracuse on a cruise against the enemy, in which adventure Escalona trusted to Sherley's valor and prudence and wished him good luck.[62] A week after receiving these final instructions and good wishes from Escalona, Count Sherley sent a farewell message to the King. "Your Armada," he announced, "is in a flourishing condition, and I hope to perform great feats with it. May God prosper it for the glory and service of your royal highness and preserve your royal highness for the good of Christianity." [63] Sometime later he sailed for Messina and wrote to the King again from there. He was preoccupied in this letter not only with the problems of the fleet, but with the question of diverting the silk trade to Ormuz, and with the difficulties encountered by the merchants in that far-off port.[64] It was now November, and Escalona noted that the fleet had already exceeded its budget by three thousand escudos, a matter which he thought would be of minor importance if Sherley proceeded with prudence and followed instructions.[65]

At the end of December Sherley was still in Syracuse. It was nearly three months since Escalona had issued his final orders and sailing instructions. He complained to Sherley about the continual delays and about the frauds and confusion in the fleet's accounts.[66] Perhaps as a result of the Viceroy's insistence, the squadron put to sea a few days later. It had hardly gotten outside the harbor before it was hit by a storm and driven back to Syracuse. A month later the fleet was still there. "I have reported to Your Majesty," wrote Escalona, "the work and care which were necessary to get the fleet ready for sea, and I had provisioned the ships for five months . . . the fleet put in at Messina to take on supplies and artillery and from there went to Syracuse to embark several companies of Italian infantry. In spite of my insistence that the fleet sail, Count Sherley delayed longer in these ports than was necessary. . . . Having left Syracuse . . . and being some miles at sea, he ran into a storm in which he lost a number of ships. . . . Through bad seamanship he came close to losing his flagship. Subsequently he set out to collect the fleet, leaving behind a large vessel called the *Carraca* to be repaired . . . but the storm of 10 January was so violent that it [the *Carraca*] heeled over near Rijoles and although only nine persons were lost it received so much damage that it will be difficult for it to sail again . . . another ship fled to Barbary . . . the whole fleet has disintegrated to such an extent that I doubt that it will be able to sail from Syracuse. . . . I have sent there 500 quintals of biscuit and other victuals which I am informed the men of the fleet are assiduously consuming, and under various pretexts avoiding work . . . the lack of discipline is apparent. I have thought best to relate these facts to Your Majesty so that you may send such instructions as you think best. I am anxious to avoid the difficulties which a number of people are apprehensive will befall the fleet in view of the Count's talents." [67]

From Syracuse, Sherley had written to the King justifying himself. Even in harbor, he contended, the fleet was fulfilling its mission since the Turkish attacks on Sicily had not materialized. The delays in sailing were not his fault. The armada had been ready long before, but the peace with Holland had frustrated his original plan for financing the squadron by preying on Dutch commerce. His second plan to raise money by a tax on notaries had been evaded by the officials in Sicily. His intentions had always been sincere, he insisted, and His Catholic Majesty had no one who served him with more love, fidelity, and diligence. He had gotten together, armed, and equipped a fleet when it was direly needed, and he had done it in Sicily where supplies and provisions of all kinds were lacking. He had performed the task in six months whereas the King's ministers with all the great weight of government behind them would have taken two years to complete it.[68]

The fleet finally sailed on 7 February. Sherley reconnoitered the islands of Corfu, Cephalonia, and Zante and after a number of minor adventures landed on the island of Schiato on 21 March with a thousand men, unaware that the previous night the Turks had also landed several hundred men. The invaders marched inland eight miles, harrying the Greek peasants as they went, and walked into a Turkish ambush. Taking advantage of both the ruggedness of the mountains and the thick woods, and repeatedly skirmishing with the invaders, the Turks and Greeks forced Sherley and his men to retreat to their ships, which they did in an orderly manner, according to a Spanish report, and reembarked with the loss of only twenty men while the Turks and Greeks lost many more. This was the major accomplishment of the expedition. Count Sherley later pillaged Mytilini, was reported to have landed on Braccio de Maino, and also captured a Venetian ship, which he had been expressly ordered not to do. The fleet was back in port before the beginning of June 1610.

"Count Don Antonio Sherley has returned," Escalona reported to Madrid, "with seven of the eight ships with which he left . . . they have returned in such bad condition that it is easy to see the treatment they have had and the neglect they have suffered. The fleet brought back no booty of value and nothing of importance occurred except that on one occasion, as Your Majesty will see by the report on the voyage, Sherley came close to losing his battle flag and all his men with it. I have been very much surprised that having express orders not to effect a landing, he should have carried out a foolhardy one, an act deserving the severest reprimand. I expressed this sentiment to him . . . he has been totally unable to justify his plan of action. I have considered depriving him of his command before he got into irreparable trouble, but being aware of the large number of pirates cruising these seas, the damage they are doing, and the meager coastal defenses available . . . it would appear unwise to leave this kingdom without any maritime forces whatever. I have therefore decided that Count Sherley should strengthen and repair the four best ships, and that these should act as armed escort vessels for the protection of Your Majesty's shipping and not as an independent fighting fleet. The eighth ship which Count Sherley took to the Levant seas, and which did not return, he says he left in eastern waters to obtain information about Turkish ship movements, but some say the ship deserted the fleet, and left the Levant in company with a number of French and English vessels. . . . The matter presents considerable problems . . . this fleet employs men of various nations who lack military discipline. It is under the command of a person who is not one of Your Majesty's subjects, and therefore not too punctilious about carrying out your orders. The result has been that instead of the seas being cleared of corsairs, thus enabling merchant shipping to operate freely, the pirates are more numerous than ever. Under the guise of carrying out Your Majesty's orders, many excesses have been committed which are unworthy of Your Majesty, contrary to your gracious desires, and the welfare of your subjects. My duty and the interests of the royal service compel me to report these facts to your Majesty." [69]

Count Anthony really ceased to be an admiral at this time. As a matter of fact, the King's council in Madrid had decided he should cease to be one some months previously when Escalona's report on the condition of the fleet after the storm at Syracuse had been received. "Considering the mode of life of this man," the council observed on that occasion, "his status and qualities, one is led to the conclusion that little more could be expected of him than what the Duke of Escalona reports, and perhaps it were better if the armada did not put to sea again for fear of even more serious disorder. It would appear that in order to avoid greater damage and difficulties, the fleet should cease to exist." [70] Count Anthony probably left Sicily soon after returning from the cruise. In November he was reported as being at Naples, "in great want." [71]

Meanwhile his brother Robert had arrived in Spain on his embassy from the Shah of Persia to the European courts. It is known that Count Anthony returned to Spain in January 1611, for in that month he informed on an Irishman, John Talbot, then at Alicante, who had been involved in a mutiny, and caused Talbot to be jailed.[72] Sherley was so poor that Sir John Ferne sent four hundred ducats to the port in order that he might travel to Madrid. He reached the city in February 1611 and was welcomed by his brother Robert and lodged in his house. He was, reported Cottington, "extreme poor both in purse and reputation; these people in my opinion do begin much to despise him, which he well perceives, and talks sometimes of his going for England, and sometimes of a journey into Persia with his brother, and daily (as I am told) utters very mutinous words against this state, but mine opinion is, that unless he governs his tongue with more discretion, his progress will shortly be at an end." [73] About two months later, Count Anthony repaid his brother's kindness in taking him into his home by doing him a remarkable disservice.

"Some six days past," wrote Cottington, "Mr. Robert Sherley sent somewhat hastily and earnestly for me, and coming to him he seemed much perplexed, and troubled and in such sort as he was hardly able to speak to me, at length said these words, 'Oh Mr. Cottington, I am betrayed where I am most trusted,' whereupon desiring him to explain himself, he gave me a letter out of his bosom, directed unto his brother Anthony, willing me to open it, which I did, and found it was from Secretary Prada (whose hand I am well acquainted withal) and to this effect,—'I have given an account to His Majesty of your plot, by which the Ambassador your brother may be secured from proceeding with his intention of going into England, or unto the rebels, who commands me to give you thanks in his name, and to let you know how well he takes your endeavors, which I have thought fit to do in writing, and also to desire you to proceed in your work, assuring you that you need not fear any want of secrecy.' This letter I read twice over, and can only remember thus much of it. The Ambassador told me he lighted upon it by a great chance that very morning. Sir Anthony lies in his house and is so extreme poor, as if his brother did not relieve him, he would doubtless suffer much misery. The Ambassador fears they will find some means to poison him; myself am now of opinion that he shall hardly be able to get from hence except by stealth." [74]

The following month the King's ministers decided it were best that Anthony should leave Madrid and return to Naples. The decision was apparently made by Juan de Idiaquez, the Comendador Mayor of Leon, but the news was broken to Sherley by Secretary Andrés de Prada. "I have informed Don Antonio Sherley of the decision of Your Lordship," Secretary Prada wrote to Idiaquez, "and I have asked him to reply to me in writing. That reply together with a copy of it rendered into more intelligible language are attached herewith. I thought it best to forward these papers to you since the decision was yours. Your Lordship will decide the best action to take." Idiaquez added a note to Prada's message and returned it to him. "I have seen the letter of Don Antonio Sherley, together with the more legible copy," he wrote, "and I am sending you another letter which I received from Don Antonio last night together with my answer by which I endeavored to appease him. I should like to say now that I interfered in this affair because Don Antonio appeared so hurt by the decision handed him by Secretary Arostegui. . . . I know Your Honor has told him that you are not happy about sending him to Naples . . . and being sent to Naples is what he resents. . . . It appears that he wants either to be given his liberty absolutely, or that he may have permission to go to the Indies and die in obscurity. I have followed the whole affair and I do not think he should be allowed to go to the Indies. . . . In view of the remuneration he has been granted he should be happy to serve wherever His Majesty should command . . . the decision to send him to Naples does not preclude his being sent elsewhere, when it seems advisable. In the meantime we should not lose sight of this gentleman whom I could use under a capable leader who knew how to utilize his good qualities without paying attention to his speeches. Don Antonio could stay here a few months and in the meantime it could be decided what was best to do with him." [75]

About two weeks after writing the note to Prada, Idiaquez talked to Count Sherley. Don Antonio thought that he ought to be paid the nine thousand ducats which were owed to him by the Kingdom of Naples. He asked that he be given the Isle of Capri, that he be appointed governor there, and that the title of count be conferred upon him. If the title and the island were given him he was willing that a reduction should be made in his annual stipend. Harking back to his proposed stamp tax in the Kingdom of Sicily on drafts, payments, and other documents, he felt that the debts which he had incurred there in the service of the King, amounting to forty-five thousand ducats, should be paid from the proceeds of the tax. If he were personally granted the privilege to collect such a tax for eight or ten years, he could sell the patent and so clear off his debt to the crown immediately, an arrangement advantageous both to himself and to the King. If the tax he had proposed were not acceptable, then he proposed alternative taxes. Should His Majesty not wish to grant what was owing to him in Naples then he ought to be allowed to go to the Indies, where he was unknown, or any place where his presence would not be a disservice to the crown.

In reporting his conversation to the King, Idiaquez suggested that Sherley should be paid half of what was owed him so that he would have money to leave Madrid. The Island of Capri, it could be pointed out to Sherley, was a possession of the Crown of Aragon and not separable from it. The tax which Count Sherley proposed could be referred to the proper authorities and an opinion on its legality and desirability obtained. The request that he be allowed to go to the Indies ought to be denied. Concerning the request that he be allowed to select some other place of retirement, Idiaquez thought that "it will be difficult to deny it to him since he is a free and honorable gentleman. To avoid any appearance of being curt with him, Your Majesty could suggest to Don Andrés de Prada that he insinuate to Sherley that if he wished to remain in the service of Your Majesty as had been suggested, then Your Majesty would honor and esteem him. . . . If he should still wish to go elsewhere he would continue to be treated as an upright Christian gentleman who could be counted on to act prudently and wisely, and who would choose to go to such places as were convenient to Your Majesty, so that Your Majesty would be in a position to continue to make grants and favors to him under your royal seal." [76]

A month after these proposals and counterproposals had been exchanged, Count Anthony was still in Madrid, living very poorly and inclined to talk about the great sums which the crown owed him.[77] To this period apparently belongs an undated letter of Sherley's probably addressed to Secretary Prada.

"Your Honor may dispose of me as you see fit," he wrote, "for the love of God be pleased to obtain some clothes for me." [78] At one time Don Antonio thought of going to the Canary Islands, but did not do so and continued "in great want" in Madrid.[79] Sir John Digby wrote to Dudley Carleton that the Cloak of the Order of Santiago had been sent to Count Anthony, "but I think they should have done better to have sent him a suit of clothes . . . for he hath scarce any to put on his back. He hath titles enough before of Conde General. And they think he hath shifted so long he now can make shift with titles. . . . He hath scarce money to buy him bread and is lodged in a Bodegon, which is little worse than an English ale house." [80] Even in poverty Don Antonio had his eyes fixed on that mystical thing called honor. Years before he had received the badge of the Order of Santiago; now he had received the cloak, but it was not enough. He pointed out to the King's ministers that he had served Christianity with all his strength and fortune. At great personal danger he had gained the friendship of the King of Persia and fomented war among the Moslems, but no one had rewarded him for this service to Christianity, and so he now asked that he should be given the full regalia of the order such as was accorded to those born and bred in Catholicism.[81] The Duque de Lerma promised to look into the matter. There is no record that Don Antonio got what he desired, but shortly afterward, in September 1611, perhaps as a substitute for the full regalia, he had his pension increased.[82] Probably in the same month he retired to Granada, where except for journeys to Bayza or to Madrid or elsewhere in Spain, he lived for the rest of his life.

CHAPTER XI

Robert Sherley, Persian Ambassador

ROBERT, of course, was only one in a series of ambassadors and agents dispatched by the Shah, having been preceded among others by his brother Anthony, Husein Ali Beg, the merchants Assad Beg and Fetchi Beg, and the ambassador who arrived in Vienna in 1604. About the time the Shah dispatched Sherley he also sent Jangiz Beg and Ali Quli Beg. The reasons for sending Robert have been touched upon previously, and differ according to who is telling the story and where and when he is telling it.

Sherley departed for Europe on 12 February 1608, "well accompanied and furnished," [1] and took with him his Circassian wife, Teresa, his old companion Thomas Powell, and Powell's Persian wife. The company went by way of the Caspian Sea and the Volga to Moscow, where they overtook the ambassador Ali Quli Beg, who had left Persia before them. They were received in great state, costly presents were exchanged, and Robert experienced there none of the difficulties which Sir Anthony had encountered. On leaving Moscow, Robert went overland to Poland, arriving at Cracow in the fall of 1608, where he, his companions, and Ali Quli Beg were sumptuously entertained at the court of Sigismund III. At this time there were some English and many Scots at the Polish court, who may have made Robert's stay more pleasant. Sherley wintered in Cracow, but sent one Master Moore to England with news of his coming. Moore carried copies of the laudatory speeches and verses with which Sherley had been entertained in Cracow, and these, together with other news about Robert which has been alluded to previously and which he to some extent invented, were published in a little book by Thomas Middleton.[2]

Leaving Teresa in a convent in Poland, Sherley and Ali Quli Beg proceeded in the spring to the court of the Emperor at Prague, where they arrived at the end of April 1609. They were received with courtesy and their expenses were defrayed by the Emperor, but actually aside from urging war with Turkey, which was a continuing duty of Persian ambassadors, Robert had few affairs to occupy him at the Imperial court. The most notable events of his stay were that the Emperor conferred upon him the title of Count Palatine which he had previously conferred upon his brother, and that the new Count Robert paid off a large debt which Count Anthony had left behind.[3]

Sherley left sometime after the middle of July, going by way of Milan to Florence, where he arrived in the latter part of August. The Venetians, fearing that Sherley would divert the silk trade from the Mediterranean, invariably took a dim view of his activities. The resident of that republic at Florence reported that Count Robert "has put his household in silk of various colors. He gets the stuff but does not pay. He has asked the Grand Duke for four thousand crowns for his needs. It is thought that he will get it in place of a present." [4] A week later the same gentleman declared that Count Robert would only get "one thousand crowns . . . the whole Court wishes him away." [5] William Trumbull, the English representative at Brussels, on the contrary heard that Count Robert "hath been very favorably entertained in his passage thitherward, both at Milan and Florence. It is said that in his journey he hath paid a good part of his brother Sir A. Sherley's desperate debts." [6]

From Florence, Robert traveled to Rome, arriving there in the last days of September. "He was dressed," dutifully reported the Venetian ambassador, "in a cloak of black velvet trimmed with gold. He wore a turban with a cross on the top of it to show he is a Catholic. He has had an audience of the Pope in the presence of some Cardinals, and after presenting his credentials he made an elaborate oration, setting forth the esteem in which the King held His Holiness . . . [and] the hope that His Holiness would take steps to unite [the] Christian Sovereigns against the

Count Robert in 1609, from an engraving by Diego de Astor. The vignette below the portrait depicts Count Robert's audience with the Pope. (Reproduced with the permission of the Trustees of the British Museum from the engraving in the Department of Prints and Drawings.)

common foe." [7] Sherley also presented a letter from the Shah to the Pope, in which he asked the Pontiff to induce the King of Spain to invade Cyprus, "an island abounding with provisions of all kinds, with ports most suitable for wintering his [the King of Spain's] fleet, and near at hand for an attack later on Syria and . . . Aleppo, and so join up with the Persian army." [8] He also asked the Pope to persuade the King of Poland to fight the Turks in Wallachia, to induce the Emperor to fight them in Hungary, and to use his influence to have the European powers break off relations with Turkey.

The Pope made Count Robert a count and a chamberlain of honor,[9] and what was more lucrative, granted him the right to sell blessed rosaries, crosses, medals, and images, although of course the Papal letter was not quite worded in that way. The Pope granted to these blessed objects certain indulgences and graces. The possessor of one of them, if he performed certain devotional acts, might deliver a soul from purgatory and obtain plenary indulgence; by performing other religious exercises he might obtain fifty or a hundred years of indulgence, and in fact there were some sixteen ways in which the possessor might utilize his blessed object. From this Papal letter arose wild tales of great sums made by Count Robert in peddling Papal indulgences.[10]

Sherley probably departed for Spain in the latter part of November and arrived at Barcelona in the first days of January 1610. From there he went to Alcalá and for at least two weeks was officially ignored. "Out of a desire to understand the reason of this strange fashion towards my countryman," the English ambassador Cottington wrote, "I not long since took notice of it in a merry fashion unto the Secretary Prada, who told me that they had been so often cozened with embassies from those far countries, as his Majesty was resolved before he admitted him to see what record, as he termed it, he brought to make him accepted as an ambassador, and besides, said he, we have no great opinion of his wisdom for coming with a turban upon his head." [11]

A few days later Count Robert had an audience with the King and Queen at Aranjuez. "To the king he gave two letters," reported Cottington, "and spake much in persuading him to join with some other princes in making an effectual war against the Turk, to all which the King answered in so few words as he remains very ill satisfied. . . . The next day (Wednesday) he had his access unto the Duke [Lerma], to whom as I am advertised, in very round terms he complained of the strange entertainment he receives here, but the Duke gave him so small satisfaction as both began to talk very loud. What is since become of him I have not yet understood." [12]

One of the two letters which Count Robert handed to Philip III was from himself, and the other from the Shah. To a considerable extent they said the same things. The Shah urged that the Turk should be attacked by way of Aleppo and in Anatolia. Count Robert pointed out the trade which could be developed at Ormuz, especially if Spain gained control of the Red Sea, and he urged that a Castilian ambassador be sent to Persia.[13] Sherley got no answer to his proposals, and a few weeks after making them he talked with Cottington. "I do not perceive," the latter observed, "that he is possessed with those vanities which do so much govern his brother Anthony. He is not pleased with his entertainment here. He tells me he resolves to go from hence directly into England, and that by kind letters received from your Lordship [Salisbury] he hath understood His Majesty is contented that he also perform his embassage there." [14]

The Spanish were alarmed at Sherley's plan to go to England and resolved either to persuade him to change his mind, or if necessary prevent him from going. Don Juan Rodrigo de Calderón, the Marqués de Siete Iglesias, interviewed Count Robert and reported his interview to the King, that is to say, to Lerma. Calderón got the distinct impression that this embassy of Sherley's was different from previous Persian embassies, that if the offer of a trade treaty and a pact against the Turk was rejected, then Perso-Spanish friendship would be at an end. The Marqués warned that although Count Robert was not very prepossessing in appearance, those who had dealings with him found him well informed and resolute. Calderón observed that Sherley had a high regard for honor and was completely faithful to the mission which had been entrusted to him. Indeed it was these very qualities which were creating difficulties, for having been unable to obtain a treaty in Spain, Count Robert had resolved to go to England. He felt, he told Calderón, that the Shah's proposals had not been studied with the necessary care in Spain, and therefore he must, following the Shah's instructions, continue to England. When Calderón chided him for intending to do business with heretics, Count Robert replied that eminent theologians in Rome had assured him that the continuance of the war between the Persians and the Turks was the overriding consideration; and that in Flanders, His Majesty, Philip III himself, "makes use of Germans, ragamuffins, and other heretic soldiers . . . whole regiments of them." On his own part Calderón urged that a treaty be made for Persian silk, and that a partly private, partly royal association be formed to get the silk to Spain, for, he observed, "in this manner were carried out the enterprises of Queen Isabella in the Indies." He also noted that in Amsterdam there was a company for the Indies trade, and in England there was "an association of merchants who voyage to India, who pay the King duties for each hundredweight of pepper imported, from which he gets a great revenue." In the opinion of the Marqués, Sherley's proposals were the most important which had come to Spain in many years, and he urged that there should be no further delay in reaching an agreement with the Shah's ambassador.[15] As a consequence it was decided to send an ambassador to the Shah, as Sherley had urged, and it was arranged that Sherley and a Spanish ambassador should leave together for Persia in October 1610. Spain's ambassador would be instructed to conclude a new treaty of peace and amity with Persia. In the meantime, to ensure a good reception for the Spanish envoy, everything possible was to be done for the comfort and pleasure of Sherley, the Shah's ambassador. For the same reason, their envoy was to carry a letter to the Shah praising Count Robert's services.[16] Sherley and the Spanish ambassador would go by sea and debark at Ormuz. It was noted, "The sooner Don Roberto were to leave that island [Ormuz] so much less information he will be able to give about it." [17] To induce Count Robert to return directly to Persia, the Spanish gave him a purse of 2,000 ducats and an additional

2,000 ducats for the expenses of the journey.[18] As a result of these efforts Count Robert was mollified. He decided to remain in Spain, and sent word to his wife in Poland to join him in Madrid.[19] Cottington noted that Sherley "is made much of and still entertained at the King's charge." [20]

Still the Spanish court did nothing about the Persian proposals which Sherley had conveyed, and by December 1610 Count Robert had again become impatient and discouraged, and once more talked of going to England. In the last part of January or the beginning of February, Teresa Sherley arrived in Lisbon. Sherley wrote her to await him there. In a short time, he said, he would join her, and together they would go to England. His plan became known to Don Cristóbal de Moura, the old and trusted advisor of Philip II who had been sent to Portugal as viceroy by Philip III. Moura duly reported it to Secretary Antonio de Arostegui in Madrid.[21] As a result, Moura was advised from Madrid that he need not go to any expense on account of Teresa Sherley,[22] and Sherley's relations with the court in Madrid deteriorated badly until the Duke of Lerma cast in his teeth "the baseness of his brother Anthony." [23] Count Robert broached the subject of his going to England with Ambassador Cottington. He feared that "His Majesty would not hold it fit to give him that kind of entertainment (being born his subject) which from other princes he had received and peradventure was fitting the person he represented, yet were he not attended with Persians (whose relations at home might peradventure breed him no small disgrace) he would expect no more ceremony than was due unto the person of Robert Sherley." [24] He summarized the proposals he would submit if he were received in England: the English would have the free use of two good ports; silk would be sold to them at such a price as would yield them a profit of 700 per cent; they would have their goods passed free of customs and might maintain consular agents in Persia; the Shah would accept gold and precious stones for his silk so as not to deplete England's supply of silver. The terms were so attractive that Cottington asked why they had not been accepted in Spain. "Because," Sherley replied, "I do require that this King do make invasion of the

Turk and that the imposition [excise tax] of 23 per one hundred be taken off at Lisbon so that Portuguese commodities be sold at easier rate; but in England I will only propound the settling of a trade, and because you shall understand why the Persian shall be contented with that trade only, it is because by it will be diverted that great course of traffic to Constantinople and Aleppo, to the great loss of his enemy the Turk." The proposals, Cottington wrote, "in my poor judgment will not be amiss for England, if he can perform what he promiseth," [25] and later noted that "Mr. Sherley hath here gotten very great reputation through his wise and discreet carriage, he is judged both modest and moreover brave in his speech, diet and expenses, and in my poor opinion to those vices which in Sir Anthony do so abound, in this man may be found the contraries." [26] As they had been the year before, the Spanish were troubled that Sherley wanted to go to England. They pointed out that it was a disservice to the Catholic Church to place such a rich trade in the hands of heretics, that Spain had expended 40,000 ducats for his expenses in addition to the rent on a house, and that it was an ill jest to leave them in this manner.[27]

At this point there was an occurrence which proved a misfortune for Sherley and an advantage to the Spanish. Soon after Count Robert had left Persia, the Shah did what he had so often done before, he dispatched two more ambassadors to Europe in order that their reports might be checked against each other. The two additional ambassadors were the Augustinian, Father Gouvea, and a Persian, Jangiz Beg. According to Father Gouvea, the Shah had originally proposed that Gouvea should be a single ambassador. This Augustinian had had a checkered career and seems to have been governed at times by personal ambition rather than Christian piety; but when it is remembered how eager Shah Abbas was to get rid of Gouvea and how lightly he esteemed the office of ambassador, Gouvea's statement sounds reasonable. Having appointed the friar an ambassador, Shah Abbas then appointed Jangiz Beg an ambassador also. The Shah explained privately to Gouvea (according to the latter) that although Jangiz Beg was nominally his ambassador, actually he was only sending the Persian because he might be useful to the friar.[28] The Carmelites in Persia maintained that Jangiz Beg was not an ambassador but simply a merchant sent to sell silk.[29] Gouvea and Jangiz Beg arrived in Lisbon in September 1610. News of their arrival reached Madrid during the time that Sherley was having his unhappy altercations with the Spanish court. Sherley being still determined to go to England, Philip III's ministers pointed out that it would be only wise for him to wait and learn what message Father Gouvea and Jangiz Beg, then on their way from Portugal, brought from the Shah, and commanded him to remain. Count Robert replied that he was sure the latest emissaries would have no new proposals, nor could they know all the instructions which the Shah had given to himself. Father Gouvea, he declared, had worked to get himself and Jangiz Beg sent as ambassadors. He produced a letter from the Discalced Carmelites in Persia in which those religious declared that when Gouvea had first arrived in Persia from Goa he had claimed to be an ambassador from the King of Portugal, that the Shah was displeased with him, thought him insane, and had asked the Carmelites to get him out of the court.[30] Count Robert feared the harm the two might do him, and his fears were to prove well founded.

In February 1611, Gouvea and Jangiz Beg arrived in Madrid, the latter being recognized by the Venetian ambassador as a merchant who had been at Venice six years previously selling silk.[31] Gouvea advised the King's ministers that although there was some danger in allowing Robert to go to England, he was sure that Sherley had already communicated to Spain's enemies all that he knew about Spain. Fortunately, the friar assured the Spanish court, his companion Jangiz Beg was so trusted by Abbas that by simply writing a letter to the Shah, advising him to treat only with the Spanish, Jangiz Beg could nullify all the evil efforts of Sherley. Jangiz Beg himself declared to the King's councilors that Count Robert was not an ambassador and that the Persian letter of credence he carried did not give him that title.[32] He also assured the court that it was the Shah's wish that Gouvea should be designated Bishop of the Armenians, and upon the urging of Philip III the Pontiff reluctantly created the friar Bishop of Cyrene with jurisdiction over all Armenians in

Persia.[33] Jangiz Beg had brought with him 200,000 ducats worth of the best silk that had been seen in Spain, and the greater part of this he gave as presents to the King and Lerma. He was lodged better and shown more respect than had been accorded Sherley. A month after his arrival Count Robert still had not spoken to him. When, eventually, Gouvea and Jangiz Beg returned to Persia, the former was thrown into prison and the latter was beheaded for giving away silk he had been sent to sell and for maligning Sherley, but at the time the Spanish had no way of knowing how Shah Abbas actually felt about the pair.[34]

Count Anthony Sherley arrived in Madrid about the same time as did the two travelers from Persia. Soon after his arrival, Anthony warned the King's ministers of the damage to Spain his brother could do.[35] He lent his aid to the machinations of the Spanish ministers to detain Robert in Spain, and in April occurred the painful scene, described in the last chapter, when Robert discovered that his brother was plotting against him. Actually Count Robert did not leave Madrid until June. His wife had joined him there in March, and thenceforth she accompanied him on his travels. Sir John Digby, appointed to succeed Cottington as English ambassador at Madrid, met the Sherleys on their way out of Spain as he was on his way to his new post. Digby remarked that the Shah's ambassador seemed to have left Spain without the King's leave, and added "he maketh show to be resolved to come for England," [36] which indicated he rightly suspected that Sherley was not actually headed there. Sir Robert, his lady, and his retinue, which now included Sir John Ferne, traveled to Bayonne and there took passage not for England, but for Rotterdam, where they arrived toward the end of June 1611.

When Count Anthony had been in Morocco there was also a certain Dutchman there, Gilles della (or de la) Faille. Like Anthony, Faille migrated to Spain, and Count Robert may have met him through his brother. In any event, Robert and Faille had planned to form a Dutch company to trade in Persian silk. The merchandise was to be sent to Holland by way of the Cape of Good Hope, and Faille was to be the active director of the company with a salary of 2,000 florins per year.[37] On 1 July 1611, the States General considered the proposals made by the merchant Faille, formerly of Amsterdam, recently of Madrid, and more recently returned to Holland as the representative of Sherley, ambassador of the Shah of Persia. Their High Mightinesses of the States General agreed to preserve the utmost secrecy in their discussions, for Sherley was believed to be still in Spain and would be in the utmost danger if his proposals became known.[38] Actually, although they did not know it, Sherley was at that time no farther away than Rotterdam. Sherley's proposal to divert the Persian silk trade, which went to Portugal by way of Ormuz, to Holland by way of the Cape of Good Hope, was discussed by the States General, as was also the proposal to form a company to carry on the trade. Both proposals were referred to a committee which was instructed to discuss this matter with the directors of the Dutch East India Company. The directors produced four letters written by one Theodore Rodenburg, then in Spain, to the directors of the Guinea Company, which showed more knowledge of the affair than the communications of Faille. The East India Company officials averred that it would be better to send someone directly to Spain to talk to the Persian ambassador than to deal through Gilles de la Faille. They felt, in fact, that both Faille and Sherley were suspect. Faille was thinking only of his own profits, and Sherley was wholly unqualified to deal in such matters. The Levant trade, they advised, ought to be developed on a safe and sane basis. For the past two years the Dutch East India Company's admiral in India had sought to establish a Persian trade, and the matter ought to be left to him.[39] Part of the Dutch lack of confidence in Sherley, says the historian Emanuel Van Meteren, arose from the fact that since Count Robert had long lain in Spain, it was suspected that his real purpose might simply be to make trouble for the Dutch East India Company.[40]

Sir Ralph Winwood reported that while the States General were deliberating, Sherley "hath sent to the States to know if he may have audience, which they have granted, and likewise to be lodged by their appointment [i.e. at their expense] to which demand they make a cold and doubtful answer." [41] As another

English observer put it, "Answer was only made unto Sir John Ferne who he sent unto them, that he was welcome into the country and that if he did come unto The Hague they would so receive him as a public minister, and so returned that knight unto him. He having received this answer, and finding that the States sent not unto him coaches and such like fit conveyance for him and his train as he expected . . . made them to understand that he took it not well . . . and so embarked himself for this place [Flushing]." [42] Sir John Throckmorton, the English governor at Flushing, describing these occurrences to his predecessor, Viscount Lisle, added: "Truly my Lord, he is in my judgment a very fine gentleman and of a good assured speech and fashion and is very well followed." [43]

From Flushing Sir Robert took ship for England, and arriving there went immediately to Wiston. It was a sad homecoming. "It may please your good Lordship," he wrote to Lord Salisbury, "my father at this present, being very sick, is exceedingly troubled in his mind about a seizure which he feareth will shortly come upon him, and all his tenants, in respect of an arrearage of rent which he sayeth is due from him to the King's Majesty for certain parsonages granted by His Highness unto him. . . . The great disreputation which now would happen unto him upon the execution of this business doth beyond measure grieve and trouble my father in this time of his sickness. . . . My father cannot remove the same out of his memory, or take any rest, or contentment for it." [44] To deepen the gloom, Count Robert found that his eldest brother Thomas had been jailed for debt.

In September Robert had a short audience with the King and in the following month was received as the Shah's ambassador. "He went in English dress," said the Venetian ambassador, describing the ceremony, "three paces from the dais he made submission, sinking on his knees and imploring His Majesty's pardon, if he, while still His Majesty's subject, had ventured to accept that office, for he had done so on the express order of the King of Persia. . . . The king was pleased at this manner of proceeding . . . and dismissed him, praising his prudence, eloquence, and modesty after he had retired. So in a few days he will explain his proposals which as far as I understand are two, one is commercial, the other relates to a union of arms against the Turk." [45]

What Sherley had to propose Ambassador Cottington had already outlined for the home government. The English would be accorded two good ports, freedom from customs, and silk at a cheap price. Sherley asked in addition "that His Majesty should admit gentlemen to adventure in fashion of trade and that they might have His Majesty's letters patents for declaration to encourage those that are already well disposed." [46] He did in fact obtain King James's permission to fit out a pinnace and a ship, to be the joint venture of himself, his friends, and the King, who, Sherley explained, "promised graciously to give me assistance likewise in that particular." [47]

King James and Cottington believed that Sherley's proposals promised good profits, but those already in oriental trade had forebodings of large losses. When Count Robert proposed that the King, his friends, and himself should fit out ships for Persia, it was remarkable how many immediately pointed out the sinful inclination of English seamen to take to piracy in distant seas. The Levant merchants who made money from oriental goods carried overland to Aleppo and other Mediterranean ports regarded with virtuous hostility this renegade Papist who proposed to take the bread out of their mouths by sending those same goods around the Cape of Good Hope. For the merchants of the East India Company this proposal to invade their territory with a company of gentlemen, headed by the King, adventuring in fashion of trade, was one more exasperating instance of a tendency which King James had already exhibited a number of times previously. The East India Company had been chartered in December 1600 by Queen Elizabeth. The early voyages were very profitable, seldom yielding a gain of less than 100 per cent. Such gains interested quite a number of people, and previous to Sherley's arrival King James had granted subsidiary licenses to private traders on a number of occasions, licenses which were, of course, infringements of the Company's charter. Count Robert's group of gentlemen adventurers was another case in which the rights of the Company were being disregarded. The view of the Company could not be that of Sherley.

"The merchants make needless oppositions," Sherley complained to Lord Salisbury, "so that it seems they have no will to the Persian business." He warned that "this great business can bear no delays, for of necessity they that first come shall be best welcome." [48] He reminded Salisbury that "I have an earnest desire to speak with you, to know what I am to expect in answer of those things I have proposed in the name of the King which sent me." [49] In December he discussed his proposals with the members of both the Levant Company and the East India Company, but met only evasion and hostility. The merchants were not the only ones who opposed him. The dispatches of the Venetian ambassador were invariably hostile, and this being so it is hardly likely that the diplomat would have let slip other opportunities to disparage Sherley. Archbishop Abbot, the diligent metropolitan of the Church of England, so courageous and God-fearing that he did not hesitate to burn Arians, was also an enemy of Sherley as he was of all Papists. Since the Persians and Turks had agreed on points of trade there was no point, Abbot insisted to the King, in Count Robert's mission and he might just as well go back to Persia.[50]

The Spanish ambassador in England, Don Alonso de Velasco, had orders both to discredit Sherley whenever possible and to hinder him from coming to an agreement with King James. In fact, Velasco was advised that Sherley intended to stir up trouble for Spain in Persia, and Spain's ambassador was admonished to prevent his return to Ispahan. The letter containing this admonition fell into the hands of King James who gave it to Count Sherley.[51] After discovering that Count Robert had gone to Holland, the Spanish did not stick, reported the English ambassador in Spain, to lay every imputation upon him. Whereas previously he had been extolled as a good Catholic, after his departure it was said he had lived in Persia as a Moslem. The Spanish were particularly put out that Sherley had been cordially received by King James, reported Sir John Digby from Madrid, and sought "to discredit and disparage both his person and commissions, not sparing to give him the name of a cozener and of a counterfeit. I tell them that if he be so it is not *he,* but the other princes of Christendom that have deceived the King my master, especially the Emperor, the Pope, and this King; the Emperor having received him with great honors and made him Count of the Empire; the Pope, besides many other favors, making him of his Chamber; and this King entertaining him with much honor, more than a year, and with the expense of at least 50,000 crowns, and none of them seeming to make any doubt or question of the truth or authenticalness of his commission." [52]

The Spanish spread the word that Count Robert had appropriated 15,000 florins of the Shah's money, a charge that grew out of the fact that the same Angelo Gradenigo who had been involved in the trial of Anthony Sherley at Venice had sold in that city in about 1602 a quantity of silk belonging to the Shah of Persia and had kept the money. When Robert arrived at Prague, Gradenigo was at the court. Sherley complained about Gradenigo to the Emperor, whereupon the latter consigned to Count Robert 15,000 florins belonging to the Italian; these were the 15,000 florins of the Shah's money he was said to have appropriated. Count Robert's reply to the Spanish libel was that not only was he empowered to spend that fifteen thousand but he could show letters from the Shah empowering him to spend an additional 25,000 florins.[53] As is usually the case the charge attracted more attention than the rebuttal.

Against the opposition of Spanish, Venetians, East India merchants, Levant merchants, and the Archbishop of Canterbury, Count Robert could make no headway. The East India merchants were resolute that he should return in one of their ships. "Mr. Robert Sherley with his Persian lady," wrote John Chamberlain, "are slipt away homeward in a ship that goes for the East Indies, leaving their little son behind, and bequeathing him to the favor and care of the Queen. He hath stayed here well but to little purpose, having no great reason to haste away, seeing he had allowance of four pounds a day of the King during his abode here." [54]

About a month before noting Count Robert's departure, on 17 December 1612, Chamberlain had also recorded the death of "old Sir Thomas Sherley." [55] Sir Thomas had preserved his amazing versatility almost to the end. "My father (being a man of most excellent and working wit)," wrote young Sir Thomas, "did find out the device for making of baronets which brought to Your Majesty's coffers well nigh a hundred thousand pounds for which he was promised . . . good recompense which he never had." [56] There is little doubt that, as his son said, he had dreamed up the idea of baronets, an honor first sold in 1611, the year prior to his death.[57]

Sir Thomas had not been particularly fortunate. At least one man had made a fortune as paymaster of the forces by the same means that brought Sir Thomas to ruin. Others had made money rather than lost it on impropriate tithes and parsonages and by financing West Indian voyages and privateering expeditions. Still, he had been more fortunate than Sir Philip Sidney and many another who, like himself, had gone soldiering in the Low Countries; and his adventures had led him to a less unhappy end than that of Sir Walter Ralegh, Essex, or others who had ventured much. His acceptance of bribes and presents and his use of funds which did not belong to him were standard practice for the Queen's servants in his day. He ventured into so many things that a very large proportion of the books on the Elizabethan age contain some mention of him, though not all the comments are laudatory. Perhaps old Sir Thomas was not far from being a typical Elizabethan gentleman of parts.

As has been mentioned, when Count Robert first returned to England in the summer of 1611, his brother was in the King's Bench prison for debt, the unfortunate result of a scheme he had embarked on some years earlier. Soon after his release from prison early in 1608 he had obtained a patent to collect old debts due the crown.[58] He agreed to pay £9,000 for his privilege, payable in installments over a period of years. He had failed to keep the agreement and his imprisonment in 1611 was the result. He was again in the King's Bench jail the following year when Count Robert, ambassador from the Shah, was negotiating with the King, and Count Anthony, a retired admiral on a pension, was basking in the sun at Granada. To sit in prison, brooding perhaps on the disparity between their fortunes and his own, was perhaps too much for Sir Thomas and he took poison. Doomed to be thwarted, he was unsuccessful, and recovered.[59] When his father died, he inherited not only the burden of the heavily encumbered Sherley estates but also his father's prerogatives and perquisites. Doubtless remembering how his parent had solved the same problem, Sir Thomas secured immunity from debtors' prison by serving as a member of Parliament. He is listed in 1613 as representing Hastings, and in 1614 and 1615 as representing his own pocket borough of Steyning. These dates do not coincide with those of the Parliaments, but probably he represented Hastings in the Parliament of 1604–1611, and Steyning in the following Parliament. Having achieved a precarious freedom, he turned to the problem of the estates his father had bequeathed him and endeavored by various machinations to salvage something from them, efforts which were to stretch over a decade.

CHAPTER XII

The Further Travels of Count Robert and the Tribulations of Sir Thomas the Younger

AS John Chamberlain had noted, at the beginning of 1613 Count Robert Sherley and his lady, Teresa, slipped away quietly, homeward. "The seventh of January we set sail from Gravesend for the East Indies, in the good ship the *Expedition* of London . . . ," wrote Walter Payton, a factor of the Company who chronicled the voyage, "which carrieth in her fifty-six persons, besides a Persian ambassador and his followers, who are in number fifteen, which we had order to receive into our ship, to be transported into the kingdom of Persia, at the costs and charges of the Worshipful Company [the East India Company] aforesaid. The names of the ambassador and his people are these: Sir Robert Sherley, the ambassador; Teresa, his lady, a Circassian; Sir Thomas Powell; Tomasin, his lady; Leylye, a Persian woman; Morgan Powell, gentleman; Captain John Ward; Francis Bubb, secretary; John Barber, apothecary; John Herriot, musitioner; John Georgson, goldsmith and Hollander; Gabriel, an old Armenian; Nazer Beg, Scander Beg and Molhter, all Persians." [1] The vessel was commanded by Christopher Newport, and Count Robert agreed that for the return trip from Persia he would lade the vessel with silks, carpets, and indigo, on condition that he received one-third of the proceeds from the sale of the goods. The voyage probably was much like that of any other to the East Indies at that time, characterized chiefly by sickness, bad food, spoiled beer, and a general aura of discomfort. By May, some four months after leaving England, the *Expedition* reached Saldanha Bay near the Cape of Good

Hope, where were at anchor two other ships of the East India Company, the *Hector* and *Thomas,* and four Dutch East Indiamen, all homeward bound. On 10 May, a few days after the *Expedition* reached Saldanha, another ship of the East India Company, the *Peppercorn,* homeward bound under Captain Nicholas Downton, arrived in the bay. "She having been long out," said Payton, "was not very well fitted with necessaries which we supplied out of our small store, as well as we could spare." The *Peppercorn* had sailed in company with another Company ship, *Trade's Increase,* commanded by Sir Henry Middleton, the "General" of the voyage, in 1610. The two ships had anchored off Surat and had been scurvily treated there. In revenge they sailed for the Red Sea and there plundered what Indian vessels they could find, not being careful to exclude Turkish vessels. The two ships had then sailed to Java, where Middleton had died, and the *Trade's Increase,* which was riddled with worms, was abandoned. When Captain Downton, a truly valorous and remarkable man, brought the *Peppercorn* into Saldanha Bay, the ship had been at sea about three years. "The haste I made on my way," Downton reported to the Company, "was with most industry; the misfortunes by leaks bred me much disquietness, the sickness and death of my men was to me most grievous, and the long foul weather and adverse winds, before I came to Cape Bona Speranza, was to me (in regard of the imminent peril and want of ropes and sails) most tedious." [2] Payton's remark that the *Peppercorn* was not well fitted with necessaries was an understatement. While in Saldanha Bay, Downton became well acquainted with Sherley, and more than a year later he wrote to Count Robert that "besides the ancient desire long dwelling in me for to understand or find out fit place for ships safely to ride and do business within the King of Persia his dominions, the little conference I had with your Honour at Saldanha of the hopes within land for sales of cloth and other of our country commodities, or to barter and exchange them for the commodities of those countries, together with your report of the magnanimity and noble virtues of that King, much increase my desire that our countrymen may have intercourse into Persia." [3] After remaining in Saldanha Bay some days, the *Hector, Thomas,* and *Peppercorn* departed homeward, while those aboard the *Expedition* were bent upon "determining their course for towards the confines of Persia, to some place where they might in safety land Sir Robert Sherley."

The *Expedition* coasted along Baluchistan hunting a suitable spot to land Count Sherley. The country was largely inhabited by nomadic tribes of various races, and the laws of Shah Abbas hardly reached the coasts of that region. It was decided that the most suitable place was Gwatar Bay and there the ship dropped anchor. The inhabitants brought aboard as presents two goats, fresh fish, and dates, "so that," says Payton, "what with their exterior show of unfeigned love and kindness towards us, together with all men's speeches . . . we were thoroughly persuaded, without any kind of distrust, that they meant us as well as they said; especially, the Lord Ambassador was exceedingly well conceited of them, being joyful to arrive in Persia in twenty days [from Saldanha Bay], and we not sorry in bringing to perfection our long desired hopes." [4] Before Sherley and his party were put ashore it was fortunately discovered "that the Viceroy and governor did entice so many of us as they could ashore, of purpose to cut our throats, which being done, they meant to have set upon our ship, and to have made spoil of all. . . . Also, that they had made enquiry of every particular man in our ship both of our places, profession and estates; for they had consulted and concluded upon the massacre of us all." The attempt to land in Baluchistan was given up, and the ship sailed for India, dropping anchor at the mouth of the Indus, off Diul Sinde, or Larbandar, the port for Tatta, a day's journey up river. There was a Portuguese settlement at Diul Sinde and it was decided to leave Sherley there. "At the Ambassador's departing out of the ship," relates Payton, "we entreated his Lordship that he would send us word how he found the country, and whether we might have trade there or not." Accordingly Sherley enquired of the governor of Diul Sinde whether the East India Company would be permitted to trade there, and on being assured by the governor that he would be interested in trade proposals, he sent Payton and another Company servant, Joseph Salbank, ashore to negotiate.

Although Payton and Salbank did not know it, Captain Best of the Company's ship *Red Dragon*, having proved his valor by decisively defeating a fleet of Portuguese vessels off Surat, had already obtained in January 1613 from the Moghul or Emperor the right to establish a factory (i.e. a trading post) at Surat and at three other places around the Bay of Cambay. Now, five months later, Payton and Salbank were informed by this Indian governor that "we were very welcome, and that he was glad to see Englishmen in those parts; and proceeded to further talk concerning our business, and told us (whereas we desired trade) the Portugals would not consent that we should drive any trade, or have to do where they were, threatening to be gone if he did entertain us." The English did, in fact, meet with instant hostility from the Portuguese, for when Sherley showed the governor his credentials as the Shah's ambassador, "as also the King of Spain's pass, thinking thereby to satisfy and resolve the jealous doubts of the Portugal's lieger there (who reported, upon intelligence from Ormuz, that Don Roberto Sherley was come forth of England with three ships into the Indies of purpose to steal) . . . they [the Portuguese] peremptorily denied credence to any writing he showed them." After that encounter relations between the Portuguese and the English grew worse. On one occasion, as the Portuguese crowded about Sherley and his companions, Payton told them "that they were a shameless and lying people in spreading of so many devised scandals and slanderous reports of our nation. . . . Also I told them," continued Payton, "that if they did not contain themselves within the compass of better peace, reforming themselves hereafter . . . they should be all rooted out of the Indies, and a more honest and royal nation placed in their rooms." [5] The Indian governor of Diul Sinde was little more than a tool of the Portuguese, and after the departure of the *Expedition* both the Indians and Portuguese grew bolder in their maltreatment of the English.

A letter was received at Ormuz from Philip III warning the Portuguese there that Sherley had negotiated in England to buy vessels with which to attack that fortress. The Spanish king insisted that Ormuz be strengthened against the attack and sent instructions that no means should be spared to capture Sherley. As a consequence, it was reported that twelve men were sent from Ormuz to Diul Sinde to assassinate Count Robert. Count Sherley himself stated that as a matter of fact twenty-five or thirty-five Portuguese soldiers arrived by ship from Ormuz with orders to do him in. "He [Sherley] sought liberty to go to Tatta," Payton was later told, "but the governor not permitting (as was thought of evil purpose), he went without leave, and was by the way to pass a river, where none durst carry him or his, being prohibited on pain of death by the said governor. They therefore made rafts of boards and timbers, on which the Ambassador shipped himself with Nazer Beg, one of his followers, to help him over, and were no sooner put off, but twenty or thirty horsemen came from the governor in great haste to stay them. Thus they were brought back, men swimming to the raft, which Nazer Beg was not able to guide against the tide, and they narrowly escaped drowning. His followers, disdaining this rude dealing, one Master John Ward shot off his pistol in their faces, and was instantly slain by another shot, and the rest carried away prisoners to Diul Sinde, being pillaged by the way of the soldiers."

News of Sherley's treatment at Diul Sinde reached the Great Moghul, who dispatched a letter, "commanding the governor to treat him courteously, to give him assistance and send him to the Court, who [the governor] now fearing the event of the injuries done conspired with the Portingals to mischief the English, which they put in practice, and in the dead of night some forty or fifty of them with pots of powder and suchlike provision, burnt their house, yet in the end they were expulsed without effecting their purposes." According to Count Robert, he lay very ill in his house for twenty days, and it was while in this condition, unable to defend himself, that the Portuguese set fire to his house. He himself, he declared, had been almost miraculously pulled from the burning building by his wife, but a number of his servants were killed, and in fact only six escaped.[6] Since there was no alternative, the governor at Diul Sinde allowed Sherley to go to Tatta, but his treatment in that city was not much better. Nicholas Withington, a Company factor who had arrived in India with Captain Best in 1612, reported that, on one occasion, "toward night I met with a Banian [a pedlar] who came that day from Tatta, who told me that Sir Robert Sherley, with his wife and three or four English women with seven or eight Englishmen, were in Tatta. . . . He told me how Sir Robert had been much abused at Loribander [Diul Sinde] . . . and likewise at his arrival at Tatta. . . . Mirza Rustam, then governor of Tatta for the Mogul, used him very unkindly and took from him jewels and what else soever pleased him, purposing to send him up to the Mogul. In this estate he left Sir Robert this last night when he was at Sir Robert's house."[7] Sherley remained at Tatta two months before going on to Ajmer where the Great Moghul, or Emperor, then was. The latter received him kindly, giving him 12,000 rupees and half as much again in jewels. When he heard the details of Count Robert's maltreatment at Diul Sinde, the Great Moghul ordered that the governor be put in irons and that his house should be sacked, both of which commands were carried out. The Great Moghul, related Count Robert, also imprisoned the Portuguese who had assaulted him, confiscated their property, and offered to give Sherley both the lives and the property of the recreant Portuguese.

At Ajmer Sherley became good friends with Thomas Kerridge, an East India Company servant who became president of the factory at Surat, and Robert wrote for Kerridge a description of the ports on the Persian side of the Arabian Sea which later proved useful to the Company; he also warned Kerridge, "if the English come not shortly into Persia as he hath advised, that then he will bring the Dutch into that trade, who as he saith have been very importunate on him for it."[8]

Count Robert left Ajmer on 10 September for Agra, where he arrived five days later; and on 25 September 1614, almost exactly a year after he had first landed in India, he left Agra for Persia by the overland caravan route. "He stayed here only ten days . . . and so departed," wrote Nicholas Withington, "carrying the Frenchman's elephant with him, and swore to me, he would make him juggle for another. . . . He seemeth to be no great friend to the Company, yet makes show to do something concerning our trade in Persia." [9] Of Count Robert's original party there remained only Teresa Sherley, her maid, the old Armenian, and the three Persians. "The English that came with him since their landing are all dead," Thomas Kerridge remarked, "an apothecary only excepted who left his service." [10] As Count Robert was making his way to Persia, he met that inveterate sightseer Thomas Coryate. "About the middle of the way, betwixt Ispahan and Lahore," reported the latter, it then being about Christmas 1614, "I met Sir Robert Sherley and his lady . . . so gallantly furnished with all necessaries for their travels that it was a great comfort unto me to see them in such a flourishing estate. . . . Besides other rarities that they carried with them out of India, they had two elephants and eight antelopes. . . . These they meant to present to the Persian king." Count Sherley and his lady provided Coryate with funds, but what seemed equally important to him, "they seemed to exult for joy to see me." [11]

About the middle of June 1615, two and a half years after leaving England, and six and a half years after leaving Ispahan, Count Robert arrived back in that city, where, Sherley related, "the Shah, King of Persia, received him with very great honors and expressions of joy as is well known; and he [the Shah] was so well satisfied with what he had done in his service that he could not say enough about it to his nobles and repeated his praises many times." He was also, declared Count Robert, given greater gifts and privileges than the Shah had ever before bestowed. During his absence the Shah had greatly improved the position of Persia. Kandahar had been recovered from the Great Moghul, and peace had been signed with the Turk in 1611. Being at last free to deal with the Portuguese, Abbas had captured their port of Gombroon on the mainland and renamed it Bandar Abbas. Ormuz was on an island, and to reduce that fortress shipping and landing craft were needed, but the Shah could and did cut off the supply of water and provisions going into Ormuz. At the time Sherley returned, Abbas had resolved to send another mission to Europe, chiefly to reassure and lull the Spanish while he negotiated with one of the maritime powers, England or Holland, for help in reducing Ormuz. The embassy was also to buy the needed ships, an order which later caused trouble for Count Robert. "After having read the letters which he [Sherley] brought from the Christian sovereigns," wrote the Carmelite Father Redentor de la Cruz, who subsequently returned to Europe with Sherley, "and seen the laudatory mention they made of his good sense, and his method of procedure, so prudent in dealing with business, the Shah determined to send him back once more, not caring to dispatch a Muslim on account of the bad reports he had had of all those who had gone to Europe, how they committed a thousand outrages and got drunk to the great disgust of the European sovereigns and to his own discredit and dishonor, so different to Count Robert's methods." [12]

Accordingly, the Shah told Sherley "that it would be rendering him a great service, were he to turn back and undertake once more this journey and embassy. At those words he [Sherley] became very upset, his heart transfixed by an arrow as it were, recalling in his imagination all that he had suffered on (his last) so lengthy a journey. So he refused to go . . . saying . . . that he had not had a single day's rest after . . . so many trials that he had suffered in company with his wife, and they would greatly desire that the Shah should desist and not send him to Spain, where he had been so discredited and made the object of baseless calumnies." [13] Count Robert later consulted the Carmelites on whether or not he should undertake the embassy for the Shah. They advised him to go and he acquiesced. In giving the Shah his decision, perhaps remembering the credence Assad Beg had enjoyed in Spain through the support of Friar Gouvea, Sherley said that unless he had permission to take one of the Discalced Carmelites with him to Spain he would not go, even if the Shah ordered his body to be chipped to pieces. The Shah assented, adding that if Robert did not return to Ispahan he would cut the remaining six Carmelites into bits. In the letters which Sherley was to carry to foreign princes, the Shah stated that not only was Count Robert his ambassador on this occasion, but that he had been his ambassador on his first visit to Europe. Before Count Robert left Persia, the first representatives of the East India Company, Richard Steel and

John Crouther, arrived in that country. "Richard Steel reached thither [Ispahan] the fifteenth [of September] at noon," wrote John Crouther, "and found Sir Robert Sherley dispatched from the Persian King in embassage to the King of Spain, with him his lady, and for his chaplain a friar of the barefoot order. . . . The purpose is, that seeing the Portugals are not able to stand, the Spaniards may be brought in, six friars remaining in hostage till his return at Ispahan, whom otherwise the king hath vowed to cut in pieces, which he is likely enough to do." [14] The official instructions for Crouther and Steel on being ordered to Persia were that they should proceed to Ispahan and inform themselves on the possibilities of trade in the country; that they should deliver the letters to Sir Robert Sherley; and that they should keep two copies of a joint journal, one copy to be carried to London by Steel and the other to Agra by Crouther. The two Company servants carried letters for Sherley from both Kerridge and Nicholas Downton. Kerridge had provided Steel and Crouther with a copy of Sherley's notes on Persian ports which Count Robert had given him in India, and also wrote to Count Robert, soliciting his efforts "for his furtherance in their business." [15] Captain Downton wrote to Sherley that "when in the *Peppercorn* I parted from you at Saldanha . . . I little thought . . . to have written to your Honor into Persia." Downton then related that having consulted with Thomas Aldworthe (in charge of the Company factory at Surat), with Richard Steel, and with others, he was desirous of opening trade in the Shah's dominions. "I purpose to put the India Company," he wrote, "to that expense in sending this bearer Richard Steel to you into Persia, desiring your help in this business. . . . If it prove well, the India Company will not fail to be thankful to you. . . . The thing principally to entreat you for is to move the king, and know his Majesty's pleasure, whether he will grant and give his firman and chop [edict] for the subjects of the King of England to have free intercourse and peaceable commerce throughout all his dominions, which if His Highness will grant, then that it may please him that Jask may be prepared by his directions for the courteous entertainment of the English . . . and also that it may please you to give Richard Steel, who is now the India Company's servant, all furtherance for his information concerning merchandising business, as also your help for his quiet passage out of Persia homewards." [16]

Richard Steel delivered his letters to Sir Robert, who, declared Crouther, "durst scarcely read them, but now and then by stealth, fearing the Portugals should know of them. He after said it was too late to look after that business for our nation, and seemed discontent with the Company, and the master and merchants which landed him. But at last said he was an Englishman, and promised to effect our desires, and (the Friars being absent) carried both on the nineteenth to the Master of the ceremonies or maimondare, and took us with him to the Great Vizier, Sarek Hogea, who presently called his scrivans and made draughts of what we desired; viz., three firmans, one which John Crouther hath for Surat, one for Richard Steel to carry into England; the third sent to Jask to the Governor. All are sealed with the King's great seal, and to this effect, that all governors of sea ports within His Majesty's dominions shall kindly entertain the English shipping, etc. The same day that these firmans were ended, departed Sir Robert Sherley, being the last of September, toward Shiraz, with great pomp and much honor." [17] In his report Richard Steel remarked that they had spent twenty-five days at Ispahan, "the one-half was in following of Sir Robert Sherley for this firmans received."

Sherley, with the Carmelite, Father Redentor, left Ispahan on 10 October 1615. He had persuaded the Shah to empower him to gather up the Portuguese who had been taken prisoner at Gombroon when the Persians had captured that Portuguese port and to return them as a peace offering to the Portuguese governor at Ormuz. These unfortunate Europeans were held as slaves by various people scattered over the countryside, who hid them on the approach of Count Robert. Sherley nevertheless gathered up the greater number of the enslaved Portuguese and, says Father Redentor de la Cruz, "attended to their bodily necessities giving them food and clothing." With seventy of these freed men Count Robert entered Ormuz amid great jubilation. In accordance with the Shah's new benevolent policy, which was to endure until he was in a position to take a hostile one, Sherley re-established friendly relations between Persia and the Portuguese. About a month later Count Robert and his entourage sailed from Ormuz to Goa, which they reached on 24 February 1616. Having missed the annual convoy going to Spain, they were forced to remain in Goa the whole of the year 1616. There were those in that city, recounts Father Redentor de la Cruz, who said that Count Robert and his wife were heretics, that Sherley had conspired against the King of Spain, and that he was now returning to Spain with a deceitful intent.

At this time there was in Goa a Spanish noble, Don García Silva y Figueroa, who had been dispatched from Spain as ambassador to Shah Abbas. It will be remembered that in 1610, when Count Robert was previously in Spain, Sherley had urged that a Spanish ambassador should be dispatched to Persia that very year. The Spanish crown had appointed Silva y Figueroa, "an ancient decayed gentleman," and by 1616, four years later, in the good Spanish tradition, he had gotten as far as Goa. Don García had heard the suspicions and calumnies regarding Sherley which were rife after Count Robert had left Spain for the Netherlands and England in 1611, and since he later lost no opportunity to disparage Sherley he probably did so while the two were in Goa.

There must also have been many in Goa who remembered that Count Robert was the Englishman who had left Spain without the King's permission and had gone to Holland and England, and whom the officials of Goa had been instructed at all costs to prevent from returning to Persia. A renegade named Reeve escaped from Goa and reported that the Portuguese there, fearing that Sherley would learn too much about their shipping and fortifications, kept him practically a prisoner, being only allowed out of his home by the Viceroy's order, although Count Robert occasionally escaped for a short breath of liberty disguised as a Spaniard.[18] His retinue was likewise kept cooped up. Sherley and his companions did not actually leave Goa on the return journey to Spain until early in 1617. When the water supply ran short on the long voyage the religious aboard were supplied from the casks of the Shah's ambassador, and the poor aboard were given food and drink by Sherley and his lady. The ship arrived at Lisbon on 27 September 1617, almost nine months after leaving India.

The new mission to Spain was in many respects a repetition of that of 1609–1611. Sherley did not finally leave that country until the end of March 1622, after four and a half years of interviews, questions, proposals, postponements, and frustrations. The Spanish sought at first to avoid the expense of entertaining the Persian ambassador by taking the view that since he had come to discuss trade at Ormuz his business was with Portugal and that he ought to remain at Lisbon, where he had disembarked, and take up the matter with the Viceroy for Portugal. Sherley maintained that he was accredited to the King and refused to enter into discussions until he had been received by the King. In the end Madrid capitulated. Count Robert was given 1,800 ducats per month for his expenses and the use of a coach and four by the Spanish crown, but Sherley was so displeased with his reception that he sent a letter to the Shah asking that the Spanish ambassador in Persia, García Silva y Figueroa, should be detained until he was himself given more satisfactory treatment. A copy of this letter fell by accident into the hands of Silva y Figueroa.[19] That unfortunate diplomat had been having a most difficult time in Persia. The Shah had seen him briefly in the summer of 1618, but he was kept waiting a year for a second audience. At the second interview, he demanded from the Shah restitution of Gombroon and other Portuguese possessions; the Shah interrupted him and finally turned his back on the Castilian. When Sherley's letter to the Shah fell by accident into his hands, Silva y Figueroa took it as final proof that the Shah had no feeling of amity for Spain and that he had sent Count Robert, not to negotiate in good faith, but simply to divert the Spanish with talk of friendship and profitable trade until such time as he felt strong enough to strike at Ormuz, an estimate of the Shah's attitude which was, in fact, perfectly accurate.

The news of Robert's arrival brought his brother up from Granada. "Sir Anthony is also here," the English ambassador noted, "but a very poor man and much neglected, yet the King gives him 3,000 ducats every year by quarterly payments but he hath so pawned and spent it, as he is sometimes like to starve for want of bread; the poor man comes sometimes to my house and is as full of vanity as ever he was, making himself believe that he shall one day be a great prince, when for the present he wants shoes to wear; the two brothers are much fallen out, and both by word and writing do all the harm they can in defaming each other, but I must needs confess that the ambassador is the discreeter of the two." [20]

While Count Robert had been cooped up in Goa, suffering the long voyage home, and spending frustrating years in Spain, the English East India Company had continued its efforts to establish trade in Persia. Sir Thomas Roe had been appointed ambassador to the Moghul, and although he was officially the envoy of King James, he was paid by the Company. Roe arrived at Surat on 15 September 1615. He reached India, then, after the East India Company's servants in India had dispatched Crouther and Steel to Persia and, indeed, about the same time Crouther and Steel saw Count Robert before the latter's departure for Europe. By sending Crouther and Steel to Persia, the merchants of the Company had infringed Roe's prerogative and wounded his ambassadorial dignity, for he was accredited not only to the Great Moghul but also to the kings of "the bordering nations." Partly from pique, as the merchants became more eager for this new trade, Roe became more reluctant to embark on it, and since Sherley had urged trade with Persia he became anti-Sherley. Soon after Count Robert left Persia, Crouther and Steel sent word to Roe from Ispahan that Sherley had been dispatched to Spain by the Shah "with an offer unto the King of Spain of the whole trade of his gulf, and place to fortify, and they to have all the trade of his silks and other commodities solely to themselves, which is thought will be a great hindrance to our trade here." [21] Such a report confirmed Roe in his opinion that the merchants of the Company had been totally unwise in trusting Sherley and in venturing upon the Persian trade without proper protocol and investigation. The merchants attempted to mollify Roe. "What Sir Robert Sherley could say I have often heard," Kerridge wrote to King James's ambassador to justify the Persian trade, "and in that I knew his ends, I think I erred not; which perchance I might declare to your satisfaction, but why should I wrong him that trusted me? . . . For the benefit to be expected by the Persian trade I know no more than he promised which is enough to encourage prosecution." [22] In September 1616, when the Indian market for cloth was already saturated, a Company fleet arrived in Swally Road, the anchorage off Surat, laden with shiploads of unsalable textiles. On 2 October the Company servants, both those who had come with the fleet and those stationed at Surat, faced with the fact that the Company had "sent divers sorts of commodities at present not vendible in these parts," met to consider what could be done. They noted that John Crouther had brought from Persia "a firman or command from the King of Persia, directed to his viceroy, governor of ports, etc., importing the fair entertainment of the English nation into any port or ports of his dominions," and also "very large encouragement . . . to settle trade and commerce in these parts of Persia . . . as also the King's exceeding great desire to entertain traffic with our nation." The merchants further noted "that Sir Robert Sherley is now absent . . . who would either hinder us, or to our great charge (as we suppose) lend us his furtherance; that the war between the Turk and the Persian having (as we understand) shut the intercourse of merchandise between the two countries, it is likely that both a dearth of cloth, wontedly brought thither from Turkey, and the cheapness of silk thence formerly transported into Turkey, must consequently follow." [23] In view of these propitious circumstances it was resolved to send a small ship, the *James,* laden principally with cloth, to the port of Jask, not far from Ormuz, to explore the possibility of trade. That the merchants had sent Steel and Crouther to Persia without his approval had made Roe indignant; that they should dispatch a ship to that country made him furious. It indicated, he thought, their "haste and lack of respect to me." He observed to Sir Thomas Smythe that "however your factors love to run without me, I will look out to mend their faults and, like patient Job, pray and sacrifice for them, as he did for his sons while they banqueted." [24] Yet it appeared to Roe that possibly the rash acts of the merchants, by the sagacity of a discreet ambassador, might yet be turned to a useful purpose.

"The use can be made . . . of this ship [the *James,* previously sent to Jask]," Roe wrote to Sir Thomas Smythe, "is that, seeing Sir Robert Sherley hath been stayed at Goa by God's providence this year, that His Majesty will be pleased to command his Ambassador resident in Spain to be attentive upon the arrival of Sherley, that when he [Sherley] hath delivered his message . . . he may require an audience and take notice of the Persian overture, and require the King of Spain in the name of His Majesty not to prejudice the subjects of England by this new contract, for that the Persian hath already, by his command sealed, given them free trade, and upon assurance thereof you have sent a ship: that it is a free kingdom, and if the peace or league be made to the expulsion of our nation, it is a just occasion of breach . . . and withal to declare that if they proceed to exclude us they must resolve of a war in that quarter, for if they [the East India Company merchants] cannot trade like merchants, they will like men of war." [25] A few days after writing to Smythe, Roe wrote to Sir Ralph Winwood. "Some few days since," he declared, "I received advice from Ispahan that Sherley hath written to the King [the Shah] that with much joy and ready embracement he hath so far proceeded with the Viceroy of Goa in a conclusion of this league as his [the Viceroy's] commission hath power, and that he is ready to embark for Spain to accomplish it fully. If it proceed and take effect . . . it will revive and strengthen all the ruins and decays of the Portugalls in the Indies." [26] Roe could not let the matter rest there, but on the same day wrote to a "Right Honorable Councillor" suggesting that "when Sir Robert Sherley shall arrive in Spain . . . the ambassador of His Majesty resident may crave audience, and produce the letters granted to us, and urge our possession of the port [Jask]; and therefore require in the name of His Majesty that in this new contract [between the Shah and Spain] either the English may be comprehended or at least that nothing pass on the part of the King of Spain prejudicial to the subjects of His Majesty." [27]

Count Robert had a good friend in Ispahan, one William

Robbins, who made a living dealing in jewels and who acted as Sherley's agent during his absence. Roe made efforts to enlist Robbins' support and to undermine his friendship for Sherley. "This business [the Company's trade in Persia] sincerely and discreetly handled," Roe advised him, "may be a fortune to you as great as unexpected. You know not whether God in his providence sent you out to do service to that land that gave you life. Trust not too much to him [Sherley] whom you know in religion is opposite to us and in his practices but lukewarm. He may deceive you, when a Company will not." [28] He had further advice for Robbins. "Open the King's [Shah's] eyes that he be not blinded with the smoky air of Spanish greatness. . . . You are an Englishman; show it rightly." [29] He later complained to Robbins that "I find in all your letters you have a belief that Sir Robert Sherley is a well wisher to his country and an enemy to the Portugals. I would persuade you out of this error. His actions show little reason. He hath not only procured for them a peace, but is engaged to procure for them the whole traffic, and to that end he is employed." [30] Roe was encouraged in his anti-Sherley efforts by that great and good man Archbishop Abbot. "Sherley's children," the latter observed to his friend Roe, "have all been shifters, venturing on great matters, carrying high shows, and in the end coming to beggary. . . . Sir Thomas is in the Fleet for debt, Sir Anthony in Spain has his pension seized for debt and is barely kept from starving; Sir Robert if he have any religion is a Papist . . . in a word you know that he is a hungry fellow and liveth merely by his wit." [31]

While Sir Robert was on the voyage to Spain the chief merchant of the East India Company, Edward Connock, was in Ispahan. He was greatly impressed by the quantity of Persian silk available. One could easily buy, he observed, a million pounds worth of silk per year. The opportunities for trade in Persia were greater than the Company could handle. Since Count Robert was then on his way to Spain, "you may please to pause and well consider," he admonished the Company, "that as well your Aleppo and Turkey trade (Sir Sherley effecting his embassy) will wholly decay, as the trade of silks from China (which I take you aim at), when these great quantities shall be yearly brought even at your doors, will soon turn to nought. The Spaniard besides will hereby grow rich, strong, and yet prouder in these seas . . . when then will follow that as well we, as the French, Hollanders, and Italians shall be forced of them to rebuy." [32] With regard to any treaty the Shah might make with Spain, he proposed to say frankly to the Shah "that the commodity of silk, having and still being our chiefest trade from out of Turkey, we may so rightly challenge to be due to us alone; that justly we may require whatsoever prince . . . to desist from intercepting such our trade and without breach of peace thereto require him by the bullet." Connock promised "in the interim, for a full stop to Sir Sherley's embassy to contact with the Spaniard, I will endeavor that this King by his letters do suspend, if not restrain, his conditions and order for treaty, and if I obtain I will speedily send them you." [33]

The fears of Sir Thomas Roe, Edward Connock, and other Company servants were groundless. As has been indicated, Count Robert spent four and a half frustrated, futile years in Spain. In March 1622 Sir Walter Aston, the English ambassador in Madrid, reported that "Sir Robert Sherley who hath now been here some years with a Persian embassage is at length dispatched and ready to be gone, but I do not understand that he hath concluded anything of importance. He hath here been well entertained, and hath now 8,000 ducats given him for the charges of his way." [34] Aston also noted that there had departed from Lisbon "four caraques with a new vice king for Goa, and in their company four tall ships of war with soldiers and a new governor for Ormuz." Aston was convinced that there was some truth in a rumor "lately spread in the Court that the King of Persia quarrels with the Portuguese for what they possess in the Gulf of Persia, but considering the Persian hath no shipping, he will doubtless be able to do little hurt unto Ormuz." [35]

Actually the Shah no longer needed shipping. Ormuz was taken in April 1622 with the reluctant help of ships of the East India Company, which Shah Abbas forced into the operation by the threat that unless the vessels took part in the attack the Company would be excluded from further trade in Persia. In return the Company got a small share of the plunder; their goods were passed free of Persian customs; and it was agreed that the English would receive half the customs collected at Ormuz, which they never did, although they received part of the customs for a long time.

About three and a half years previously Count Robert had written for the Spanish court "a description of my voyage and pilgrimage and of the hardships and shipwreck which overtook me until my arrival in Spain, . . . the danger to which I was exposed in the service of God and of Your Majesty, and also . . . what the Portuguese have done to me." After the fall of Ormuz someone, probably Secretary Arostegui, got out the account and reread it. "It would be as well to read this statement of Count Robert Sherley," he wrote in the margin, "so as to appreciate how he was treated here, because it can be inferred that as this ambassador was not listened to in Spain, the King of Persia opened hostilities and through his orders Ormuz was taken." [36]

On leaving Spain Count Robert went first to Florence and then to Rome, being received courteously and entertained generously both by the Grand Duke of Tuscany and by the Pope. He then went on to Poland, and may even have gotten as far as Moscow, but suddenly turned back. Perhaps his courage failed him when he contemplated the long road ahead. Perhaps he intended to go to England when he left Spain, but remembering the sinister Spanish efforts in 1611 to prevent his reaching England he threw the Spanish off the scent by leading them to think that he was on his way back to Persia. Later the East India merchants charged that he had actually attempted to reach Persia but had been turned back by the Czar who had forbidden him to pass through Russia. The precise movements of Count Robert after reaching Poland remain a mystery.

Suddenly in December 1623, twenty months after leaving Spain, he appeared in England. "Sir Robert Sherley with his Persian wife is come hither again out of the clouds I think," wrote Chamberlain to Carleton, "for I cannot learn where he hath been all this while, but he requires audience in quality of an ambassador, which I hear is granted him at Newmarket, because he lies not far off at his sister's the Lady Crofts which is the best retreat and means he hath here." [37] By this time Sir Thomas the younger had sold Wiston and moved to the Isle of Wight, so that except for his sister's house Robert was homeless. On this occasion he remained three years and three months in England, a sojourn remarkably and discouragingly like his first appearance as Persian ambassador. He was given an audience by the King on 27 January 1624 and presented his letters of credence, "un-understood," says Sir John Finett, "for want of an interpreter, nowhere to be found in England."

The English, as had the Spanish, sought to avoid the expense of so distinguished a visitor. Secretary Conway advised both the Levant Company and the East India Company that Count Robert had come with an offer of free trade and that his expenses would have to be defrayed. At the mention of defraying an ambassador's expense, because of previous sad experiences both companies took fright. In 1617, for example, an ambassador had arrived from Russia. The Muscovy Company was at that time in financial straits, and King James had insisted that the Muscovy and East India Companies should merge for two years. Bowing to the royal command the East India Company merged with the Muscovy merchants, and the new joint company had then been saddled with the expenses of the Russian ambassador. That event had occurred seven years previously; in the case of the Persian embassy of Count Robert, the Levant Company made haste to say that they were "very confident it can be no way advantageous nor appertaining unto us as merchants trading into the dominions of the Grand Signor . . . and so we conceive that proposition made by Sir Robert Sherley concerning the trade into Persia cannot properly appertain unto us nor be profitable or useful in our trade and so the charge no way belonging unto us." [38] The East India Company were equally sure that they could not be held responsible for Sherley's expenses. In March 1624, all else failing, James granted Sherley thirty pounds per week. Later the sum was increased to forty pounds, but still later the crown repented such generosity.

The prospects of large profits to be made in the Persian trade were so attractive that, as on Count Robert's first embassage, James I became personally interested. "The King has long since taken to heart the proposition of the Persian ambassador for drawing the trade of Persia silks into this kingdom," wrote Secretary Conway to Sir John Coke, "but jealousy, malice, or covetousness hath made the East India Company so averse that all the reasons urged by the Privy Council could not move them." [39] Conway sought Coke's advice on the kind of a commission that should be issued, the number of ships needed, and what profits could be held out to draw in adventurers to join with the Prince, Duke, and other nobles in this enterprise of the Persian trade. Sherley had the sympathy of Conway, but he was an ally of doubtful value. He was a good soldier, although as a secretary of state he was able only to think whatever Buckingham thought at the moment. King James jocularly observed that "Steenie [Buckingham] . . . had given him a secretary who could neither read nor write."

A few weeks after Conway sought the advice of Coke, the Governor of the East India Company reported to the court of the Company that King James "was now resolved, with the assistance of his nobility and such others as would join with him, to pursue that trade his own way, hoping to bring the whole trade of the Persian silk upon freight hither into England by contract between the two kings." [40] The Privy Council, taking up the matter, considered "*First,* whether it were feasible to have all or the greatest part of the Persian silks to be brought into England and here to have the staple made of that rich commodity . . . ; *Secondly,* whether it would be profitable for this kingdom in case it may be effected." The Privy Councilors consulted the merchants of the East India Company, and decided "that in case it would be effected . . . it must needs be very beneficial to this kingdom." [41] Later at a meeting at the house of Sir Thomas Smythe, the Governor of the East India Company (the frugal Company used Smythe's house as its headquarters for a number of years), a treaty between the Shah and the King was again discussed, and it was "agreed by all parties to be the only means to draw the greatest part of Europe's money hither, in making the staple of the Persian raw silks here." [42] It was also decided that a ship should be dispatched immediately to load raw silk in Persia. Unfortunately, King James died in March 1625, and Sir Thomas Smythe, who had at least acquiesced in the scheme, died about five months later. These two events sounded the death knell of a royal monopoly of the silk trade in England. The new Governor of the Company, Morris Abbot, a brother of the zealous Archbishop, declared "the Company's resolution to follow the trade as merchants. . . . The Company have no need of Sir Robert's help, and neither desire to have anything to do with him . . . that the King [Shah] would not trust his silk for England, and never trusted them with more silk than they had stock in his kingdom to satisfy." [43] The Company now proclaimed on all possible occasions that Count Robert was an impostor, and subsequently produced a Persian ambassador of their own to prove it. Since, as the reader is by now well aware, multiple Persian ambassadors frequently appeared anyway, and since the Dutch East India Company had, at the cost of 100,000 florins, persuaded Shah Abbas to send a Persian ambassador to Holland, the action of the Company was adroit but neither difficult nor original. The Shah, of course, regarded ambassadors lightly. When the English East India Company had first sent one of its servants to his court, Abbas was puzzled to know the Englishman's status. It was explained to the Shah that the Englishman was a company agent rather than an ambassador, but there was no Persian word for agent. It was finally decided that an agent was an *elchee cachit*, or petty ambassador. When the East India Company asked for an ambassador to take to London at their expense he gave the Company one, Nuqd Ali Beg, designating him an *elchee cachit*, or agent, or petty ambassador, but what the designation meant and why the Shah had used it was not known in England. When he arrived there in February 1626, aboard a Company ship, Nuqd Ali Beg promptly and dutifully proclaimed that Sherley was an impostor and that his credentials were forgeries. The Company, to welcome the Persian "with an affected honor, beyond that done to the other Persian ambassador, Sir Robert Sherley," remarked Sir John Finett, "had procured the King's coach to be drawn with eight horses as with the more grace to the latter to disgrace the former." [44] Sherley's friend, the Earl of Cleveland, arranged an interview between Count Robert and Nuqd Ali Beg, which was described by Sir John Finett in detail: "Entering the hall (where he was then sitting in a chair on his legs double under him, after the Persian posture), and affording no motion of respect to any of us, Sir Robert Sherley gave him a salutation, and sat down on a stool near him, while my Lord of Cleaveland, by an interpreter signified in three words, the cause of the Ambassador Sherley's and his and our coming to him, but with little return of regard from him, till I informing the interpreter of the new Ambassador what my Lord's quality was, he let fall his trussed-up legs from his chair, and made a kind of respect to his Lordship. This done, Sir Robert Sherley, unfolding his letters, and (as the Persian use is in reverence to their King,) first touching his eyes with them, next holding them over his head, and after kissing them, he presented them to the Ambassador, that he receiving them, might perform the like observance, when he suddenly rising out of his chair, stepped to Sir Robert Sherley, snatched his letters from him, tore them, and gave him a blow on the face with his fist, and while my Lord of Cleaveland stepping between kept off the offer of a further violence, the Persian's son [who later in Persia dared not face Sherley] next at hand, flew upon Sir Robert Sherley, and with two or three blows more, overthrew him; when Master Maxwell of the bedchamber, and my Lord of Cleaveland, nearest to him, pulling him back, (while we of the Company laid hands on our swords, but not drawing them, because not any one sword or dagger was drawn by the Persians), my Lord of Cleaveland remonstrated to the Ambassador the danger and insolency of the fact, saying, that if he, and the gentlemen there with him, had not borne more respect to that King whom he represented than he [the Ambassador] had done to the letters shewed him for justification of the other's quality, neither he, nor those about him, that had committed that insolency, should have gone alive out of that place. After these words, he made some show of acknowledgment, and said he was sorry he had offended his Lordship and us, by his act, which he had performed." Nuqd Ali Beg then excused himself by saying he was outraged that Sherley should impersonate an ambassador and should have presumed to say he had married the Shah's niece. To this Finett says, "Sir Robert Sherley (who was in the meantime retired behind the company, amazed and confounded with his blow and treatment) stepped in and answered, that he never said he had married the King's niece, but the Queen's kinswoman." After which, says Finett, the Earl of Cleveland, Sherley, and the rest of the party departed "with little or no respects" being paid to Nuqd Ali Beg.[45] The incident was reported to King Charles, who thereupon cancelled the audience he had arranged for Nuqd Ali Beg for that afternoon.

Subsequently Nuqd Ali Beg did have an audience with Charles I. The King and the Persian confronted each other, neither speaking, until the Persian broke the silence by apologizing and withdrew. Subsequently a second Persian arrived in England who refreshingly made no claims to being an ambassador but insisted he was simply a merchant selling silk. The second Persian proved to be no help to the Company. "The merchant . . . desired to leave his silks in their [the Company's] hands," the court minutes of the Company read, "and be paid for same a year or two hence. It was thought fit, in case the Court should conclude a bargain with him, to have the ambassador [Nuqd Ali Beg] present, but he [the merchant] said he was answerable for the silk to the King of Persia only, neither hath he anything to do with the ambassador, nor the ambassador with him." [46] Subsequently Nuqd Ali Beg asked the help of the Company in getting money from the merchant, Shaswar Beg, and the Company sent a deputy to the merchant to intercede for their man. Shaswar Beg took the position that "if the Ambassador could show the King of Persia's hand, he might have what he would, otherwise not; and desired to know whether the Ambassador could take his silk from him by violence; the deputy [for the Company] made answer, no such thing was intended. . . . He [the merchant] complained that the Ambassador [Nuqd Ali Beg] had disgraced and beat him and threatened to rip up his belly." [47] Later upon an appeal from Robert Sherley, Shaswar Beg (or Hogga Shan su war, as Sherley gives his name) was taken under the special protection of Secretary Conway to secure him from the molestations of Nuqd Ali Beg. Hogga Shan su war, or Shaswar Beg, subsequently died in England and was buried near the Church of Saint Botolph, Bishopsgate.

When Sir Dodmore Cotton, Count Robert, and Nuqd Ali Beg all went to Persia together in a Company fleet, Nuqd Ali Beg committed suicide just before landing, but that was in 1628. In 1626 Nuqd Ali Beg was for Sherley a painful experience. One of the most telling points made by the Company against Count Robert was that he wanted to purchase galleys for the Shah. When Sherley left Persia, Shah Abbas had captured Gombroon and was preparing to move against Ormuz. He needed galleys or landing craft of some sort and hence the instructions to Count Robert to negotiate for galleys. By the time Sherley was negotiating in England the capture of Ormuz was already two to four years in the past, and the Shah had no further interest in galleys. The Company merchants at Ispahan wrote to ask why Sherley, who "falsely pretendeth himself to be an ambassador," should want to buy galleys for the Shah, "when there are at least twenty good frigates and galliots [rowing craft] lie unprofitable at the port." [48]

Curiously enough, while the Company was complaining that Sherley was an impostor, and no representative of the Shah, at the same time they feared that he would use his great influence with that monarch to wreak vengeance upon them in Persia. In April 1626, the Company complained "that Sir Robert Sherley has practiced with the Persian merchant here [Shaswar Beg] and his son against the Company and has both written himself and procured them to write to the King of Persia to seize all the Company's goods and servants, and therefore if he should go into Persia, he would not only destroy the trade, but practice against their factors." [49] About the same time the Company stated that in the previous year they had sold 2,500 pieces of cloth, 80 tons of tin, and other commodities and had thought in the present year to double their sales, but "because they perceive that they shall be constrained to transport Sir Robert Sherley into Persia, of whose fair proceeding there, the Company having just cause to be jealous do therefore surcease to send any further supply for preservation of that trade, and have already given order to clear that country both of their goods and servants." [50]

The Company's attitude toward Sherley's expenses was also puzzling. The crown had agreed to defray the cost of the embassage. It later appeared to the King's ministers that the East India Company ought to pay part of the expense, and until this question was decided no one paid. "It pleased God so to direct the course of my business at my first coming, as to fall in the hands of so worthy and noble a gentleman, as yourself," Sherley wrote to Secretary Conway, "who would not suffer me, and my barge, tossed with the tempest of envious calumnies to be cast away; for which favor I come to give your Lordship most humble thanks. Your Lordship knows that at my first coming hither, I had the honor to kiss His Majesty's hands at Newmarket, who promised according to my humble request, that I should have nothing at all to do with the merchants, but should be dispatched in all things immediately from himself, as being sent ambassador from a King to a King, which also your Lordship can witness who brought me the same message, yet since now it hath pleased His Majesty to ordain otherwise, and to command the merchants to pay me some part of that allowance it pleased His Majesty to vouchsafe me, to the end Your Lordship may see how the same sum is to be bestowed for redeeming of my wife's jewels, empawned for my necessities, I send your Lordship a list thereof." [51] Count Robert then listed debts amounting to £1,899 besides which he said he had arrived with £1,400 which was likewise spent. He had actually been paid £1,040 and the crown owed him £3,360. The crown made what would seem a fair proposal to the Company. If it were found upon Count Robert's return to Persia that he was no true ambassador, as the Company stoutly maintained, then the crown would pay all Sherley's debts. If it were found that Count Robert was an authentic ambassador of the Shah, then as reparation for their false allegations the Company would pay £2,000 of Sherley's debts. When this fair and equitable proposal was announced at the Company court, "one of the generality alleged the Company's inability, and that Sir Robert had been rather their enemy than their friend; another added that it is not long since £22,000 was forced from the Company, and if the State shall continue to put such burthens upon them, it were better to divide while there is something left, and surcease the trade, others alleged that the stock is at an end, that they are now upon a losing trade; for £100 after eight years payment is not now worth above £80; that the money belongs to orphans and other poor people who lie in prison for debt, moreover that the Company are themselves indebted £200,000 and that it were more conscience to pay their own than Sir Robert Sherley's debts. Mr. Governor being then pressed to put it to the question framed it in this manner: 'as many of you as shall think fit upon his Majesty's command to allow, give, or lend upon privy seal or otherwise anything towards the payment of Sir Robert Sherley's debts hold upon your hands,' the which by a general consent and erection of hands was utterly denied." [52]

In March 1626, the Company was informed that the King had resolved to send Sir Dodmore Cotton to Persia as his ambassador to determine whether or not Count Robert was an impostor and required the Company to transport both Cotton and Sherley to that country. The Company was as reluctant to do anything for Cotton as they had been to aid Sherley. The new governor of the Company told Cotton bluntly that "he [Cotton] hath labored for this employment long, having offered Mr. Bacon, the Company's late secretary, above a year since £100 to effect the same." [53] Governor Abbot also said that in his conversation with Cotton the latter had "let fall thus much . . . that so long as he had hoped to be employed by the Company into Persia as an ambassador, he had a stomach to the journey, but being rejected he is now not so forward to undertake so long and tedious a voyage." [54] The Privy Council asked that the Company should provide Cotton with funds which would be repaid to the Company in London. The members of the Company after debating "what answer to give their Lordships; agreed to deliver this much as their just excuse, that they have now recalled their estates out of Persia, where they have little or nothing remaining, by which means the Company shall be altogether unfurnished, and can in no sort accommodate Mr. Cotton as is desired." [55] This was not true of course. Although it had been arranged that Sherley, Cotton, and Nuqd Ali Beg were to be transported to Persia in the Company's ships, all three missed the fleet when it sailed in April. Sherley and Cotton got aboard the Company ship *Expedition,* which had not sailed with the fleet and which was bound for Jacarta. They endeavored to have the ship ordered to Persia instead, but in this they were unsuccessful. On 12 February of the following year, the fleet being about ready to sail, "Sir Robert Sherley before the Lords [of the Council] protested his affection to the Company, and that he had been exceedingly wronged, but forgave those that had done it; whereupon some of the Lords desired a reconciliation between him and the Company, and Mr. Governor answered that the Court had no particular difference with Sir Robert, but what they had done was for the good of the Company." [56] A few days later Count Robert made another attempt at reconciliation. "Letter read from Sir Robert Sherley," the Company minutes noted, "offering his best services to the Company, now their differences were settled; was answered that they never had any particular difference with him, but what was done was only for the Company's cause." [57]

On Robert's first visit to England, his brother Sir Thomas had been living dangerously in the usual Sherley style; he needed money, he was a member of Parliament, and he was trying desperately to maintain a hold on the ancestral properties in Sussex. It will be remembered that the King had granted the ancestral lands to old Sir Thomas Sherley at an annual rental of a thousand odd pounds per year, but that Sir Thomas the elder neglected to pay the rent for so many years that the lands were finally extended to the crown; that is, the crown took over the lands until such time as the debts owed the crown had been paid.

In 1614 King James granted both the Sherley lands and the arrearages in rent to Robert Carr, Earl of Somerset, that beautiful young man of whom it was said that "James leaned continually upon his arm, smoothed his hair, pinched his cheek, rearranged his clothes whenever they were disordered and frequently embraced him in public." Preoccupied with such matters, His Majesty was a difficult person with whom to do business. "I went to the Court with a purpose to become a humble suitor to your Majesty for a release of my rent charge," Sir Thomas the younger later reminded King James, "then the Earl of Somerset, being in great favor, crossed my suit and begged it for himself. With him I compounded, and have paid him the whole sum agreed, saving seven thousand pounds for raising of which money already paid, I was forced to sell land and at half the value to mine utter undoing." [58] The facts were that Somerset had agreed to transfer the Sherley lands to young Sir Thomas for £10,550. The amount paid by young Sir Thomas was £3,550, and he never paid the rest. In 1614, the very year he got the Sherley lands, Somerset was replaced as the King's favorite by Buckingham, an even more beautiful young man of whom Sir John Oglander remarked that "I never yet saw any fond husband make so much or so great dalliance over his beautiful spouse as I have seen King James over his favorites, especially Buckingham." [59] Sherley took advantage of the change in favorites to try once more to get back his lands. "Vouchsafe to bend forward your gracious eye upon this enclosed paper," he implored the King, "wherein Your Majesty may behold, if you please, the true anatomy of a most ruined poor gentleman. Unless it will please your Highness, out of your princely benignity, to raise me out of the dust and enable me to do Your Majesty better service than hitherto I have done; and this Your Majesty may easily do (if you please) without any charge to you; only in forgiving me the four thousand pounds which is yet unpaid to the Earl of Somerset for my ransoms from him whereby Your Majesty may enable me to an estate able to live and only give me that which you have formerly bestowed upon another and I must pay out of my poor means to mine utter ruin. It is the work of God to return this power into Your Majesty's hands that thereby I may be relieved and saved from perdition. . . . To Your Majesty I vowed my life and service twenty years since. To Your Majesty's grace I most humbly desire to be bound." [60]

Unfortunately King James was not inclined to save Sir

Thomas from perdition. From the time the lands had been first extended to the crown until 1621, a number of people acquired claims to the properties or part of them, or to the rents from them or part of the rents, so that, several people testified, it was next to impossible to discover precisely what encumbrances there were on the lands. "My land is subject to so many cross entanglements," young Sir Thomas complained, "as very few would buy any of it." [61] In a long letter Sherley complained bitterly to King James. "My late father and myself have (with all our best endeavors)," he wrote, "served Your Majesty both in the late Queen's time and sithence to both our own great charges and mine extreme peril. . . . When I returned home from my long and tedious captivity, Your Majesty was graciously pleased to afford me good countenance and to pity and commiserate my miserable estate, but never have gave me the worth of one groate." [62] In 1621 Lionel Cranfield, Earl of Middlesex, set about buying up the claims and clearing the titles to the Sherley manors. Among other payments he paid the creditors of the Earl of Somerset £7,000, the amount young Sherley had left unpaid; he also paid £5,400 to Sir Thomas, his mother, and his sisters and a £500 annuity to Lady Sherley, the widow of Sir Thomas the elder. In return King James then granted Wiston and the other Sherley properties to the Earl of Middlesex.[63]

Early in 1622 Middlesex received a letter from the son of Sir Thomas the younger, also called Thomas. "May it please your Honorable Lordship," he wrote, "having heard by Sir Edward Grevill and others of a noble intention of Your Lordship to do me good, I was ambitious to embrace any opportunity wherein I might express myself to be Your Lordship's servant already in mine affection before I am made so happy in condition. Mr. Jordan, the Counselor, did entreate me to go with him to my grandmother to the intent that by his reasons and my entreaties we might win my grandmother's affections from Wiston that Your Lordship might have present possession thereof which undertaking we found so difficult to effect at the first that both Mr. Jordan and myself were in doubt to have lost our labours, but since she is [now] more tractable to our desires in this I am confident Your Honor will deal nobly with her. I did specify some particulars in a letter to Sir Edward Grevill concerning those terms which my grandmother stands upon, and I would have taken the boldness to have done the same to your Lordship at large: but that Mr. Jordan (who hath been the chiefest instrument in this) hath promised me to satisfy Your Lordship fully by word of mouth this week. I humbly beg your Lordship's pardon for this rudeness of mine and humbly beseech you to accept these lines as a testimony of the true affection and future service." [64] Not long after receiving this letter from her grandson, Middlesex received one from Lady Sherley, the widow of old Sir Thomas. "Seeing my son hath been so unhappy as to be constrained to part with his inheritance through his necessities and wants," she wrote, "I cannot but grieve (being his mother) when I remember it; yet when I consider how truly nobly your Lordship hath dealt both with my son and me, I then strive to forget altogether that I ever had such a place to live in and altogether endeavor to remember your honorable dealing to me and mine." [65]

So Sir Thomas and his mother and his children moved out of Wiston, and that summer Roger Townshend, writing the latest gossip to his father, noted that the new owner, Lord Treasurer Middlesex, had given a great entertainment in Sussex at the new home which he had bought from Sir Thomas Sherley, the Duke of Buckingham and many other illustrious personages being present.[66]

Wiston is still there, not too much changed in many respects from the time when it was occupied by the Sherleys. The last of the line, Thomas Sherley, great-grandson of old Sir Thomas Sherley and physician to Charles II, wore himself out in his unsuccessful efforts to recover the family estates. The house passed to the Faggs, then to the Gorings, one of whom immortalized himself by planting the trees of Chanctonbury Ring.

CHAPTER XIII

The Last Days of the Brothers

SIR DODMORE COTTON and Count Robert were ready to sail for Persia, but Sir Dodmore complained that although the merchants of the East India Company had been in a very great hurry to depart as long as he and Count Robert were still on shore, after they arrived aboard the merchants showed leaden heels. They richly accommodated Nuqd Ali Beg and gave kennels to himself and Count Robert. The Persian had two butts of Canary for his own mouth, but never a drop of wine was there for Sherley or Cotton. Sir Robert had brought, to take with him, cloth to the value of £100 by warrant of the Lord Treasurer, but it was held up for nonpayment of customs so that the ship was likely to sail before it came aboard, and so Sir Robert would be cozened of his goods.[1] The fleet eventually sailed in March 1627, the last voyage, as it turned out, for all three, Sherley, Cotton, and Nuqd Ali Beg. In the party of Sherley and Cotton were Lady Teresa Sherley and three who left accounts of the embassage: Thomas Herbert (later knighted), Robert Stodart, a valet, and Henry Gooch, the chaplain, the narrative of the last being especially valuable.

The Privy Council had ruled, in accordance with a petition presented by Lady Teresa Sherley, that Count Robert and Nuqd Ali Beg should not be allowed to go ashore for exercise at the same time lest the Persian inflict harm on Sherley, and this admonition was conscientiously obeyed. Count Robert and Sir Dodmore asked that they might from time to time leave their own ship and go aboard the admiral's for a few days as a change and recreation. The Company court, apprehending that such visits "will be a means of feasting and superflous spending of wine and other provisions, it was thought fit to admonish Captain Hall that though he be not absolutely denied to admit them, yet by no means to suffer them to lie aboard at night, and at these meetings to use no wasteful expense of wine or other provisions." [2] Happily during the voyage there was no quarrel between Sherley and the Persian, no riotous and expensive merrymaking, no unpleasant incident until the fleet neared Surat. Four days before reaching that port, Nuqd Ali Beg, despite the entreaties of his son, began to take excessive amounts of opium, and died the day the fleet reached port. "Now this tragic end of Nogdibeg," says Thomas Herbert, "was not without cause, for it seems, despairing of his master's favor and conscious to himself of his abusive carriage in England, both to Sir Robert Sherley and some other misdemeanours of his which begot a complaint against him to Shah Abbas and made known by the way of Aleppo after his departure out of England, he gave himself this desperate exit." [3] Having arrived at Swally Road on 30 November 1627, the ambassadors remained at Surat until 18 December, when the fleet sailed for Gombroon, arriving there on 6 January 1628.

When eventually Cotton and Sherley reached the court of the Shah, they received a cold welcome, which can be explained by recalling some incidents which had occurred during Sherley's absence and others which had occurred during Abbas' long reign. It will be recalled that before the Sherleys had arrived in Persia, Shah Abbas had suppressed his own rebellious satraps, and when Anthony and Robert reached Qazvin he was mopping up the Uzbegs, who had occupied large parts of his country. Having eliminated this tribe, he defeated the Turks, who had also appropriated large parts of Persia. With his western borders safe he had turned eastward and recovered Kandahar from the Great Moghul. He then allied himself with the English to get the Portuguese out of Ormuz and to break their power in the Persian Gulf. Although he had sought English help, he strove to avoid allowing this ally to obtain a firm foothold in the country. In January 1623, the Company merchants at Surat complained that after the taking of Ormuz, the Persians "not only defeated them of their shares in the spoils but of residence also in the Castle." [4]

Imam Quli Khan, the Shah's great general, subsequently

urged the English to join with him on an expedition against the Portuguese possession of Muscat, but the East India Company merchants were by this time disillusioned; they stated bluntly that they had gotten very little of what the Persians had promised them for the Ormuz enterprise and refused to take part in further joint adventures. Two years later they were still bitter. "Although the English were to share in all conquests," the merchants complained, "the Persians had kept both Kishm [near Ormuz] and Ormuz; while the 165 pieces of brass ordinance taken had been very unequally divided." [5] Shortly before Sherley arrived at Gombroon the Company's servants at Surat observed that "the King [Shah] hath given ample denial of any fort within his Persian dominion with such further addition of distrust as will ascertain you that [the] King seeks his own ends and never intended any such division as was contracted. . . . If he make all that is gained by your people's assistance to be his Persian continent, you will have little reason to assist him in Muscat, lest by title thereof, he claim all the continent of Arabia also." [6] By the time Sherley and Cotton reached Gombroon, not only did the English distrust the Shah, but the latter obviously regretted that he had ever allied himself with the English. Throughout his long reign, he had made unremitting efforts to get the foreigners out of Persia, only to find at the age of seventy that he had unwittingly let in a nation which obviously planned to stay a long, long time.

Although the Shah and his ministers were disillusioned, Persians generally were not aware that the English were a menace. At Lar on the way to the Shah's court, Cotton and Sherley were given a hearty welcome. "A Persian anticly habited, out of a poetic rapture (for the Persians are for the most part poets) sang our welcome," wrote Herbert, "the epilogue was resounded upon kettle drums, timbrels, and other barbarous jangling unmusical instruments. . . . A homely Venus, attired like a Bacchanal, attended by many morris dancers, began to caper and frisk their best lavoltas, so as every limb strove to exceed each other; the bells, cymbals, kettle music and whistles storming such a Phrygic discord that, had it been night, it would have resembled an orgy to Bacchus." [7] Proceeding from Lar to Shiraz the embassy got its first taste of the anti-English sentiment which had developed in official circles. When the embassy arrived at Shiraz, Imam Quli Khan, the governor of the city, pointedly left to go hunting. Having ignored the English embassy for a suitable interval, Imam Quli Khan then returned and entertained the English with a sumptuous banquet, where, says Herbert, Count Robert "in a cup of pure gold drank His Eminence's health, and then (knowing it would please the Duke [Imam Quli Khan]) put it in his pocket with the merry compliment that after so unworthy a person as himself breathed in it, it was some indignity to return it; which the Duke amiably accepts as good satisfaction." [8] Proceeding toward Ispahan, at the request of one of the Shah's officials, Sherley and Cotton waited at a village a few miles outside the capital city until a welcome could be prepared for them, and while the travelers waited they were dined by the European merchants, including those of the East India Company, who came out from Ispahan to greet them. When the Englishmen finally made the short journey to the capital the highway was lined for two miles with people shouting a welcome. Later the envoys were graciously received by the Shah's courtiers but the Shah was not there. He was at Ashraf on the shores of the Caspian.

Sherley and Cotton set off for Ashraf, a long journey on which they suffered hunger, misfortune, and misery. They saw the Shah briefly at Ashraf, but they were treated with bare courtesy by the monarch and with rudeness by his ministers. When the Shah's court departed for Qazvin, the Englishmen followed. On the road to Qazvin most of the party suffered from dysentery. Good care was taken, remarked Henry Gooch, that "neither pleasure should mollify us, nor plenty cause us to surfeit. Our first lodging was at one of the King's houses, but as we lodge beggars, out of doors upon the cold earth under the eves of a stable." [9] Arriving at Tehran, two-thirds of the way to Qazvin, they waited "a long hour or two in the open street," says Gooch, "before any would give him [Dodmore Cotton] lodging; until at length, the master of the night watch took pity of him and conveyed him unto a poor butcher's house. Not a man amongst us all this day had tasted one drop of water or one crumb of bread. We expected our dinner until four in the afternoon, looking for a great feast after so long time for preparation. At length appeareth a dish of cherries, another of apricots, a third of cheese to digest the same withal. After a while they brought us (as I take it) for our supper, a few cucumbers and an handful of onions and some ice to cool our wine withal, when we could get it." [10] A few days later the party "were feasted with two eggs."

At their first audience with the Shah at Ashraf, Cotton and Sherley had discussed the proposals for trade which Count Robert had put forward in England on behalf of Persia. The Shah declared that "the king of Great Britain should, if he pleased, receive ten thousand bales of silk at Gombroon every January, and for payment [he] would accept of so many thousand English cloths as should be adequate in value; for as he [Shah Abbas] well knew the silk was a greater quantity than he [King James] could use in his own dominions, so were the cloths to him [Shah Abbas]; but he would hazard the venting them by his merchants to serve his neighbors so that neither we nor he should need to traffic or hold correspondence with Turkey." Concerning Count Robert, the Shah declared that he had known Sherley many years and had granted him as many favors as he had to any Persian. As for Nuqd Ali Beg and the charge that he had insulted or slandered Count Robert, he believed the charge might well be true since, Sir Thomas Herbert quoted the Shah as saying concerning Nuqd Ali Beg, "in some sort he presaged my rigour, for had he come, and been found faulty, by my head (an oath of no small force) he should have been cut in as many pieces as there are days in the year and burnt in the open market with dog's turds." [11]

The Shah's chief minister at that time was Mahomet Ali Beg, who is notable in Persian history as a remarkably honest and faithful servant of the crown. At Qazvin, Sir Dodmore had several interviews with Mahomet Ali Beg. The latter felt sure, he told Cotton, that the Shah had not authorized Count Robert to make the proposals for trade which he had made in England. The English were welcome as were all other nations to trade in Persia, and when they no longer desired to trade they were free to depart. Mahomet Ali Beg declared that Sherley's letters of credence were not genuine, and that when he had showed them to Shah Abbas, the latter had destroyed them in a rage. The English by this time were truly in a rage. They were sure that Mahomet Ali Beg was a black-hearted villain and that his hostility arose from the fact that they had not brought rich presents for himself and for other Persian officials. They were also certain that he was simply lying about Sherley's letters of credence.

Count Robert was now very ill, without energy to utilize his customary versatility, and actually had not long to live. "Presently from my Lord," relates Gooch, "I acquaint the Lord Sherley herewith whom I found sick in his bed. I demonstrate unto him, how nearly it concerned his honour to justify himself, and vindicate his letters. I put him in remembrance what himself was wont often, upon occasion, to tell me, that the copies of all such letters, etc., were kept among the records of the kingdom, and advise him to cause due search to be made for the same. But, whether the violence of his sickness, which daily increased more upon him, took away, at that time, the wonted sense of his honour, as commonly it doth the care of all things else; or whether it be the nature of small injuries to speak, of extreme to stand amazed, I know not; he replieth nothing, but falleth off into other discourse, especially into bitter invectives against the English agent [of the East India Company] and per adventure not without just cause." [12]

Sir Robert died on 13 July 1628. He was, says Gooch, who had traveled thousands of miles in his company, "a noble gentleman." Sir Thomas Herbert, who had also endured many hardships in his company, remarked that "this gentleman made good the old proverb that 'tis better to die honorably than to live with obloquy. And (wanting a fitter place for burial) we laid him under the threshold of his door without much noise or other ceremony. . . . Rank me with those that honor him." [13] When one considers what Count Sherley endured, the respect he won in trying circumstances from honorable men, his efforts to keep his word and finish the tasks assigned to him, it would be difficult not to say with Herbert, "Rank me with those that honor him."

Cotton, ill with dysentery, died ten days after Sherley, and the embassy leadership was taken over by Henry Gooch. With a loan from the agent of the Dutch East India Company, Hubert Visnich, and very little help from the English East India Company, the survivors of the embassage got back to Gombroon and finally to England. Lady Teresa Sherley, after many hardships, traveled to Constantinople, where she remained three years, and finally to Rome, arriving there in December 1634. She purchased a house near the church of Santa Maria della Scala in Travestera, where she lived the rest of her long life and where she died in 1668. She had brought, or caused to be brought, to Rome the bones of Count Robert. There is in the church of Santa Maria della Scala in Travestera a plaque reading:

DOM
ROBERTO SHERLEYO
ANGLO NOBILISSIMO
COMITI CESAREO EQUITI AURATO
RODULFI II IMPERAT LEGATO AD SCIA ABBAM
REGEM PERSARUM EIUSDEM REGIS SECUNDO
AD ROMANO PONTH IMPERATO REGES
HISPANIAE ANGLIAE POLONIAE MOSCOVIAE
MOGORRI ALIOSQUE EUROPAE PRINCIPES
INCLITO ORATORI
THERESIA SAMPSONIA AMAZONITES
SAMPHUFFI CIRCASSIAE PRINCIPIS FILIA
VIRO AMANTISSIMO ET SIBI POSVIT
ILLINS OSSIBUS SUIS QUE LARIBUS
IN URBEM E PERSIDE
PIETATIS ERGO TRANLATIS
ANNOS NATAL XXIX
MDCLXVIII

Sir Thomas Sherley the younger had, in 1617, taken a second wife, Judith Taylor, née Bennet. He had a total of eighteen children, seven by Frances Vavasour, and eleven by Judith Taylor. After selling Wiston, he moved with his numerous progeny to the Isle of Wight. In 1625 he applied for and obtained from Secretary Conway the keeping of the Royal Park [Parkhurst Forest]. "I do not desire the same," he wrote to Conway, "in respect of matter of profit, but because of the conveniency of the house, for I am old and infirm and do dwell in a place of much trouble whereas this is quiet and void of trouble." [14] When one remembers the number of his children and the fact that he was past sixty, his desire for a quiet house is understandable. He lived at the manor of Cosham, an ancient house with secret chambers and passages, which stood at the corner of South Street and Church Litten, well within the present limits of the town of Newport.[15] Sherley was a relative of Sir John Oglander, the great man of the island, and figures in the latter's commonplace book. "Sir Thomas Sherley," says Oglander, "having sold Wiston, married a whore and spent all, came to end his days miserably in our Island." Under the notable events of 1633, Oglander notes that "I lent to Sir Thomas Sherley, Knight, on a feather bed, a bolster, and a rug, four pounds. To his lady after his death on six spoons, two pounds. I lend them my money freely and ever have done. When they want, they always repair to me as his kinsman and friend; yet I knew him to be so ill a paymaster that I was forced to make him honest by taking a pawn for my money." [16] Since Sir John makes these comments under the year 1633, the implication is that Sir Thomas Sherley died in that year. Of Sir Thomas' children the best known to posterity are Henry and Thomas. The former was a playwright. His play, *The Martyred Soldier,* was published in 1638, long after his death, and he wrote a number of plays which were never published. Henry was killed in October 1627. "There was a foul murder committed here on Friday last," one account of his death runs, "by Sir Edward Bishop, of Sussex, on Mr. Henry Sherley of the same shire, whom he ran through with his sword (having no weapon about him) as he came to him in his lodging in Chancery Lane to demand of him an annuity of 40 pounds which he said Sir Edward Bishop was to give him, whose lands (which are reported to be of £1,500 or £2,000 by the year) were presently begged and given away, but himself not yet found out." [17]

Henry's brother Thomas became the third Sir Thomas Sherley. A professional soldier, he served in the army of the United Provinces, but gave up his commission to serve in the English expedition of 1627 to the Isle of Rhé and Rochelle, where he was wounded and where, he says, he "lost all his friends in whom his hopes lay for preferment." [18] He fought on the side of King Charles during the Civil War and was knighted by His Majesty at Oxford in February 1645. His son, Dr. Thomas Sherley, physician to Charles II, made a futile attempt to recover Wiston, and he is the last of the Wiston Sherleys (but far from the last Shirley) to figure in the annals of his country.

After Count Anthony retired to Granada in 1611 he caused less stir in the world, but he was often in Madrid endeavoring to interest the court in his projects for the betterment of Spain and himself. In 1613 the English ambassador noted that "Sir Anthony Sherley our undertaking countryman hath now great hopes by a copper mine which he hath discovered and procured a grant from this King, and truly I am informed, it may prove a matter of great consequence. He hath for divers months past lived in a town called Veza [Baeza] near unto his mine in the kingdom of Granada where he hath 3,000 ducats per annum very punctually paid him, and never lived so well or orderly as at this present." [19]

In 1617 the Spanish government, having word that Sir Walter Ralegh intended a voyage to the Orinoco, consulted various people on his probable intentions, among them Count Anthony. "I have looked at the papers," Sherley wrote, "and the recommendations therein indicate the method by which to put an end to this enterprise as well as the lives of all who go with Don Gualtero Rauli. But Señor, if the decision on every contretemps that arises in the West Indies, which is so far away, is to rest [with the authorities] here in Spain, there will be no end to them. It is essential that the decision and execution should proceed from the governors on the spot. . . . I am certain that if the plan that I wot of were put into operation, within two or three years neither Virginia nor the Bermudas nor any rebels or trace of them would be left in the Indies—I stake my life on it. If I am acceptable for the carrying out of this task, I offer my life and labor for it, or alternatively I will serve in Poland, Milan, or on any duty that His Majesty may command. But if I am of no use for any service, it seems to me to be unreasonable that His Majesty should give me such an ample salary." [20]

Two years later, in 1619, Count Anthony notified the king that the English had offered Shah Abbas a fleet for the conquest of Ormuz in return for the privilege of getting the Persian silk trade into their hands. The Counts of Gondomar and Benavente consulted Sherley on what had best be done in the circumstances. Count Anthony warned that if some action were not taken to stop the penetration of English and Dutch in the Orient, the whole Spanish empire there would be lost. He proposed that a company of wealthy merchants should be formed, as had been done in Holland and England, for trade in drugs, spices, and Persian silk. He also advocated blocking the English port of Surat by sinking two ships loaded with stone in the narrow channel leading to the port. Unprotected by their naval guns, those English already at Surat, and those who might attempt to land in small boats from ships standing off the port, could be easily liquidated. A second company of merchants, Sherley advised, could be formed at Acapulco. These traders would import spices from the Moluccas to Acapulco which would be transported overland to the Atlantic coast and eventually brought to Seville by the treasure fleet which sailed annually from New Spain. An international market in spices could be established at Final in Sicily, and from this central point the spices could be sold throughout Europe. In addition to the profits to be made, this scheme had the advantage that a great mart for oriental goods in Sicily would damage the prestige and power of Genoa and Venice. These schemes impressed Counts Gondomar and Benavente as being of great value. They recommended that these proposals should be examined by experts, and that in the meantime Count Sherley, a man of wide experience in world affairs, should receive royal thanks for his zeal and labor. Benavente and Gondomar also suggested that if perchance Count Sherley had a favor to ask of His Catholic Majesty, the favor should be granted, but there is no record of favors being granted to Count Anthony at this particular time.

He now signed himself, and even the King addressed him, as El Conde de Leste, which may have meant simply the Count of the East (i.e., Conde de l'Este). There is no official record of such a Spanish title, but such records were not consistently or accurately kept. As the years went by his exploits underwent a transformation in his mind and became increasingly unselfish acts of heroism and virtue. In 1622 he remembered that many years before as an admiral in Sicily "in raising the fleet that I formed I spent a large sum of money with which I defended the kingdoms of Naples and Sicily . . . forcing the powerful fleet of the Turk to retire." He pictured himself as "having sacrificed and offered to your royal service my time, estate, life and honor." [21] He had forgotten that the money he spent on the fleet was not his, that no powerful Turkish fleet had threatened Sicily at the time, and that he had no estate. He addressed a series of rhetorical questions to the King's ministers: "Am I not the man who roused the Persians against the Turk? . . . Did I not bring at my own expense and without being remunerated twenty-five slaves from Barbary? . . . Did I not give aid with one hundred pieces of artillery? . . . Did I not arm a fleet in Sicily?" [22] The reader will know how to answer these questions, but possibly Count Anthony no longer was able to do so accurately.

In this same year of 1622 Sherley made a determined effort to get the attention of the Conde Duque de Olivares, who was then at the beginning of his power. In November he finished a book, *Peso politico de todo el Mundo,* addressed to the Conde Duque, which has since been published.[23] It is a survey of the countries and regions of the world, followed by a detailed plan for reforming and resuscitating the commercial and industrial life of Spain, and restoring Spain's political greatness. In describing the various countries and regions, Sherley drew on his own experience and from such books as he had at hand, which obviously were not numerous. He incorporated in the book the various projects which he had advanced over the years: control of the Strait of Gibraltar, the establishment of the cloth trades in the territories of Spain, an embargo on the importation of manufactured goods. He suggested a number of ways in which Olivares might employ his talents. There were, for example, shameful frauds in the refining and transportation of silver and gold from America, by which, Sherley estimated, roughly 30 per cent of the gold was being embezzled and lost to the crown. Count Anthony would be an ideal person to investigate this situation. He saw great advantages in making peace with Spain's ancient enemy, the Turk, and indeed of forming an alliance with the Porte. Such a rapprochement would be difficult; it would require a negotiator of sagacity. He was forced "without arrogance" to the conclusion that except himself "no one has the skills or experience which must inevitably be required to handle such a treaty." [24]

In the following year (1623) one Juan Nicholas, who styled himself the agent of the Conde de Leste, pointed out to the Conde Duque de Olivares the numerous occasions on which the government to the detriment of the country had disregarded the wise counsel of Sherley. Count Anthony had advised that the Dutch should be excluded from the salt pans at Punta Araya in Venezuela. No notice was taken of him, with the result that Dutchmen grew rich on Spanish salt. He had suggested that the friendship of the King of Denmark be cultivated. He was ignored and Spain lost a useful friend. Living with his brother Robert he had discovered him to be a fraudulent ambassador. His discovery was not appreciated and the English entered the Persian trade by way of Ormuz, a very serious occurrence, and eventually Ormuz was lost.[25]

In 1624 Count Anthony summarized a number of his projects in a single document. He again urged that Spain should obtain control of the Strait of Gibraltar. "I assert," he said, "that with closing or obstructing the passage of the Strait, Your Majesty is placing his foot on the necks of the princes of Italy and of the Turk, for passage through the Strait is crucial to their commercial life." He advocated a regular mail service between Spain and the Indies and offered to establish it. He suggested that a company should be formed in Mexico to sell spices. He pointed out the wisdom of establishing a market for dyes, spices, and drugs at Final, of fortifying the island of Mogador, of basing a merchant fleet on Cartagena, of making peace with the Turk.

But the King's ministers were jaded and annotated his document with such comments as "No," "Nothing," and "Nothing in this." [26]

Two years later he put forward his most ambitious proposal, which was that he and his Spanish descendants, his son Don Diego is mentioned specifically, should be given proprietary rights to a town on the island of Fadala and another in Anafa, or Mogador in Barbary, to hold as vassals of the King of Spain with the title of Señorio, or Seigneur, or Lord. He and his descendants would have the right to fortify these towns, to develop the fishery in the vicinity, to buy wheat, hides, meat, and other products in Barbary, and to sell these products in Spain. In return for these privileges Sherley agreed to maintain a fleet of fifty ships which would be at the disposal of the King four months of the year, and in the other eight months might be used by the Conde de Leste in his trading operations. He was also to give the crown 60,000 ducats as a guarantee that he would carry out the agreement and would not inflict damage on any of the King's subjects, friends, or allies. This last clause was the unfortunate one. He did not furnish the guarantee at the time stipulated; he made excuses and the time was extended, but there is no record that he ever paid it, or that he ever became Seigneur of Fadala, Mogador, or Anafa.[27]

At the time the Conde made the proposal, he was sixty-one. He lived in Granada, somewhere in the narrow streets of the parish of Saint Peter and Saint Paul. Doubtless he was a famous man, full of stories of the wars in Flanders, of the magnificence of the Persian court, of sea fights in the Indies, of the horrible machinations of the famous English heretics, Queen Elizabeth, Essex, Cecil, Sir Walter Ralegh, all of whom he had known. Can it be doubted that often in the cool streets, with the Alhambra above him and the Sierra Nevada in the distance, his black doublet somewhat spotted and rusty, but his manner still persuasive, his accent still slightly foreign, still using an occasional *italianismo,* he explained to the other great men of that provincial town, his far-reaching plans for restoring the grandeur of Spain?

And so he passed his days until 1633. In that year, in the

Anales de Granada of Francisco Henriquez de Jorquera, the chronicler notes that "this year there died in the city of Granada, the valiant cavalier, the Conde de Leste, the Englishman who sacked the city of Cadiz, during the time of King Philip II. He did it against his will, for afterward he came fleeing to Spain, and His Majesty helped him with a pension taken from the taxes of this city where he lived modestly. He was buried in the parochial church of Saint Peter and Saint Paul of this city. He has left a son of outstanding quality whom His Majesty will employ in his service for he is capable in many matters."

When he died Anthony had lived in Spain more than twenty years. There was a Spanish adage current in his day that if there are six Spaniards, there are six adventurers. Of these six one will go to Flanders, one to Italy, one to the Indies, one will be engaged in lawsuits, one will be in prison, and one will go into the church. Count Anthony had all of these experiences except that of entering the church. Though English, he was the epitome of the Spanish adventurer.

One must inevitably ask oneself if the story of the Sherleys is important, and the answer is, of course, that it is not. The Sherleian adventures point no moral, embody no inspiration, and are remarkable only in that one family should have had so many of them. These men shaped no great moments in history, but they were typical of their age, and in certain aspects, of any age. The grasping, greedy world of old Sir Thomas was more typically Elizabethan than the good fellowship of the Mermaid Tavern. A father busily scheming and getting, assiduously initiating his sons in all the wrong ways of living and getting, is not uncommon. To have fought in the Low Countries, as did the Sherleys, was an experience shared by many, and Anthony and Robert were typical of a multitude of English travelers to faraway places. There were hordes of men in Europe who gained a livelihood, as did Anthony, by serving as minor diplomats and spies for one European monarch after another, their knowledge of the secrets of a number of courts making them valuable if dangerous servitors. The Spain of Philip III and Philip IV swarmed with foreign adventurers seeking to interest the crown in schemes profitable to themselves. The tragedy of an individual like Robert, sacrificed to a national policy or victimized by a corporation, occurs in any age, and pathetic Thomas the younger, inept and incompetent, frustrated by the world and betrayed at home, could be paralleled many times over.

J. Robert Oppenheimer once remarked that one of the effects of the spectacular advances in science has been to cause the methods of science to be imitated and adapted in nonscientific fields. Mr. Oppenheimer's observation is true for the study of the past, for certainly attempts to measure and define scientifically the elephant "history" have been common enough. Mr. Oppenheimer adds that the impressive victories of science may have done disservice to other fields by obscuring for investigators the role of the contingent and the particular. "It is true," he concludes, "that many particulars can be understood and subsumed by a general order. But it is probably no less a great truth that the elements of abstractly irreconcilable general orders can be subsumed by a particular. And this notion might be more useful to our friends who study man and his life than an insistence on following the lines which in natural science have been overwhelmingly successful." The disparities and conflicts, if not irreconcilables, subsumed under the contingent and the particular, "Sherley," are numerous enough: Catholic, heretic, and Shi'ah Moslem; Turkey and Persia, Poland and Russia, Spain and England; seaman and soldier; traitor and patriot; scoundrel and gentleman. The Sherleys' story may be arresting enough to cause one to pause and consider Mr. Oppenheimer's notion. In any event, one may agree with G. M. Trevelyan that history is attractive because it is poetic and sufficient records of this family have survived to enable one to glimpse, even in this halting narrative, the stumbling, striving, courage, and cowardice, the tragic and comic poetry of four lives lived so long ago and so far away.

Notes

ABBREVIATIONS USED IN THE NOTES

AGS	Archivo General de Simancas, Simancas
PRO	Public Record Office, London
CSP	*Calendar of State Papers* for the years 1581–1629, published in London, 1865–1964
HMC	*Historical Manuscripts Commission Calendars*
Sherley Brothers	Evelyn P. Shirley, *The Sherley Brothers, an historical memoir of the lives of Sir Thomas Sherley, Sir Anthony Sherley, and Sir Robert Sherley, Knights, by one of the Same House* (Chiswick, 1848; printed for members of the Roxburghe Club)

CHAPTER I. THE FAMILY OF SHIRLEY AND THE SHERLEYS OF WISTON

1. S. F. Surtees, *William Shakespeare of Stratford on Avon: His Epitaph Unearthed and the Author of the Plays Run to Ground* (London, 1888).
2. E. P. Shirley, *Stemmata Shirleiana, or The Annals of the Shirley Family* (2nd ed.: Westminster, 1873), p. 10.
3. T. W. Horsfield, *The History, Antiquities, and Topography of the County of Sussex* (Lewes, 1835), II, 234.
4. W. Page, ed., *The Victoria History of the County of Sussex* (London, 1907), I, 370, 445.
5. As quoted by J. B. Black, *The Reign of Elizabeth, 1558–1603* (Oxford, 1936), p. 225.
6. All the quotations concerning the office of sheriff are from E. P. Cheyney, *A History of England from the Defeat of the Armada to the Death of Elizabeth* (New York, 1926), II, 357–358. Other information on the duties of a sheriff has been obtained from A. Fitzherbert, *In this Booke is conteyned the offices of Shyriffes, baylyffes of liberties, Eschea-*

tours, Constables & Coroners, and sheweth what euery one of them may do by vertue of their offices (London, 1556); and from C. H. Karraker, *The Seventeenth Century Sheriff: A Comparative Study of the Sheriff in England and the Chesapeake Colonies, 1607–1689* (Chapel Hill, 1930).

7. Cheyney, *History of England,* II, 344.

8. The will of Thomas Sherley of West Grinstead, Esquire, in Shirley, *Stemmata Shirleiana,* p. 303.

9. Sir John E. Neale, *The Elizabethan House of Commons* (London, 1949), p. 68.

10. S. D'Ewes, *Journal of all the Parliaments during the reign of Queen Elizabeth* (London, 1682), pp. 246–247; S. E. Lehmberg, *Sir Walter Mildmay and Tudor Government* (Austin, 1964), pp. 130–133.

11. D'Ewes, *Journal,* p. 288.

12. *Ibid.,* pp. 355–357.

13. G. S.Thomson, "The Origin and Growth of the Office of Deputy-Lieutenant," in Royal Historical Society, *Transactions* (4th ser.; London, 1922), V, 159.

14. *CSP, Domestic, 1581–1590,* p. 171 ("Interrogatories ministered to the Countess of Arundell by Sir Thomas Sherley," 9 April 1584).

CHAPTER II. THE SHERLEYS TAKE UP ARMS

1. M. Waldman, *Elizabeth and Leicester* (London, 1944), p. 174.

2. *CSP, Foreign, 1585–1586,* XX, 320 (Sherley to Burghley, 25 Jan. 1586).

3. *Ibid.* (Sherley to Walsingham, 25 Jan. 1586).

4. Robert Dudley, Earl of Leicester, *Correspondence of Robert Dudley, Earl of Leycester, during His Government in the Low Countries in the Years 1585 and 1586,* ed. James Bruce (London, 1844), pp. 160–161.

5. *Ibid.,* pp. 171–172.

6. *Ibid.,* p. 172.

7. *Ibid.,* pp. 172–174.

8. *Ibid.,* p. 174.

9. T. Digges, *An Arithmeticall Militare Treatise named Stratioticos* (London, 1579), A4, verso.

10. *Correspondence of Robert Dudley, Earl of Leycester,* p. 228 (Leicester to Walsingham, 16 April 1586).

11. W. Garrard, *The Art of Warre* (London, 1591), p. 5.

12. C. G. Cruickshank, "Dead Pays in the Elizabethan Army," *English Historical Review,* LIII (1938), 95.

13. Sir John E. Neale, "Elizabeth and the Netherlands," *English Historical Review,* XLV (1930), 389.

14. *CSP, Foreign, Jan.–July 1589,* XXIII, 111 (A. de Wael to George de Bye, 25 Feb. 1589); p. xl of the introduction; and p. 159 (musters of the discharged horsebands).

15. *Ibid.* See also pp. 142–143. The figures are sometimes conflicting, which is to be expected.

16. *Ibid., April–Dec. 1587,* XXI, Part III, 463 (Articles of instruction to be put into execution by the Lord Willoughby, 24[?] Dec. 1587).

17. Neale, "Elizabeth and the Netherlands," p. 384.

18. *CSP, Foreign, June 1586–March 1587,* XXI, Part II, 66 (Leicester to the Queen, 27 June 1586).

19. *Ibid.,* pp. 82–83 ("A Memorial for Sir Thomas Sherley," 9 July 1586).

20. *Ibid.,* p. 380. Huddlestone was dismissed in February 1587, and Sherley was given his place. Sherley's patent was dated 27 Feb. 1587.

21. *Ibid., April–Dec. 1587,* XXI, Part III, 141–142.

22. *Ibid.,* pp. 174–175 (Leicester to the Privy Council, 15 July 1587).

23. *Ibid.,* p. 211 (Leicester to Burghley, 31 July 1587).

24. *Ibid.,* p. 369 (Sir Thomas Sherley to Burghley, 14 Oct. 1587).

25. PRO, State Papers, Foreign, Holland, SP 84/14, fol. 119 (Sir John Norris to Burghley, 26 April 1587); calendared in *CSP, Foreign, April–Dec. 1587,* XXI, Part III, 30–31.

26. *Ibid.,* SP 84/23, fol. 5 (Arthur Champernowne to Walsingham, 2 April 1588); calendared in *CSP, Foreign, Jan.–June 1588,* XXI, Part IV, 247.

27. *CSP, Foreign, Jan.–June 1588,* XXI, Part IV, 271 (Morgan Coleman to Burghley, 7 April 1588).

28. *Ibid., Jan.–July 1589,* XXIII, 219 (endorsed by Burghley "Lord Willoughby," 15 April 1589).

29. Hatfield House Library, Cecil Papers, 167/80 (petition of Lord Willoughby *et al.*); calendared in *HMC Calendar of the Manuscripts of the Most Honourable the Marquis of Salisbury,* IV (London, 1892), 50 (endorsed by Burghley "Willoughby, Lord Burgh, Sir William Russell, Sir John Burgh, contra Sherley, 5 July 1590").

30. *CSP, Foreign, Jan.–July 1589,* XXIII, 258–259 (Sir Thomas Sherley's Declaration of His Entertainment and Expenses," 3 May 1589).

31. *CSP, Domestic, 1591–1594,* p. 54 (Sherley to Burghley, 5 June 1591).

32. *Ibid.,* pp. 373–374 ("Declaration of Sir Thos. Sherley's yearly entertainment and ordinary charges in the Low Countries," 26 Sept. 1593).

33. *Ibid., 1595–1597,* pp. 44–45 ("Complaints against Sir Thomas Sherley and his answers," 23 May 1595).

34. Neale, "Elizabeth and the Netherlands," p. 387.

35. *Ibid.*

36. *CSP, Foreign, June 1586–Mar. 1587,* XXI, Part II, 94 (Elizabeth to Leicester, 19 July 1586).

37. *Ibid., April–Dec. 1587,* XXI, Part III, 395–396 (memorial in Burghley's hand, Oct. 1587).

38. *Ibid.*

39. *Ibid., Jan.–July 1589,* XXIII, 398 ("The Privy Council to Sir John Conway," 27 July 1589).

40. *Ibid., 1586–1587,* XXI, Part II, 423 (Buckhurst to Walsingham, 26 March 1587).

41. *Ibid., April–Dec. 1587,* XXI, Part III, 25–26 (Sherley to Burghley, from The Hague, 20 April 1587); *ibid.,* p. 30 (Gilpin to Wilkes, 25 April 1587).

42. *Ibid., July–Dec. 1588,* XXII, 278 (States of Zeeland to Burghley, 22 Oct. 1588).

43. *Ibid.,* pp. 188-189 ("Petition of the Soldiers of Ostend to the Queen," before 8 Sept. 1588).

44. *Ibid., April–Dec. 1587,* XXI, Part III, 406–407 (Sir Thomas Sherley to the Privy Council, 6 Nov. 1587).

45. *Ibid.,* p. 427 (Leicester to the Lord Chancellor and the Lord Treasurer, 21 Nov. 1587).

46. *Acts of the Privy Council of England, 1586–1587,* XIV (London, 1897), 374.

47. *CSP, Foreign, April–Dec. 1587,* XXI, Part III, 56 (the Privy Council to Lord Buckhurst, 9 May 1587).

48. Neale, "Elizabeth and the Netherlands," p. 389.

49. *CSP, Foreign, Jan.–July 1589,* XXIII, 398–399 ("Order for the payment of Weekly Imprests to Her Majesty's Forces in the Low Countries," 27 July 1589).

50. *Ibid., April–Dec. 1587,* XXI, Part III, 3 (Edward Burnham to Walsingham, 2 April 1587).

51. *CSP, Domestic Addenda, 1580–1625,* pp. 306–307 (Thomas Digges to Burghley, 2 May 1590).

52. *Ibid.,* p. 309 (Thomas Digges to Willoughby, 25 July 1590).

53. Lincolnshire County Archives, Grimsthorpe MSS, III/1588/18 and 20 (the defeat on 4 Feb. N.S.); calendared in *HMC Report on the Manuscripts of the Earl of Ancaster Preserved at Grimsthorpe* (London, 1907), pp. 79–81.

54. *CSP, Foreign, Jan.–June 1588,* XXI, Part IV, 93–94 (Willoughby to Burghley, 16 Feb. 1588). Reports on the skirmish are to be found in the references given in note 53; see also *CSP, Foreign, Jan.–June 1588,* XXI, Part IV, 66 (G. de Prounincq to Sir William Russell, 7 Feb. 1588).

55. *Acts of the Privy Council, 1587–1588,* XV (1897), 390.

56. *CSP, Foreign, Jan.–June 1588,* XXI, Part IV, 209 (Willoughby, Killigrew, and Wilsford to Burghley, 20 March 1588).

57. Grimsthorpe MSS, VI/1589/236 (notes by Lord Willoughby); calendared in *HMC Manuscripts of the Earl of Ancaster,* p. 284.

58. *CSP, Foreign, July–Dec. 1588,* XXII, 264.

59. *Ibid., April–Dec. 1587,* XXI, Part III, 168.

60. *HMC Manuscripts of the Earl of Ancaster,* p. 59 (Willoughby to Leicester, Sept. 1587).

61. *Ibid.,* pp. 108–109 (magistrates of Arnhem to Willoughby, 27 March 1588; and Adolf Count of Nieuwenaar to Willoughby, 27 March 1588).

62. *Ibid.,* p. 110 (Stephen Le Sieur to Willoughby, 28 March 1588).

63. *Ibid.,* pp. 77, 133, 139.

64. *Ibid.,* p. 134 (James Digges to Willoughby, 3 May 1588).

65. *CSP, Foreign, July–Dec. 1588,* XXII, 57 (Lord Willoughby to the Privy Council, 18 July 1588).

66. Grimsthorpe MSS, IV/1588/72 (Anthony Sherley to Killigrew, 17 June 1588); calendared in *HMC Manuscripts of the Earl of Ancaster,* p. 153.

67. *CSP, Foreign, July–Dec. 1588,* XXII, 93 (Sir Thomas Morgan to Walsingham, 31 July 1588).

68. *Ibid.,* p. 57 (Lord Willoughby to the Privy Council, 18 July 1588).

69. Grimsthorpe MSS, IV/1588/159 (Adolf Count of Nieuwenaar to Willoughby, 5 Aug. 1588); calendared in *HMC Manuscripts of the Earl of Ancaster,* p. 175.

70. *CSP, Foreign, July–Dec. 1588,* XXII, 163 ("The petition of the Captains of the horse bands to Lord Willoughby," 28 Aug. 1588).

71. Grimsthorpe MSS, IV/1588/169 (Council of State to Lord Willoughby, 25 Aug. 1588); calendared in *HMC Manuscripts of the Earl of Ancaster,* p. 177.

72. *HMC Manuscripts of the Earl of Ancaster,* p. 191 (magistrates of Utrecht to Willoughby, 19 Sept. 1588).

73. *CSP, Foreign, July–Dec. 1588,* XXII, 216, 264.

74. Grimsthorpe MSS, V/1588/211 (Council of State to Willoughby, 23 Dec. 1588); calendared in *HMC Manuscripts of the Earl of Ancaster,* p. 233.

75. Grimsthorpe MSS, VI/1589/28 ("List of troops, both horse and foot, to be employed under Sir John Norris and Sir Francis Drake. To be delivered to Sir Edward Norris," 16 Jan. 1589).

76. *Acts of the Privy Council, 1588–1589,* XVII (1898), 116 (28 March 1589).

CHAPTER III. THE SHERLEYS LAY DOWN THEIR ARMS

1. Ian Dunlop, *Palaces and Progresses of Elizabeth I* (London, 1962), pp. 151–154.

2. Hatfield House Library, Cecil Papers, 34/91 (Sir Thomas the younger to Sir Thomas Heneage, 4 Sept. 1595); calendared in *HMC Calendar of the Manuscripts of the Most Honourable the Marquis of Salisbury,* V (London, 1894), 361.

3. *Ibid.*

4. *Sherley Brothers,* pp. 5–7 (Cecil to Sir Thomas the elder, 21 Sept. 1591); calendared in *HMC Salisbury MSS,* V, 361.

5. *Ibid.*

6. *HMC Salisbury MSS,* IV (1892), 137–138 (Sir Thomas the elder to Cecil, 22 Sept. 1591).

7. *Ibid.*

8. *Ibid.*

9. *CSP, Domestic, 1591–1594,* p. 109 (Sir Thomas the elder to Burghley, 29 Sept. 1591); see also *Sherley Brothers,* p. 7.

10. *Ibid.,* pp. 105–106 (Katherine Paget to Sir Thomas the elder, 18 Sept. 1591).

11. British Museum, Lansdowne MSS, 68/106; also in *Sherley Brothers,* pp. 7–8.

12. *HMC Report on the Manuscripts of Lord De L'Isle and Dudley, Preserved at Penshurst Place, Kent,* II (London, 1934), 249 (Rowland Whyte to Sir Robert Sidney, 12 March 1597).

13. *Acts of the Privy Council of England, 1597,* XXVII (London, 1903), 209.

14. *Ibid.,* XXVII, 30–31.

15. Cecil Papers, 165/145 (Sir Thomas the younger to Sir Robert Cecil, 30 April 1597); calendared in *HMC Salisbury MSS,* VII (1899), 180.

16. *Acts of the Privy Council, 1597–1598,* XXVIII (1904), 143; *HMC Salisbury MSS,* VII, 245 (Sir Robert Sidney to the Earl of Essex, 7 June 1597).

17. *Acts of the Privy Council, 1597–1598,* XXVIII, 143 (23 Nov. 1597); pp. 179–180 (11 Dec. 1597); pp. 260–261 (22 Jan. 1598).

18. E. P. Cheyney, *A History of England from the Defeat of the Armada to the Death of Elizabeth* (New York, 1926), I, 224.

19. A. Dupouy, *Histoire de Bretagne* (Paris, 1941), p. 227.

20. T. Churchyard, *A Journal of the Honorable Service of the Renowned Knight Sir John Norris, General of the English and French Forces, Performed against the French and Spanish Leaguers in France: 1591.* The *Journal* is attached to the author's partial translation of Emanuel Van Meteren's history of the Netherlands, to which Churchyard gives the title *A true discourse historicall of the succeeding Governours in the Netherlands, and the civil warres there begun in the yeere 1565, with the memorable services of our honourable English generals, captaines and souldiers* (London, 1602). The *Journal* begins at fol. 119.

21. *Ibid.,* p. 132.

22. Sir H. Unton, *Correspondence of Sir Henry Unton, Ambassador from Queen Elizabeth to Henry IV., King of France, in the years 1591 and 1592: From the originals and authentic copies* (London, 1847; printed for members of the Roxburghe Club), p. 320.

23. Dupouy, *Histoire de Bretagne,* p. 227.

24. PRO, State Papers, Foreign, France, SP 78/30, fols. 72–75, 83–84 (1 and 10 Feb. 1593: "Instructions for Colonel Sherley dispatched to Her Majesty this first of Feb. 1592/93," and Sherley's request addressed to the Lords of the Council, pursuant to Norris' instructions).

25. *Ibid.*

26. T. Birch, *An Historical view of the negotiations between the courts of England, France, and Brussels, from the year 1592 to 1617* (London, 1749), p. 9.

27. Cecil Papers, 169/139 (Sherley to Sir Robert Cecil, 23 Oct. 1593); calendared in *HMC Salisbury MSS,* IV, 396. See also *HMC Manuscripts of Lord De L'Isle and Dudley,* II, 146; Bibliothèque Nationale, manuscrit français, 22275, fol. 97, and 32869, fol. 72.

28. *Seventh Report of the Royal Commission on Historical Manuscripts* (London, 1879), p. 523a (G. E. Frere to his brother, 2 May 1594).

29. *Sherley Brothers,* pp. 8–9, quoting British Museum, Harleian MSS, 6996, fol. 82.

30. Cecil Papers, 26/40 and 26/50 (the Lord Keeper Puckering and Lord Buckhurst to Sir Robert Cecil, 26 April and 2 May 1594); calendared in *HMC Salisbury MSS,* IV, 516, 521–522.

31. Cecil Papers, 31/32 (Thomas Arundel to Sir Robert Cecil, 20 March 1596); calendared in *HMC Salisbury MSS,* VI (1895), 105. See also G. G. Butler, ed., *Edmondes Papers: A selection from the correspondence of Sir Thomas Edmondes* (London, 1913), pp. 141–142.

32. Cecil Papers, 31/96 (Sir Anthony Sherley to Sir Robert Cecil, 17 April 1595); calendared in *HMC Salisbury MSS,* V, 176.

33. PRO, State Papers, Domestic, Elizabeth, SP 12/252, fol. 29. ("Complaints against Sir Thomas Sherley and his answers," 23 May 1595); calendared in *CSP, Domestic, 1595–1597,* pp. 44–45.

34. *Ibid.*

35. Joyce Mousley, "Sussex County Families" (unpublished Ph.D. dissertation, University of London), p. 740.

36. A. Collins, *Letters and Memorials of State in the reigns of Queen Mary, Queen Elizabeth, King James, King Charles the First, part of the reign of King Charles the Second, and Oliver's usurpation* (London, 1746), I, 359.

37. Cecil Papers, 54/80 (Sir Thomas the elder to Sir Robert Cecil, 24 Aug. 1597) and 54/79 (Sir Thomas the elder to Burghley, 24 Aug. 1597); calendared in *HMC Salisbury MSS,* VII, 363.

38. PRO, State Papers, Foreign, Holland, SP 84/39, fol. 171.

39. *HMC Manuscripts of Lord De L'Isle and Dudley,* II, 234 (Rowland Whyte to Sir Robert Sidney, 18 Feb. 1597).

40. *Ibid.,* II, 247; Collins, *Letters and Memorials,* II, 27 (Whyte to Sir Robert Sidney, 8 March 1597).

41. Collins, *Letters and Memorials,* II, 27–28; *HMC Manuscripts of Lord De L'Isle and Dudley,* II, 248–249 (Whyte to Sidney, 12 March 1597).

42. *HMC Manuscripts of Lord De L'Isle and Dudley,* II, 252 (Whyte to Sidney, 17 March 1597).

43. *Ibid.* (19 March 1597).

44. Cecil Papers, 39/31 (Sir John Fortescue to Sir Robert Cecil, 19

March 1597); calendared in *HMC Salisbury MSS,* VII, 118–119. See also *CSP, Domestic, 1595–1597,* p. 380 (notes by Attorney-General Edward Coke, 4 April 1597).

45. Cecil Papers, 49/101 (Sir Thomas the elder to Sir Robert Cecil, 4 April 1597); calendared in *HMC Salisbury MSS,* VII, 142.

46. *CSP, Domestic, Addenda, 1580–1625,* p. 382 ("Brief of the reckonings between Sir Thomas Sherley, plaintiff, and William Beecher, defendant, taken by virtue of a Chancery commission," April[?] 1597).

47. PRO, State Papers, Domestic, Elizabeth, SP 12/264, fol. 95 (Sherley to Burghley, 28 Aug. 1597); calendared in *CSP, Domestic, 1595–1597,* p. 493.

48. PRO, State Papers, Domestic, Elizabeth, SP 12/264, fol. 133 (Sherley to Burghley, 5 Oct. 1597); calendared in *CSP, Domestic, 1595–1597,* p. 509.

CHAPTER IV. THE SHERLEYS TAKE TO THE SEA

1. W. J. Harte, *Gleanings from the Common Place Book of John Hooker* (Exeter, 1926), p. 39, as quoted by K. R. Andrews, *Elizabethan Privateering* (Cambridge, 1964), p. 4.

2. R. C. Anderson, ed., *The Book of Examinations, 1601–1602* (Southampton, 1926), p. xiii.

3. T. Birch, *Memoirs of the Reign of Queen Elizabeth from the year 1581 till her death* (London, 1754), I, 456.

4. E. P. Cheyney, *A History of England from the Defeat of the Armada to the Death of Elizabeth* (New York, 1926), II, 47–52.

5. Birch, *Memoirs,* I, 457.

6. Hatfield House Library, Cecil Papers, 47/103 ("Commission of [Lord Admiral Howard and the Earl of Essex] The Lord Generals to Sir Anthony Sherley to levy, muster, and arm all volunteers for her Majesty's service to the number of 1,500 and also to be captain and commander of all ships set forth at the charge of himself and Sir Thomas Sherley, Treasurer at War, in this expedition," April 1596); calendared in *HMC Calendar of the Manuscripts of the Most Honourable the Marquis of Salisbury,* VI (London, 1895), 162.

7. Birch, *Memoirs,* I, 490.

8. *Ibid.*

9. "A true relation of the voyage undertaken by Sir Anthony Sherley Knight in Anno 1596. intended for the Ile of San Tomé, but performed to S Iago, Dominica, Margarita, along the coast of Tierra firma, to the Ile of Jamaica, the bay of the Honduras, 30 leagues up Rio Dolce, and homewarde by Newfoundland: With the memorable exploytes atchieved in all this voyage," in R. Hakluyt, *The Principal Navigations, Voyages, Traffiques & Discoveries of the English Nation* (Glasgow, 1904), X, 267.

10. *Ibid.,* pp. 269–271.

11. *Ibid.*, p. 272.

12. *Ibid.* p. 274.

13. I. A. Wright, "The Spanish Version of Sir Anthony Sherley's Raid on Jamaica," *Hispanic American Historical Review,* V (1922), 227–248.

14. *Ibid.*

15. *Ibid.*

16. *Ibid.*

17. "A true relation of the voyage undertaken by Sir Anthony Sherley," in Hakluyt, *Principal Navigations,* X, 274–276.

18. *HMC Report on the Manuscripts of Lord De L'Isle and Dudley, Preserved at Penshurst Place, Kent,* II (London, 1934), 259 (Rowland Whyte to Sir Robert Sidney, 3 April 1597).

19. Cecil Papers, 49/83 (Sir Thomas the elder to Sir Robert Cecil, 29 March 1597); calendared in *HMC Salisbury MSS,* VII (1899), 134.

20. Cecil Papers, 52/46 (Sir Anthony to Cecil, 23 June 1597); calendared in *HMC Salisbury MSS,* VII, 265–266.

21. *Sherley Brothers,* p. 10, citing A. Collins, *Letters and Memorials of State in the reigns of Queen Mary, Queen Elizabeth, King James, King Charles the First, part of the reign of King Charles the Second, and Oliver's usurpation* (London, 1746), II, 35. See also *CSP, Ireland, July 1596–Dec. 1597,* p. 361 (Sir Robert Cecil to the Lord Deputy Burgh, July 1597).

22. "The Storm" in *The Poems of John Donne,* ed. H. J. C. Grierson (Oxford, 1912), I, 176.

23. S. Purchas, *Hakluytus Posthumus or Purchas His Pilgrimes,* XX (Glasgow, 1907), 44.

24. *Ibid.*

25. Cecil Papers, 54/26 (the Earl of Essex to Sir Robert Cecil, 11 Aug. 1597); calendared in *HMC Salisbury MSS,* VII, 346.

26. *Ibid.*

27. PRO, State Papers, Domestic, Elizabeth, SP 12/264, fol. 67 (Sir Robert Cecil to the Earl of Essex, July[?], 1597); calendared in *CSP, Domestic, 1595–1597,* p. 482. The letter is also printed in W. B. Devereux, *Lives and Letters of the Devereux* (London, 1853), I, 347.

28. W. L. Clowes, *The Royal Navy, a History From the Earliest Times to the Present* (London, 1897), I, 524.

29. M. Oppenheim, ed., *The Naval Tracts of Sir William Monson* (London, 1902), II, 29.

30. Purchas, *Hakluytus Posthumus,* XX, 92.

31. Sir Francis Vere as quoted in Oppenheim, *Naval Tracts,* II, 72.

32. Purchas, *Hakluytus Posthumus,* XX, 33.

33. Cecil Papers, 57/118 (Sir Thomas Sherley to Sir Robert Cecil, 30 Dec. 1597); calendared in *HMC Salisbury MSS,* VII, 526.

34. Thomas Nashe, *Lenten Stuffe* (London, 1599), as quoted by Andrews, *Elizabethan Privateering,* p. 5.

35. Cheyney, *History of England,* I, 463–464.

36. *CSP, Venice, 1617–1619,* XV, 416 (relation of England of Piero Contarini, Venetian Ambassador, 1618).

37. K. R. Andrews, "Economic Aspects of Elizabethan Privateering" (unpublished Ph.D. dissertation, University of London, 1951), pp. 50, 54; C. Ewen L'Estrange, "Organized Piracy round England in the Sixteenth Century," *Mariners Mirror,* XXXV (1949), 33. Examples of letters of marque are to be found in R. G. Marsden, ed., *Documents Relating to Law and Custom of the Sea* (London, 1915), Vol. I.

38. Cecil Papers, 63/49 (Sherley to Sir Robert Cecil, 14 Aug. 1598); calendared in *HMC Salisbury MSS,* VIII (1899), 305–306.

39. *Ibid.*

40. Cecil Papers, 64/7 (Sherley to Sir Robert Cecil, 10 Sept. 1598); calendared in *HMC Salisbury MSS,* VIII, 340.

41. Cecil Papers, 64/22 (Sherley to Sir Robert Cecil, 14 Sept. 1598); calendared in *HMC Salisbury MSS,* VIII, 346.

42. Cecil Papers, 64/98 (Owyn Tottye, mayor, and others, to the Earl of Nottingham and Sir Robert Cecil, 9 Oct. 1598); calendared in *HMC Salisbury MSS,* VIII, 385. See also *HMC Salisbury MSS,* VIII, 367 (Sir Thomas Sherley the elder to Sir Robert Cecil, 28 Sept. 1598), and *Acts of the Privy Council of England, 1598–1599,* XXIX (London, 1905), 193–194.

43. Cecil Papers, 67/6 (Sir Thomas Sherley the younger to Sir Robert Cecil, 29 Dec. 1598); calendared in *HMC Salisbury MSS,* VIII, 523.

44. *Acts of the Privy Council, 1598–1599,* XXIX, 437–438, 596.

45. Oppenheim, *Naval Tracts,* II, 106.

46. *Ibid.,* p. 103.

47. *Ibid.,* p. 84.

48. *Ibid.,* p. 105.

49. *Ibid.,* p. 84.

50. *Ibid.,* p. 107.

51. Cecil Papers, 71/102 (Sir Thomas the younger to Cecil, 31 July 1599); calendared in *HMC Salisbury MSS,* IX (1902), 254.

52. Cecil Papers, 74/30 (Sir Thomas the elder to Cecil, 13 Oct. 1599); calendared in *HMC Salisbury MSS,* IX, 371.

53. Cecil Papers, 74/98 (John Skinner to Sir Robert Cecil, 24 Nov. 1599); calendared in *HMC Salisbury MSS,* IX, 399.

54. Cecil Papers, 78/43 (Sir Thomas the younger to Sir Robert Cecil, 6 April 1600); calendared in *HMC Salisbury MSS,* X (1904), 103.

55. Cecil Papers, 78/58 (Sir Ferdinando Gorges to Sir Robert Cecil, 13 April 1600); calendared in *HMC Salisbury MSS,* X, 108.

56. Cecil Papers, 78/43 (Sir Thomas the younger to Sir Robert Cecil 6 April 1600); calendared in *HMC Salisbury MSS,* X, 103.

57. Cecil Papers, 78/59 (Sir Thomas the younger to Sir Robert Cecil, 13 April 1600); calendared in *HMC Salisbury MSS,* X, 109.

58. Cecil Papers, 78/58 (Sir Ferdinando Gorges to Sir Robert Cecil, 13 April 1600); calendared in *HMC Salisbury MSS,* X, 108–109.

59. *Acts of the Privy Council, 1599–1600,* XXX (1905), 318 (11 May 1600).

60. *Ibid.,* pp. 281–282 (last of April).

61. Cecil Papers, 186/145 (merchants interested in the goods taken by Sir Thomas Sherley the younger to Sir Robert Cecil, May 1609); calendared in *HMC Salisbury MSS,* XIV (1923), 128–129.

62. Cecil Papers, 181/8 (Sir Julius Caesar to the Earl of Nottingham, 2 Sept. 1600); calendared in *HMC Salisbury MSS,* X, 302.

63. Marsden, *Documents,* I, 303–304.

64. *Ibid.,* pp. 302, 306.

65. Sir John E. Neale, *Queen Elizabeth I* (Penguin ed.; London, 1961), p. 392.

66. National Library of Scotland, Advocates MSS, 33.1.7, Vol. XXII, no. 51.

67. Cecil Papers, 85/94 (Sherley to Cecil, 19 March 1602); calendared in *HMC Salisbury MSS,* XII (1910), 78.

68. *CSP, Domestic, 1601–1603,* p. 187 (John Chamberlain to Dudley Carleton, 8 May 1602). The account of the voyage is given in a unique pamphlet in the British Museum, *A True Discourse of the Late Voyage made by the Right Worshipful Sir Thomas Sherley* (London, 1602; British Museum no. C.123.d.16).

69. *Sherley Brothers,* p. 13; *CSP, Domestic, 1601–1603,* p. 209 (John Chamberlain to Sir Dudley Carleton, 27 June 1602).

70. Anderson, *Book of Examinations,* pp. xvi–xviii.

71. *Sherley Brothers,* pp. 33–34 (Father Persons to [Ralph?] Eure in England, 30 April 1601, from Rome).

72. Cecil Papers, 107/75 (Francis Mitchell to Viscount Cranborne, 20 Oct. 1604); calendared in *HMC Salisbury MSS,* XVI (1933), 333.

CHAPTER V. SIR ANTHONY AND ROBERT SHERLEY, THEIR JOURNEY TO PERSIA

1. P. M. Handover, *The Second Cecil: The Rise to Power, 1563–1604, of Sir Robert Cecil, Later First Earl of Salisbury* (London, 1959), p. 175.

2. *Ibid.,* p. 164.

3. PRO, State Papers, Domestic, Elizabeth, SP 12/284, fol. 78 (Sir Anthony to Chief Justice Popham, 20 July 1602).

4. *Sherley Brothers,* p. 15 (Sir Anthony to Chief Justice Popham, 30 Aug. 1601).

5. *HMC Calendar of the Manuscripts of the Most Honourable the Marquis of Salisbury,* VIII (London, 1899), 116-117.

6. PRO, State Papers, Domestic, Elizabeth, SP 12/284, fol. 78 (Sir Anthony to Chief Justice Popham, 20 July 1602).

7. Hatfield House Library, Cecil papers, 57/118 (Sir Thomas the elder to Sir Robert Cecil, 30 Dec. 1597); calendared in *HMC Salisbury MSS,* VII (1899), 526.

8. A. Collins, *Letters and Memorials of State in the reigns of Queen Mary, Queen Elizabeth, King James, King Charles the First, part of the reign of King Charles the Second, and Oliver's usurpation* (London, 1746), II, 79 (George Gilpin to Sir Robert Sidney, 12 Jan. 1597); see also *HMC Report on the Manuscripts of Lord De L'Isle and Dudley, Preserved at Penshurst Place, Kent* (London, 1934), II, 308.

9. *CSP, Domestic, 1601–1603,* p. 223 (Sir Anthony to the Lord Chief Justice, 20 July 1602).

10. T. Coryate, *Coryat's crudities, hastily gobbled up in five moneths travells* (Glasgow, 1905), I, 318, 402.

11. There are four accounts of Sir Anthony's journey to Persia. Sir Anthony himself published an account in 1613. This was entitled *Sir Antony Sherley his relation of his travels into Persia: The dangers, and Distresses, which befell him in his passage, both by sea and land* (London, 1613). Sir Anthony's account was abridged in S. Purchas, *Hakluytus Posthumus or Purchas His Pilgrimes,* VIII (Glasgow, 1905), 375–441. Abel Pinçon's account was first published in Paris in 1651 with the title "Relation d'un Voyage faict és années 1598 et 1599 par un gentilhomme de la suitte du Seigneur Scierley, Ambassadeur du Roy d'Angleterre," in C. B. Morisot, ed., *Relations Veritables et Curieuses de l'Isle de Madagascar et du Bresil, avec l'Histoire de la derniere guerre fait au Bresil entre les Portugais et les Hollandois, trois relations d'Egypte et une du Royaume de Perse* (Paris, 1651). William Parry's narrative, *A New and Large Discourse of the Travels of Sir Anthonie Sherley Knight by Sea and over Land to the Persian Empire* (London, 1601), was abridged in Purchas, *Hakluytus Posthumus,* VIII, 442–449, and later published in full by J. Payne Collier in the series of reprints which are entitled *Illustrations of Early English Popular Literature* (London, 1863–1864). Parry's narrative is no. 2 in Vol. II (1864) of that series. George Manwaring's account, "A true discourse of Sir Anthony Sherley's Travels into Persia, what accidents did happen in the waye, both goeinge thither and returning backe, with the businesse he was employed in, from the Sophie," was printed in part in *The Retrospective Review* (London, 1820), II, 351–381, and the remainder of it was published in *The Three Brothers, or The Travels and Adventures of Sir Anthony, Sir Robert, & Sir Thomas Sherley, in Persia, Russia, Turkey, Spain* (London, 1825). Sir E. Denison Ross republished the accounts of Manwaring, Pinçon, and Parry in his *Sir Anthony Sherley and His Persian Adventure* (London, 1933). The quotations in this chapter from the accounts by these three companions of Sherley's are from Ross's reprint. Page citations have not been given, since the accounts are chronological

and the passages are easily located. Complete bibliographical information on the narratives may be found in Ross.

12. Parry, "New and Large Discourse," in Ross, *Sir Anthony Sherley,* p. 101.

13. Cecil Papers, 174/100 (endorsed: "Advertisement touching Ant. Sherley written from Venice to a merchant of Frankfort," undated, but probably written in March 1598); calendared in *HMC Salisbury MSS,* VIII, 116–117. See also *HMC Salisbury MSS,* VIII, 151 (George Gilpin to the Earl of Essex, 30 April 1598).

14. PRO, State Papers, Domestic, Elizabeth, SP 12/284, fol. 78 (Sir Anthony to the Lord Chief Justice, 20 July 1602); calendared in *CSP, Domestic, 1601–1603,* p. 223.

15. Cecil Papers, 61/49 (Thomas Chaloner to Anthony Bacon, 2 June 1598); calendared in *HMC Salisbury MSS,* VIII, 188–189.

16. *CSP, Venice, 1592–1603,* IX, 291 (Agostino Nani, Venetian Ambassador in Spain, to the Doge and Senate, 20 Oct. 1597).

17. Cecil Papers, 174/108 (De Moucheron to Essex, 19 Jan. 1598); calendared in *HMC Salisbury MSS,* VIII, 10–11. Also Cecil Papers 204/109 (De Moucheron to Essex, 26 March 1598); calendared in *HMC Salisbury MSS,* VIII, 86. See also Davis to Essex, 1 Aug. 1600, in A. H. Markham, *The Voyages and Works of John Davis the Navigator* (London, 1880), p. 129.

18. Cecil Papers, 75/67 (Davis to Essex, undated); calendared in *HMC Salisbury MSS,* XIII (1915), Addenda, 599.

19. Cecil Papers, 61/49 (Thomas Chaloner to Anthony Bacon, 2 June 1598); calendared in *HMC Salisbury MSS,* VIII, 188–189.

20. *Ibid.*

21. The quotations are from the accounts referred to in note 11 above, as are the quotations from Manwaring, Parry, and Pinçon which follow.

22. Cecil Papers, 61/49 (Thomas Chaloner to Anthony Bacon, 2 June 1598); calendared in *HMC Salisbury MSS,* VIII, 188–189.

23. PRO, State Papers, Domestic, Elizabeth, SP 12/284, fol. 78 (Sir Anthony Sherley to the Lord Chief Justice, 20 July 1602); calendared in *CSP, Domestic, 1601–1603,* p. 223. See also *CSP, Venice, 1592–1603,* IX, 447.

24. A. Sherley, *His relation of his travels* (1613), p. 10.

25. *Sherley Brothers,* p. 17 (H. Lello to Cecil, 6 Aug. 1598).

26. A. Sherley, *His relation of his travels,* p. 8.

27. John Eldred, as quoted in W. Blunt, *Pietro's Pilgrimage; A Journey to India and back at the beginning of the Seventeenth Century* (London, 1953), p. 95.

28. A. C. Wood, *A History of the Levant Company* (London, 1935), p. 24.

29. P. R. Harris, "The Letter Book of William Clark, Merchant at Aleppo, 1598–1602" (unpublished Ph.D. dissertation, University of London), p. 214.

30. *Ibid.*

31. *Ibid.*

32. A. Sherley, *His relation of his travels,* p. 17.

33. J. Chamberlain, *Letters written by John Chamberlain during the reign of Queen Elizabeth* (Westminster, 1861), p. 32.

34. Harris, "Letter Book of William Clark," p. 215.

35. Cecil Papers 64/79 (Sir Anthony to the English Counsel at Aleppo, before 3 Oct. 1598); calendared in *HMC Salisbury MSS,* VIII, 376–377.

36. Cecil Papers, 130/150, 179/7, and Petitions, no. 1178; calendared in *HMC Salisbury MSS,* XIV (1923), 88, 90, 116.

37. A. Sherley, *His relation of his travels,* pp. 20–21.

38. *Ibid.,* pp. 23–24.

39. *Ibid.,* p. 25.

40. Harris, "Letter Book of William Clark," pp. 215–216.

41. A. Sherley, *His relation of his travels,* p. 28.

CHAPTER VI. THE PERSIA OF THE SHERLEYS

1. L. Lockhart, *The Fall of the Safavi Dynasty and the Afghan Occupation of Persia* (Cambridge, 1958), pp. 2–11.

2. *Ibid.,* p. 11.

3. Sir T. Herbert, *Travels in Persia, 1627–1629,* ed. Sir William Foster (London, 1928), p. 247.

4. Sir P. M. Sykes, *A History of Persia* (London, 1930), II, 126.

5. *Ibid.,* pp. 202–207.

6. *Ibid.,* pp. 198–202.

7. "Extracts from the Travels of Pietro della Valle in Persia," in J. Pinkerton, ed., *A General Collection of the Best and Most Interesting Voyages and Travels* (London, 1811), IX, 23.

8. Sykes, *History of Persia,* II, 201.

9. J. Cartwright, *The Preacher's Travels* (London, 1611), p. 61.

10. Herbert, *Travels in Persia,* p. 132.

11. Cartwright, *Preacher's Travels,* p. 61.

12. *Ibid.,* pp. 50–51.

13. Sir J. Chardin, *Sir John Chardin's Travels in Persia, with an Introduction by Sir Percy Sykes* (London, 1927), p. xxii.

14. Herbert, *Travels in Persia,* pp. 217–219.

15. Cartwright, *Preacher's Travels,* p. 59.

16. Sykes, *History of Persia,* II, 187–188.

17. For accounts of the Papacy's attempts to unite the Christian princes in an alliance with Persia, see *A Chronicle of the Carmelites in Persia and the Papal Mission of the XVIIth and XVIIIth Centuries* (London, 1939) and Ludwig von Pastor, *The History of the Popes* (London, 1891–1953), *passim.*

18. G. Le Strange, ed., *Don Juan of Persia, a Shi'ah Catholic, 1560–1604* (New York, 1926), p. 21 of introduction.

19. G. Manwaring, "A true discourse of Sir Anthony Sherley's Travels into Persia, what accidents did happen in the waye, both goeinge thither and returning backe, with the businesse he was employed in, from the Sophie," in Sir E. D. Ross, *Sir Anthony Sherley and His Persian Adventure* (London, 1933), p. 201.

20. *Ibid.*

21. A. Pinçon, "A Relation of a Journey taken into Persia in the Years 1598 and 1599," in Ross, *Sir Anthony Sherley,* p. 155.

22. Sir A. Sherley, *Sir Antony Sherley his relation of his travels into Persia* (London, 1613), p. 64.

23. Herbert, *Travels in Persia,* p. 248.

24. Manwaring, "True discourse," in Ross, *Sir Anthony Sherley,* p. 210.

25. W. Parry, "A New and Large Discourse of the Travels of Sir Anthonie Sherley Knight by Sea and over Land to the Persian Empire," in Ross, *Sir Anthony Sherley,* p. 120.

26. A. Sherley, *His relation of his travels,* pp. 65–66.

27. Pinçon, "Relation of a Journey," in Ross, *Sir Anthony Sherley,* p. 157.

28. Herbert, *Travels in Persia,* p. 262.

29. *Ibid.,* p. 243. The words of Angelo Corrai are from Guglielmo Berchet, *Raccolta Veneta,* Vol. I, ed. N. Barozzi (1st ser.; Venice, 1866), as printed in Ross, *Sir Anthony Sherley,* p. 29.

30. Manwaring, "True discourse," in Ross, *Sir Anthony Sherley,* p. 222.

31. A. Sherley, *His relation of his travels,* p. 58.

32. Folger Shakespeare Library MSS, V.b.142 ("Abstract of a letter sent from Sir Anthony Sherley to Mr. Robert [i.e. Anthony] Bacon").

33. A. Sherley, *His relation of his travels,* p. 79.

34. *Ibid.,* p. 73.

35. *Ibid.,* p. 80.

36. *Ibid.,* p. 106.

37. *Ibid.,* p. 109.

38. *Ibid.,* p. 120.

39. Folger Shakespeare Library MSS, V.b.142 ("An abstract of a letter written by Sir Anthony Sherley to the Earl of Essex in April last").

40. P. R. Harris, "The Letter Book of William Clark, Merchant at Aleppo, 1598–1602" (unpublished Ph.D. diss., University of London), p. 216.

CHAPTER VII. THE PERSIAN EMBASSY TO THE COURTS OF EUROPE

1. *CSP, Venice, 1592–1603,* IX, 445.

2. *Ibid.,* p. 439.

3. W. Parry, "A New and Large Discourse of the Travels of Sir Anthonie Sherley Knight by Sea and over Land to the Persian Empire," in

Sir E. D. Ross, *Sir Anthony Sherley and His Persian Adventure* (London, 1933), p. 126.

4. Ross, *Sir Anthony Sherley,* pp. 238–239 (letter from Sir Anthony Sherley from Russia). See also *Sherley Brothers,* pp. 23–24.

5. Folger Shakespeare Library MSS, V.b.142 (abstract of a letter from Anthony Sherley to Anthony Bacon).

6. Parry, "New and Large Discourse," in Ross, *Sir Anthony Sherley,* p. 125.

7. Sir A. Sherley, *Sir Antony Sherley his relation of his travels into Persia* (London, 1613), p. 126.

8. A. Pinçon, "Relation of a Journey taken to Persia in the Years 1598 and 1599," in Ross, *Sir Anthony Sherley,* p. 167.

9. *Ibid.,* pp. 168–169.

10. Parry, "New and Large Discourse," in Ross, *Sir Anthony Sherley,* p. 128.

11. *Ibid.,* pp. 126–127.

12. Ross, *Sir Anthony Sherley,* p. 239 (letter from Sir Anthony Sherley from Russia). See also *Sherley Brothers,* p. 24.

13. *Ibid.*

14. Parry, "New and Large Discourse," in Ross, *Sir Anthony Sherley,* p. 128.

15. Sir B. Pares, *History of Russia* (New York, 1953), pp. 137–138.

16. Parry, "New and Large Discourse," in Ross, *Sir Anthony Sherley,* pp. 129–130.

17. *Ibid.,* p. 131.

18. I. I. Lyubimenko, *Les relations commerciales et politiques de l'Angleterre avec la Russie avant Pierre Le Grand* (Paris, 1933), p. 63.

19. *Sherley Brothers,* p. 24 (Sir Anthony Sherley to Anthony Bacon, 12 Feb. 1600). The details of the subsequent fate of Melo are in *A Chronicle of the Carmelites in Persia and the Papal Mission of the XVIIth and XVIIIth Centuries* (London, 1939), I, 71; A. Gouvea, *El Glorioso Triunfo de Tres Martires Españoles, dos Portugueses, y frailes de la Orden de S. Augustin, y uno Castellano hijo de Madrid* (Madrid, 1623); L. Lockhart, "El Glorioso Triunfo de Tres Martires Españoles," *Journal of the Royal Central Asian Society,* XVIII (1931), 570–573. The quotations on the Englishmen's fear of being exiled by the Czar are from Parry, "New and Large Discourse," in Ross, *Sir Anthony Sherley,* p. 132.

20. G. Le Strange, ed., *Don Juan of Persia, a Shi'ah Catholic, 1560–1604* (New York, 1926), pp. 252–253, 256.

21. *Sherley Brothers,* pp. 25–26 (Sir Anthony Sherley to Anthony Bacon, 12 Feb. 1600).

22. Sir A. Sherley, *Le "Peso Politico de Todo el Mundo" d'Anthony Sherley, ou un aventurier anglais au service de l'Espagne,* ed. Xavier-A. Flores (Paris, 1963).

23. Lyubimenko, *Relations commerciales et politiques,* p. 63.

24. *Ibid.,* pp. 61–62.

25. Parry, "New and Large Discourse," in Ross, *Sir Anthony Sherley,* p. 134.

26. Le Strange, *Don Juan,* p. 261, 284.

27. *Sherley Brothers,* p. 33 (Father Persons to [Ralph?] Eure in England, 30 April 1601).

28. W. Coxe, *History of the House of Austria* (London, 1852), II, 94–95.

29. *CSP, Venice, 1592–1603,* IX, 430–431, 444. (Piero Duodo, Venetian ambassador in Germany, to the Doge and Senate, 30 Oct. 1600 and 22 Jan. 1601).

30. *Ibid.,* pp. 430–431.

31. *Ibid.,* p. 437 (Piero Duodo to the Doge and Senate, 25 Dec. 1600).

32. Sir W. Foster, ed., *The Travels of John Sanderson in the Levant, 1584–1602* (London, 1931), pp. 176–177 (Richard Colthurst to John Sanderson, 26 July 1599, from Aleppo).

33. National Library of Scotland, Advocates MSS, 33.1.7., Vol. XXI, no. 23 (Sir Anthony Sherley to James VI of Scotland, 10 July 1600).

34. *Sherley Brothers,* pp. 28–29 (Sir Anthony Sherley to Robert Cecil, 10 June 1600).

35. *Ibid.*

36. Hatfield House Library, Cecil Papers, 180/117 (Sir Anthony Sherley to the Earl of Essex, 20 June 1600, from Archangel); calendared in *HMC Calendar of the Manuscripts of the Most Honourable the Marquis of Salisbury,* X (London, 1904), 190.

37. *Sherley Brothers,* pp. 28–29 (Sir Anthony Sherley to Sir Robert Cecil, 10 June 1600).

38. Cecil Papers, 180/108 (Sir Anthony Sherley to his father, 12 June 1600); calendared in *HMC Salisbury MSS,* X, 180.

39. Cecil Papers, 67/90 (Sir Thomas the elder to Sir Anthony, 6 Jan. 1600); calendared in *HMC Salisbury MSS,* X, 3.

40. *Sherley Brothers,* pp. 30–31 (Sir Robert Cecil to Mr. Lello, 17 Oct. 1600).

41. Henry IV, King of France, *Receuil des lettres missives de Henri IV,* ed. J. Berger de Xivrey (Paris, 1843–1876), V, 334.

42. *CSP, Venice, 1592–1603,* IX, 446–447 (Agostino Nani, Venetian Ambassador in Constantinople, to the Doge and Senate, 20 Feb. 1601).

43. This document was first published in Guglielmo Berchet, *Raccolta Veneta,* Vol. I, ed. N. Barozzi (1st ser.; Venice, 1866). The translation given here is that published in Ross, *Sir Anthony Sherley,* 25–31.

44. AGS, Estado, Leg. K. 1630, fol. 121 ("Relación de la Embajada que el Rey de Persia envió con Don Antonio Sirley, inglés, y Cussain Alibech, persiano. En Roma 8 de junio 1601").

45. Ludwig von Pastor, *The History of the Popes,* XXIII (London, 1933), 298.

46. *Chronicle of the Carmelites,* I, 80.

47. Ross, *Sir Anthony Sherley,* pp. 31–32.

48. AGS, Estado, Leg. K. 1630, fol. 121 ("Relación de la Embajada que el Rey de Persia envió con Don Antonio Sirley, inglés, y Cussain Alibech, persiano. En Roma 8 de Junio 1601"). See also A. Gouvea, *Relation des grandes guerres et victoires obtenues par le Roi de Perse Chah Abbas contre les Empereurs de Turquie Mahomet et Achmet son fils* (Rouen, 1646), pp. 140–148.

49. *Ibid.*

50. Pastor, *History of the Popes,* XXIII, 298–300.

51. Le Strange, *Don Juan,* p. 277.

52. *CSP, Venice, 1592–1603,* IX, 437–438 (Piero Duodo, Venetian ambassador in Germany, to the Doge and Senate, 25 Dec. 1600, from Prague).

53. *Ibid.,* p. 445 (Piero Duodo, Venetian ambassador in Germany, to the Doge and Senate, 12 Feb. 1601, from Prague).

54. Le Strange, *Don Juan,* p. 282.

55. A. M. Crinò, *Fatti e figure del Seicento anglo-toscano* (Florence, 1957), pp. 12–13, quoting Archivio di Stato di Firenze, Fondo Mediceo, filza 896, c. 283. Details of Sir Anthony's visit to Florence are reported in Archivio di Stato di Firenze, Guardaroba medicea, Diario d'etichetta, Vol. III (1589–1612), cc. 163–164.

56. AGS, Estado, Francia, Leg. K. 1630, C. 36, fol. 88 ("El Duque de Sessa al Rey. Entrada en Roma de dos embajadores del Persiano, el uno inglés y otro moro," 10 April 1601, from Rome).

57. *Ibid.*

58. *CSP, Venice, 1592–1603,* IX, 451 (Giovanni Mocenigo, Venetian ambassador in Rome, to the Doge and Senate, 7 April 1601).

59. Ross, *Sir Anthony Sherley,* p. 47 (letter of Cardinal D'Ossat to King Henry IV of France, 11 April 1601).

60. AGS, Estado, Leg. K. 1630, fol. 121 ("Relación de la Embajada que al Rey de Persia envió con Don Antonio Sirley, inglés, y Cussein Alibech, persiano. En Roma 8 de junio 1601"). See also *Sherley Brothers,* pp. 32–33 (Father Persons to [Ralph?] Eure in England).

61. *CSP, Venice, 1592–1603,* IX, 451–452 (Giovanni Mocenigo, Venetian ambassador in Rome, to the Doge and Senate, 14 April 1601).

62. *Chronicle of the Carmelites,* I, 75 (citing Fondo Borghese, ser. III, no. 107). See also AGS, Estado, Francia, Leg. K. 1630, fol. 119 ("El Duque de Sessa al Rey: Con diversos papeles sobre la embajada del Rey de Persia. De Roma 8 junio 1601").

63. AGS, Estado, Francia, Leg. K. 1630, C. 36, fol. 88 ("El Duque de Sessa al Rey. Entrada en Roma de dos embajadores del Persiano, el uno inglés y otro moro," 10 April 1601, from Rome).

64. *Ibid.*

65. *Ibid.,* Leg. K. 1630, fol. 100 ("Inglaterra, 1601. Diferentes pareceres enviados en marzo y abril con la relación del parecer de lo que Don Antonio Sirley, inglés, de las cosas de allá").

66. *Ibid.*

67. *Ibid.*

68. Ross, *Sir Anthony Sherley,* pp. 49–50 (Cardinal D'Ossat to M. De Villeroy, 28 March 1601).

69. Cecil Papers, 182/44 (Sir Anthony Sherley to Anthony Bacon, 3 June 1601); calendared in *HMC Salisbury MSS,* XI (1906), 215–216. See also AGS, Estado, España, Leg. K. 1630, fol. 116 ("De Roma 4 de junio 1601"; endorsed: "Copia de carta del Duque de Sesa al de Feria. De Roma, 4 de junio 1601, y en esta conformidad se escribio al Duque de Albuquerque con el mismo Cussain Halibech").

70. AGS, Estado, Leg. K. 1630, fol. 121 ("Relación de la Embajada que al Rey de Persia envió con Don Antonio Sirley, inglés, y Cussein Alibech, persiano, en Roma 8 de junio 1601").

71. *CSP, Venice, 1592–1603,* IX, 462 (Marco Venier and Giovanni Mocenigo, Venetian ambassadors in Rome, to the Doge and Senate, Rome, 2 June 1601).

72. Ross, *Sir Anthony Sherley,* p. 50 (Cardinal D'Ossat to King Henry IV of France, 11 June 1601).

73. Cecil Papers, 182/80 (Matthew Greensmith to Sir Robert Cecil, 3 July 1601); calendared in *HMC Salisbury MSS,* XI, 264.

74. AGS, Estado, Nápoles, Leg. 1097, fol. 147 ("De Nápoles a 15 de julio 1601. El Conde de Lemos"; endorsed: "Al Rey nuestro señor. En manos de Don Pedro Franqueza su secretario").

75. *Ibid.,* fol. 175 ("Nápoles. El Conde de Lemos a Su Majestad, de 26 de agosto 1601. Descifrada").

76. *Ibid.,* fol. 217 ("Intención del Inglés Antonio Sirley de hacer juntamente con Don Manuel hijo del prior de Crato, empresa en las Indias portuguesas. Consulta del Consejo de Estado, entre otros asuntos sobre la carta del Conde de Lemos de haber llegado a Ragusa Don Antonio Sirley. Madrid, septiembre 1601"; endorsed: "Consejo de Estado"); fol. 147 ("De Nápoles a 15 de julio 1601. El Conde de Lemos"; endorsed: "Al Rey nuestro señor. En manos de Don Pedro Franqueza su secretario"); fol. 195 ("De Nápoles, 8 noviembre 1601. Don Francisco de Castro"; endorsed: "Al rey nuestro señor. En manos de Don Pedro Franqueza su secretario de Estado").

77. Gouvea, *Relation des grandes guerres,* pp. 140–148.

78. *Sherley Brothers,* pp. 36–37, 104.

79. AGS, Estado, Nápoles, Leg. 1097, fol. 175 ("Nápoles. El Conde de Lemos a Su Majestad, de 26 de agosto 1601. Descifrada"); *Sherley Brothers,* pp. 34–35 (citing SP, Turkey [Mr. Lello at the Porte to Robert Cecil, 2 Aug. 1601]). A Latin letter in the Cassel archives of the Landgrave Maurice of Hesse Cassel (from his agent in Florence, dated Florence, 7 July 1602) gives the impression that Sherley intended to return to Persia, but the agent's information was out of date.

NOTES

CHAPTER VIII. SIR ANTHONY AS A SECRET AGENT

1. AGS, Estado, Flandes, Leg. 2847, n.fol. ("Granada y enero 31 de 1623 años [i.e. 1624] Humilde servidor de Vuestra Excelencia, El Conde de Sherley"; endorsed: "Granada. Al Conde, mi señor. 1623. El conde de Cherley 31 de enero"; endorsed in another hand: "Visto y consultado sobre algunos puntos en 24 de abril") ; *ibid.,* Leg. 1171, fol. 92.

2. *Ibid.,* Francia, Leg. K. 1678, fol. 37 ("El Caballero Pagliarini al Rey de España. Venise 17 mayo 1608").

3. A. F. Allison, ed., *Biographical Studies* (Bognor Regis, 1951), II, 275; M. S. Rawson, *Penelope Rich and Her Circle* (London, 1911), pp. 234–238.

4. H. G. Stafford, *James VI of Scotland and the Throne of England* (New York, 1940), pp. 254–256; Sir D. Dalrymple, Lord Hailes, ed., *The Secret Correspondence of Sir Robert Cecil with James VI of Scotland* (London, 1766), pp. 155–157.

5. J. Bruce, ed., *Correspondence of King James VI of Scotland with Sir Robert Cecil and Others in England during the Reign of Queen Elizabeth* (London, 1861), pp. 40–41.

6. National Library of Scotland, Advocates MSS, 33.1.13, Vol. XXX, no. 2 (instructions for Captain Lawson to the King's Most High and Excellent Majesty, 28 Sept. 1602).

7. *Ibid.*

8. *Ibid.,* no. 18 (Sir Anthony Sherley to King James VI of Scotland, 14 Sept. 1602, from Venice).

9. *Ibid.*

10. *Ibid.,* no. 2 (instructions for Captain Lawson, 28 Sept. 1602).

11. *Ibid.,* no. 9 (Sir Anthony Sherley to King James VI of Scotland, 14 Sept. 1602, from Venice).

12. *Ibid.,* no. 2 (instructions for Captain Lawson, 28 Sept. 1602).

13. *Ibid.,* no. 19 (instructions for Captain Lawson to the King's Most High and Excellent Majesty).

14. *Ibid.,* no. 2 (instructions for Captain Lawson, 28 Sept. 1602).

15. J. F. Mozley, *John Foxe and His Book* (London, 1940), p. 9.

16. P. M. Handover, *The Second Cecil: The Rise to Power, 1563–1604, of Sir Robert Cecil, Later First Earl of Salisbury* (London, 1959), p. 268.

17. *HMC Calendar of the Manuscripts of the Most Honourable the Marquis of Salisbury,* XII (London, 1910), 323 (Thomas Wilson to Sir Robert Cecil, 27 Aug. 1602).

18. *Sherley Brothers,* p. 40 (Thomas Wilson to Sir Robert Cecil, 23 June 1602).

19. PRO, State Papers, Domestic, Elizabeth, SP 12/284, fol. 110 (Sir Anthony Sherley to Chief Justice Popham, 30 Aug. 1602, from Venice); calendared in *CSP, Domestic, 1601–1603,* p. 236.

20. *Sherley Brothers,* p. 40 (Thomas Wilson to Sir Robert Cecil, 3 July 1602).

21. *Ibid.,* p. 39 (Sir Anthony Sherley to the Countess of Cumberland, 20 July, 1602, from Venice).

22. *Ibid.,* p. 40 (Thomas Wilson to Sir Robert Cecil, 9 Aug. 1602, from Venice).

23. Advocates MSS, 33.1.13, Vol. XXX, no. 2.

24. *Sherley Brothers,* p. 41 (Simon Fox to Sir Robert Cecil, 20 June 1602); Handover, *Second Cecil,* p. 267.

25. B. Penrose, *The Sherleian Odyssey, Being a Record of the Travels and Adventures of Three Famous Brothers, during the Reigns of Elizabeth, James I, and Charles I* (London, 1938), p. 118.

26. Hatfield House Library, Cecil Papers, 95/12–14 (Thomas Wilson to Sir Robert Cecil, 27 Aug. 1602); calendared in *HMC Salisbury MSS,* XII, 323–325.

27. *Ibid.*

28. Advocates MSS, 33.1.13, Vol. XXX, no. 18 (Sir Anthony Sherley to King James VI of Scotland, 14 Sept. 1602, from Venice).

29. *Ibid.,* no. 2.

30. Cecil Papers, 96/2 (Sir Anthony Sherley to Sir Robert Cecil, 15 Oct. 1602, from Venice); calendared in *HMC Salisbury MSS,* XII, 442.

31. *Sherley Brothers,* p. 38 (Sir Anthony Sherley to the Countess of Cumberland, 20 July 1602).

32. PRO, State Papers, Domestic, Elizabeth, SP 12/284, fol. 78 (Sir Anthony Sherley to Chief Justice Popham, 20 July 1602); calendared in *CSP, Domestic, 1601–1603,* p. 224.

33. *Sherley Brothers,* p. 39 (Sir Anthony Sherley to the Countess of Cumberland, 20 July 1602).

34. Sir E. D. Ross, *Sir Anthony Sherley and His Persian Adventure* (London, 1933), p. 55 (citing a letter from the agent of the Landgrave of Hesse Cassel at Florence, 7 July 1602).

35. Cecil Papers, 99/163–164 (Aurelian Townsend to Sir Robert Cecil, 24 Oct. 1602, from Venice); calendared in *HMC Salisbury MSS,* XII, 455.

36. The investigations by the College, the discussions of Sherley's case before the Senate, his interrogation before the College or Commission appointed by the Senate, and the judgment rendered in his case are all contained in Venice, Archivio de Stato, Quarentia criminal, filza 114, 1603 ("Processo formato contro Antonio Sceles, Inglese, Fu spedito nel eccellentissimo Senato X maggio 1603"). The quotations given here are from that document.

37. G. Cappelletti, *Storia della Republica di Venezia* (Venice, 1855), IX, 291.

38. *CSP, Venice, 1603–1607,* X, 23, 29 (the proceedings of the Senate of 10, 14, 15, and 17 May 1603).

39. *Sherley Brothers,* p. 30 (Cecil to Lello, endorsed 17 Oct. 1600); *ibid.* (Sir Anthony Sherley to Sir Robert Cecil, 3 March 1602, from Venice);

CSP, Domestic, 1601–1603, p. 159 (Antony Tracy to Sir Robert Cecil, 5 March 1602).

40. A. M. Crinò, *Fatti e figure del Seicento anglo-toscano* (Florence, 1957), pp. 31-32 (Sir Henry Wotton to the Grand Duke of Tuscany, 14 Feb. 1604, from Venice).

41. Cecil Papers, 99/163–164 (Sir Anthony Sherley to the King, 9 May 1603); calendared in *HMC Salisbury MSS,* XV (1930), 77–80.

42. *CSP, Venice, 1603–1607,* X, 35 (Scaramelli to the Doge and Senate, 22 May 1603).

43. *Ibid.,* p. 72 (Scaramelli to the Doge and Senate, 30 July 1603).

44. *Ibid.,* pp. 73–74 (Scaramelli to the Doge and Senate, 6 Aug. 1603); *ibid.,* p. 100 (Scaramelli to the Doge and Senate, 5 Oct. 1603); *ibid.,* p. 88 (minutes of the Venetian Senate, 2 Sept. 1603); *Sherley Brothers,* p. 46; *CSP, Domestic, 1603–1610,* p. 76 ("Licence to Sir Anthony to remain beyond the seas," 8 Feb. 1604).

45. L. Hicks, "The Embassy of Sir Anthony Standen in 1603," *Recusant History,* VI (1962), 170–179.

46. Cecil Papers, 105/72 (Sir Anthony Sherley to Cecil, 22 May 1604); calendared in *HMC Salisbury MSS,* XVI (1933), 109–110.

47. *Ibid.,* 105/71 (Sherley to King James I, 22 May 1604); calendared in *HMC Salisbury MSS,* XVI, 109.

48. *Sherley Brothers,* pp. 47–48 (Sir Anthony Sherley to Sir Robert Cecil, 27 Feb. 1605).

49. Penrose, *Sherleian Odyssey,* p. 254 (Sir Anthony Sherley to the Imperial ambassador at Venice, 28 Feb. 1604).

50. *Ibid.,* p. 255 (Sir Anthony to the Emperor Rudolph, 19 June 1604, from Venice).

51. *Ibid.,* p. 256 (Sir Anthony to the Emperor Rudolph, 9 July 1604, from Venice).

52. *Ibid.*

53. *Ibid.*

54. *Ibid.,* p. 257 (Sir Anthony to the Emperor Rudolph, 11 Sept. 1604, from Venice).

55. *Ibid.,* p. 258 (Sir Anthony to the Emperor Rudolph, 3 Oct. 1604, from Venice).

56. *CSP, Venice, 1603–1607,* X, 194 (minutes of the Council of Ten, 1 Dec. 1604).

57. Sir A. Sherley, *Le "Peso Politico de Todo el Mundo" d'Anthony Sherley, ou un aventurier anglais au service de l'Espagne,* ed. Xavier-A. Flores (Paris, 1963), p. 69.

58. Penrose, *Sherleian Odyssey,* pp. 259–260 (Sir Anthony to the Emperor Rudolph, 26 Jan. 1605, from Ferrara).

59. *Ibid.,* p. 260 (Sir Anthony to the Emperor Rudolph, 10 Feb. 1605).

60. F. C. H. Babinger, *Sherleiana: I, Sir Anthony Sherley's persische Botschaftreise, 1599–1601; II, Sir Anthony Sherley's marokkanische Sen-*

dung 1605/1606 (Berlin, 1932), p. 35, quoting PRO, News Letters, no. 41.

61. Penrose, *Sherleian Odyssey,* pp. 128–129.

62. *Sherley Brothers,* p. 47 (Sir Anthony to Sir Thomas the elder, 20 Feb. 1604).

63. *Ibid.,* p. 45 (Sir Thomas the younger to Sir Anthony, 31 May 1605).

64. PRO, State Papers, Foreign, Turkey, SP 97/5, fol. 16 (Sir Thomas the younger to William Burton, 31 May 1605).

CHAPTER IX. WHAT BEFELL ROBERT IN PERSIA, HIS BROTHER SIR THOMAS IN TURKEY, AND SIR THOMAS THE ELDER IN ENGLAND

1. J. Cartwright, *The Preacher's Travels* (London, 1611), p. 70.

2. *A Chronicle of the Carmelites in Persia and the Papal Mission of the XVIIth and XVIIIth Centuries* (London, 1939), I, 143–144 (citing Fondo Borghese, II, no. 20, 181).

3. *Ibid.,* pp. 90–92.

4. A. Gouvea, *Relation des grandes guerres et victoires obtenues par le Roi de Perse Chah Abbas contre les Empereurs de Turquie Mahomet et Achmet son fils* (Rouen, 1646), pp. 102–103.

5. *Ibid.,* p. 107.

6. *Chronicle of the Carmelites,* I, 143–144 (citing Fondo Borghese, IV, no. 52, 346).

7. *Ibid.,* pp. 143–144 (citing Fondo Borghese II, no. 20, 181).

8. G. von der Jabel Tectander, *Iter Persicum, ou description du voyage en Perse entrepris en 1602 par Etienne Kakasch de Zalonkemeny envoyé comme ambassadeur par l'empereur Rudolph II à la cour du grand-duc de Moscovie et à celle de Chah Abbas, roi de Perse, Relation redigée en allemand et presenté a l'empereur par Georges Tectander von der Jabel, traduction publiée et annotée par Ch. Schefer* (Paris, 1877), pp. 42–46.

9. *Sherley Brothers,* p. 56 (Lello to Sir Robert Cecil, 7 May 1603).

10. A. Nixon, *The Three English Brothers, Sir T. Sherley his travels, Sir A. Sherley his embassage to the Christian princes, Master R. Sherley his wars against the Turkes* (London, 1607), fols. K2, verso–K4, recto.

11. *Sherley Brothers,* p. 61.

12. Cartwright, *Preacher's Travels,* p. 70.

13. *Sherley Brothers,* pp. 56–57.

14. *Sherley Brothers,* pp. 58–59.

15. *Ibid.,* p. 58.

16. *Chronicle of the Carmelites,* I, 119–124.

17. *Ibid.,* p. 126.

18. *Ibid.,* p. 131.

19. García de Silva y Figueroa, *L'Ambassade de D. Garcias [sic] de Silva*

Figueroa [*sic*] *en Perse, contenant la politique de ce grand Empire, les moeurs du roy Schah Abbas et une relation exacte de tous les lieux de Perse et des Indes, traduite de l'espagnol par M. de Wicqfort* (Paris, 1667), preface.

20. A. Nixon, *Three English Brothers,* fol. B2, recto. All of the quotations unless otherwise noted are from Nixon. Nixon's account of Robert Sherley bears all the marks of being a fabrication, while his report on the activities of Sir Thomas gives evidence of having been gotten directly from Sir Thomas. Possibly, since in 1607 Robert's embassy was news, Nixon attached his fictitious account of Robert to a factual account of Sir Thomas in order to take advantage of the public interest in Robert.

21. *CSP, Venice, 1592–1603,* IX, 544 (from Don Francesco de Heredi in Zante, 10 Feb. 1603; translated from Greek into Italian; enclosed with a letter of 6 March 1603 from Michiel to the Doge).

22. B. Penrose, *The Sherleian Odyssey, Being a Record of the Travels and Adventures of Three Famous Brothers, during the Reigns of Elizabeth, James I, and Charles I* (London, 1938), p. 37 (Lello to Sir Robert Cecil, 26 Feb. 1603).

23. *Sherley Brothers,* pp. 12–13 (quoting SP, Domestic, Feb. 1602).

24. Nixon, *Three English Brothers,* fol. D3, verso.

25. *Ibid.,* fol. E3, verso.

26. *Ibid.,* fol. F1, verso.

27. *HMC Calendar of the Manuscripts of the Most Honourable the Marquis of Salisbury,* XV (London, 1930), 137 (Sir Thomas Sherley to Sir Robert Cecil, 17 June 1603).

28. *Ibid.,* XVI (1933), 371 (Sir Thomas Sherley to Lord Cecil, 30 Nov. 1604).

29. *Ibid.,* p. 21 (Sir Thomas Sherley to the King, 3 Feb. 1604).

30. *Sherley Brothers,* pp. 44–45 (Sir Thomas the younger to Sir Anthony, last of May 1605).

31. *CSP, Venice, 1603–1607,* X, 311 n. (Lello to Robert Cecil, Earl of Salisbury, 19 Dec. 1605; the note is given in connection with a letter from Ottaviano Bon, Venetian ambassador in Constantinople, to the Doge and Senate, 6 Jan. 1606).

32. *Ibid.,* p. 311 (Ottaviano Bon, Venetian ambassador in Constantinople, to the Doge and Senate, 6 Jan. 1606).

33. Hatfield House Library, Cecil Papers, 116/72 (Sir Thomas Sherley to the Earl of Salisbury, 28 May 1606); calendared in *HMC Salisbury MSS,* XVIII (1940), 147.

34. Sir T. Sherley, *Discourse of the Turkes,* ed. E. Denison Ross (London, 1936), p. 21 n.

35. Cecil Papers, 116/71 (Sir Thomas Sherley to the King, 28 May 1606); calendared in *HMC Salisbury MSS,* XVIII, 147.

36. A. M. Crinò, *Fatti e figure del Seicento anglo-toscano* (Florence, 1957), p. 108 (Anthony Standen to Belisario Vinta, 27 Jan. 1607).

37. G. F. Warner, ed., *The Voyage of Robert Dudley, afterwards styled Earl of Warwick and Leicester and Duke of Northumberland, to the West Indies, 1594–1595, Narrated by Capt. Wyatt, by himself, and by Abram Kendall, master* (London, 1899), p. xii.

38. J. T. Leader, *Life of Sir Robert Dudley, Earl of Warwick and Duke of Northumberland* (Florence, 1895), App. II.

39. Archivio di Stato di Firenze, Mediceo del Principato, filza 942, c. 510.

40. *HMC Salisbury MSS,* XIX (1965), 173 (Sir Thomas Sherley the younger to the Earl of Warwick, 6 July 1607).

41. *Ibid.,* p. 174 (Sir Thomas Sherley the younger to Sir Anthony Sherley, 6 July 1607).

42. *Ibid.,* p. 474 (Sir Thomas Sherley the younger to the King, spring or summer of 1607).

43. *Ibid.,* p. 173 (Sir Thomas Sherley the younger to Giovanni Basadonna at Venice, 6 July 1607, from London).

44. *Sussex County Magazine,* IX (1935), 708 (Rowland Whyte to the Earl of Shrewsbury, 17 Sept. 1607).

45. *CSP, Venice, 1607–1610,* XI, 41 (Zorzi Giustiniani, Venetian ambassador in England, to the Doge and Senate, 3 Oct. 1607).

46. *HMC Salisbury MSS,* XIX, 474 (Sir Thomas Sherley the younger to the Earl of Salisbury, Sept. 1607).

47. PRO, State Papers, Foreign, Turkey, SP 97/5, fol. 257 (the questions put to Sir Thomas Sherley in the Tower and his answers).

48. *Sussex County Magazine,* IX (1935), 708 (Sir Thomas Sherley the younger to the Earl of Salisbury, 17 Sept. 1607).

49. Sir Thomas Sherley's *Discourse of the Turkes* (London, 1936), was edited by Sir E. Denison Ross and published by the Camden Society.

50. S. A. Moore, *A History of the Foreshore and the law relating thereto* (London, 1888), pp. 169–172.

51. British Museum, Lansdowne MSS, 50/69.

52. *Ibid.*

53. *CSP, Foreign, Sept. 1585–May 1586,* XX, 368 (Sir Thomas Sherley the elder to Burghley, 11 Feb. 1586); see also *ibid., April–Dec. 1587,* XXI, Part III, 72–73 (Sir Thomas Sherley to Burghley, 24 May 1587); *ibid.,* p. 174 (Sherley to Burghley, 13 July 1587).

54. J. Strype, *Annals of the Reformation* (Oxford, 1824), III, Part II, 577–579.

55. *Ibid.,* p. 56 and ff. Strype is mistaken in presuming that Sir Thomas Sherley actually secured a 99-year lease on the Cathedral's lands. The quotation is on p. 60.

56. Lansdowne MSS, 50/70; see also *HMC Salisbury MSS,* XIV, 272 (Thomas Fanshaw, Remembrancer of the Exchequer to the Queen, undated).

57. Cecil Papers, Petitions, no. 96 (Thomas Fanshaw, Remembrancer

of the Exchequer to the Queen, undated); calendared in *HMC Salisbury MSS,* XIV (1923), 272.

58. Strype, *Annals of the Reformation,* II, Part I, 450.

59. Cecil Papers, Petitions, no. 151 (Casper Vansenden, merchant of Lübeck, to the Queen, Nov. [1600?]); calendared in *HMC Salisbury MSS,* XIV, 143.

60. *Ibid.*

61. *Ibid.,* X, 399, 431.

62. G. W. Prothero, "The Parliamentary Privilege of Freedom from arrest and Sir Thomas Sherley's case, 1604," *English Historical Review,* VIII (Oct. 1893), 733–740.

63. The details concerning Sir Thomas Sherley's lands are contained in the Cranfield MSS deposited by Baron Sackville with the Historical Manuscripts Commission.

64. H. Lansdell, *The Sacred Tenth; or Studies in Tithe-giving, ancient and modern* (London, 1906), II, 306.

65. C. Hill, *Economic Problems of the Church from Archbishop Whitgift to the Long Parliament* (Oxford, 1963), p. 116.

66. *Ibid.,* p. 115.

67. *Ibid.,* p. 141.

68. Cecil Papers, 110/147 (Sir Thomas Sherley to the Earl of Salisbury, 11 May 1605); calendared in *HMC Salisbury MSS,* XVII (1938), 199, 218, 281.

69. Cecil Papers, 116/7 (Roger Manners to the Earl of Salisbury, 17 April 1606), and 116/23 (Sir Thomas Sherley to the Earl of Salisbury, 27 April 1606), calendared in *HMC Salisbury MSS,* XVIII, 113, 124; *CSP, Domestic, 1603–1610,* p. 297 (Roger Manners to the Earl of Salisbury, 9 March 1606).

70. Cecil Papers, 117/79 (Sir Thomas Sherley to the Earl of Salisbury, 29 Aug. 1606); calendared in *HMC Salisbury MSS,* XVIII, 266.

71. Cecil Papers, 118/4 (Sir Thomas Sherley to the Earl of Salisbury, 13 Oct. 1606); calendared in *HMC Salisbury MSS,* XVIII, 322.

72. E. P. Shirley, *Stemmata Shirleiana, or The Annals of the Shirley Family* (2nd ed.; Westminster, 1873), p. 255; Lansdowne MSS, 166, fol. 256 (fol. 260 in the new numbering).

73. Inner Temple Library, MS no. 538, fol. 27.

CHAPTER X. SIR ANTHONY, DIPLOMAT, ADMIRAL, AND COUNT PALATINE

1. Captain Melchior, a Portuguese, on the advantages of the Moroccan trade in 1561, as quoted by T. S. Willan, *Studies in Elizabethan Foreign Trade* (Manchester, 1959), p. 107.

2. Comte H. de Castries, *Les sources inédites de l'histoire du Maroc de 1530 à 1845* (Paris, 1918–1935), *Ser. I, Archives et Bibliothèques d'Angleterre,* II, 299–300 (citing British Museum, Harleian MSS, 1875, fol. 634); *ibid., Ser. I, Archives et Bibliothèques des Pays-Bas,* II, 109 (P. M. Coy to the States, 16 Dec. 1605).

3. *Ibid., Ser. I, Archives et Bibliothèques de France,* II, 336–340 (citing Bibliothèque Nationale, fond français, 16145, fols. 24–27 [A. De L'Isle to Villeroy, 10 April 1606]); *ibid., Ser. I, Archives et Bibliothèques des Pays-Bas,* I, 161 (P. M. Coy to the Estates General, 3 Oct. 1606).

4. *Ibid., Ser. I, Archives et Bibliothèques d'Angleterre,* II, 318–321 ("Muley Hamet's Rise"). Castries believes this work to be by George Wilkins.

5. *Ibid., Ser. I, Archives et Bibliothèques de France,* II, 330–335 (De Lisle to Villeroy, 29 Jan. 1606).

6. *Ibid., Ser. I, Archives et Bibliothèques des Pays-Bas,* I, 148 (P. M. Coy to the Estates General, from Marrakesch, 18 May 1606); *ibid.,* p. 151 (P. M. Coy to the Estates General, 21 June 1606); *ibid.,* p. 161 (P. M. Coy to the Estates General, 3 Oct. 1606).

7. Castries, *ibid., Archives et Bibliothèques d'Angleterre,* II, 292–293 (citing Harleian MSS, 1875, fol. 607); *ibid.,* pp. 274–282; *ibid., Ser. I, Archives et Bibliothèques de France,* II, 345–346 (Barrault to Villeroy, 16 Oct. 1606, from Madrid); *ibid., Ser. I, Archives et Bibliothèques des Pays-Bas,* I, 151 (P. M. Coy to the Estates General, 21 June 1606).

8. *Ibid., Ser. I, Archives et Bibliothèques d'Angleterre,* II, 274–282.

9. *Sherley Brothers,* p. 53 (Hugh Lee, English consul in Portugal, to the Earl of Salisbury, 8 Sept. 1606).

10. W. C. Atkinson, *A History of Spain and Portugal* (London, 1961), p. 169.

11. P. Aguado Bleye, *Manuel de Historia de España* (Madrid, 1958–1964), II, 697.

12. M. A. S. Hume, *The Court of Philip IV, Spain in Decadence* (London, 1907), p. 20.

13. M. A. S. Hume, *Spain, Its Greatness and Decay, 1479–1788* (Cambridge, 1925), p. 209.

14. Hume, *Court of Philip IV,* p. 17.

15. *CSP, Venice, 1603–1607,* X, 418 (Francesco Priuli, Venetian ambassador in Spain, to the Doge and Senate, 1 Nov. 1606).

16. AGS, Estado, Leg. 1171, fol. 70 (Anthony Sherley to one of the King's ministers, almost certainly Villalonga, late 1606 or early 1607).

17. *Sherley Brothers,* p. 54 (Sir Anthony Sherley to the Earl of Salisbury, 7 Sept. 1606).

18. AGS, Estado, Leg. 1171, fol. 77 (Count Anthony Sherley to the Count of Villalonga, endorsed: "Para veer el Signore Conde de Villalunga [sic]," Dec. 1606).

19. *CSP, Venice, 1603–1607,* X, 436–437 (Francesco Priuli, Venetian ambassador in Spain, to the Doge and Senate, 27 Nov. 1606).

20. *Ibid.,* p. 458 (Francesco Priuli, Venetian ambassador in Spain, to the Doge and Senate, 28 Jan. 1607).

21. Castries, *Les sources inédites, Ser. I, Archives, et Bibliothèques d'Angleterre,* II, 299–300 (citing Harleian MSS, 1875, fol. 634).

22. AGS, Estado, Sicilia, Leg. 1171, fol. 206 ("Relación de lo que se trato con Sirley, desde el año de 1607 hasta el presente en que estamos de 1611"); *ibid.,* fol. 71 ("De mi posada a los 28 de noviembre de 1606. De Vuestra Sacra Católica Real Majestad, Humilissimo criado, Don Antonio Sherley"; endorsed: "Para ver al Señor Conde de Villalonga").

23. *Ibid.,* fol. 52 (endorsed: "Para la contratación del Brasil. Consultado en 13 de enero de 1607"); *ibid.,* fol. 7 ("En Madrid, a 14 de enero de 1607," endorsed: "Consulta de la Junta de Tres, sobre lo que parece cerca de los papeles que ha propuesto Don Antonio Sirley").

24. The writer has been unable to locate Cafia precisely. It is not a misreading of the manuscripts. There are the Iles Chafarines on the Mediterranean coast of Morocco, but since Sir Anthony only knew the Atlantic coast, he probably did not refer to those islands.

25. AGS, Estado, Sicilia, Leg. 1171, fol. 7 ("En Madrid, a 14 de enero de 1607," endorsed: "Consulta de la Junta de Tres, sobre lo que parece cerca de los papeles que ha propuesto Don Antonio Sirley").

26. *Ibid.,* fol. 16 (at the head of the document: "Los papeles que Vuestra Majestad ha visto de Don Antonio Sirley, contienen en suma lo que se sigue"; at the end of the document: "Vuestra Majestad lo mandará ver y proveer lo que mas fuere servido. En Madrid a 10 de febrero de 1607"; endorsed: "El Consejo de Estado. A 10 de febrero 1607. Sobre las propuestas de Don Antonio Sirley").

27. *Ibid.*

28. *Ibid.,* fol. 8 ("Lo que Su Majestad ha resuelto sobre las propuestas de Don Antonio de Sirley").

29. Sir R. Winwood, *Memorials and Affairs of State in the Reigns of Q. Elizabeth and K. James I* (London, 1725), II, 273.

30. *Ibid.,* p. 319 (Sir Charles Cornwallis to the Earl of Salisbury, 14 June 1607).

31. AGS, Estado, Sicilia, Leg. 1171, fol. 35 ("En Madrid a 5 de marzo de 1607"; endorsed: "La Junta de dos. A 5 de marzo 1607. Sobre lo que contiene un papel de Don Antonio Sirley, en lo de la conquista de Tonbotu").

32. *Sherley Brothers,* p. 65 (Mr. Offeley to Mr. R. Cocks, Madrid, 14 March 1607).

33. *CSP, Venice, 1603–1607,* X, 498 (Francesco Priuli, Venetian ambassador in Spain, to the Doge and Senate, 20 May 1607).

34. *Sherley Brothers,* pp. 65–66 (Sir Charles Cornwallis to the Earl of Salisbury, 31 March 1607, from Madrid).

35. *Ibid.,* p. 66 (John Jude to Thomas Wilson, 9 June 1607, from Madrid).

36. *Ibid.,* p. 67 (Sir Henry Wotton to the Earl of Salisbury, 2 Oct. 1607); *CSP, Venice, 1603–1607,* X, 478 (Francesco Priuli, Venetian ambassador in Spain to the Doge and Senate, 8 March 1607); AGS, Estado, Sicilia, Leg. 1171, fol. 206 ("Relación de lo que se trato con Sirley, desde el año de 1607 hasta el presente en que estamos de 1611").

37. AGS, Estado, Sicilia, Leg. 1171, fol. 40 (on the document cover: "Nápoles. A Su Majestad. 1607. Don Antonio Sirley. a 19 de julio. Recibida a 22 de agosto. Avisa de su llegada a Nápoles y toca diversos puntos, así sobre su viaje como sobre otras cosas").

38. *HMC Calendar of the Manuscripts of the Most Honourable the Marquis of Salisbury,* XIX (London, 1965), 234–235 (Anthony Tracy to Sir Thomas Sherley, the younger, 30 Aug. 1607, from Florence).

39. *Ibid.,* p. 240 (John Ingram to George Rooke, in my Lord Ambassador's House, Venice, 1 Sept. 1607, from Leghorn).

40. AGS, Estado, Alemania, Leg. 2494, fol. 44 ("De Praga, 5 enero 1608. Don Guillén de San Clemente"; endorsed: "Praga, A Su Majestad. Avisa la llegado allí de Don Antonio de Sirley"; another endorsement: "Al Rey Nuestro Señor: En manos de Andrés de Prada, su secretario").

41. F. C. H. Babinger, *Sherleiana: I, Sir Anthony Sherley's persische Botschaftreise, 1599–1601; II, Sir Anthony Sherley's marokkanische Sendung 1605/1606* (Berlin, 1932), p. 39.

42. AGS, Estado, Alemania, Leg. 2494, fol. 44 ("De Praga, 5 enero 1608. Don Guillén de San Clemente"; endorsed: "Praga, A Su Majestad. Avisa la llegado allí de Don Antonio de Sirley"; another endorsement: "Al Rey Nuestro Señor: En manos de Andrés de Prada, su secretario").

43. *CSP, Venice, 1607–1610,* XI, 117 (the secretary of the English ambassador speaking before the Cabinet in Venice, 8 April 1608).

44. *Sherley Brothers,* p. 67 (G. Rooke, "to his bedfellow and cousin," 18 April 1608).

45. AGS, Estado, Leg. K. 1678, G. 7, fol. 28 ("Alonso de la Cueva al Rey. Descifrado. Con notas"; endorsed: "Venecia. A Su Majestad. Don Alonso de la Cueva, 5 abril. Recibida en 2 de mayo").

46. *Sherley Brothers,* pp. 67–68 (citing British Museum, Lansdowne MSS, 90/68 [Count Anthony to his sister, Lady Tracy, 12 May 1608, from Milan]).

47. AGS, Estado, Francia, Leg. K. 1678, G. 7, fol. 42 ("De Venecia, 29 de mayo 1608. Don Alonso de la Cueva y Benavides"; endorsed: "Al Rey, nuestro señor, en manos de Andrés de Prada, su secretario de Estado"; another endorsement: "Don Alonso de la Cueva a 29 de mayo. Recibida a 27 de junio. Envia una que la ha dado Tomas Pagliari, secretario que ha sido de Don Antonio Sirley").

48. *Ibid.,* fol. 37 ("De Venetia a 12 maggio 1608. Che iddio fellicīti Vostra Maesta Catolico, infiniti secoli. Di Vostra Maesta Catolica humillissimo servitor, Il cavagliero Pagliarini"; endorsed: "Allá Sua Maesta Catolica, del Re nostro signore").

49. *Ibid.,* Sicilia, Leg. 1171, fol. 206 ("Relación de lo que se trato con Sirley, desde el año de 1607 hasta el presente en que estamos de 1611").

50. *Ibid.,* Leg. 1163, fol. 163 ("De Mallorca a 3 de marzo 1609. El Conde Don Antonio Sherley" [Count Sherley to the King]); *ibid.,* fol. 166 ("En Palermo a 20 de marzo de 1609 años. El Conde Don Antonio Sherley" [Count Sherley to the King]); *ibid.,* Flandes, Leg. 626, fol. 53 (endorsed: "De cartas del Conde Don Antonio Serley de Mayorca y de Palermo, de 21 de marzo de 1609"; the letter from Majorca is dated 3 March 1609, that from Palermo, 21 March 1609); *ibid.,* Sicilia, Leg. 1163, fol. 164 ("En Malloca [sic] a 10 de marzo 1609. Don Juan Vilaragur").

51. *Ibid.,* Sicilia, Leg. 1171, fol. 124 ("En Palermo a los 3 de abril de 1609 años. El Conde Don Antonio Sherley"; endorsed: "Palermo. A Su Majestad"; another endorsement: "Don Antonio Sirley a 3 de abril 1609. Recibida a 30 de mayo").

52. *Ibid.,* Leg. 1163, fol. 166 ("En Palermo a 20 de marzo de 1609 años. El Conde Don Antonio Sherley" [Count Sherley to the King]).

53. *Relation of the most famous kingdoms and commonweals through the world* (London, 1616), p. 240. This book is a translation by Robert Johnson of a work by Giovanni Botero, but in this, the 1616 edition, Johnson incorporated a section on Sicily taken from George Sandys, *A Relation of a Journey begun An. Dom. 1610. Foure Bookes. Containing a Description of the Turkish Empire, of Ægypt, of the Holy Land, of the remote parts of Italy, and Ilands adjoyning* (London, 1615). The writer has not had an opportunity to see Sandys' work.

54. AGS, Estado, Sicilia, Leg. 1171, fol. 166 (endorsed: "Sobre la patente de capitán general de los navíos de alto borde de Vuestra Majestad en el mar Mediterráneo"). In the same legajo (fol. 167) is the patent that Sherley requested.

55. *Ibid.,* fol. 124 ("En Palermo a los 3 de abril de 1609 años. El Conde Don Antonio Sherley"; endorsed: "Palermo. A Su Majestad. Don Antonio Shirley a 3 de abril 1609. Recibida a 30 de mayo").

56. Winwood, *Memorials and Affairs of State,* III, 38–40 (Sir Charles Cornwallis to the Lord Treasurer, 10 May 1609).

57. AGS, Estado, Sicilia, Leg. 1171, fol. 125 ("De Palermo a 9 de abril de 1609. El Conde Don Antonio Sherley"; endorsed: "Palermo. A Su Majestad. 1609 Don Antonio Sirley a 9 de abril"); *ibid.,* fol. 130 ("En Palermo a 30 de abril 1609. El Marqués, Duque de Escalona"; endorsed: "Palermo. A Su Majestad. El Duque de Escalona a 30 abril 1609. Recibida a 26 de mayo"); *ibid.,* fol. 176 (no date; endorsed: "Sobre la fabrica de atarazanas y almacenes par la provision de la armada de Vuestra Majestad en Trapana o en Siragoza, etcetera. A consulta que pues el Virrey ha escrito que no se puede dar el gobierno de Trapana, a Don Antonio Sirley, conforme a los privelegios del Reino, se puede omitir la respuesta de este punto"); *ibid.,* fol. 112 (no date; endorsed: "Don Antonio Sirley. Propone medios por los cuales le parece conviene subir

la moneda en España"); *ibid.*, fol. 127 ("En Palermo a 30 de abril de 1609 años. El Conde Don Antonio Sherley"; endorsed: "Palermo. A Su Majestad. Don Antonio Sirley, a 30 de abril 1609. Recibida a 26 de mayo"); *ibid.*, fol. 101 (no date; "Don Antonio de Sirley sobre el arbitrio de los leonicos, moneda de Polonia"; endorsed: "Sobre la estampa de los leonicos en Sicilia"); *ibid.*, fol. 206 ("Relación de lo que se trato con Sirley, desde el año de 1607 hasta el presente en que estamos de 1611").

58. Actually a small number of Moriscos were deported as late as 1614. The number deported has been estimated by different historians at 104,000; 310,000; 340,000; 400,000; 600,000; 900,000; a million. The figure given here is that arrived at by Henri Lapeyre in his most admirable study, *Geographie de l'Espagne Morisque* (Paris, 1959), which is based on careful and exhaustive study of the reports on the number of Moriscos deported from the various parts of Spain which were made to the government at the time. Lapeyre shows that while most contemporary historians had a fairly accurate idea of the number of Moriscos, and the number deported, there were already at that time writers who, in an effort to demonstrate that the Moriscos were a menace, placed their numbers higher than they actually were. The same desire motivated writers to increase the number in the following centuries. In the nineteenth century a new motive appeared for exaggerating the number. Some non-Spanish writers wished to show that the economy of Spain was ruined by intolerance and bigotry, and so they increased the number deported and exaggerated the importance of the Moriscos in the economy of Spain. It was in the nineteenth century that the figure reached a million. Two writers of the present day, Mr. Earl J. Hamilton and Señor Ignacio Olagüe, have concluded (for different reasons) that the figure (140,000) given by the commissioners of the King who planned and carried out the deportation was probably the correct one. Mr. Hamilton in his study of prices in Spain could find only negligible indications that the deportations had affected the economy and concluded therefore that the Moriscos must have been far fewer than had been supposed. Señor Olagüe believes that Spanish historians have been too much inclined to look for internal and superficial causes of Spanish decadence; for example, that the decadence of Spain was caused by the Inquisition, the incompetent Hapsburgs, or by the Moriscos. In support of his thesis he argues that the Moriscos were few in number and hence their deportation could have had little effect upon Spain's fortunes. Lapeyre charitably concludes that the records at Simancas are in an out-of-the-way place and that this has caused historians to neglect them.

59. AGS, Estado, Sicilia, Leg. 1171, fol. 206 ("Relación de lo que se trato con Sirley, desde el año de 1607 hasta el presente en que estamos de 1611").

60. *Sherley Brothers*, p. 71 (Count Anthony Sherley to Sir Thomas Sherley the elder, 9 Sept. 1609, from Palermo).

61. *Ibid.*, p. 70 (Francis Cottington to the Earl of Salisbury, 3 Nov.

1609). Concerning Skipper Carleson, see H. Lonchay and J. Cuvelier, eds., *Correspondance de la Cour d'Espagne sur les affaires des Pays Bas au XVIIe siècle* (Brussels, 1923), I, 350–351, as quoted by Xavier-A. Flores in his edition of Sir Anthony Sherley's *Le "Peso Politico de Todo el Mundo" d'Anthony Sherley, ou un aventurier anglais au service de l'Espagne* (Paris, 1963), pp. 31–32.

62. AGS, Estado, Sicilia, Leg. 1171, fol. 182 ("Data en Palermo a quatro de octubre, 1609. El Marqués, Por mandado de Su Excelencia: Roque de Osma"; the document begins: "Don Juan Fernandez Portocarrero, Marqués de Villena, Duque de Escalona, Virrey, Lugarteniente y Capitán general por Su Majestad en este reino de Sicilia," and at the end of the document are the words, "Instruccion para el Ilustre Conde Don Antonio Sirley").

63. *Ibid.,* Leg. 1163, fol. 252 ("De la real, 11 de octubre 1609. El Conde Don Antonio Sherley" [Count Anthony to the King]).

64. *Ibid.,* fol. 251 ("De Micina, 29 de octubre 1609. El Conde Don Antonio Sherley"; endorsed: "Don Antonio Sirley. No hay que responder").

65. *Ibid.,* Leg. 1171, fol. 183 (summary of a letter of the Duke of Escalona, 13 Nov. 1609, from Palermo).

66. *Ibid.,* Leg. 1163, fol. 260 ("En Palermo, 23 de diciembre 1609. El Marqués"; at the foot of the letter: "Señor Conde Sirley"; endorsed: "Del Marqués de Villena").

67. *Ibid.,* Leg. 1164, fol. 6 ("En Palermo, 5 de febrero de 1610. El Marqués"; endorsed: "El Rey nuestro señor. En manos de Andrés de Prada, su secretario de Estado"; another endorsement: "El Duque de Escalona, a 5 de febrero, recibida a 12 abril").

68. *Ibid.,* Leg. 1171, fol. 184 ("De este Puerto de Zaragoza a dos de enero de 1610. El Conde Don Antonio Sherley" [Count Sherley to the King]).

69. *Ibid.,* Leg. 1164, fol. 34 ("En Palermo a 2 de junio 1610. El Marqués"; endorsed: "Palermo, A Su Majestad"; another endorsement: "El Duque de Escalona, a 2 de junio, recibida a 28").

70. *Ibid.,* fol. 6 (*consulta* appended to Escalona's report of 5 Feb. 1610; see note 67 above).

71. Berkshire County Record Office, Trumbull MSS, 21/37 (Francis Cottington to William Trumbull, 11 Nov. 1610, from Madrid); calendared in *HMC Report on the Manuscripts of the Marquess of Downshire,* II (London, 1936), 393.

72. AGS, Estado, Leg. 229, n.fol. ("Del real de Valencia a 25 de enero 1611. El Marqués de Caracena"; endorsed: "Valencia. A Su Majestad. 1611"; another endorsement: "El marqués de Caracena, a 25 de enero. Recibida en 31").

73. *Sherley Brothers,* p. 75 (Francis Cottington to the Earl of Salisbury, 22 Feb. 1611).

74. *Ibid.,* pp. 75–76 (Francis Cottington to the Earl of Salisbury, 10 April 1611).

75. AGS, Estado, Sicilia, Leg. 1171, fol. 209 ("En Madrid a 14 de mayo de 1611. Andrés de Prada"); *ibid.,* fols. 210, 211 (fol. 211 is the original letter from Count Anthony in which he asks that he be allowed to go to the Indies to die, and in which he protests the order that he return to Naples; fol. 210 is the more coherent or more legible copy. The letter ends: "De Casa a 14 de mayo 1611. Besa las manos de Vuestra Merced, su verdadero servidor, El Conde Don Antonio Sherley").

76. *Ibid.,* fol. 207 (from the Comendador Mayor de Leon to the King; endorsed: "El Comendador Mayor de Leon a 30 de mayo de 1611. Sobre particulares de Don Antonio Sirley").

77. *HMC Reports on the Manuscripts of the Earl of Eglinton, Sir J. Stirling Maxwell, Bart., C.S.H. Drummond Moray, Esq., C.F. Weston Underwood, Esq., and G. Wingfield Digby, Esq.* (London, 1885), p. 522 (Sir J. Digby to Sir T. Edmonds, 22 June 1611).

78. AGS, Estado, Flandes, Leg. 626, fol. 291.

79. *HMC G. Wingfield Digby MSS,* p. 526 (Sir John Digby to Sir Thomas Edmonds, 14 Aug. 1611, from Madrid).

80. *Ibid.,* p. 527 (Sir John Digby to Sir Dudley Carleton, 17 Aug. 1611).

81. AGS, Estado, Sicilia, Leg. 1171, fol. 180.

82. *HMC G. Wingfield Digby MSS,* p. 534 (Sir John Digby to Sir Dudley Carleton, 14 Sept. 1611, from Madrid).

CHAPTER XI. ROBERT SHERLEY, PERSIAN AMBASSADOR

1. *Sherley Brothers,* pp. 61–62 (Thomas Glover to the Earl of Salisbury, 2 July 1608, from Constantinople).

2. T. Middleton, *Sir Robert Sherley, sent Ambassadour in the name of the King of Persia to Sigismond the third, King of Poland and Swecia* (London, 1609).

3. *A Chronicle of the Carmelites in Persia and the Papal Mission of the XVIIth and XVIIIth Centuries* (London, 1939), I, 145; F.C.H. Babinger, *Sherleiana: I, Sir Anthony Sherley's persische Botschaftreise, 1599–1601; II, Sir Anthony Sherley's marokkanische Sendung, 1605/1606* (Berlin, 1932), p. 49.

4. *CSP, Venice, 1607–1610,* XI, 330 (Giacomo Vendramin, Venetian resident in Florence, to the Doge and Senate, 5 Sept. 1609).

5. *Ibid.,* XI, 341 (Giacomo Vendramin, Venetian resident in Florence, to the Doge and Senate, 12 Sept. 1609).

6. *HMC Report on the Manuscripts of the Marquess of Downshire,* II, (London, 1936), 123 (William Trumbull to Sir Thomas Edmondes, 13 Sept. 1609). This letter is presently deposited in the Berkshire County

Records Office. It is a draft of a letter in the British Museum (Stowe MSS, 171/163).

7. *CSP, Venice, 1607–1610,* XI, 361 (Giovanni Mocenigo, Venetian ambassador in Rome, to the Doge and Senate, 3 Oct. 1609).

8. *Chronicle of the Carmelites,* I, 147–149.

9. *Ibid.,* p. 145. See also Biblioteca Nacional, Madrid, MS no. 8180, fol. 128, verso ("Brebe Relación de la Justificación que da El Conde Dn Roberto Sherley a la Magd. Catholica de España"). According to Robert Sherley, these honors were accorded him by an Apostolic Brief dated 7 October 1609.

10. British Museum, Additional MSS, 29546, SP 43820; Biblioteca Nacional, Madrid, MS no. 8180. Count Robert states in the latter manuscript that at this time he formed a friendship with Cardinal Borghese and that the Cardinal corresponded with him for some time. The Cardinal's papers may contain additional Sherley material.

11. *Sherley Brothers,* p. 72 (Francis Cottington to the Earl of Salisbury, 18 Jan. 1610); see also Sir R. Winwood, *Memorials and Affairs of State in the Reigns of Q. Elizabeth and K. James I* (London, 1725), III, 98 (Francis Cottington to William Trumbull, 20 Dec. 1609, from Madrid).

12. *Sherley Brothers,* p. 72 (Francis Cottington to the Earl of Salisbury, 20 Jan. 1610).

13. AGS, Estado, Leg. 229, n.fol. ("Sumario de los papeles tocantes a Don Roberto Serley y a otro embajador persiano que ha venido por Lisboa"; endorsed: "Papeles tocantes a Don Roberto Serley y a otro embajador de Persia que vino por Lisboa. En Madrid a primero de Febrero 1611").

14. *Sherley Brothers,* pp. 72–73 (Francis Cottington to the Earl of Salisbury, 5 Feb. 1610).

15. Biblioteca Nacional, Madrid, MS no. 8180, fols. 124–130 ("Brebe Relación"); AGS, Estado, Leg. 229, n.fol. ("Sumario de los papeles").

16. AGS, Estado, Alemania, Leg. 2864, fol. 82 (extracts of a *consulta* chiefly concerned with how to deal with Robert Sherley to Spain's best advantage).

17. *Ibid.,* fol. 78 (extracts of a *consulta* on the instructions and secret instructions to be given to a Spanish ambassador to be sent to Persia).

18. *Ibid.,* fol. 68 ("De El Espinar a 27 de febrero 1610. El Duque al Presidente del Consejo de Hacienda").

19. PRO, State Papers, Foreign, Spain, SP 94/17, fol. 74 (Francis Cottington to the Earl of Salisbury, 29 April 1610); calendared in *CSP, Colonial Series, East Indies, China, and Japan, 1513–1616,* p. 215.

20. PRO, State Papers, Foreign, Spain, SP 94/17, fols. 158–160 (Francis Cottington to the Earl of Salisbury, 10 Aug. 1610, from Madrid); calendared in *CSP, Colonial Series, East Indies, China, and Japan, 1513–1616,* pp. 205–206.

21. AGS, Estado, Leg. 229, n.fol. ("De Lisboa a 5 de febrero 1611. Don Cristóbal [de Mora]"; at the foot of the document: "Señor Secretario

Antonio de Arostigui"; endorsed: "Lisboa A.A. 1611. Don Cristóbal de Mora, a 5 de febrero. Recibida a 11").

22. *Ibid.*, n.fol. ("Lisboa a 8 de enero de 1611. Cristóbal de Moura"; endorsed: "Lisboa. A Su Majestad. 1611. El Marqués de Castel Rodrigo, 8 de enero").

23. *CSP, Colonial Series, East Indies, China, and Japan, 1513–1616,* pp. 209–210 (Francis Cottington to the Earl of Salisbury, 5 Jan. 1611, from Madrid); *Sherley Brothers,* p. 74.

24. *Sherley Brothers,* p. 74.

25. Winwood, *Memorials and Affairs of State,* III, 250 (Francis Cottington to William Trumbull at Brussels, 10 Jan. 1611, from Madrid).

26. *Sherley Brothers,* p. 74 (Francis Cottington to the Earl of Salisbury, 5 Jan. 1611, from Madrid).

27. *CSP, Colonial Series, East Indies, China, and Japan, 1513–1616,* pp. 209–210 (Francis Cottington to the Earl of Salisbury, 5 Jan. 1611).

28. A. Gouvea, *Relation des grand guerres et victoires obtenues par le Roi de Perse Chah Abbas contre les Empereurs de Turquie Mahomet et Achmet son fils* (Rouen, 1646), pp. 454–459.

29. *Chronicle of the Carmelites,* I, 146 n.

30. AGS, Estado, Leg. 229, n.fol. ("Sumario de los papeles").

31. *CSP, Venice, 1610–1613,* XII, 124 (Piero Priuli, Venetian ambassador in Spain, to the Doge and Senate, 12 March 1611).

32. AGS, Estado, Leg. 229, n.fol. ("Sumario de los papeles").

33. *Chronicle of the Carmelites,* I, 202.

34. Biblioteca Nacional, Madrid, MS no. 8180, fol. 127, verso ("Brebe Relación"); A. T. Wilson, *Early Spanish and Portuguese Travels in Persia* (Guildford, 1927), pp. 24–25.

35. AGS, Estado, Flandes, Leg. 626, fol. 279 ("Sustancia de los tres papeles de Don Antonio Sirley").

36. PRO, State Papers, Foreign, Spain, SP 94/18, fol. 91 (Sir John Digby to the Earl of Salisbury, 4 June 1611); calendared in *CSP, Colonial Series, East Indies, China, and Japan, 1513–1616,* p. 224.

37. Comte H. de Castries, *Les sources inédites de l'histoire du Maroc de 1530 à 1845* (Paris, 1918–1935), *Ser. I, Archives et Bibliothèques des Pays-Bas,* I, 189 n.; H. Dunlop, ed., *Bronnen tot de Geschiedenis der Oostindische Compagnie in Persië* (The Hague, 1930), I, lxii of introduction.

38. Dunlop, *Oostindische Compagnie in Persië,* I, 1–4.

39. *Ibid.*

40. *Ibid.*, pp. lxii–lxiii.

41. Berkshire County Record Office, Trumbull MSS, 47/35 (Sir Ralph Winwood to William Trumbull, 2 July 1611); calendared in *HMC Downshire MSS,* III (1938), 101.

42. *HMC Report on the Manuscripts of Lord De L'Isle and Dudley, Preserved at Penshurst Place, Kent,* IV (London, 1942), 277 (Sir John Throckmorton to Lord De L'Isle, 8 July 1611, from Flushing).

43. *Ibid.*

44. *Sherley Brothers,* p. 77 (Count Robert to the Earl of Salisbury, 30 Aug. 1611, from Wiston).

45. *CSP, Venice, 1610–1613,* XII, 226 (Antonio Foscarini, Venetian ambassador in England, to the Doge and Senate, 21 Oct. 1611).

46. *Sherley Brothers,* p. 80 (Count Robert to the Earl of Salisbury, 2 March 1612).

47. *Ibid.*

48. *CSP, Colonial Series, East Indies, China, and Japan, 1513–1616,* p. 231 (Count Robert Sherley to the Earl of Salisbury, 12 Dec. 1611).

49. PRO, Colonial Office, East Indies, CO 77/1, fol. 32 (Count Robert Sherley to the Earl of Salisbury, 12 Dec. 1611); calendared in *CSP, Colonial Series, East Indies, China, and Japan, 1513–1616,* pp. 232–233.

50. *CSP, Domestic, 1611–1618* (London, 1858), p. 140 (Archbishop Abbot to King James I, 3 Aug. 1612, from Croydon).

51. *Ibid., Colonial Series, East Indies, China, and Japan, 1513–1616,* p. 238; Biblioteca Nacional, Madrid, MS no. 8180, fol. 127, verso ("Brebe Relación"; the letter, Count Robert says, was dated 15 June 1611).

52. *Sherley Brothers,* p. 78 (Sir John Digby to the Earl of Salisbury, 19 Jan. 1612, from Madrid).

53. *CSP, Venice, 1607–1610,* XI, 281, 317–318, 325, 343, 361, 372; *ibid., Colonial Series, East Indies, China, and Japan, 1513–1616,* p. 231.

54. Winwood, *Memorials and Affairs of State,* III, 428 (John Chamberlain to Sir Ralph Winwood, 29 Jan. 1613).

55. *CSP, Domestic, 1611–1618,* p. 162 (John Chamberlain to Sir Dudley Carleton, 17 Dec. 1612).

56. E. P. Shirley, *Stemmata Shirleiana, or The Annals of the Shirley Family* (2nd ed.; Westminster, 1873), p. 256; National Library of Scotland, Advocates MSS, 33.1.7, Vol. XXII, no. 51.

57. Shirley, *Stemmata Shirleiana,* p. 256 (citing Sir D. Dalrymple, Lord Hailes, *Memorials and letters relating to the History of Britain in the reign of James I* [Glasgow, 1766], p. 69; and J. G. Nichols in the *Herald and Genealogist,* Vol. III, but no pagination given by Shirley).

58. *CSP, Domestic, 1603–1610,* p. 451 (Sir Thomas Sherley the younger to the Earl of Salisbury, 9 Aug. 1608).

59. *Ibid., 1611–1618,* p. 135 (John Chamberlain to Sir Dudley Carleton, 17 June 1612).

CHAPTER XII. THE FURTHER TRAVELS OF COUNT ROBERT AND THE TRIBULATIONS OF SIR THOMAS THE YOUNGER

1. W. Payton, "A Journall of all principall matters passed in the twelfth Voyage to the East-India, observed by me Walter Payton, in the good ship

the Expedition: the Captaine whereof was M. Christopher Newport, being set out Anno 1612," in S. Purchas, *Hakluytus Posthumus or Purchas His Pilgrimes,* IV (Glasgow, 1905), 180.

2. East India Company, *Letters received by the East India Company from its servants in the East; transcribed from the 'Original Correspondence' series of the India Office records, 1602–1613,* I (London, 1896), 291.

3. East India Company, *Letters from its servants, 1613–1615,* II (1897), 209–211 (Captain Nicholas Downton to Count Robert Sherley).

4. Payton, "Journall of all principall matters," in Purchas, *Hakluytus Posthumus,* IV, 193.

5. *Ibid.,* pp. 201–209.

6. The account of what happened at Diul Sinde after the departure of the *Expedition* is from W. Payton, "The second Voyage of Captaine Walter Peyton into the East-Indies, in the Expedition, which was set forth by the East-India Company, together with the Dragon, Lyon, and Pepper-Corne, in January 1614. gathered out of his large Journall," in Purchas, *Hakluytus Posthumus,* IV, 296–297. The account of the attempt to burn down Sherley's house is in East India Company, *Letters from its servants, 1613–1615,* II, 106–108 (Thomas Kerridge to the East India Company, 20 Sept. 1614). Sherley's own account is contained in Biblioteca Nacional, Madrid, MS no. 8180, fol. 128 ("Brebe Relación de la Justificación que da el Conde Dn Roberto Sherley a la Magd. Cathólica de España").

7. "The Journal of Nicholas Withington, 1612–1616," in Sir W. Foster, *Early Travels in India, 1588–1619* (Oxford, 1921), p. 212.

8. *Sherley Brothers,* p. 83 (Thomas Aldworth and William Biddulph to Sir Thomas Smith, 19 Aug. 1614, from Surat).

9. East India Company, *Letters from its servants, 1613–1615,* II, 141 (Nicholas Withington to Thomas Aldworth, agent at Surat, 29 Oct. 1614, from Agra).

10. *Ibid.,* pp. 106–108 (Thomas Kerridge to the East India Company, 20 Sept. 1614, from Ajmir).

11. Purchas, *Hakluytus Posthumus,* IV, 471 ("A Letter of Mr. Thomas Coryat, which travailed by Land from Jerusalem to the Court of the Great Mogol, written to Mr. L. Whitaker").

12. *A Chronicle of the Carmelites in Persia and the Papal Mission of the XVIIth and XVIIIth Centuries* (London, 1939), I, 214–221 (quoting "Relación breve del viaje que hizo el Fr. Redento de la Cruz en compañía del Conde Don Roberto Serleo ambasre [embajador] del Rey de Persia a su Majestad Católica desde Aspahan corte de aquel rey hasta Lisboa," a manuscript in the Carmelite library, O.C.D. 234e). Sherley's account of his reception is contained in Biblioteca Nacional, Madrid, MS no. 8180, fol. 127, verso, fol. 130, recto ("Brebe relación").

13. *Chronicle of the Carmelites,* I, 215.

14. "A Journall of the Journey of Richard Steel and John Crowther,

from Azmere in India, the place of the Great Mogols residence, to Spahan the Royall Seat of the King of Persia, in the affaires of the East-Indian Society, Ann. 1615, 1616," in Purchas, *Hakluytus Posthumus,* IV, 267–277.

15. East India Company, *Letters from its servants, 1615,* III (1899), 70–71.

16. *Ibid.,* II, 209–211.

17. Purchas, *Hakluytus Posthumus,* IV, 277; East India Company, *Letters from its servants, 1615,* III, 178.

18. B. Penrose, *The Sherleian Odyssey, Being a Record of the Travels and Adventures of Three Famous Brothers, during the Reigns of Elizabeth, James I, and Charles I* (London, 1938), p. 201. The report that Sherley occasionally escaped disguised as a Spaniard is in García de Silva y Figueroa, *Comentarios de d. García de Silva y Figueroa de la embajada que de parte del rey de España don Filipe III hizo al rey xa Abas de Persia* (Madrid, 1905), II, 143–149.

19. García de Silva y Figueroa, *L'Ambassade de D. Garcias* [*sic*] *de Silva Figueroa* [*sic*] *en Perse, Contenant la politique de ce grand Empire, les moeurs du roy Schah Abbas et une relation exacte de tous les lieux de Perse et des Indes, traduite de l'espagnol par M. de Wicqfort* (Paris, 1667), pp. 270–272.

20. *Sherley Brothers,* p. 87; *CSP, Colonial Series, East Indies, China, and Japan, 1617–1621,* pp. 330–331 (Francis Cottington to Sir Robert Naunton, 12 Dec. 1619).

21. East India Company, *Letters from its servants, 1616,* IV (1900), 303.

22. *Ibid.,* p. 328 (the factors at Surat, Thomas Kerridge, Thomas Barker, and Thomas Mitford, to Sir Thomas Roe, 23 July 1616).

23. *Ibid.,* pp. 189–192.

24. *CSP, Colonial Series, East Indies, China, and Japan, 1513–1616,* pp. 482–483 (Sir Thomas Roe to Sir Thomas Smith, 27 Nov. 1616); the letter is printed in full in Penrose, *Sherleian Odyssey,* App. G.

25. East India Company, *Letters from its servants, 1616,* IV, 247 (Sir Thomas Roe to Sir Thomas Smith, 27 Nov. 1616).

26. Penrose, *Sherleian Odyssey,* p. 201 (Sir Thomas Roe to Sir Ralph Winwood, 30 Nov. 1616).

27. Purchas, *Hakluytus Posthumus,* IV, 459.

28. East India Company, *Letters from its servants, Jan.–June 1617,* V (1901), 50–52 (Sir Thomas Roe to William Robbins at Ispahan, 17 Jan. 1617).

29. *CSP, Colonial Series, East Indies, China, and Japan, 1617–1621,* pp. 10–11 (Sir Thomas Roe to William Robbins, agent to Sir Robert Sherley in Persia, 17 Jan. 1617).

30. East India Company, *Letters from its servants, July–Dec. 1617,* VI (1902), 76 (Sir Thomas Roe to William Robbins, 21 Aug. 1617).

31. *CSP, Colonial Series, East Indies, China, and Japan, 1617–1621,* pp. 13–14 (Archbishop Abbot to Sir Thomas Roe, 20 Jan. 1617).

32. East India Company, *Letters from its servants, Jan.–June 1617,* V, 189–192 (Edward Connock to the East India Company, 2 April 1617).

33. *Ibid.*

34. PRO, State Papers, Foreign, Spain, SP 94/25, fol. 46 (Sir Walter Aston to Lord Digby, 25 March 1622); also printed in *Sherley Brothers,* p. 88.

35. *Ibid.*

36. AGS, Estado, Inglaterra, Leg. 7038, n.fol. ("De la posada a 22 de noviembre de 1618. El Conde Don Roberto Sherley").

37. *Sherley Brothers,* p. 88 (John Chamberlain to Sir Dudley Carleton, 17 Jan. 1624).

38. PRO, Colonial Office, East Indies, CO 77/3, fol. 3, fol. 104 of the new numbering (Hugh Hammersley, Governor, and the Company of Turkey Merchants to Secretary Conway, 4 Feb. 1624); calendared in *CSP, Colonial Series, East Indies, China, and Japan, 1622–1624,* p. 243.

39. *CSP, Colonial Series, East Indies, China, and Japan, 1622–1624,* p. 444 (Secretary Conway to Sir John Coke, 18 Nov. 1624).

40. *Ibid.,* p. 460 (court minutes of the East India Company, 6 Dec. 1624); *ibid.,* p. 444 (Secretary Conway to Sir John Coke, 18 Nov. 1624).

41. *Acts of the Privy Council of England, 1623–1625* (London, 1933), pp. 427–428 (an Act of Council about the Persian trade, 13 Jan. 1625).

42. PRO, Colonial Office, East Indies, CO 77/3, fol. 44, fol. 58 of the new numbering (consultation at Sir Thomas Smith's house concerning the Persian voyage, 28 Jan. 1625); calendared in *CSP, Colonial Series, East Indies, China, and Japan, 1625–1629,* p. 17.

43. *CSP, Colonial Series, East Indies, China, and Japan, 1625–1629,* p. 72 (court minutes of the East India Company, 30 May 1625).

44. Sir J. Finett, *Finetti Philoxenis, som choice observations of Sr. John Finett, Knight* (London, 1656), p. 173.

45. Penrose, *Sherleian Odyssey,* pp. 214–216.

46. *CSP, Colonial Series, East Indies, China, and Japan, 1625–1629,* p. 185 (court minutes of the East India Company, 10 April 1626).

47. *Ibid.,* p. 197 (court minutes of the East India Company, 10 May 1626).

48. *Ibid.,* pp. 212–213 (Thomas Barker, John Purifey, Robert Loftus, and George Smith to the East India Company, 14 June 1626, from Ispahan).

49. *Ibid.,* p. 186 (minutes of business to be submitted to the King, April[?] 1626).

50. PRO, Colonial Office, East Indies, CO 77/4, fol. 10 (memorandum concerning the East India Company and the Persian trade); calendared in *CSP, Colonial Series, East Indies, China, and Japan, 1625–1629,* p. 185.

51. *Sherley Brothers,* p. 92 (Count Robert Sherley to Secretary Conway).

52. *CSP, Colonial Series, East Indies, China, and Japan, 1625–1629,* p. 179 (minutes of a general court, 28 March 1626).

53. Sir T. Herbert, *Travels in Persia, 1627–1629,* ed. Sir William Foster (London, 1928), p. xx (report of a meeting of the Directorate of the Company, quoted by Sir William Foster in his introduction).

54. *Ibid.*

55. *CSP, Colonial Series, East Indies, China, and Japan, 1625–1629,* pp. 186–187 (court minutes of the East India Company, 14–19 April 1626).

56. *Ibid.,* pp. 318–319 (court minutes of the East India Company, 12 Feb. 1627).

57. *Ibid.,* p. 320 (court minutes of the East India Company, 14–16 Feb. 1627).

58. National Library of Scotland, Advocates MSS, 33.1.7, Vol. XXII, no. 51.

59. M. P. Ashley, *The Stuarts in Love* (London, 1963), pp. 113, 118.

60. Advocates MSS, 33.1.7, Vol. XXII, no. 49 (21 Jan. 1616).

61. *Ibid.,* no. 51.

62. *Ibid.*

63. Uncalendared Cranfield papers on deposit at the Historical Manuscripts Commission.

64. *Ibid.*

65. *Ibid.*

66. *HMC Eleventh Report, Appendix, Part IV, the Manuscripts of the Marquess of Townshend* (London, 1887), p. 21 (Roger Townshend to his father, Sir Roger Townshend, 31 Aug. 1622).

CHAPTER XIII. THE LAST DAYS OF THE BROTHERS

1. *CSP, Colonial Series, East Indies, China, and Japan, 1625–1629,* pp. 333–334 (Sir Dodmore Cotton to Secretary Conway, 18 March 1627).

2. *Ibid.,* p. 335 (court minutes of the East India Company, 21–30 March 1627).

3. Sir T. Herbert, *Travels in Persia, 1627–1629,* ed. Sir William Foster (London, 1928), p. 31.

4. Sir W. Foster, ed., *English Factories in India, 1622–1623; A Calendar of Documents in the India Office, British Museum, and Public Record Office* (Oxford, 1908), p. 183.

5. Foster, *English Factories in India, 1624–1629* (1909), pp. 43–44.

6. *Ibid.,* p. 198 (President Kerridge, Richard Wylde, John Skibbow, Joseph Hopkinson, William Martin, and George Page to the East India Company, 4 Jan. 1628, from Surat).

7. Herbert, *Travels in Persia,* pp. 54–55.

8. *Ibid.,* p. 80.

9. R. Stodart, *The Journal of Robert Stodart; Being an Account of His*

Experiences as a Member of Sir Dodmore Cotton's Mission in Persia in 1628–1629 (London, 1935), p. 27 (this quotation is from the "Journal" of Henry Gooch, which is printed in full in Sir E. Dennison Ross's introduction to Stodart's account); E. Hyde, 1st Earl of Clarendon, *State Papers collected by Edward Earl of Clarendon, commencing from the year 1621, containing the materials from which his history of the Great Rebellion was composed* (Oxford, 1767), I, 39.

10. Gooch, "Journal," in Stodart's *Journal,* pp. 27–28; Clarendon, *State Papers,* I, 39.

11. Herbert, *Travels in Persia,* pp. 156–157.

12. Gooch, "Journal," in Stodart, *Journal,* pp. 31–32; Clarendon, *State Papers,* I, 41.

13. Herbert, *Travels in Persia,* pp. 205–206.

14. PRO, State Papers, Domestic, James I (Conway Papers), SP 14/183, fol. 46 (Sir Thomas Sherley to Secretary Conway, 12 Feb. 1625); calendared in *CSP, Domestic, 1623–1625,* pp. 472–473.

15. R. J. Eldridge, *Newport, Isle of Wight, in Bygone Days* (Newport, 1952), p. 61.

16. Sir J. Oglander, *A Royalist's Notebook; the Commonplace Book of Sir John Oglander* (London, 1936), pp. 182, 238.

17. E. P. Shirley, *Stemmata Shirleiana, or The Annals of the Shirley Family* (2nd ed.; Westminster, 1873), p. 270.

18. *Ibid.,* p. 288.

19. Berkshire County Records Office, Trumbull MSS, 22/119 (Sir John Digby to William Trumbull, 28 Feb. 1613); calendared in *HMC Report on the Manuscripts of the Marquess of Downshire,* IV (London, 1940), 48.

20. V. T. Harlow, *Ralegh's Last Voyage* (London, 1932), p. 141.

21. AGS, Estado, Flandes, Leg. 626, fol. 311 (to Olivares, "En Madrid, a 14 de abril de 1622. Besa las manos de Vuestra Excelencia su verdadero servidor, El Conde de Sherley").

22. *Ibid.* The quotation immediately preceding is also from this letter.

23. Sir A. Sherley, *Le "Peso Politico de Todo el Mundo" d'Anthony Sherley, ou un aventurier anglais au service de l'Espagne,* ed., Xavier-A. Flores (Paris, 1963), pp. 175–181.

24. *Ibid.,* p. 47.

25. *Ibid.,* pp. 175–176.

26. AGS, Estado, Flandes, Leg. 2847, n.fol. ("Granada y enero 31 de 1623 años. Humilde servidor de Vuestra Excelencia, El Conde de Sherley"; endorsed: "Granda. Al Conde, mi señor. 1623"; another endorsement: "El conde de Cherley 31 de enero"; another endorsement: "Visto y consultado sobre algunos puntos en 24 de abril").

27. *Ibid.,* Estado, Leg. 2853, n.fol.

Index

INDEX

INDEX

Spring Valley Library
Colorado Mountain College
3000 County Road 114
Glenwood Springs, CO 81601